ASSASSINATION of LINCOLN

A History of the Great Conspiracy

TRIAL OF THE CONSPIRATORS
BY A MILITARY COMMISSION

And a Review of the Trial of John H. Surratt

by

T. M. Harris

LATE BRIGADIER-GENERAL U.S.V. AND MAJOR-GENERAL BY BREVET

A MEMBER OF THE COMMISSION

HERITAGE BOOKS
2011

HERITAGE BOOKS
AN IMPRINT OF HERITAGE BOOKS, INC.

Books, CDs, and more—Worldwide

For our listing of thousands of titles see our website
at
www.HeritageBooks.com

A Facsimile Reprint
Published 2011 by
HERITAGE BOOKS, INC.
Publishing Division
100 Railroad Ave. #104
Westminster, Maryland 21157

Entered according to Act of Congress, in the year 1892,
By T. M. Harris,
In the Office of the Librarian of Congress at Washington.

— Publisher's Notice —
In reprints such as this, it is often not possible to remove blemishes from the original. We feel the contents of this book warrant its reissue despite these blemishes and hope you will agree and read it with pleasure.

International Standard Book Numbers
Paperbound: 978-1-55613-230-8
Clothbound: 978-0-7884-8631-9

EXPLANATION.

It is perhaps necessary that the author should explain the sense in which the term, "Great Conspiracy," in the title of his book, is used. It is not at all in the same sense in which it is used by General Logan in his book. In that it is used as the equivalent of the Great Rebellion, only that it broadly covers all that led to and culminated in the war against the government, designated as "The Rebellion." It is only here used to designate the conspiracy that resorted to the policy of assassination as a means to give aid to the rebellion; and the reader who follows the author through will then be able to perceive why he designates this a "Great Conspiracy."

PREFACE.

It is now more than twenty-seven years since the assassination of Abraham Lincoln, President of the United States, — an event of the greatest importance at the time, not only to the people of the United States, but to the civilized world. The trial of the conspirators by a military commission created the greatest possible interest; and the proceedings and testimony were published from day to day by all of the great newspapers of the country, and read with avidity. The judgment of those who carefully studied the testimony at the time was formed upon a competent knowledge of the facts.

And yet, even then, the fate of the prisoners on trial before the Commission, to be found innocent or guilty according to the evidence, constituted the great point of interest, and thus tended to divert attention from the evidence against the other parties charged not only with being co-conspirators, but as being the instigators of the plot.

Since that time a new generation has come on to the stage of action, and as the official report of the trial by Ben Pittman, published at the time, is in the hands of but comparatively few people, a concise history of this great event, in popular form, but founded on the evidence, seemed to the writer to be due and called for at the present time.

The necessity for this has been emphasized by a recent revival of efforts that have been made from time to time, ever since the execution of the assassins that were condemned to death, to prejudice public sentiment against the government by the assumption of the innocence of one of the parties executed — Mrs. Surratt.

Only a few months since (May 30, 1891), La Salle Institute in New York City was crowded by an audience that came together expecting to hear Cardinal Gibbons and Father Walter review the case of Mrs. Surratt. Neither the cardinal nor the father appeared, but a Mr. Sloane arose and read to the audience a letter from Father Walter on the subject. This letter contained nothing new to those who were familiar with the case at the time of its occurrence. It was substantially the same that was published over his signature shortly after her execution. After stating that he was her confessor, and that his priestly vows did not permit him to reveal the secrets of the confessional, he very calmly and positively states his belief in her entire innocence, basing that belief on what he professes to know. He then relates the efforts he made to get a reprieve and a postponement of her execution for a few days, and expresses the belief that could he have succeeded in this for only ten days he could have saved her life.

He then complains of the manner in which he was treated by the President, Andrew Johnson, and Judge Holt, who referred him back and forth, each to the other, and that between them he could get nothing accomplished.

A story has also been gotten up of a Union soldier who was a member of the conspiracy and knew all of its members and secrets, who affirms the innocence of Mrs. Surratt. The most rational and, at the same time, charitable thing to be said about this story is, that this Union soldier was manufactured for the occasion.

That portion of the press of to-day that inherits the old copper-head animus, greedily publishes all such things as these, and indulges in the wildest latitude of editorial comment and false statements. They have buried all of the members of the Commission but one many times; have followed all of the principal actors in the scene to violent and miserable deaths; and have made it manifest that had the Almighty Ruler of the Universe viewed the matter in their light, and been as swift in his retributions as they would have had him to be, not one who had any connection with the arrest, trial, and execution of the assassins of the great and good President would have been left alive.

They have manifested an especial venom of feeling against the then Secretary of War, Hon. E. M. Stanton, iterating and reiterating the absurd and false statement that he died from the violence of his own hand, being crazed with remorse. Why they should thus select Mr. Stanton as the especial object of their hatred cannot be seen from any connection he had with this case. His part, though important and involving great responsibility, was, in fact, a very subordinate one. He selected the officers to be embraced in the order of detail for the Commission, under the order of the President, that was all. Judge Holt conducted the trial and recorded the proceedings under the President's order, and when he handed that record over to the President his connection with the case ended. President Johnson then held the temporal destiny of this woman, as well as that of all the others convicted, in his own hand. He and he alone was responsible.

From all this it appears that the time has come when a clear, concise history of this conspiracy and trial should be given to the world. To this task the writer has addressed himself, and he offers this volume as the result of his labors. The facts herein narrated in regard to the assassination, as well as to the parts enacted by each of the individual members of the conspiracy, are drawn from the testimony before the Commission. They have been thrown into the form of a connected narrative, and there has been nothing stated as a fact but what is fully sustained by the evidence which formed the basis of the decisions of the Commission. Nothing has been admitted into this narrative but what rests on the specific testimony of unimpeachable witnesses. The author only deems it necessary that the opinion, or belief, of Father Walter, and all others of his persuasion, shall be confronted by the testimony in the case, in order that an intelligent judgment shall be reached. At the time of this trial there were just two classes of people in this country — the friends and the enemies of the government. The former were united and determined in their purpose and effort to preserve and perpetuate the government established by our fathers under the constitution that included in its purpose and provisions the union of the states and made us a nation. The latter were madly bent on its overthrow, and so judged favorably or unfavorably of the occurrences of the times, as they tended to favor or hinder the accomplishment of their purposes. The feelings of both parties had been wrought up to the highest pitch of intensity because the matters at issue had been submitted to the arbitrament of the sword. The result of this appeal was clearly foreshadowed at the time of the assassination of the President, and before the conclusion of the trial of his murderers the cause of the Confederacy had collapsed. The rebellion was virtually overcome. The deep political scheme to give it a new lease of life and bring to its aid new elements of success by the assassinations that had been planned, had been too long delayed, and its execution had become utterly impracticable. The soldiers of the rebellion had fought their fight — a brave and plucky and protracted fight. They realized the hopelessness of their cause and, though greatly disappointed and mortified at their failure, they had the consciousness that they had done all that brave men could do to win success, and so were ready to accept the result, return to their homes, and resume citizenship under the government they were unable to overthrow. Not so with the secret active enemies of the government. They were not willing to accept defeat, but were, nevertheless (happily for the country), in a condition that they could only show their enmity by maligning and villifying the authorities they were unable to overthrow; and of this privilege they fully availed themselves. Thus it has come to pass that the magnitude, scope, and purpose of the assassination conpiracy are unknown to the present generation. All that a large majority of those who have come upon the stage of action since that time know of this, in many respects, one of the most important trials that has ever occurred in our history, is what they have learned through the efforts of these vituperators; and they have never seen it referred to other than as the trial of Mrs. Surratt. The Commission was not called upon to render a decision as to the innocence or guilt of the persons charged by the government with being co-conspirators with John H. Surratt and John Wilkes Booth, who were not in the custody of the government and so not before the Commission; but the government, having assumed the responsibility of charging Jefferson Davis, George N. Sanders, Beverly Tucker, Jacob Thompson, William C. Cleary, Clement C. Clay, George Harper, George Young, and others, with thus conspiring to kill and murder Abraham Lincoln, Andrew Johnson, Wm. H. Seward, and Ulysses S. Grant, was under the necessity of vindicating its honor and dignity before the world by presenting the evidence in its possession on which its charge was founded. It will be my purpose to present this evidence, and to show the full significance and purpose of the plot, and with whom it originated. Many of the prominent actors in this tragedy have been summoned before a higher tribunal to answer for the deeds done in the body. There we are content to leave them, assured that "all things are naked and open to the eyes of Him with whom they have to do," and that there will be no mistakes made in the decisions there rendered. And toward those who yet remain, it is with no feelings of personal enmity that the author shall write. He only knows them as they are revealed in the testimony, and by this he shall endeavor to deal fairly and candidly. They made themselves conspicuous in their connection with public affairs of the greatest importance, and so their acts belong to the public. If they have made a bad record, it is due to the truth of history that their acts shall be fully unfolded. History is a truthful narration of events that have occurred; and its conclusions must be based on a consideration of all of the facts, taken in their proper order and relation to the events. The aim of the writer has been to give a candid and reliable history of the Great Conspiracy as deduced from the evidence before the Commission and to be found in the official report of the proceedings published by Ben Pittman immediately after the trial.

The asperities of the great conflict have been largely obliterated by the many happy years of peace that have intervened since that unhappy period. We have but one country and one flag, which almost all have learned to love as of old. Let us draw wisdom and virtue from the history of the past, learning as well from our errors and mistakes as from our virtues, that we may, by a course of well-doing, gain the favor of Him who holds the destiny of nations in His hands, and who pulls down one and sets another up.

The stability of a popular government must rest n the virtue and intelligence of its people. Our institutions were established on this basis alone, and on this alone can they stand. The divorcement of Church and State by the framers of our constitution was one of the wise conclusions which they drew from the past; but it was no part of their purpose to divorce religion from the State. On the contrary, their politics was a part of their religion and was deduced from the teachings of God's word. Let us beware of the effort of the present time to divorce politics from religion because we rightly divorce the Church from the State.

There is no morality that can make a man a valuable and a reliable citizen of a free state except the morality of the Christian religion as taught in God's word. It is the duty, therefore, of every parent and every teacher to instill into the minds of our youth this Christian morality as a basis for the highest patriotism and noblest citizenship. Let the American flag float over every school-house, and the morality of the Bible be taught with the authority inherent in God's word. Then will the days of assassinations, whether political or religious, come to an end. Owing to a variety of causes, the facts connected with this most important event in our nation's history have been slurred over and obscured. Scarcely one in a thousand of our people to-day have any knowledge of their existence.

The object of the writer will be to revive them and bring them out clearly to the knowledge of all.

T. M. HARRIS.

RITCHIE C. H., W. Va.

CONTENTS.

EXPLANATION 3
PREFACE 5
CONTENTS 13

CHAPTER I.
INTRODUCTORY 17

CHAPTER II.
PREPARATIONS FOR THE EXECUTION OF THE PLOT 24

CHAPTER III.
ASSASSINATION OF THE PRESIDENT AND ATTEMPTED ASSASSINATION OF SECRETARY SEWARD 34

CHAPTER IV.
THE NEWS COMMUNICATED TO THE WORLD, AND ITS EFFECT . . 47

CHAPTER V.
UNRAVELLING THE PLOT — PURSUIT AND CAPTURE OF BOOTH AND HEROLD — DEATH OF BOOTH 51

CHAPTER VI.
UNRAVELLING THE CONSPIRACY — ARREST OF SPANGLER, O'LAUGHLIN, ATZERODT, MUDD, AND ARNOLD 60

CHAPTER VII.
QUESTIONS PRELIMINARY TO THE TRIAL — WHAT SORT OF TRIAL SHOULD BE GIVEN, CIVIL OR MILITARY 82

CHAPTER VIII.
A MILITARY COMMISSION — ITS NATURE, CONSTITUTION, DUTIES, AND JURISDICTION 96

CHAPTER IX.
CONSTITUTION OF THE COMMISSION, AND TRIAL 98

CHAPTER X.
EVIDENCE IN REGARD TO ATROCITIES NOT EMBRACED IN THE CHARGE AND SPECIFICATIONS, FOR WHICH DAVIS AND HIS CANADA CABINET WERE RESPONSIBLE 118

CHAPTER XI.
EVIDENCE PRESENTED BY THE GOVERNMENT TO SUSTAIN ITS CHARGE AND SPECIFICATIONS 147

CHAPTER XII.
THE GOVERNMENT WITNESSES AGAINST DAVIS AND HIS ASSOCIATES IN THIS CRIME 163

CHAPTER XIII.
A CRITICISM OF NICOLAY AND HAY 177

CHAPTER XIV.
JACOB THOMPSON'S BANK ACCOUNT — WHAT BECAME OF THE MONEY . 182

CHAPTER XV.
THE CASE OF MRS. SURRATT 192

CHAPTER XVI.
FATHER WALTER 204

CHAPTER XVII.
CONCLUSION 211

CHAPTER XVIII.
FLIGHT AND CAPTURE OF JOHN H. SURRATT 212

PART II.

CHAPTER I.
INDICTMENT AND TRIAL 229

CHAPTER II.
A CRITICISM OF THE DEFENSE 253

CHAPTER III.
TREATMENT OF WITNESSES AND EVIDENCE BY THE COUNSEL FOR THE DEFENSE, AND THEIR ANIMUS TOWARD THE GOVERNMENT AND APPEALS TO THE POLITICAL PREJUDICES OF JURORS . . . 259
APPENDIX 317
PREFACE TO APPENDIX 319
ARGUMENT OF JOHN A. BINGHAM 325
CONTROVERSY BETWEEN PRESIDENT JOHNSON AND JUDGE HOLT . . 407

Part I.

ASSASSINATION OF LINCOLN.

CHAPTER I.

INTRODUCTORY.

THE rebellion of the slave-holding states, and the attempt to establish a separate government by force of arms, was solely in the interest of the institution of slavery. The Southern Confederacy was to rest on this institution as its corner-stone. By the establishment of the Confederacy it was intended to end, forever, the agitation of this question, and establish the system of human slavery as one of the permanent institutions of the world. And all this in the nineteenth century of the Christian era! Preparatory to this the pulpit and the press had been suborned, the Christian conscience of the country had been debauched, and the doctrine that slavery was a Divine institution was taught, and accepted as true, by one-half of the American people.

A doctor of divinity, or even a common preacher, who could prove this to his own satisfaction, and that of his hearers, at once achieved popularity, and had his great learning and ability heralded by the secular press throughout the South land. Neither was this kind of preaching confined to the South. It found a distinct and earnest echo in many places in the North. It was argued, and no doubt sincerely believed, that slavery was the best condition for securing the happiness and welfare of the African race — the condition in which the negro could be most useful to the world; that his condition had been greatly improved by his transplantation from a heathen land and the environments of barbarism to a Christian land and civilized and Christian environments; and that subjection to a higher and superior race was necessary to his deriving the highest benefit from the change. Slavery, it was taught, was a patriarchal institution, and that it was only through it that the highest ideal of human civilization could be attained. It was natural that a people whose judgment had crystalized around such opinions as these should be intolerant of opposition, as they had closed the door to discussion on this question; and so for several generations a contrary opinion was not tolerated, or allowed to find expression, in the slave-holding states. The agitation of this question, in its moral aspects, by constantly increasing numbers of earnest, able men in the North, at last led to the organization of a political party opposed to this institution, and the question of slavery thus became a political question.

The friends of the institution instinctively recognized the danger that thus confronted them, and began to strengthen their fences by most stringent measures to repress discussion and shut out the light. This was a tacit admission that they felt themselves unable to stand before the world in argument. It may be laid down as an axiom, that whenever a political party forecloses discussion on any subject, but more especially on a great moral issue, it is not only on the wrong side of that issue, but has an intuitive perception of that fact.

It may also be accepted as an axiom, that the more inconsistent a man's attitude is on any great moral question the more intolerant will he be of opposition. Not only were the most stringent laws passed to prevent the discussion of the institution of slavery in its moral aspects in the Southern States, but also the most lawless and violent measures were resorted to, so that it was as much as a man's life was worth to undertake to make a public argument against slavery in a slave-holding state, and even to be found earnestly opposed to the institution in sentiment was to put personal safety in jeopardy. The making of this question a political question tended largely to de-sectionalize it. No party could hope to succeed, as a National party, without the vote of the South, and this could only be secured by concessions to the demands of the slave holders in the interest of that institution; and so the party that was willing to concede the most to their demands became the dominant party in the nation. Thus the leading Democratic politicians, all over the North, became the staunch advocates of slavery; and we all know with what blind confidence, and fierce determination, the masses follow their political leaders. The culmination of the contest over this question, resulting in the election of Abraham Lincoln to the Presidency by a party openly opposed to slavery, caused its friends to take their appeal from the ballot box to the sword; and this appeal found those who were the friends of the institution from political party considerations scattered all over the North in quite formidable numbers, constituting an enemy in the rear of our armies that gave to the administration of President Lincoln no little anxiety and embarrassment, making it necessary for him, as early as September, 1862, to proclaim martial law and suspend the writ of *habeas corpus* in respect to all persons in the United States who were found to be actively disloyal, and engaged in efforts to aid the rebellion. The following is a copy of his proclamation: —

GENERAL ORDERS NO. 141.

WAR DEPARTMENT,
ADJUTANT GENERAL'S OFFICE,
WASHINGTON, Sept. 25, 1862.

The following Proclamation by the President is published for the information and government of the Army and all concerned:

By the President of the United States of America.

A PROCLAMATION.

Whereas it has become necessary to call into service not only volunteers but also portions of the militia of the States by draft, in order to suppress the insurrection existing in the United States, and disloyal persons are not adequately restrained by the ordinary processes of law from hindering this measure and from giving aid and comfort in various ways to the insurrection: Now, therefore, be it ordered: First, That during the existing insurrection, and as a necessary measure for suppressing the same, all rebels and insurgents, their aiders and abettors, within the United States, and all persons discouraging volunteer enlistments, resisting militia drafts, or guilty of any disloyal practice affording aid and comfort to rebels against the authority of the United States shall be subject to martial law, and liable to trial and punishment by court-martial or military commission. Second, That the writ of *habeas corpus* is suspended in respect to all persons arrested, or who are now, or hereafter during the rebellion shall be, imprisoned in any fort, camp, arsenal, military prison, or other place of confinement, by any military authority, or by sentence of any court-martial or military commission. In witness whereof I have hereunto set my hand, and caused the seal of the United States to be affixed.

Done at the city of Washington, this twenty-fourth day of September, in the year of our Lord one thousand eight hundred and sixty-two, and of the Independence of the United States the eighty-seventh.

ABRAHAM LINCOLN.

" By the President,
  " WILLIAM H. SEWARD, *Secretary of State.*
" By order of the Secretary of War,
  " L. THOMAS, *Adjutant General.*"
      " Official."

This disloyal element was rendered much more formidable by the fact of its perfect combination, through secret, oath-bound organizations under the names of Knights of the Golden Circle and Order of American Knights. These secret orders no doubt had their origin in the South, preparatory to secession and war; but after the war had been commenced it was chiefly in the North that they were useful to the rebel cause, and it was through these that the assassination of the President-elect was to have been accomplished at Baltimore when on his way to the Capital in 1861, and thus his inauguration as President was to have been prevented. We thus see the desperate character of the political leaders of the rebellion, who were ready to frustrate the expressed will of the people by resorting to assassination. We need not think strange that a rebellion which was ready to resort to such means in its incipiency should finally expire under the weight of this infamy.

By these secret organizations, the enemies of the government, wherever they might be, possessed the means of a secret recognition amongst their members. And under whatever circumstances they might be placed, the obligations of their oath afforded them confidence and security. They constituted a brotherhood, and by their secret grips, signs, passwords, etc., they had a guarantee of unity of sentiment and of purpose, and of faithfulness to each other and to the obligations of their oath.

These organizations were regarded as allies by the rebel government, and were counted on as a valuable factor to secure the success of its arms. This element in the North kept itself in constant communication with the rebel government and the rebel armies, and thus, in a large degree, filled the place of spies in giving information. To furnish facilities for communication with its friends in the North, as also for various other purposes in aid of the rebel cause, the Confederate Government sent a number of its ablest civilians to Canada, at an early period of the war, as its secret agents, who established their headquarters at Montreal. This cabal consisted of the following persons: Jacob Thompson, who had been Secretary of the Interior under Buchanan's administration; Clement C. Clay, who had been a United States Senator from Alabama; Beverly Tucker, who had been a Circuit Judge in Virginia; George

N. Sanders, William C. Cleary, Prof. Holcomb, George Harper, and others. Of these, Thompson, Tucker, and Clay seem to have held semi-official positions, and we will designate them as Davis's Canada Cabinet. The others named, as also others unnamed above, appear to have acted as aids, in a subordinate capacity, in the execution of their plots. They all claimed to be acting as agents of the Rebel Government upon their oaths on the trial for the extradition of the St. Alban's raiders.

The proclamation of martial law and suspension of the writ of *habeas corpus* in September, 1862, had the effect of restraining the open, active efforts of these secret disloyal organizations to cripple the resources at Mr. Lincoln's command for suppressing the rebellion, inasmuch as any such efforts were met by arrest, military trial, and imprisonment; yet, inasmuch as they created a necessity for a military police at all important points in the North, they felt that they were still rendering valuable service to the rebellion by thus weakening the force at the front; and whilst it was necessary to conduct their operations with much more secrecy, their organizations were not disbanded. They went on to effect a complete military organization, thoroughly officered and drilled, and in many cases armed, holding themselves ready to take the field in any emergency that might arise that would justify so bold a measure. The Canada Cabinet watched over these organizations with great interest, and directed their operations, and by many schemes sought to bring about an emergency that would enable them to bring this army, which they had hidden away in secrecy, into the field of active operations for the success of their cause. The officers of these secret military organizations were chosen from the local political leaders in the different localities where they existed, and kept themselves in communication with the Canada Cabinet, and through this medium the Confederate Government was kept informed of their strength, organization, plans, and purposes. So bold and active did they become, in spite of the efforts of the military police for their suppression, that the government finally found it necessary, through its secret service department, to possess itself of a thorough knowledge of these organizations, and in this way was enabled to capture the arms and munitions of war which had been secured and were hidden away in secrecy by them, and also to arrest the leading officers of these organizations in several states. Whilst by these means these treasonable combinations were seriously crippled, they were unchanged in animus and still struggled to maintain their existence. They kept themselves in communication with the Canada conspirators, and ready to co-operate with them for the success of their schemes should the conditions become sufficiently promising to justify them in declaring themselves openly.

It was in the summer of 1864 that Jacob Thompson, according to the testimony before the Commission, declared that he had his friends all over the Northern States, who were willing to go to any length in order to serve the cause of the South. Jefferson Davis's Canada Cabinet kept up a constant correspondence with their chief, through secret agents who travelled directly through the states, and even through the city of Washington.

So potent was the aid of secret signs, grips, pass-words, etc., as a means of recognition, and so universally were the members of these secret orders diffused over the country, that they could go anywhere. Should one agent find it necessary to stop his task for fear of detection, another would take it up; and where men could not go, women went, to carry communications. The Canada Cabinet was well supplied with money by the government at Richmond, and in this department of the service Jacob Thompson seems to have been Secretary of the Treasury. He kept his deposits largely in the Ontario Bank of Montreal, and his credits there arose from Southern bills of exchange on London. The object of the writer in this introductory chapter has been to place clearly before his readers the formidable character of the conspiracy, which, with the President of the Confederacy at its head, and organized by his Canada Cabinet, was intended to throw the loyal North into a state of chaotic confusion and bring to the aid of their sinking cause the disloyal element all over the North, by a series of assassinations which would leave the nation without a civil and military head and without any constitutional way of electing another President, and at the same time would deprive the armies of the United States of a lawful commander. This was the last card of the political leaders of the rebellion, the last desperate resort to retrieve a cause that had been manifestly lost in open warfare. It may seem like temerity in the writer to make such a charge involving a total disregard of the laws of civilized warfare, and such utter moral depravity on the part of these conspirators, and to claim for their wicked project the approval of Jefferson Davis, but the evidence in the possession of the government and adduced before the Commission, it will be seen, fully justified the government in making this charge. The persons brought before the Commission, though in full sympathy in sentiment with their employers, were merely the tools and hired assassins of the Canada Cabinet, acting under the advice and sanction of their chief. I shall now proceed to bring before my readers the denouement of their plot, and, from the evidence given before the Commission, show that the origin, scope and purpose of the conspiracy have been truly indicated above.

CHAPTER II.

PREPARATIONS FOR THE EXECUTION OF THE PLOT.

The evidence which will be hereafter referred to shows that John Wilkes Booth and John H. Surratt had, as early as the latter part of October, or early in November, 1864, entered into a contract with Davis's Canada Cabinet to accomplish the assassinations they had planned, and that they immediately entered upon their work of preparation. It would seem from the evidence, that at that time the purpose was to execute their designs at a much earlier date than they did; and that this delay was occasioned by the Canada conspirators.

Surratt and Booth, however, were busied from that time on in making their preparations. The first step was to enlist in the conspiracy a sufficient number of competent and reliable assistants, to each one of whom was assigned the part he was to take in it, and to train, equip, and prepare him for the part assigned him. The assassination of President Lincoln had fallen to Payne by lot; and to him was entrusted the task of making all needed preparations. Payne had visited Canada during the fall of 1864, and probably there made the acquaintance of Booth. To a man of Booth's sagacity, a mere glance at Payne would be sufficient to impress him with the idea that he was one of the helpers he wanted; and as we find him as early as February, 1865, transplanted to Washington City by Booth and Surratt, and from that time on associating with them very intimately but very secretly, and without employment, or visible means, passing back and forth between Washington and Baltimore, and finally provided with quarters in Washington by Surratt, there can be no doubt that he was early enlisted in the conspiracy, and supported by the Canada Cabinet through their agents in Washington — Booth and Surratt. The author is led to

J. WILKES BOOTH.

conclude from studying the evidence that Booth and Surratt were acting under a considerable latitude of provisional instructions, and that to them was entrusted the selection of the time and place for the accomplishment of their purpose. There were a number of persons in Canada, members of the conspiracy, who were expected to take an active part in its execution; and it is altogether probable that the original plan contemplated the accomplishment of these assassinations as opportunities could be found or made, and that for each one a man had been assigned.

John Wilkes Booth and John Harrison Surratt were the leaders of the conspiracy in Washington, they having proposed to their co-conspirators in Canada to accomplish for them the assassinations they had planned.

They were stimulated by their intense hostility to the administration of President Lincoln and desire for the establishment of the Southern Confederacy, and also by the delusive idea of winning enduring fame and the lasting gratitude of their countrymen of the South for being thus the instruments of retrieving the fortunes of their dying cause. But in addition to these considerations, they had large promises of pecuniary reward. They were, in fact, the hired assassins of Jefferson Davis and his Canada Cabinet.

These two men had been engaged for months in making their preparations for the assassination of the President, Vice-President, Secretary Seward, and General Grant. They visited and conferred with the Canada conspirators from time to time during the summer and fall of 1864, and early winter of 1865. They traversed the counties of Prince George, Charles, and St. Mary's, Maryland, lying along the north side of the Potomac below Washington, to prepare the way for escape by securing confederates along the contemplated route who would assist in facilitating their flight by aiding them in their progress, or by concealing them if necessary. Booth had spent some time in this work during the fall and early winter, making himself familiar with the geography of the country, roads, etc., under the pretence that he desired to purchase lands in Maryland. He found in Charles County Dr. S. A. Mudd, who sympathized with his plans, and entered into them at least so far as to pledge him any assistance he could give him in making his escape. Mudd also visited Booth two or three times in Washington during the winter, introducing him on the occasion of his first visit to John H. Surratt; and in the course of these visits he was always found in company with Booth and others of the conspirators who were to take an active part in its accomplishment, and was no doubt kept well informed of the progress of their preparations, and of the time when it would be attempted after that had been determined upon. Surratt also spent much time during the winter in this part of Maryland, in preparation for the work. Being at home there, he could render Booth valuable assistance by procuring friends who would aid him in his flight, and in getting him across the Potomac at the selected point. As this was on the line of a regular underground mail route between Washington and Richmond, with which Surratt was familiar, he, of course, had no difficulty in making satisfactory arrangements, the great mass of the population in all of these counties being intensely disloyal.

They had selected and arranged with Payne, Atzerodt, O'Laughlin, Arnold, Herold, Spangler, and numerous other parties who were never made known, to take an active part in the work of assassination, or to aid them in their escape. Booth and Surratt had provided horses for the occasion, and, with Atzerodt and Herold, were known to a number of liverymen of whom they were liberal and frequent patrons.

Surratt provided quarters for Payne at the Herndon House, representing him to be a delicate gentleman, and stipulating that his meals should be served to him in his room. Atzerodt, who was to have assassinated the Vice-President, had taken a room at the Pennsylvania House. Booth, being an actor, and familiar with the routine of the play and the work of the assistants on the stage, having selected Ford's Theatre as the place for the accomplishment of his purpose, proceeded to make himself at home amongst the *habitues* of that establishment. He was a very handsome man, stylish in his dress, dissolute in his habits, a constant and free drinker, generous in the expenditure of his money on his vices of smoking and drinking, and of great personal magnetism. He soon ingratiated himself with the employees of the theatre, and became a general favorite.

It was necessary that he should have a co-conspirator at the theatre to assist him in making his escape. He had labored hard with an actor in New York by the name of Chester, with whom he was acquainted, to engage him in the conspiracy, that he might station him at the door of his exit, to see that his way should be clear and the door open at the critical moment, for which service he offered to pay him three thousand dollars; but Chester, after several interviews and much importunity, absolutely declined, and begged Booth never to mention the matter to him again. Failing to secure Chester, he turned his attention to Edward Spangler, an employee at the theatre. Spangler was a man of dissipated habits, low moral tone, and little intellectual culture, and being politically in sympathy with Booth, he was easily led by him into the conspiracy. Booth had had a shed fitted up as a stable in an alley back of the theatre, and had kept his horse in it occasionally for some time previous, that he might have it convenient when the supreme moment should have arrived, without exciting suspicion. To reach the private box fitted up on the occasion for the occupancy of the President and General Grant, with their wives, it was necessary to pass through two doors. The first led into a passage behind the box, the second from this passage into the box. To prevent any one from following him into the passage and hindering the accomplishment of his purpose, Booth had cut, himself, or more likely had had Spangler, who was a kind of rough carpenter, cut a mortise in the plastering of the passage wall, in such a position with reference to the door that the end of a wooden bar, three and a half feet long, which had been prepared for that purpose, could be inserted in the mortise, and the other end placed against the panel of the door so that it could not be opened from the outside.

That ingress to this passage might not be prevented by the bolting of the door by the President and his party after entering, the screws of the fastenings had been drawn, so that it could be easily pushed open. A hole had been bored through the door to the box, opposite where the President's chair was placed, with a small bit, and reamed out with a knife, so that Booth could, after gaining the passage and barring the door behind him, peep through this hole and assure himself of the exact position of his intended victim. The manner in which all of these arrangements had been made, the mortise in the plastered wall, the bar of wood fitted to the mortise, and in length having been exactly prepared to fit against the panel of the door and act as a brace, show that all these preparations had been made with the greatest forethought and care.

About three weeks previous to the assassination, John H. Surratt, Herold, and Atzerodt brought to the tavern at Surrattsville, in Maryland, about ten miles below Washington City, owned by Mrs. Surratt, and at the time occupied by a man by the name of Lloyd, two carbines, with ammunition, a monkey-wrench, and a piece of rope. Surratt asked Lloyd to take charge of these things and keep them secreted, saying they would be called for before a great while, at the same time showing him a suitable place about the house in which to hide them. The Surratt family had lived in this house and kept a country tavern until within a few months previous, when they had removed to Washington, renting their tavern to Lloyd, so that Surratt was much more familiar with the house than Lloyd. These things, as we shall see, were placed there for the use of Booth and his companion in their flight after the assassination. As a precautionary measure, Booth, on the Tuesday before the assassination, sought an interview with Mrs. Surratt, who shortly after that interview discovered that she had some private business at Surrattsville that had to be attended to that day, and so she asked Mr. Wiechmann, a young man who had been a boarder at her house for several months, to drive her down, saying that she wanted to go and see a Mr. Nothey who owed her some money. She then sent Wiechmann to Booth, to get his horse and buggy for the drive. Booth told Wiechmann that he had sold his horse and buggy, but gave him ten dollars with which to procure one. Meeting Lloyd on the way down, driving up to Washington, they stopped; Lloyd got out of his buggy and went to the side of Mrs. Surratt's buggy, on which she was sitting, when Mrs. Surratt told Lloyd, as he afterwards testified, in a low voice, so that Wiechmann did not hear what she said, to have those shooting irons ready, or handy, as they would be called for before long. On the day of the assassination Booth again had a private interview with Mrs. Surratt, after which she again asked Wiechmann to drive her down to Surrattsville, claiming the same errand as before. On this occasion she sought an opportunity for a private interview with Lloyd, when she told him to have the carbines handy, as they would be called for that night, at the same time handing him a field-glass, which Booth had given to her, and telling him to have two bottles of whiskey ready.

John H. Surratt left Washington for Richmond on the 25th of March and returned to Washington on the 3d of April, leaving for Montreal on the evening of the same day. He showed to Wiechmann — an old college friend and, at this time, a boarder in his mother's house — nine or eleven twenty-dollar gold pieces, and sixty dollars in greenbacks, on his return from Richmond. Surratt, in his Rockville lecture, admits that he received two hundred dollars in gold from Benjamin to pay expenses and remunerate for services. Surratt left Washington for Canada on the evening of the 3d of April, and we find him, by the evidence, in Montreal on the 6th, where he delivered to Thompson a cipher dispatch from Jefferson Davis, and a letter from Mr. Benjamin, of Davis's Richmond Cabinet. After reading these documents, Thompson, laying his hand on them, said, "This makes the thing all right." The sanction of the rebel president to his arrangements with the assassins had been obtained, and authority also for the expenditure of funds to fulfil the contract. The Canada conspirators who were to take a part prepared at once, and started for the States, boasting to their friends that they would hear of the death of Old Abe and others before ten days. This was on the 8th of April, and nothing now remained but to find, and use, an opportunity; and Booth selected the appearance of the President at the theatre as affording the opportunity he sought, and proceeded to make all his arrangements accordingly.

All things were now ready. Booth had selected the route for his escape and had provided to be furnished with a field-glass, two carbines, and two bottles of whiskey at Surrattsville, having sent a notice to Lloyd to have them ready, as they would be called for that night. He had provided horses from a livery-stable for himself and Herold, who was to accompany him. He had also provided a horse for Payne, whose part was to murder Secretary Seward. He had assembled his assistants in Washington, to one of whom, Michael O'Laughlin, he had assigned the task of the assassination of General Grant; and having made these preparations, he spent the day and afternoon of the 14th of April looking after the matter generally, and keeping up his courage, or rather recklessness, with frequent potations of whiskey. To Payne he had given a one-eyed bay horse, which he had purchased of a man by the name of Gardner, a neighbor of Dr. Samuel Mudd, in Charles County, Maryland. Mudd accompanied him, and introduced him to Gardner as a man who was desirous of purchasing land in that part of Maryland, and who wished a good driving horse that he could use for a short time. During the afternoon of the 14th, Booth, Herold, and Atzerodt hired horses from liverymen, and were to be seen riding here and there about the streets of Washington, frequently stopping at saloons to refresh themselves with that which obtunds all moral sensibility and makes men reckless in wickedness. Booth was acting the part of a general mustering his forces for the conflict, part of which he thus displayed openly, but keeping another part in concealment. He kept himself in active communication with all, and delivered his orders and instructions. Feeling the full force of the responsibility of his engagment, and earnestly intent on its complete and thorough accomplishment, he attended in person to every detail to make failure, if possible, an impossibility.

It would seem that a previous attempt had been made to assassinate the President, which had resulted in a failure. It was known that President Lincoln was in the habit of riding out to the Soldiers' Home of evenings, passing through a lonely suburb of the city unguarded. Some time in March, John Wilkes Booth, John H. Surratt, Payne, Atzerodt, Herold, and two others, left the house of Mrs. Surratt about two o'clock in the afternoon, on horseback, armed with revolvers and bowie-knives, and returned about six o'clock under the greatest possible excitement of rage and disappointment. All the evidence went to show that this expedition was regarded by them as one of the greatest importance, involving the necessity of leaving the city, perhaps for good, as their return in the evening was as much of a surprise to their friends as it was an occasion of dissatisfaction to themselves. I think there can hardly be a doubt that they expected to intercept the President on his way to the Home, and were lying in wait for him with the purpose of there assassinating him, and then making their escape. The President, however, upon the earnest advice of his cabinet, had yielded the point of riding unprotected and alone, and had accepted the protection of an escort of cavalry on these rides. Booth and his party finding him thus guarded had been compelled to abandon the idea of thus finding an opportunity to assassinate him, and so had to prepare a new plan of operations. There was a rumor, which found its way into the papers about this time, that there was a plot to capture the President and carry him a prisoner to Richmond; but however much Booth's pride and vanity might have impelled him to achieve the notoriety that would have attended the accomplishment of such a feat, the difficulties and dangers attending its accomplishment must have been too obvious to a man of Booth's sagacity, and its success involved in too much uncertainty, to have justified him in making such an attempt.

In view of all the facts, I conclude that the real purpose of Booth and his party on the occasion referred to was to murder the President, and trust to flight for concealment and safety. But now Booth was fully possessed with the idea of the practicability of his present plan, and was determined to know no such word as fail; and that it was entirely possible that, but for a Providential interference, he might have made good his escape after murdering the President, we shall hereafter see.

President Lincoln had been convinced by the most undoubted proofs that a plan for his assassination at Baltimore whilst on his way to Washington, in 1861, to assume the responsibilities of the office to which he had been called by the choice of the people, had been arranged and prepared for by his enemies, and had only been prevented of its execution by the strategic movement planned by his friends, by which he passed through that city during the night previous to the morning on which he was expected.

"From the very beginning of his Presidency Mr. Lincoln had been constantly subject to the threats of his enemies and the warnings of his friends. The threats came in every form: his mail was infested with brutal and vulgar menace, mostly anonymous, the proper expression of vile and cowardly minds.

"The warnings were not less numerous; the vaporings of village bullies, the extravagancies of excited secessionist politicians, even the drolling of practical jokers, were faithfully reported to him by zealous or nervous friends. Most of these communications received no notice. In cases where there seemed a ground for inquiry it was made, as carefully as possible, by the President's private secretary and by the War Department, but always without substantial results.

"Warnings that appeared to be most definite, when they came to be examined proved too vague and confused for further attention. The President was too intelligent not to know he was in some danger. Madmen frequently made their way to the very door of the executive offices, and sometimes into Mr. Lincoln's presence.

"He had himself so sane a mind, and a heart so kindly even to his enemies, that it was hard for him to believe in a political hatred so deadly as to lead to murder. He would sometimes laughingly say, 'Our friends on the other side would make nothing by exchanging me for Hamlin,' the Vice-President having the reputation of more radical views than his chief. He knew, indeed, that incitements to murder him were not uncommon in the South. An advertisement had appeared in a paper of Selma, Alabama, in December, 1864, opening a subscription for funds to affect the assassination of Lincoln, Seward, and Johnson before the inauguration."[1]

In view of all this danger he would say "that he could not possibly guard against it unless he were to shut himself up in an iron box, in which condition he could scarcely perform the duties of a President. By the hand of a murderer he could only die once; to go continually in fear would be to die over and over."

To his faithful and devoted friend, Father Chiniquy, who on several occasions warned him of his danger, and of the ultimate source of its inspiration, he said, "I see no other way than to be always prepared to die. I know my danger; but man must not

---

[1] "Life of Lincoln," by Nicolay and Hay, *Century Magazine*, pp. 431–32.

care how and where he dies, provided he dies at the post of honor and duty."

We have come to the point now where we find, on the part of his murderers, all things ready for his taking off; and their intended victim prepared in mind for his fate, and ready to "die at the post of honor and duty." What a fearful, and at the same time, sublime spectacle! The powers of light and the powers of darkness were contending, as ever, for the supremacy. Satan, the usurper, claims this world for his kingdom. He has seduced and enslaved the human race, and, by every false and cunning device, is always resisting every movement that looks to the disenthralment of mankind, and bringing the world back to its allegiance to God, its rightful sovereign. How sublime was the faith of President Lincoln in the ultimate triumph of the right! How sincerely and believingly could he have sung,

> "Thy saints in all this glorious war,
> Shall conquer though they die;
> They see the triumph from afar,
> By faith they bring it nigh."

CHAPTER III.

ASSASSINATION OF THE PRESIDENT AND ATTEMPTED ASSASSINATION OF SECRETARY SEWARD.

ON the morning of the 14th of April, 1865, the President's messenger went to Ford's Theatre in Washington City and engaged a private box for the President and General Grant, with their wives, to witness the play of "Our American Cousin," which was to be rendered there that night. The heavy burden of responsibility, the weight of cares and anxieties which had for four long years rested on the head of President Lincoln in his official position of President of the United States and Commander-in-Chief of its army and navy, employed during all that time in suppressing a gigantic rebellion of the slave-holding States of the South against the constitutional and lawful authority of the government, and which had followed him into his second term of office, upon which he had just entered, had been partially lifted by the signal success of the Union arms at Appomattox, and the surrender of Lee's army. General Grant, who had just accepted the unconditional surrender of that army, and finished the work of dismissing to their homes the officers and men who had composed it (and who for four long years had fought with such magnificent bravery, and manifested such earnestness and determinedness of purpose in a cause which, though bad, was no doubt esteemed by them to be just), under no other condition than that they should return to their homes and the pursuits of peaceful life, and desist from all further acts of hostility against the government they had sought, but failed, to overthrow, had gone to Washington to talk over the situation with the President and Secretary of War, and to decide on future operations for the speedy establishment of peace. With the surrender of Lee's army, and the successful march of Sherman from Atlanta to the sea, and his almost unresisted progress up the coast toward the Nation's Capital, it was obvious that the rebellion had collapsed, and that the return of peace was just at hand. All loyal hearts throughout the land throbbed with joy, and praise and thanksgiving ascended to Him who had stamped the righteousness of the union cause with the signet of His approbation, in thus giving us the victory after a long and bloody contest. The years of sacrifice, toil, suffering and danger were almost forgotten in the gladness of that hour; and the war-scarred veterans in the field, and their friends at home, were rejoicing at the prospect of a speedy re-union, under skies of peace. It was an hour big with the memories of the past and hopes of the future. When we think of what President Lincoln had endured through all these years of the war; of his unfaltering purpose to discharge all the duties of his official oath, by protecting, defending and preserving the constitution of his country; of the formidable difficulties that had to be met and overcome — difficulties thrown across his pathway often by friends, always by foes; when we remember his largeness of soul, his unbounded love of, and sympathy with, mankind; his all controlling love of his country and her institutions of freedom; his patient toleration of opposing views of martial and of political policy; his self-poise, and almost infallible appreciation of the situation and its demands, in whatever circumstances he might be placed; his kindness of nature and goodness of heart, we can well conceive what must have been his fullness of joy on this the last day of his sojourn on earth. God, in his providence, led him to the opening of a vista through which his patriotic and philanthropic soul could swell with delightful anticipations of the greatness, the glory, and the happiness that should accrue to mankind through his faithfulness to the obligations of his official oath, by which he had vindicated his authority, and brought to a right solution the great moral question underlying the contest, and thus had made our beloved land a land of freedom in fact, as well as in name. He saw a new and glorious era about to dawn on his country. Like Moses, however, he was only permitted, in vision, to look over into the promised land — the great future of his beloved country.

It is consoling to thus know that to the great Lincoln his last day on earth was the happiest, and at the same time, the meekest day of his life. His biographers, Nicolay and Hay, who were able to write from personal association with, and observation of, this great man, inform us that on this day his soul was filled with the kindliest feelings toward his enemies, and in his last conference with his cabinet his policy of dealing with them was shadowed forth as free from feelings of revenge or desire for the punishment of any. He desired that no man should lose his life for the part he had taken in the rebellion. He held "malice toward none," and was filled with "charity for all." His passage from time to eternity, though brought about by the bullet of an assassin, was a passage through a triumphal arch, whose further portal was the gate of heaven.

The presence of General Grant was known to the city, and it was noised abroad that both he and President Lincoln would honor the theatre with their presence on that evening. The public knowledge of this fact was calculated to bring out a brilliant and large assemblage of people. The loyal citizens would be there to give to the President and the successful and popular commander of his armies in the field a heartfelt and royal ovation in this the hour of their triumph. All felt happy and secure. That they were coming together to witness, on that night, the awful tragedy of the assassination of the nation's head, President Lincoln, was not dreamed of by any except those who had made every preparation in advance for accomplishing the murderous plot, and who were stealthily slipping about through the assembling crowds, like fiends, to assure themselves that every arrangement for the successful accomplishment of their hellish purpose was complete. During the day General Grant received a telegram that called him to Philadelphia on business, and owing to this apparently providential circumstance he was prevented from accompanying the President to the theatre on that eventful night, and also, in all probability, from being, with the President, a victim of the plot, in which there is good reason to conclude, from all the evidence, his life was included, and that for him an assassin had been provided.

In lieu of General and Mrs. Grant, President Lincoln had taken Major Rathbone and Miss Harris, the step-son and daughter of Senator Harris, of New York, into the Presidential party. On reaching the theatre at a somewhat late hour, and after the play had commenced, as soon as the presence of the President became known, the actors stopped playing, the band struck up " Hail to the Chief," and the audience rose and received him with vociferous cheering.

The party proceeded along the rear of the dress circle, and entered the box that had been prepared for them, the President taking the rocking chair that had been placed there for him on the left of the box, and nearest to the audience, about four feet from the door of entrance to the box. Major Rathbone and the ladies found seats on the President's right. During this time the conspirators were on the alert, scanning the situation, passing about so as to keep up a communication with each other, in preparation for their work. Booth had arranged with Payne to assassinate Secretary Seward at the same time that he would assassinate the President; and no doubt had planned for Payne, after accomplishing his task, to join him and Herold in their flight, crossing the Eastern Branch at the Navy Yard bridge, and then to pass down through Maryland and cross the Potomac, at a selected point, into Virginia, where they might consider themselves as being safe amongst their friends. Secretary Seward was known to have received severe injuries from the upsetting of his carriage, and to be lying in a critical condition under the care of Dr. Verdi. Booth had planned to take advantage of this circumstance for gaining admittance for Payne into the sick chamber, where, by springing with the ferocity of a tiger upon the sick man, he might make quick work in dispatching him with his dagger. To this end he had prepared a package rolled up in paper, and had schooled Payne in the artifice, teaching him to represent himself as having been sent by Dr. Verdi with this package of medicine, which it was necessary he should deliver in person, as he had important verbal directions as to the manner of its use, which required him to see the Secretary.

About ten o'clock Booth rode up the alley back of the theatre where he had been accustomed to keep his horse, and having reached the rear entrance, called for Ned three times, each time a little louder than before. At the third call Ned Spangler answered to his summons by appearing at the door. Booth's first salutation was in the form of a question: "Ned, you will help me all you can, won't you?" To which Spangler replied, "Oh, yes!" Booth then requested him to send "Peanuts" (a boy employed about the theatre), to hold his horse. Spangler gave the boy orders to do this, and upon the boy making the objection that he might be out of place at the time he had a duty to perform, Spangler bade him go, saying that he would stand responsible for him. The boy then took the reins, and held the horse for about half an hour, until Booth returned to reward him with a curse and a kick, as he jerked the rein from him preparatory to remounting for his flight. After entering the theatre, Booth passed rapidly across the stage, glancing at the box occupied by his intended victim, and looking up his accomplices, he passed out of the front door on to the walk where he was met by two of his fellow conspirators. One of these was a low, villainous-looking fellow, whilst the other was a very neatly-dressed man. Booth held a private conference with these by the door where he and the vulgar-looking fellow had stationed themselves. The neatly-dressed man crossed the walk to the rear of the President's carriage and peeped into it. One of the witnesses, who was sitting on the platform in front of the theatre, had his attention arrested by the manner and conduct of these men, and so watched them very closely.

It was at the close of the second act that Booth and his two fellow conspirators appeared at the door. Booth said, "I think he will come down now"; and they alligned themselves to await his coming. Their communications with each other were in whispered tones. Finding that the President would remain until the close of the play, they then began to prepare to assassinate him in the theatre. The neatly-dressed man called the time three times in succession at short intervals, each time a little louder than before. Booth now entered the saloon, took a drink of whiskey, and then went at once into the theatre. He passed quickly along next to the wall behind the chairs, and having reached a point near the door that led to the passage behind the box, he stopped, took a small pack of visiting cards from his pocket, selected one and replaced the others; stood a second with it in his hand, and then showed it to the President's messenger, who was sitting just below him, and then, without waiting, passed through the door from the lobby into the passage, closing and barring it after him. Taking a hasty, but careful, look through the hole which he had had made in the door for the purpose of assuring himself of the President's position, and cocking his pistol and with his finger on the trigger, he pulled open the door, and stealthily entered the box, where he stood right behind and within three feet of the President. The play had advanced to the second scene of the third act, and whilst the audience was intensely interested Booth fired the fatal shot — the ball penetrating the skull on the back of the left side of the head, inflicting a wound in the brain (the ball passing entirely through and lodging behind the right eye), of which he died at about half-past seven o'clock on the morning of the fifteenth. He was unconscious from the moment he was struck until his spirit passed from earth. An unspeakable calm settled on that remarkable face, leaving the impress of a happy soul on the casket it had left behind.

Thus died the man who said, "Senator Douglass says he don't care whether slavery is voted up, or voted down; but God cares, and humanity cares, and I care."

As soon as Booth had fired his pistol, and was satisfied that his end was accomplished, he cried out, "Revenge for the South!" and throwing his pistol down, he took his dagger in his right hand, and placed his left hand on the balustrade preparatory to his leap of twelve feet to the stage. Just at this moment Major Rathbone sprang forward and tried to catch him. In this he failed, but received a severe cut in his arm from a back-handed thrust of Booth's dagger. Time was everything now to the assassin. He must make good his escape whilst the audience stood dazed, and before it had time to comprehend clearly what had happened. With his left hand on the railing, he boldly leaped from the box to the stage. The front of the box had been draped for the occasion with the American flag, which was stretched across its front, and reached down nearly or quite to the floor. In the descent, Booth's spur caught in the flag, tearing out a piece which he dragged nearly half way across the stage. The flag, however, was avenged for this double insult which he had put upon it; for by this entanglement his descent was deflected, causing him to strike the stage obliquely, and partially to fall, thus fracturing the fibula of his left leg, on account of which injury his flight was impeded, and his permanent escape made impossible. As he recovered himself from his partial fall and started to run across the stage with his dagger brandished aloft, he cried out in a theatrical tone, "*Sic semper tyrannis!*" and quickly passed out at a little back door opening into the alley where he had left his horse, and, though closely pursued, succeeded in mounting, and rode rapidly away.

Of course he could not afford to run any risks in regard to his escape, and for all this he had made his arrangements in advance. Spangler had faithfully redeemed his promise to render him all the aid he could by keeping the passage to the door clear at the critical moment, and also by doing all he could to retard pursuit. When a fellow-employee cried out, "That was Booth!" Ned ordered him to shut up, saying "You don't know who it was." Booth was closely pursued by a man by the name of Stewart, who followed him into the alley, making every effort he could to stop him; but Booth kept his horse in motion, so that Stewart failed to get hold of the rein, and the assassin was soon off at a rapid pace.

Stewart testified that Spangler, or a man resembling him, stood near the door, and could have prevented Booth's exit had he been so disposed. It is evident his purpose was to aid, rather than hinder, his escape. All the occupants of the stage, actors and assistants, male and female, were in a state of confusion and intense excitement except this man, who evidently had not been taken by surprise, but was prepared in mind for what had happened, and had played his part in the tragedy.

At the same hour that Booth fired the fatal shot, Payne appeared at the door of Secretary Seward's house, in the guise of a messenger from Dr. Verdi, holding in his hand the package that Booth had prepared for him, and demanded to see the Secretary, saying that he had a verbal message which was of particular importance in regard to the use, or application of, the medicine, and that he must see the Secretary himself. Dr. Verdi had left his patient but a short time previous, and had consoled the family that had for days been suffering the greatest anxiety on account of the Secretary's condition by taking a favorable view of the symptoms. The family, worn with watching and anxiety, were disposing of themselves for the night. Major A. H. Seward had retired to his room. Sergeant George F. Robinson, acting as attendant nurse, was watching by the bedside, in company with Miss Seward, the Secretary's daughter. Frederick Seward occupied the room at the head of the stairs. All the rooms occupied by the Secretary and his family were on the second floor, and were reached by a flight of stairs in the hallway.

The second waiter, William H. Bell, a colored lad of nineteen, was stationed at the hall door. Being somewhat relieved of their anxiety by the doctor's favorable view of the case, all were anticipating a night of quiet rest. The door bell rang, and was responded to by Bell, the colored waiter. Immediately upon his opening of the door, Payne stepped into the hall. He was a tall, broad-shouldered, muscular man, as agile and ferocious as a panther; a low-browed, scowling, villainous-looking specimen of humanity, the animal preponderating largely in every feature of his visage and expression of his countenance. There he stood, holding in his left hand the package, and keeping his right hand in his overcoat pocket. He demanded of the boy to be allowed to see the Secretary, telling his story about being sent by Dr. Verdi to deliver the medicine with his directions. The porter told him that his orders were to admit no one, and that he could not see Mr. Seward; that he would deliver the package himself. To this Payne would not consent, but persisted in saying that he *must* see Mr. Seward. After considerable parleying, he started up stairs, and the porter, seeing that he would go, and thinking that he might complain of his conduct to the Secretary, asked him to pardon him, to which Payne replied, "O, I know, that's all right."

He was wearing heavy boots, and took no pains to walk lightly as he went up the stairs, whereupon the porter requested him not to make so much noise, to which, however, he paid no attention. As he approached the head of the stairs, he was met by Mr. Frederick Seward, who had been attracted by the noise, to whom he said, "I want to see Mr. Seward." Frederick went into his father's room, and finding him asleep, returned saying, "You cannot see him." All this time Payne stood holding out the package in his left hand, grasping with his right hand the pistol in his overcoat pocket. Frederick requested him to give him the package, saying he would deliver it; but Payne persisted in saying that that would not do; he *must* see Mr. Seward, — he *must* see him.

Frederick finally said, "I am the proprietor here, and his son; if you cannot leave your message with me, you cannot leave it at all." Payne still continued parleying with Frederick for some time; but finding that his talking availed nothing, he started as if to go down stairs. This, however, was only a feint on his part in order to throw Frederick off of his guard and to get rid of the porter who stood behind him. He again walked so heavily that the porter requested him not to make so much noise; but at that moment, Payne, having prepared himself for the encounter, turned quickly, and making a spring towards Frederick, struck him two or three times with the pistol, which he had all the time held in his hand, fracturing his skull and knocking him senseless to the floor. Having learned which was the room occupied by the invalid by seeing Frederick go into it, Payne rushed past the prostrate man, opened the door of the Secretary's room, and was met by Sergeant Robinson. Having broken and thrown down his revolver in his encounter with Frederick, he had drawn his dagger, and at his first encounter with the sergeant he struck him with his knife, cutting an ugly gash in his forehead, and partially knocking him down. He then pressed rapidly forward, knife in hand, to where the invalid lay in his bed. Throwing himself upon him, he commenced striking at his face and neck with his dagger. The Secretary was reclining in a half-sitting posture, having the coverings well drawn up about his neck and chin, to which circumstance the failure of the would-be assassin to take his life was no doubt due. The sergeant, as soon as he recovered his equilibrium, sprang upon Payne, and Major Seward, having been awakened by the screams of his sister, sprang into the room in his night-dress. Finding the sergeant grappling him in such a way as to hinder the effectiveness of his thrusts at the Secretary, and probably thinking that he had accomplished his purpose, he turned his attention toward making his escape. In disentangling himself from the grasp of the two men who now had hold of him, he gave to Major Seward several severe cuts about the head and face, crying all the time, "I am mad! I am mad!" Finally, pulling himself loose, he started to make his way to the street. Meeting a Mr. Emrick W. Hansel, another nurse, on the stairs, he made a thrust at him with his knife, inflicting an ugly wound. He now left the house, leaving five of its inmates stabbed, cut, and bleeding behind him. Having reached the street, he deliberately threw his dagger away, mounted the horse which he had hitched in front of the door, and rode off. Thus, for the time being, this inhuman monster passed from sight, having made good his retreat minus his dagger, hat, and revolver. He was not a moment too soon in withdrawing from the house. The colored porter, as soon as he saw the violence done to Frederick Seward at the head of the stairs, ran down and out into the street with the cry of "murder," and did not stop until he reached General Angur's headquarters, where he reported the occurrence and ran back immediately, accompanied by two or three soldiers. They reached the house just in time to see Payne mount his horse and ride away. He was followed some distance by the porter, who kept nearly up with him for some time, as he rode slowly at first, but he then mended his pace, and was soon out of sight. The soldiers, having no orders and not comprehending the situation, made no effort to stop him, although the colored boy who gave the alarm, and who preceded them, pointed him out to them as the man who had so ruthlessly broken the quiet of that house and produced such consternation amongst its peaceful inmates.

Although Payne rode away so leisurely at the start, he put his horse to the top of his speed as soon as he had fairly cleared the streets and reached the suburbs of the city. About two hours later, a bay horse, saddled, and blind of an eye, came running up a by-road that led to Camp Barry, about three-fourths of a mile east of the capitol, and was there halted and taken charge of and placed in General Angur's stables. The horse, when found, bore marks of having been ridden at a furious rate. The sweat was streaming from every pore and dripping to the ground. This proved to be the bay horse that Booth had bought from Gardner, the neighbor of Dr. Mudd, in November, 1864, and which he sold to his co-conspirator, Arnold, in January, 1865, according to his own statement made some time before the assassination.

This was no doubt the horse rode by Payne on that night. The most probable theory is, that being pushed and urged at a furious rate, and being blind of an eye, he stumbled and pitched headlong, throwing, and probably stunning, his rider, after which he regained his footing and made his escape before Payne had sufficiently recovered to get hold of him. The fact of his being a little lame when caught goes to sustain this theory. Thus was the would-be assassin prevented from joining his comrades, Booth and Herold, in their flight, and compelled to skulk and hide in the suburbs of the city for the next two days. He was without arms and hatless, and was compelled to throw away his overcoat, which was afterwards found, on account of the bloodstains on its sleeves. He knew that the alarm would spread rapidly throughout the vicinity, and in his present condition he dared not venture out through the country, so he was compelled to spend the time in hiding and skulking until he was forced from his retreat by hunger. Making a covering for his head out of a sleeve from his under-shirt, which he drew over it like a turban, he shouldered a pick, which he had stolen from the trenches, and at near the hour of midnight on the 17th he entered the city. He went directly to the house of Mrs. Surratt, as the safest place he could find to rest, hide, and refresh himself, and obtain an outfit in which he might make his escape. Here he felt that he could trust the secret of his presence. Unfortunately for him, as well as for Mrs. Surratt, the government had by this time come into possession of such information as justified it in sending its military police to that house, with orders to arrest its inmates.

It had been discovered that the house of Mrs. Surratt had been the headquarters of the conspirators in Washington City. The officer in charge of the police, Major H. W. Smith, had reached the house but a short time before Payne arrived. Payne came with his turban on his head, and the pick on his shoulder, and rang the door-bell. Major Smith responded to the bell, and asked him to come in. Seeing the officer, he said he believed he was mistaken in the house. Being asked whose house he sought, he replied, " Mrs. Surratt's." The officer replied, " This is the place," and drawing his revolver on him, ordered him to come in. Payne entered, and the officer closed the door. He then inquired who he was, and what he wanted. To these questions he replied that he was a poor man, and a laborer, and that Mrs. Surratt had sent for him to dig a drain for her. On being asked what brought him there at that time of night, he replied that he " merely called to see what time Mrs. Surratt wanted him to go to work in the morning." The officer saw that his hands bore no marks of labor, and at once suspected he had caged one of the conspirators. He placed him under arrest and took him along with the others in the house, to General Angur's head-quarters, where he was held for identification. William H. Bell, the colored boy who was second waiter at Mr. Seward's, being sent for, at once unhesitatingly identified him as the man who had produced such consternation in the house of Mr. Seward, on the night of the 14th, by his determined efforts to take the Secretary's life. Lewis Payne, having been thus captured and identified, and Mrs. Mary E. Surratt, were the first amongst the conspirators to be held for trial.

After the attack at Secretary Seward's, Dr. Verdi and two or three other surgeons were at once called to examine and treat the Secretary and the other victims of Payne's dagger. The house in which the onslaught was made had the appearance of a charnal house or slaughter-pen. The Secretary was found to have received three or four severe cuts about the face and neck, which were only made dangerous by the loss of blood they had occasioned and the weak condition of the patient.

The Secretary made a slow but good recovery. Of the other

four wounded men, the wounds of Mr. Frederick Seward proved the most serious, as his skull had been fractured and depressed, so as to render him unconscious, from which condition he was only recalled by a surgical operation.

All finally recovered. Here again we are called to notice the providences in the case, leading to the capture of Payne, and to the bringing on his head the just reward of his deeds.

CHAPTER IV.

THE NEWS COMMUNICATED TO THE WORLD, AND ITS EFFECT.

ON the morning of the 15th of April, 1865, the telegraph wires carried to every part of the United States that was in communication with Washington, and to the rest of the civilized world, the astounding intelligence that Abraham Lincoln, President of the United States, had been assassinated on the previous night by John Wilkes Booth, at Ford's Theatre in Washington City; that at the same hour a most savage attempt had been made to assassinate the Secretary of State, Hon. William H. Seward, and that he was lying in a most critical and dangerous condition from the wounds which he had received, and would probably die. Never, perhaps, in the history of the race were so many hearts bleeding, and so many eyes suffused with tears at one time, as on that sorrowful day. The nation was filled with grief, mingled with indignation and horror at the deed. The land was literally draped in mourning. Every city, and every town and village, displayed the sable habiliments of grief. The response came back to our people, in kind, from every civilized people on earth.

The writer was at the time a member of Grant's victorious army, and had large opportunities for witnessing the effects produced by the sad intelligence on the soldiery of our country. From the highest officers down to the rank and file of the army, sorrow and grief were depicted on every countenance. From Appomattox to Richmond the victorious army that had been filled with joyful and hopeful anticipations over its successes, and the prospect of the speedy dawn of peace, and of returning to their homes and friends and to the pursuits of peaceful life, after four years of arduous military service, was at once plunged into the deepest sadness and gloom. Strong men wept. It was as though every soldier had lost his dearest friend. There was always a day of sadness in the army after every great battle, even in the triumphs of victory, at the thought of the many brave comrades who had given up their lives for their country, and would never again be seen in the ranks, — who were even then being gathered up from the field and carefully laid away in silence to await the resurrection morn; and of the others, who with loss of limbs and fearful wounds, were receiving the care of the surgeons and nurses in the hospitals improvised for the occasion; but never before had such a pall of grief been thrown over the entire army.

The depth of sorrow into which the nation was plunged by the news of his assassination revealed, as nothing else could have done, the place Abraham Lincoln held in the confidence and affections of the loyal people of the land. The first shock of the sad intelligence was almost paralytic. The people — even the army — for the moment stood dazed and bewildered. What was the meaning of all this? Was the war to be prolonged? Were we now to be called upon to turn our victorious arms upon the enemy in the rear, of whose existence we had all the time been conscious? Such were the questions that first suggested themselves. If so, the army was then in a state of mind to have made a short work of it. The victory over our armed foe in front, who had so bravely met us, and often with success, on many a hotly-contested field, would never have been yielded to the disloyal cowards who, through all of these years of the war, from their safe retreats and hiding-places, threw every obstacle they could in the way of our now martyred President, and who had planned and accomplished his taking off.

The extent of the conspiracy had not as yet been revealed; but enough was known to the government to evince the fact that this was an act of deep political significance, having behind it a very different class of men from the dissolute and depraved assassins who were executing their behests, and not merely done for the gratification of personal and political revenge. It was obvious that the occasion called for the most vigorous and decided measures on the part of the government to meet and overcome the strategy of assassinations just now entered upon. It very soon became known to the authorities that the plot had been but very partially executed, and that the purpose of the conspirators was to subvert the constitution by depriving the nation of its executive head, and leaving no constitutional way of electing a new President, and at the same time to deprive the armies in the field of a lawful commander. To accomplish this, the President, Vice-President, Secretary of State, and General Grant were all to have been assassinated. The conspirators in Canada and also the rebel president, when they heard that only President Lincoln had been killed, could not conceal their disappointment, and virtually confessed that their deep-laid scheme had proven a failure. The former still adhered to their purpose, and in their rage declared, "We are not done with them yet." We hardly dare to venture upon the consideration of what would have been the result had they completed the work they had planned. We have reason for profound thankfulness to that God who has thus far so wisely and graciously watched over our national progress, that he did not permit its accomplishment. But we, who were actors on the stage at that time, knowing how the principal actors in our national affairs, both civil and military, had been schooled in self-sacrificing, patriotic devotion to the institutions of our fathers, and their unfaltering purpose to transmit them unimpaired to their children and children's children for a perpetual inheritance, can but feel assured that even in the dire extremity now under consideration they would have proven true to their trust, and would have found a way to restore all of the machinery of government provided for in the Constitution. The people are above the Constitution even as the maker is above the thing made.

The rebel armies had been so completely overcome that they could no longer have formed even a nucleus around which the traitors in the North could have organized an opposition that could have been regarded with other than feelings of contempt by our victorious hosts. The time had passed; the opportunity was gone. No wonder the conspirators in Canada gnashed their teeth with rage and disappointment because "the boys had not been allowed to act when they wanted to." They had amongst their many schemes concocted during the summer of 1864, such as making raids, liberating rebel prisoners of war held in Northern prisons, burning cities, spreading pestilence, and poisoning reservoirs, been led also to consider this scheme of assassinations. All of these things were to be done in aid of the rebellion.

As their cause became desperate on account of the continued success of our arms, so did they become desperate in planning to retrieve. As early as January, 1865, they received a communication from Jefferson Davis suggesting these things and urging them to stop at nothing, however desperate, and plainly intimating that Lincoln ought not to be allowed to live; but it was not until the latter part of March, 1865, that they were prepared to present to him a definitely-prepared plan for the accomplishment of their purposes that he could accept and sanction. They had thus been long delayed, and now they were compelled to realize that their work was a failure. No wonder that they all, from Jefferson Davis down, felt and expressed grievous disappointment. It reminds us of Milton's description of the malignant schemes, failures, disappointments, and rage of the Prince of Devils in his contests with the Almighty.

CHAPTER V.

UNRAVELLING THE PLOT. — PURSUIT AND CAPTURE OF BOOTH AND HEROLD. — DEATH OF BOOTH.

THE most active measures were at once resorted to by the government to discover the conspirators, and to capture all who could be found of those engaged in it. The civil and military police, as also those engaged in the secret service of the government, were at once set to work. It was soon learned that Booth and a co-conspirator, which proved to be Herold, had passed over the navy-yard bridge, on horseback, very shortly after the hour at which the fatal shot had been fired, and were fleeing toward Surrattsville and Bryantown in Maryland. They had been allowed to pass by the sentinel at the bridge, having represented themselves as citizens on their way to their homes. Booth was first at the bridge, and gave his true name to the sentinel, saying that he lived close to Beautown. Five minutes later Herold came and gave his name as Smith, saying that he lived at White Plains and was on his way home. Having gotten safely on the road, they directly joined company, and pushed on rapidly, arriving at Surrattsville about midnight.

Stopping at Lloyd's tavern in Surrattsville, Herold dismounted and went into the house, saying to Lloyd, "For God's sake, make haste and get those things!" Lloyd, understanding what he wanted from the notification given him by Mrs. Surratt on the evening previous, without making any reply, went and got the carbines, which he had placed in his bedroom that they might be handy, and brought them to Herold, together with the ammunition and field-glass that had been deposited with him, and the two bottles of whiskey that Booth had ordered through Mrs. Surratt the evening before. Herold carried out to Booth one of the bottles of whiskey, drinking from his own bottle in the house before going out. Booth declined taking his carbine, saying his leg was broken and he could not carry it. As they were about leaving, Booth said to Lloyd, "I will tell you some news if you want to hear it"; and then went on to say, "I am pretty certain that we have assassinated the President and Secretary Seward." The moon was now up and shining brightly, and the two confessed criminals resumed their flight. The next heard of them was at the house of Dr. Samuel A. Mudd, near Bryantown, in Maryland, and about thirty miles from Washington, where they arrived at about four o'clock on the morning of the 15th, having travelled at the rate of six miles per hour.

Booth's leg had been broken by a fracture of the fibula, or small bone of the leg, when he fell on the stage on leaping from the President's box, and by this time had become very painful. He greatly needed the support of a splint, and quiet as well. He was in a position, however, to get neither; for although he had reached the house of a co-conspirator, who was a country doctor, and well disposed to render him all the aid he could, he appears to have made a very bungling out, dressing the broken limb with some pasteboard and a bandage that gave but a very imperfect support. As to the rest he required, that was impossible, for although Mudd placed him in an upstairs room and kept him until the afternoon, they were admonished by seeing a squad of soldiers under Lieutenant Dana passing down past Mudd's place, which was a quarter of a mile off the road to Bryantown, that there was no rest for the wicked; and as quickly as it could be done after the soldiers passed, Mudd got rid of his dangerous charge by sending them by an unfrequented route to the house of his friend and neighbor, Samuel Cox, about six miles nearer to the Potomac. Booth was on no new ground, neither amongst strangers either to his person or to his wicked purpose. He had spent a good deal of his time during the previous fall in that part of Maryland, preparing a way for his escape after accomplishing his purpose. His way had seemed clear to him in advance; his route had been selected; his friendly acquaintanceships secured. But, alas! the broken leg. Under the guise of looking at the

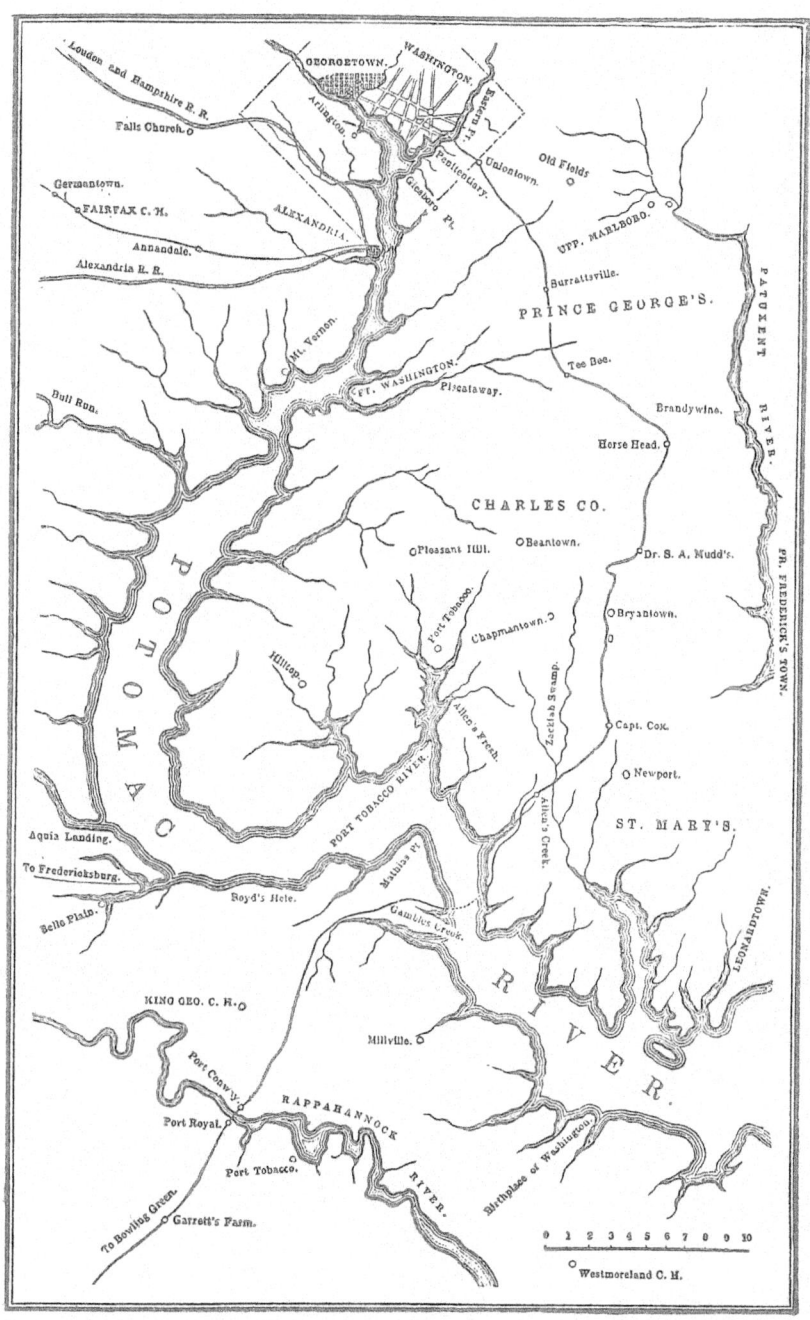

MAP OF BOOTH'S ROUTE.

country with a desire to purchase lands, he had perfected all his arrangements, and had expected to pass swiftly over his route, accompanied by Atzerodt (whose home was in this neighborhood, and who knew all about the contraband trade with the rebel capital, the underground mail route between Richmond and Washington, and all of the people engaged in these operations, and also the place and facilities for crossing the Potomac), and also by Payne and Herold. He had purposed to be safe on the soil of the Old Dominion e'er this time. Instead of realizing all this, he found himself a cripple, scarcely able to travel, and closely pursued by those whom he knew to be on his trail, with no other companion than his devoted but inefficient friend, Herold; and thus he was compelled to realize that

> "The best laid schemes o' mice and men
> Gang aft aglee;
> And lea' us nought but grief and pain
> For promised joy."

Mudd had done all he could to relieve him, but dare not try to conceal and keep him. He could only forward him to the next stage of his journey and to a safe place of concealment. This he faithfully did. Cox lived near Port Tobacco, the home of Atzerodt; and as his was too public a place to afford safety to the fugitives, he turned them over to his neighbor, Thomas Jones, a contraband trader between Maryland and Richmond, who, in the midst of a constant scouring of the country by pursuing parties, kept his charge concealed in the woods near his house, supplying them with food and doing everything he could for their comfort, waiting and watching constantly to find an opportunity to get them across the Potomac. They were hunted so closely that they could hear the neighing of the horses of the troopers, and fearing they might be betrayed by their horses answering the calls, Herold led them into a swamp near where they lay concealed in the pines and shot them.

The river was being continually patroled by gun-boats, and the task of getting his wards across proved both difficult and dangerous to Jones. The proclamation of the Secretary of War, offering one hundred thousand dollars for the capture of Booth, and warning all persons from aiding the fugitives in any way in making their escape, had been published broadcast, yet Jones was true to his trust. Neither the offered rewards nor the warnings of the proclamation had any effect on him; but for a whole week he kept them secreted in the pines on his premises, where Booth lay night and day wrapped in a pair of blankets that had most likely been furnished him by Dr. Mudd. Finally, being furnished by Jones with a boat, they took their own risks and effected a crossing; but they were seen by a colored man, upon whose report General Baker got on their track and finally effected their capture.

There can be no doubt that Booth had selected this as the route for his escape months before, and that all of his visits to this part of Maryland had been made with reference to this plan. Being at length across the Potomac, even though under such unfavorable auspices, Booth no doubt drew a free and exultant breath at having been permitted to set his foot at last on the soil of the Old Dominion. He felt that he was now amongst friends who would aid him in his progress, or help him by concealment, as the case might require; and his friend Jones no doubt breathed with a freedom he had not known for some days at finding himself cut loose from his dangerous charge. Booth was greatly disappointed at the cold reception given him by the people on whom he had counted so much after crossing into Virginia. He had expected to be lionized and honored as the hero of the age; but instead of that he received a comparatively cold reception that stung his vanity like the poison of an asp.

It is true the people showed no disposition to betray him; but, at the same time, they manifested a disposition to enter into no compromising friendship with him, or in any way to assume any responsibility in his behalf by helping him to escape. How much of this was due to abhorrence of his crime, and how much to a dread of consequences, can only be a matter of conjecture. The fact that they were willing to let him escape, if he could, would throw the preponderance on the latter as the governing motive of their conduct. Sad, indeed, was Booth's condition at this time. More than a week had elapsed since he had perpetrated his great

DAVID E. HEROLD.

crime and commenced his guilty flight; and now he found himself on foot, so lame as scarcely to be able to walk a step, even with the help of a crutch, and scarcely more than fifty miles from his starting point. His companion in crime, Herold, was now the only human being on whose friendship and fidelity he could certainly rely. A reward of one hundred and seventy-five thousand dollars offered for his capture, the brand of Cain upon him, his fractured bone cutting into the flesh at every movement of his limb, — a constant admonition of a frowning Providence, — it is no wonder that the diurnal entries in his book begin to bear evidence of a remorse that can never be appeased. We can but pity his deplorable condition, for he was a fellow-man; but then he was at the same time a monster in crime, directed by hatred of a fellow-man without just cause, and of wickedness that had brought upon him the blood of one of the greatest and best of men, not only of his own age and country, but of all the ages of the world. When we contemplate his crime, our sympathies refuse to go with him, and our sense of justice finds a grateful feeling of relief in the evidence now clearly pointing to the fact that he is a doomed man.

By the aid of his blind follower, Herold, he is able to maintain his concealment, and after a wretched fashion to resume his flight in an old wagon drawn by two miserable horses and driven by a negro. In this state he reaches Port Conway, on the Rappahannock, in King George County, Virginia. Here his driver refuses to take him any further. It is just at this juncture and in this dilemma that they are met by three confederate soldiers, Major Ruggles, Lieutenant Bainbridge, and Captain William Jett, the latter of Moseby's command.

Herold, thinking they were recruiting for the rebel service, was quick to see in them a means of assistance in getting South, and under the protection of the stars and bars, and so revealed their identity, appealing to them for assistance. A little later, Booth, getting out of the wretched conveyance, came forward, and to assure himself of their disposition toward him, accosted them with the interrogatory, "I suppose you have been told who we are?" then, throwing himself back on his crutch, and straightening himself up, with pistol cocked and drawn, he said, "Yes, I am Wilkes Booth, the slayer of Abraham Lincoln, and I am worth just one hundred and seventy-five thousand dollars to the man that captures me." His attitude and speech was that of a man at bay, under the power of a desperate purpose never to be taken alive. These three officers of the confederate army (for they were such at this time, not having been paroled), whilst mildly protesting that they did not sanction his acts as an assassin, assured him that they did not want any blood money, and promised to render him all the assistance in their power in making his escape, a promise which they faithfully kept. Major Ruggles dismounted and placed Booth on his horse, when the whole party crossed over the Rappahannock, from Port Conway, in King George, to Port Royal, in Caroline County, Virginia, and after an ineffectual effort to find quarters for Booth in the town, they took him three miles on the road to Bowling Green, the county seat of the latter county, where they succeeded in getting a man by the name of Garrett to take him in, with the understanding that he would do all he could for his comfort and safety. Garrett took Booth and Herold in with a full knowledge of all the facts in the case, and with some manifest reluctance from a knowledge of the danger he would thus incur.

Bainbridge and Herold went on to Bowling Green, whilst Ruggles and Jett remained over night in the woods near the house, Booth being hid away on the premises and cared for. On the following day Captain Jett went to Bowling Green on a visit, prompted by the tender passion, where he intended to remain a few days; and Lieutenant Bainbridge returned to the Garrett farm, where he rejoined Major Ruggles. The two started for Port Conway, but before getting there, learned that the town was full of Yankee cavalry, when they lost no time in returning to Garrett's, and gave warning to Booth, advising him to lose no time in fleeing to a piece of woods, which they pointed out to him, and then turned to look out for their own safety. The cavalry of which they got this notice was a squad detailed from the Sixteenth New York Regiment, commanded by Lieutenant Dougherty, which had been ordered to report to General L. C. Baker of the Secret Service Department, and by him placed in charge of E. J. Conger and L. B. Baker, officers belonging to his detective force.

Arriving at Port Conway on the afternoon of the day subsequent to the crossing of the parties above referred to, and finding the wife of the ferry keeper at the ferry-house sitting and conversing with another women, Colonel Conger exhibited to them a photograph of Booth, and informed them that that was the man they wanted. It at once became apparent to him, from the manner and actions of the woman, that Booth was not far off. The ferryman, a man by the name of Rollins, was sent for, and being influenced no doubt by fear of compromising himself he became very communicative. He told them all about the party that had crossed the day before, one of whom, Captain Jett, he knew well; and knowing that Jett had been paying attention to a Miss Goldman, the daughter of a Bowling Green hotel keeper, he suggested that he would most probably be found there. Colonel Conger pushed on with his squad of cavalry, commanded by Captain, then Lieutenant, E. P. Dougherty, to Bowling Green, passing the Garrett farm after dark.

Arriving at Goldman's Hotel, he inquired of Mrs. Goldman as to the men that were in the house. She answered him that her wounded son was in a room upstairs, and that he was all the man there was there. Colonel Conger then required her to lead the way upstairs, telling her at the same time that if his men were fired on he would burn the building and carry its inmates to Washington as prisoners. As he entered the room which she showed him, up one flight of stairs, Captain Jett jumped out of bed half-dressed, and admitted his identity. Colonel Conger then informed him that he was cognizant of his movements for the last two days, and proceeded to read to him the proclamation of the Secretary of War, telling him when he had done reading it that if he did not tell him the truth he would hang him; but that if he truly gave him the information that he sought he would protect him. Jett was greatly excited, and told him that he had left Booth at the Garrett Farm, three miles from Port Royal. The Colonel then had Jett's horse taken from the stable, making Jett his unwilling guide to the place of Booth's concealment.

Arriving at Garrett's, the cavalry was so disposed of as to prevent any one from escaping, and after having extorted, by threats, the information that Booth and Herold were concealed in the barn, it was at once surrounded. They were ordered to come out and surrender themselves, which Booth refused to do. After a considerable parley, Herold came to the door and gave himself up. He was followed by the maledictions of Booth, who accused him of cowardly unfaithfulness in thus deserting him. Booth still refusing to surrender, a wisp of hay was fired and thrown in on the hay in the barn. From this start the barn was soon lighted up with the flames of the burning hay. Booth was known to be armed and desperate, and as the burning hay began to illuminate the barn he was seen, carbine in hand, peering through the cracks, and trying to get an aim. He had before offered to fight the crowd for a chance of his life if the Colonel would but withdraw his men one hundred yards. Being answered that they had come to capture him, not to fight, he was preparing to sell his life as dearly as possible. At this moment, Sergeant Boston Corbett, of the Sixteenth New York Cavalry, fired at Booth through a crack in the barn, upon his own responsibility, and struck him on the back part of his head, very nearly in the same part where his own ball had struck the President, only a little lower down, and passing obliquely through the base of the brain and upper part of the spinal cord; it produced instantly almost complete paralysis of every muscle in his body below the seat of the wound, the nerves of organic life only sufficing to keep up a very difficult and imperfect respiration, and a feeble action of the heart for a few hours, when, with the coming of the morning of the 26th of April, 1865, twelve days after the commission of his crime and commencement of his flight, the malefactor expired. He was perfectly clear in his mind, but could not swallow, and was scarcely able to articulate so as to be understood, although he seemed anxious to talk. He requested the officer, who was waiting over him and trying to minister to him, to tell his mother that he died for his country. Thus was avenged, not the loyal North alone, but the cause of justice, the cause of freedom, the cause of humanity. Amongst the articles found on his person the most important as bearing on the conspiracy in which he was engaged was a bill of exchange, as follows : —

THE ONTARIO BANK,
MONTREAL BRANCH.

No. 1492.
Stamp.

Exchange for £61 12s. 10d.

MONTREAL, 27th October, 1864.

Sixty days after sight of this first exchange (second and third of same tenor and date unpaid) pay to the order of J. Wilkes Booth sixty-one pounds, twelve shillings, and ten pence sterling. Value received and charge to account of this office.

To Messrs. GLYNN, MILLS & Co., London.

[Signed]   H. STANUS, *Manager*.

The body was brought to Washington and identified fully. It was buried, for the time secretly, under the floor of the old Capitol Prison, but afterwards was given up to his friends.

Major Ruggles, in his account of his connection with Booth in his flight, gives it as his opinion that he was not shot, as claimed, by Sergeant Corbett, but that seeing escape hopeless, and knowing death to be his fate, he took his own life, holding his pistol to the back of his head; and in support of this opinion refers to the fact that one chamber of his revolver was found to be empty. He also advances the opinion that had the war still been going on, and Booth had made his escape into the confederate lines, the rebel government would have arrested him and delivered him up to the United States authorities. In this opinion he takes a charitable view of the virtue and moral integrity of the Richmond government which I shall hereafter show is not warranted by the facts and evidence in the case. In this opinion he is also giving that government credit for a degree of virtue and integrity in striking contrast with the conduct of himself and his companions, who hurriedly entered into a friendly compact with the assassins, knowing them to be such, pledging fidelity and assistance to the full extent of their ability under the circumstances in which they were placed, thus morally and legally making themselves accomplices after the fact.[1]

[1] The evidence before the Commission left Booth and Herold, from the time they left Dr. Mudd's until they arrived at Port Conway, unaccounted for. I am indebted to articles in the *Century Magazine*, by George A. Townsend, Major Ruggles, and Lieutenant Bainbridge, for the ability to fill up this interval, and to General Baker's "History of the Secret Service," for facts connected with the capture, death, and burial of Booth.— AUTHOR.

CHAPTER VI.

UNRAVELLING THE CONSPIRACY.

Arrest of Spangler, O'Laughlin, Atzerodt, Mudd, and Arnold.

NOT only was the government bending every energy to overtake and capture Booth and Herold, but also to find out who were their co-conspirators. It undertook a systematic investigation of Booth's haunts, associations, habits, and employment during the recent past. Hotel registers were overhauled, liverymen interviewed, and each clue followed up, so that in a short time enough was known to lead to the arrest of Edward Spangler, Michael O'Laughlin, George A. Atzerodt, Samuel Arnold, and Dr. Samuel A. Mudd, in addition to those heretofore spoken of as having been arrested. By this time the evidence in possession of the government made it clear that what had occurred was but a partial accomplishment of a great conspiracy, which had its origin with the agents of the rebel government in Canada; and that its execution had been entrusted to John Wilkes Booth and John H. Surratt, as leaders, and to such assistants as they should select and employ.

It was soon discovered that Booth's intimate associates, with whom he held private confidential intercourse, were John H. Surratt, and his mother, Mary E. Surratt, Lewis Payne, George A. Atzerodt, Dr. Samuel A. Mudd, David E. Herold, Samuel Arnold, and Michael O'Laughlin; and that the house of Mrs. Surratt was the headquarters of the conspirators in Washington. Arnold and O'Laughlin were intimate personal friends and associates of Booth at his home in Baltimore. Booth, Payne, and Atzerodt were frequent callers at the house of Mrs. Surratt, where they were always made welcome; their business was always of a private, confidential nature, and was with John Surratt when he

EDWARD SPANGLER

was at home, but in his absence was with Mrs. Surratt herself. Booth had every privilege granted to him in that house, his requests for a private conference being always responded to by John or his mother. To Booth it seemed to be a matter of indifference which of the two it was. In tracing his movements the last few months preceeding the assassination, it soon became evident that he was acting under the impulse of a purpose that had entire possession of his mind. Having undertaken to secure the accomplishment of the assassinations planned by Davis and his Canada Cabinet, in the latter part of October, 1864, he was constantly employed in making his preparations for the fulfillment of his contract, and gave no time or thought, apparently, to anything else. He entirely abandoned his profession, that of an actor, and lost all interest in the stage. He no longer consorted with those of his profession to any extent, except as it might be in preparation for the work to which he had devoted his life, and accepted, instead, the fellowship of such low-browed scoundrels as Payne and Atzerodt as better suited to his purpose. They became mere tools in his hands, sympathizing with him fully in his intense disloyalty, but being actuated at the same time by a mercenary motive, the evidence justifying the conclusion that they had a promise of a large pecuniary reward. He spent a great deal of time with these men, studying their characters, and schooling them in the parts they were to act. They were all known to the liverymen of the city, of whom they very frequently obtained horses to ride about the suburbs and study the roads, that they might be thoroughly familiar with the locality when the time should come for them to make their escape. They were all known, also, to go constantly armed with revolvers and bowie-knives by those who had opportunities of seeing them together in their private intercourse. They boarded at different hotels, and frequently changed their boarding-places, but were frequent visitors of each other at whatever places they might be stopping, and their intercourse was always observed to be that of privacy; and so it became a just cause for suspicion to have been an intimate companion of Booth, and finally led to the arrest of them all.

With regard to the relations existing between Booth and John H. Surratt, and his mother, Mary E. Surratt, the evidence showed that they would always retire to an upstairs room whenever a lengthy conference was desired; but that they frequently held short private conferences in the parlor, when it could be done without danger of interruption. Booth's right to thus come into the house and demand these private interviews was never questioned, but granted with the alacrity due to a common purpose that required it.

Foundation for the Arrest of Mrs. Surratt.

The agents of the government, in pursuing their investigations, obtained evidence that Mrs. Surratt's house had been the meeting-place or headquarters of the conspirators, and that she was in private, confidential intercourse with Booth. One of the principal witnesses against her was Louis J. Wiechmann, who had been for several months a boarder in her house, and whose friendly relations with the family were due to the fact that he had been a fellow-student with John H. Surratt at St. Charles College, in Maryland, and to the further fact that they were co-religionists. Wiechmann had been, during all this time that he had been a boarder at Mrs. Surratt's, employed as a clerk in the office of General Hoffman, Commissary General of Prisoners; and from him the facts above alleged were learned. Wiechmann also stated that Mrs. Surratt sent him to Booth with a message that she wanted to see him on private business, and that Booth replied that he would come that evening or as soon as he could, and that he did come that evening.

On the Tuesday previous to the assassination, Mrs. Surratt requested Wiechmann to drive her down to Surrattsville, saying that she wanted to see a Mr. Nothey who owed her some money. Upon his consenting to do so, she sent him to the National Hotel to see Booth, and request the use of his horse and buggy for the occasion. Booth said he had sold his horse and buggy, but handed to Wiechmann ten dollars with which to procure one. Wiechmann got a conveyance and drove Mrs. Surratt to Surrattsville and back. As they were on their way down, they met

Lloyd, to whom Mrs. Surratt had rented her farm and tavern at Surrattsville. Mrs. Surratt requested Wiechmann to stop; and Lloyd, stopping at the same time, got out of his buggy and came close to Mrs. Surratt, who conversed with him in so low a tone that Wiechmann did not hear what was said, but Lloyd testified before the Commission that she told him to "have those shooting-irons where they would be convenient, as they would be wanted before long." The "shooting-irons" referred to were two carbines, which, with ammunition, a monkey-wrench, and a piece of rope, had been left with Lloyd by John H. Surratt, Herold, and Atzerodt about three weeks before, with the request that he should keep them hid, Surratt at the same time showing him a safe place to secrete them. On the Friday of the assassination, Mrs. Surratt requested Wiechmann to drive her down to Surrattsville, alleging that she was going to see Mr. Nothey again on the same business as before. She gave Wiechmann money to procure a conveyance and he drove her down. Booth was with her in the parlor when he returned with the conveyance, and when Mrs. Surratt was about getting into the buggy, she requested Wiechmann to wait until she went and got Mr. Booth's things. She went back into the parlor and returned with a field-glass, which she delivered to Lloyd. They reached Surrattsville about four o'clock. Mrs. Surratt then had Wiechmann sit down and write a note to Mr. Nothey at her dictation, which she sent to him by a Mr. Bennett Gwin. Lloyd had gone to Marlboro to court, and Mrs. Surratt awaited his return which was not until about half-past six oclock. When Lloyd returned, he drove around into the back yard to unload some fish and oysters which he had purchased, and Mrs. Surratt, who had been waiting and watching for his return, seized this opportunity to see him privately, when she told him, as Lloyd testified before the Commission, to have the carbines ready, as they would be called for that night, and also two bottles of whiskey. Then going with him into the house, she gave him the field-glass.

She was now ready to return, and expressed anxiety to Wiechmann to reach home before nine o'clock, saying that she had an engagement for that hour. She reached her home just before nine, and a few moments later Wiechmann, from his place at the table in the dining-room below, heard the door-bell ring, and some one enter the parlor. The interview was very short — just long enough for Mrs. Surratt to say that all was right — when Wiechmann heard retreating footsteps, but did not know who the visitor was. In view, however, of all the foregoing, we cannot resist the conclusion that Booth was the person, and that this was their last interview. Mrs. Surratt was able to produce the letter of Mr. Calvert which she claimed required her to go to Surrattsville that day to see Mr. Nothey, but she had no appointment to meet him there, did not see him, and could just as well have written to him from her home in Washington. This excuse for her visit was a mere fabrication. Her real business was with Lloyd, and she was not ready to return until after she had an interview with him, and delivered her message from Booth, and the field-glass which he had given her. It is evident that her show of private business was gotten up as a cover to her real errand.

Again, Payne had visited the Surratt house on several occasions. The first time he came he called for John H. Surratt, and on being told by Wiechmann that John was not at home, he requested to see Mrs. Surratt. He passed this time under the alias of Wood, and was received by Mrs. Surratt, and kept over night, when he departed for Baltimore. About three weeks later, say about the 20th of March (as his first visit was about the 1st of March), he made his second visit, passing under the name of Payne, and remained three days. It was during this visit that the episode already referred to as having in all probability been an attempt to murder the President on his visit to the Soldier's Home, occurred, and from which Surratt, Booth, and Payne returned under such excitement and evident disappointment.

To such members of the family as had not been initiated into the plot, this man of many aliases — Wood, Payne, and Powell — passed as a Baptist preacher. He said that he had taken the oath whilst in Baltimore, and intended henceforth to be a good, loyal man. When this man came to the house of Mrs. Surratt on the night of the 17th of April, as heretofore related, and was placed under arrest, Mrs. Surratt, who had also upon a knowledge of the

LEWIS PAYNE.

facts just recited been arrested a few minutes before, when she was called into the hall and confronted with Payne, having heard his story as to why he had come and what he had come for, holding up her hands exclaimed, "Before God, I do not know this man, and never saw him before." He had been a guest at her table for three days only a few days previous to this, and was a man of such a marked personality that having seen him once it would have been impossible to have failed to recognize him on seeing him again, even though he might have been partially disguised. With a woman's intuitive perception, she saw the compromising effect that his visit at that time of night, and under such circumstances, was calculated to have on her own case, and so felt the necessity of this solemn disavowal of any knowledge of him. Before the government felt justified in arresting this woman, only, indeed, two or three hours after the assassination, it being known that Booth was the assassin, and that he and John H. Surratt were intimate friends, the detectives went to the house of Mrs. Surratt to see whom they could find there. When they rang the bell Wiechmann, who occupied an upstairs room, opened the window and inquired what they wanted. Upon their demanding admittance, stating that they had been sent to that house to see whom they could find in it, Wiechmann went and rapped at Mrs. Surratt's door, informing her who it was that demanded admittance, and asking her if he should let them in, when she replied, "Yes, let them in; I have been expecting them." Now, why should Mrs. Surratt at that hour, about three o'clock on the morning of the 15th, and only three or four hours after the assassination, have been expecting a visit from the detectives? A guilty conscience is its own accuser.

As Wiechmann and Lloyd were the principal witnesses against Mrs. Surratt, and their evidence so conclusively established her guilt, her counsel made an effort to discredit their testimony, but utterly failed to do so. Wiechmann was a young man who established a good character for veracity and general moral deportment by witnesses who had been intimately associated with him for months in General Hoffman's department. His manner was that of a man who was deeply affected by the fact that he found himself in a situation in which his duty to his God and his country required him to state facts that had been thrust upon him, and that were now found to be so damaging to those with whom he had been associating and whom he had regarded as friends. The attempt made by counsel for the defense in their arguments to break the force of his testimony by throwing out the unfounded insinuation that he probably knew of the existence of the conspiracy, was done for the purpose of engendering a doubt of the simple truth of his utterances which were corroborated by other testimony than his own, and of which he could have had no previous knowledge. Wiechmann's testimony, taking into consideration the lies told to him and the deceptions practiced upon him for nearly four months, is in itself absolute proof of his integrity and of his innocence. In the words of Judge Bingham in all that dread issue, "There was not a breath of suspicion found against his character, nor was a single fact to which he testified contradicted. The defense tried to kill him off with lies and insinuations, but they could not and did not do it." Wiechmann admitted that he had been puzzled to account for some of these occurrences. He could not understand why such persons as Payne and Atzerodt should be received and enjoy the privileges accorded to them by Mrs. Surratt and her son; but particularly he had had his suspicions aroused by the conduct of Surratt, Payne, and Booth upon their return from their ride as heretofore recited. He had related this occurrence to Captain Gleason, an officer with whom he was associated in his daily work. He referred to a report or rumor, which had found its way into the papers, of a plot to capture the President, and asked the Captain if he thought it could be possible that this could have been the object of their expedition. Wiechmann's character and actions in the matter could not be discredited by insinuations that had no evidence to rest on for their support.

Lloyd had rented Mrs. Surratt's farm and tavern at Surrattsville, and so was her tenant. He was a man of intemperate habits, and there was, I think, taking all things into consideration, strong reason to conclude that he had been entrusted with the secret of the plot; but of this there was no direct proof, and much less of his having been any further a party to the conspiracy. Even admitting that he had this guilty knowledge, it does not disqualify him for telling the truth as to what occurred at the private interviews referred to between himself and Mrs. Surratt, and that these private interviews did take place under the circumstances already related we have the positive testimony of Wiechmann. Lloyd's testimony was drawn out of him by questions suggested by what Wiechmann had previously stated before the Commission. The defense failed entirely to prove that he was a man not to be believed upon his oath.

They endeavored to break the force of the testimony of Major Smith in regard to Mrs. Surratt solemnly disclaiming any knowledge of Payne by claiming that her eyesight was very defective, but failed to establish any evidence of infirmity of sight beyond what was common to a person of her age of forty-five years.

The evidence of Major Smith was that the hall was well lighted when she was confronted with Payne, and her haste to disavow any knowledge of him with such unnecessary solemnity was itself evidence of guilt. Her eminent volunteer counsel, Hon. Reverdy Johnson, at that time a United States senator from Maryland, did not attempt to assail the testimony against her or to make any reference whatever to her case; but confined himself to an argument against the constitutionality of her trial by a military commission and against the jurisdiction of the court. In view of all the facts above narrated, all of which were proven by the witnesses brought before the Commission by the government, the author thinks it would be impossible for any candid mind to escape from the conclusion that Mrs. Surratt was fully informed of the purposes of Booth and her son, and gave to them her hearty approval and earnest co-operation. We have now presented in narrative form the evidence on which Mrs. Surratt was found guilty and sentenced by the Commission to be hung. Her case was evidently one of those deplorable cases, of which the rebellion furnished so many examples, of a woman so entirely under the influence of disloyalty to her government and so desirous of its overthrow, that she was ready to resort to any means whatever to accomplish that purpose, and so entered heart and soul into the schemes of Booth and her son, hoping thereby to serve the cause of the confederacy.

Arrest of Atzerodt.

George A. Atzerodt had undertaken for his part the assassination of Vice-President Johnson. He was found to have been a frequent visitor at the Surratt house, and a boon companion of Payne, Surratt, and Booth. It was found that he had taken a room at the Kirkwood House where the Vice-President was stopping at the time. He had been assigned to room number 126, on the next floor above that on which was the room occupied by the Vice-President. He had been stopping at the Pennsylvania House from the 27th of March until the 12th of April, and took this room at the Kirkwood House on the morning of the 14th of April, paying in advance for one day. On the 12th of April he visited this house, and meeting Col. W. R. Nevins in the passage leading to the dining-room, he asked him if he knew where Vice-President Johnson was. Nevins showed him the Vice-President's room, but remarked, "He is now at dinner," pointing him out to Atzerodt as he sat at the table. Atzerodt did not enter the dining-room, but simply looked in at the Vice-President. It was ascertained that Atzerodt had not occupied his room on the night of the 14th, and when the detectives who were on his track came to the Kirkwood House on the afternoon of the 15th, it was found locked, and the door had to be forced. Mr. Lee, the officer in pursuit of him, found in his room, upon gaining admission, a black coat hanging against the wall; underneath the pillow or bolster a revolver loaded and capped, and between the sheets and mattress a large bowie-knife. In the pockets of the coat were found a handkerchief marked "Mary R. Booth," another marked "F. M.," or "F. A. Nelson," and another marked "H," in one corner; also a bank-book of J. Wilkes Booth, showing a credit of four hundred and fifty-five dollars with the Ontario Bank of Montreal, and a map of Virginia. On the corner of the bank-book was written "J. W. Booth, 53." On the inside of the book, "Mr. J. Wilkes Booth, in account with the Ontario Bank of Montreal, Canada, 1864, October 27; by deposit Cr. $455."

This coat evidently belonged to Booth, and its being thus found in Atzerodt's room showed that Booth had visited him there during the day; and that he had spent some time with him schooling him in his part was shown by the fact that he had taken off his light overcoat and hung it up against the wall, and had evidently become so much absorbed in mind with the purpose of his visit that he forgot to take his coat when he left. The revolver loaded and capped, and the huge bowie-knife hidden in the bed, serve to explain the nature of the interview between Booth and Atzerodt, and the purpose of death to the Vice-President on the part of the former, and in which purpose at that time Atzerodt no doubt fully concurred. During the stay of Atzerodt at the Pennsylvania House he was frequently called on by Booth, and they were at pains always to hold their interviews in private.

Atzerodt's whereabouts from the 12th to the 14th of April are not accounted for. On the 14th, after having taken his room at the Kirkwood, we next find him at a livery-stable on Eighth and E streets, where he procured a bay mare, paying five dollars for her hire for the afternoon. He took her to Naylor's stable and had her put up. Here he was accompanied by Herold. It was about one o'clock P.M. when he had his mare put up. He left and did not return until about seven P.M. On his return he ordered his mare to be saddled, and requested that she should be left standing with the saddle and bridle on until ten o'clock, when he would call for her. He returned at ten, got his mare, and left. He returned the mare to the stable on Eighth and E streets shortly after the assassination of the President, at about eleven o'clock.

After returning the mare, he boarded a navy-yard car at Sixth Street, and rode down as far as the navy-yard. Finding a man by the name of Briscoe on the car, with whom he was acquainted, he asked him to let him sleep with him in his store. Being refused, he urged his request, and seemed excited. Briscoe asked him if he had heard the news. He replied that he had.

Not getting permission to lodge with Briscoe, he said he would return to the Pennsylvania House, which he did, arriving there on horseback about twelve M. or one o'clock A.M. He asked the colored boy in waiting at the house to hold his horse whilst he went into the bar. He then mounted his horse and left, returning again at about two o'clock on foot, in company with another man. They paid for their lodging and retired. Atzerodt, on being requested by the clerk to register before retiring to his room, hesitated, and did it with manifest reluctance. These parties arose very early on the morning of the 15th, and left. At about eight o'clock on the morning of the 15th, we find Atzerodt in Georgetown trying to sell his watch to a man with whom he was somewhat acquainted; but not being able to do so, he pawned his pistol for ten dollars, saying he was going to the country and would come, or send, and redeem it the next week. He was followed and arrested in Montgomery County, Maryland, on the 20th of April.

He ate his dinner on the 16th at the house of Mr Hezekiah Metz. There were two or three other persons at the table with him, and all were anxious to hear the news from Washington. He was asked whether it was true, as had been reported in that neighborhood, that General Grant had been killed. Atzerodt, according to the testimony of Metz, replied that " if the man who was to follow him had done so it was likely to be true." There was some conflict of statement, however, between Metz and the other two parties who were at the table, and who were used as witnesses for the defense. These thought he said if it were so, it was likely to have been done by some one who got on the train with him. There are good reasons, however, for concluding that Metz gave his real answer.

Atzerodt was known in that neighborhood as Andrew Atwood. From Metz's he went to the house of his cousin, Hartman Richter, near the little village of Germantown, and remained there until he was arrested by Sergeant L. W. Grimmell on the night of the 20th. Richter denied that there was anybody in his house when inquired of by the Sergeant. When told by the Sergeant that he would have to search the house, he admitted that his cousin was upstairs in bed. His wife then spoke up, saying, "there were three men there for that matter." Atzerodt was brought to Washington and held as a prisoner for trial, as a party to the conspiracy. There is no doubt from the evidence presented, that he was not only a party to the conspiracy, but also that Booth had arranged with him and relied on him to assassinate the Vice-President. For this purpose he had removed him from the Pennsylvania to the Kirkwood House, where the Vice-President had rooms, and was boarding. This change had been made on the morning of the 14th, and Booth had been there during the day to see that all things were properly arranged. Atzerodt's revolver was found hidden away in his bed, loaded, capped, and ready for use. His bowie-knife also was found secreted in his bed; and yet there is no evidence that he was in his room, or even in the house during the evening or night. In his defense his counsel set up the plea, and proved it, that he was incapable of committing such a crime, being constitutionally a coward. He was a low-browed, vulgar vagabond, fond of whiskey, tobacco, and vicious company; a cowardly braggart, covering up his cowardice by a great pretense of bravery when the battle was not on; low enough in moral tone to do any wicked thing, but without physical courage to face the danger connected with what he had engaged to do. Booth had mistaken his man; but being a member of the conspiracy, he was equally guilty with Booth.

Arrest of Spangler.

On the strength of the facts incidentally presented in the foregoing narrative, Edward Spangler was taken into military custody, and held as a prisoner for trial. The capture of Herold has already been given. All of these prisoners were held in military custody, and under such precautions as would have rendered any attempt at rescue or escape the height of folly.

In Booth's trunk a letter was found from Samuel Arnold to Booth, dated at Hookstown, Md., March 27th, 1865. This letter was signed simply "Sam," but was proved to be in Arnold's handwriting, and led not only to his own arrest, but also to that of his friend and fellow conspirator, Michael O'Laughlin. Arnold had evidently fallen into a hesitating frame of mind. I feel that I cannot do better than to give this letter entire. It is as follows: —

HOOKSTOWN, BALTIMORE CO., March 27, 1865.

DEAR JOHN: — Was business so important that you could not remain in Baltimore until I saw you? I came in as soon as I could, but found you had gone to Washington. I called also on Mike, but learned from his mother that he had gone out with you and had not returned. I concluded, therefore, that he had gone with you. How inconsiderate you have been! When I left you, you stated you would not meet me in a month or so. Therefore, I made application for employment, an answer to which I shall receive during the week. I told my parents I had ceased with you. Can I, then, under existing circumstances, come as you request? You know full well that the government suspicions something is going on there; therefore the undertaking is becoming more complicated. Why not, for the present, desist, for various reasons which, if you look into, you can readily see, without my making any mention thereof. You, nor any one, can censure me for my present course. You have been its cause, for how can I come now after telling them I had left you? Suspicion rests upon me now from my whole family and even parties in the country. I will be compelled to leave home any how, and how soon I care not. None, no, not one, were more in favor of the enterprise than myself, and to-day would be there had you not done as you have: by this I mean, manner of proceeding. I am, as you well know, in need. I am, as you may say, in rags; whereas to-day I ought to be well clothed. I do not feel right stalking about with means, and more from appearances a beggar. I feel my dependence: but even all this would be and was forgotten, for I was one with you. Time more propitious will arrive yet. Do not act rashly or in haste. I prefer your first query: go and see how it will be taken at R——d, and e'er long I shall be better prepared to again be with you. I dislike writing, — would sooner verbally make known my views, — yet your non-writing causes me thus to proceed. Do not in anger peruse this. Weigh all I have said, and, as a rational man and a friend, you cannot censure or upbraid my conduct. I sincerely trust this, or aught else that shall or may occur, will never be an obstacle to obliterate our former friendship and attachment. Write me to Baltimore, as I expect to be in about Wednesday or Thursday, or, if you can possibly come on, I will Tuesday meet you in Baltimore at B——. Ever I subscribe myself,

Your friend,
SAM.

Arnold got employment at Fortress Monroe, and was there at the time of the assassination; but the finding of the above letter in Booth's trunk, as also other evidence constantly turning up in the course of the investigations being made, identifying him with the conspiracy, led to his arrest on the 17th of April at Fortress Monroe. Arnold, when arrested, made a partial confession, relating the circumstances of a meeting of some of the conspirators held at the Lichau House in Washington about three weeks previous to his going to Fortress Monroe.

This meeting must have occurred within two or three days after the writing of the above letter, immediately before Surratt's visit to Richmond, and was attended by Booth, Surratt, O'Laughlin,

SAMUEL ARNOLD.

Atzerodt, Arnold, a man with the alias of Moseby, and another whose name he could not recollect. He denied that he had ever corresponded with Booth, but on being informed of the letter found in Booth's trunk he admitted that he wrote it. He also stated that Booth had letters of introduction to Dr. Mudd and Dr. Queen, but said he did not know from whom Booth got them. He claimed that an angry discussion took place at the meeting referred to. He said he told Booth then that if the thing did not take place that week he would withdraw. Booth got angry at that, and said he ought to be shot for talking in that way. He said that he replied to Booth that two could play at that game; and that he withdrew from the conspiracy at that time, and occupied his position at Fortress Monroe on the 1st of April. It is evident, I think, that as he began to contemplate the hazards of the enterprise, its dangers began to be more and more apparent to him. His heart failed him, and he was anxious for an excuse to withdraw from it, but had not the courage to peremptorily do so. This is the interpretation I put upon the above letter — of the altercation between him and Booth, and of his going to Fortress Monroe.

There is also apparent in the letter a shade of disappointment and dissatisfaction in regard to pecuniary matters, implying that promised reward had been withheld by Booth. Early in September, whilst at a grain threshing, Arnold received a letter containing a fifty-dollar bill. Reading the letter and showing it with the money to a companion, he remarked that " he was flush." He handed the letter to his friend to read, but he, after trying to read a few lines, and finding that he could not understand it on account of its ambiguity, handed it back to Arnold, asking him what it meant. Arnold replied that something big would be seen in the papers one of these days. This was no doubt a retainer's fee, or in other words, an advance payment from Booth. The rather complaining tone of Arnold's letter, hinting at pecuniary embarrassment, would seem to indicate that Booth's promises of pecuniary reward had been large, whilst his fulfillment had been far from satisfactory.

This, amongst other considerations to be named, had evidently cooled Arnold's ardor in the prosecution of the plot, and was the cause of his disposition to withdraw from it.

The probabilities are that his parents and friends suspecting that his intimacy with Booth foreboded evil, and probably suspecting something of his purpose, had so earnestly remonstrated with him as to cause him to stagger or falter in his purpose, and made him anxious for an excuse for breaking with Booth. He perhaps began to regard Booth's plan as quixotic and impracticable, full of hazard, and not likely to succeed. In fact, he stated that he so told Booth at this meeting. He was evidently restive, and thought it had been put off too long to effect the end contemplated. It does not appear to have been from any awakening of his moral nature that he faltered, neither from cowardice that he weakened; and so he failed to purge himself of complicity in Booth's guilt. But there was sufficient evidence of his desire to withdraw from any part in the execution of Booth's present purposes to extenuate his guilt in a measure, at least, in the judgment of the Commission.

Arrest of O'Laughlin.

Arnold's letter to Booth on the 27th of March, which was found in Booth's trunk, together with evidence gathered up on every hand as the investigation proceeded, led to the arrest of Michael O'Laughlin at the house of his brother-in-law, in Baltimore, on Monday, the 17th of April, the same day on which Arnold was arrested. When arrested he seemed to understand what it was for, not asking any questions about it. He had gone to Washington on the 13th and remained until Saturday, the 15th. On returning to Baltimore on Saturday night, he was met at the depot by his brother-in-law, who told him that he had been inquired for by detectives that evening. Being advised by the friend who had accompanied him to Washington and back to remain at his home, he said he would not be arrested at home, as it would kill his mother. Why was he expecting to be arrested? A man innocent of crime never fears or expects arrest. He went to the house of his brother-in-law and quietly awaited the issue. He even requested his brother-in-law to inform the officer of his whereabouts, thus seeming to court arrest.

He had carefully thought the thing over, and concluded that the government would not be able to fix guilt upon him, and so he thought to have the benefit of a seeming willingness to be arrested, as presumptive proof of his innocence. He had gone to Washington on the 13th with three companions, ostensibly to see the parade and illumination in commemoration of the surrender of Lee's army, and to "have a good time," as his companions expressed it in their evidence in his behalf on his defense.

He kept with these companions in the rounds of their drunken carousal and debaucheries enough to blind them as to the real object of his visit. They were drinking freely during the Thursday and Friday of their stay, and were evidently unable to give a connected and reliable account of O'Laughlin's whereabouts during the whole of the time. They thought he spent most of the time in company with one or the other of them; but they admitted that he had had a long interview with Booth at his room at the National Hotel on Friday, the 14th. It was positively proven, however, that he was at the house of Secretary Stanton on the occasion of the reception given to General Grant on the night of the 13th; that he seemed to be in a state of partial intoxication, and pushed himself through the crowd into the hall inquiring for General Grant, saying he wanted to see him. He was told by the Secretary's son that that was no occasion for him to see him, and to step out onto the pavement where the carriage stopped, and he could see him. He stood for some time in the hall looking in through the door at the General. He also said he wanted to see Stanton, and being asked if it was the Secretary he wished to see, he said it was. The Secretary was pointed out to him, but he did not go to him. His manner was so impertinently obtrusive and rude that he was finally requested to leave, and was escorted out of the house by the son of the Secretary. Mr. Stanton at first thought him to be intoxicated, but upon conversing with him concluded he was not. It would appear from all this that the part Booth had assigned to him was the assassination of General Grant, and that his visit to the house of the Secretary was for the purpose of so acquainting himself with the form and features of the General as to be able readily to identify him. Had not the General been called away on that Friday afternoon, — had he accompanied the President to the theatre, as he had intended doing, — there is scarcely a doubt that "Peanuts" would have had two horses to hold, or that some other arrangements would have been made for General Grant's assassination that would have made O'Laughlin a companion of Booth in his flight.

We have now seen the development of Booth's plot, and its partial success, but, as to the real object of it, its entire failure. The thing proposed by the head conspirators, whose agents we have been following up in their efforts for its accomplishment, failed of its realization. They had hoped by the policy of assassination to put the rapidly waning cause of the confederacy on its feet again under new and more favorable auspices.

The cause, at the time of this attempt to thus give it aid, was already lost on the field of military conflict beyond hope of recovery. The whole people, North and South, saw that the war was at an end; that the brief day of the so-called Southern Confederacy was over — that its sun had set; and great as must have been the disappointment of those who had so fruitlessly plunged the country into the greatest civil war that history records, they were quite content to accept and make the best of their failure.

Both parties were glad that the contest had been decided, and of the opportunity to lay down their arms, and return to the pursuits of peaceful life. Had not Booth kept himself as full of whiskey as he was of his fiendish purpose, had he given himself an opportunity to scan the situation in a duly sober frame of mind, we think it even more than probable he would have abandoned the whole project as useless. But both he and his associates were free and constant drinkers, and by their frequent visits to saloons, as shown by the whole run of the testimony before the Commission, it would seem probable that they scarcely ever drew an absolutely sober breath, and so could not realize the true situation of the cause they sought to serve.

The Canada conspirators are in like manner, according to all the testimony, shown to have been free drinkers. All of their diabolical schemes were most probably the products of minds acting

MICHAEL O'LAUGHLIN.

under the influence of alcoholic stimulants, and this may in some degree account for the obtundity of their moral perceptions. It has been said by one who was personally cognizant of the fact, that alcohol precipitated the rebellion, and that its leaders in both branches of Congress kept themselves constantly under the excitement of alcoholic stimulants and so were made reckless of consequences.

Arrest of Dr. Samuel A. Mudd.

It will be remembered that in giving the history of Booth's flight, we found him and Herold at the house of Dr. S. A. Mudd, at about four o'clock on the morning of the 15th of April, they having ridden thirty miles in about six hours after leaving Washington. They would no doubt have stopped at Mudd's, even had Booth not needed his services as a surgeon, for a short respite and refreshment, as the doctor was, as we shall hereafter see, a co-conspirator with Booth. Booth's broken leg had by this time become very painful, and this made it necessary that he should stop to have it dressed. Mudd dressed his leg, as he himself said, as well as he could with the means at his command, and giving them refreshments, he placed Booth in a chamber upstairs where he remained until about three o'clock in the afternoon. Mudd and Herold went out, as Mudd said, to find a carriage in which to take Booth on his journey; but it is more likely Mudd was showing Herold a by-way toward the Potomac, at the point where they expected to cross, whilst Booth was resting.

About one o'clock on that afternoon, Lieutenant Dana, with a squad of cavalry, passed down toward Bryantown in pursuit of Booth, and as there was no doubt a sharp look-out kept from the house of Dr. Mudd, which stood about a quarter of a mile from, and in full view of, the road, they were by this admonished of their danger and resumed their flight as soon as they could after the soldiers passed. Thus Mudd got them off of his hands, and started them on their way to his friend, Samuel Cox. On Tuesday, the 18th of April, Mudd was first interviewed, and then denied that there had been any body at his house on the 15th; but upon being pressed with questions, he finally said that two strangers had come to his house about four o'clock on Saturday morning on horseback, one of them having a broken leg, and that he had taken them in, dressed the leg, and had a crutch made for the man, and that they had left after breakfast, telling in what direction they had gone, but giving a false cue. He denied knowing either of them, and said they were entire strangers to him, going on to give a minute description of the men and their horses as though desirous of giving all the information he could, but with an appearance and manner that created distrust. Being asked if he knew Booth, he said he had been introduced to him at church in the fall before, but had no other acquaintance with him. Being asked if the man whose leg he had dressed was not Booth, he said he was not. When told by the officer that he would have to search the house, his wife went upstairs and brought down a boot that Mudd had removed from Booth's foot by ripping it down in front, and it was seen that on the inside of the boot leg, near the top, was written, " J. Wilkes," and also the maker's name. Mudd was interviewed two or three times before his arrest, and prevaricated every time so much that he frequently contradicted himself. It was noticed that he was never at home when called for, but was not far off, as he always made his appearance in a short time when sent for by his wife. He was finally placed under arrest; and upon the photograph of Booth being shown to him, and being asked if that looked like Booth, he said he thought not, but finally concluded there was some resemblance to Booth across the eyes. He was taken to Washington and held as a prisoner. Mudd was a physician, living on a farm. He had had a considerable number of slaves at the breaking out of the rebellion, most of whom had left him during the previous winter. His father also, living in the neighborhood, was a large land and slave holder, and Mudd's disloyalty was no doubt of the rabid type. His home was a place of resort for returned rebel soldiers and recruiting parties, and he had a place of concealment in the pines near his house, where they were sheltered and cared for, the doctor sending their food to them by his slaves; and if, at any time, any of these parties ventured to his house to take their meals, a slave was always placed on watch to give notice of the approach of any one.

The letter of introduction to Dr. Mudd which Booth had, as related by Arnold, had no doubt been presented in the fall, at the time Mudd admitted having been introduced to him at church; and from that time their intimacy commenced. This was in November, 1864.

About the 23d of December, 1864, Mudd visited Booth in Washington, and introduced him to John H. Surratt, under the following circumstances: Wiechmann and Surratt were on the street together, when Wiechmann heard some one call, "Surratt! Surratt!" and turning round, they were met by Dr. Mudd and Booth. Mudd introduced Booth to Surratt, and then Surratt introduced both of them to Wiechmann. They went, by invitation of Booth, to the National Hotel, where Booth had a room, and were served by him with wine and cigars. Mudd went out into a passage and called Booth. They remained out of the room for a short time, and conversed in a low tone of voice. Upon their return to the room Booth called Surratt, and the three went out again into the passage, and were engaged for some time in a private conference. Upon their return, Mudd made an explanation, by way of apology, to Wiechmann, saying that Booth wanted to buy his farm, but he did not care to sell. Booth also apologized, giving the same excuse. The three then took seats around a table, when Booth took an envelope from his pocket, and upon this, with his pencil, commenced drawing lines, as if marking roads. Whilst engaged in doing this the three were conversing in so low a tone that Wiechmann could not hear what was said.

Mudd made one or two other visits to Washington during the winter, and his business seemed always to be with Booth and Surratt. At least, he was always found in their company.

According to one of Mudd's various statements, Booth and Herold left his house between three and four o'clock in the afternoon. It will be noted that he at first denied their having been there at all. Then he admitted that two strangers had been there on Saturday morning; that he had dressed a broken leg for one of them, and had a crutch made for him, and they left after breakfast. That they remained until after Dana and his party passed down to Bryantown, there is no doubt; and that they left as soon as possible, assisted by Mudd, after the soldiers passed, as we have heretofore seen. Mudd, after his conviction and sentence, whilst being conveyed to the Dry Tortugas, admitted, voluntarily, to Captain Dutton that he knew Booth when he came to his house on the morning of the 15th of April; and also that he went to Washington in December by appointment with Booth, to introduce him to Surratt. He might just as well have admitted his complicity in the conspiracy. Mudd's expression of countenance was that of a hypocrite. He had the bump of secretiveness largely developed; and it would have taken months of favorable acquaintanceship to have removed the unfavorable impression made by the first scanning of the man. He had the appearance of a natural born liar and deceiver.

We have now Mrs. Mary E. Surratt, Edward Spangler, Lewis Payne, David E. Herold, Samuel Arnold, Michael O'Laughlin, George A. Atzerodt, and Dr. Samuel Mudd under arrest and held for trial by the government under the charge of being co-conspirators with John H. Surratt, Booth, and others yet to be named, and still others unknown and who never will be known. The evidence yet to be adduced makes it clear that there were quite a number of these conspirators in Washington at the time of the assassination who were never discovered, encouraging by their presence, and aiding and abetting, Booth and his associates.

There are good reasons for believing that the purpose of Booth and his fellow-conspirators was known to many, both in Canada and the United States, who were interested in the destruction of our government. It may yet happen that a sufficient amount of evidence may be found to justify this, or some other writer, in making explicit charges that are for the present withheld.

In regard to the persons above named who were put upon their trial, the writer will only say that, in giving an account of the grounds of arrest in each case, he has stated the facts proven by unimpeached witnesses before the Commission, whose testimony governed the decisions of the court in their respective cases, and that his statements of the facts in evidence will be found to be fully vindicated by a critical examination and study of the testimony as given by Pittman in his official report of the trial. He

GEORGE E. ATZERODT.

feels sure that no one, with that report before him, can impeach the account he has given of the parts acted by each one of the prisoners named in this great tragedy; and upon these facts must rest the judgment of mankind, as did the judgment of the court.

CHAPTER VII.

QUESTIONS PRELIMINARY TO THE TRIAL.

What Sort of Trial should be given, Civil or Military?

THE first question that presented itself to the government in regard to these prisoners was, as to what kind of a trial should be given them, whether civil or military? The civil courts were open in the District of Columbia at the time, and had been all through the war. There was no question that a form of trial could be had in the civil courts; but there was at the same time as little question that, under existing circumstances, such a trial would only result in a miscarriage of justice. The great crime had been committed during the existence of a state of war, and the courts were only able to carry on their functions under the protection of the arms of the government.

This ægis being withdrawn, the administration of justice through the civil courts would have been an impossibility, even in the capital of the nation; and with this protection it was equally impossible to secure the demands of justice through the civil courts in cases involving the issues of the war, as a jury of partizans could not be expected to decide impartially if all belonged to one party, and if divided on party lines, they could not be expected to decide at all. The latter alternative was the only one on which a jury could have been impaneled, under the rules of law, at that time, in the District of Columbia. Outside of the soldiery there were as many enemies as friends of the government in the population of the district, to say the least, and many of these enemies were passing under the guise of friends. In this state of things it was obvious that it would be futile to send these prisoners before a civil tribunal for trial. The government had evidence that a great conspiracy existed, the purpose of which was to aid the rebel cause by a series of assassinations, and that what had happened was in pursuance of that plan, but only its partial accomplishment. The extent of this conspiracy had not been fully revealed, but its spirit and purpose were known, and both wisdom and good policy required that it should be met with the utmost promptitude and suppressed with no faltering hand. These persons had been arrested by the military police, and were held as prisoners in military custody. They were held not as prisoners of war, but as *secret active enemies* of the government, guilty of a crime the purpose of which was to aid the rebellion, and this being their purpose, it took them out of the realm of *civil*, into the realm of *martial*, law. Their crime was regarded as an act of war, inasmuch as its purpose was to aid the existing armed rebellion. The means by which they thus sought to give it aid were morally reprehensible, and such as had long been rejected by the enlightened sentiment of the civilized and christian nations of the earth. The crime was a blow at the life of the nation, in the person of its chosen head, and was committed in the nation's capital, and within the intrenched lines and fortifications thereof; and so it was decided that the prisoners were properly subject to a trial by a military commission.

President Lincoln's order of September 25th, 1862, had not been rescinded and was still in force, and under this order the prisoners were, from the purpose of their crime, subject to a military trial. They could not, under the articles of war, be sent before a court-martial for trial, but could, under *martial law, which is only the common law in a state of war*, be tried by a military commission.

The chief conspirators, on whom rested the responsibility of the plot, were still at large, and in an attitude of desperate hostility towards the government. The extent of their plans, and the means at their command for their execution, could not be known, and so it was a matter of the utmost importance to deal with the prisoners in the most summary manner consistent with the ends of justice. The President requested the attorney general, Hon. James A. Speed, a Kentuckian by birth, to give his official opinion as to whether these persons implicated in this crime could be tried before a military tribunal, or must be tried before a civil court. As the reply of the Attorney General furnishes an exhaustive discussion of the different conditions existing under a state of peace and a state of war, and shows that whilst in a state of peace the Constitution throws its shield of protection over the life, liberty, and property of the citizen, even the humblest, its provisions cannot afford protection to these in a state of war, and that martial law, or the common law of war comes in in the place of the Constitution to ameliorate as much as possible the miseries of war, and secure, as far as possible, the ends of justice and mercy; and as it constitutes a most important and interesting document worthy of the careful study of every young man who desires to become well informed on the most important questions of our national life, I shall give it a place entire, and commend it to careful perusal and study.

Opinion of the Attorney General.

The President was assassinated at a theatre in the city of Washington. At the time of the assassination a civil war was flagrant, — the city of Washington was defended by fortifications regularly and constantly manned, the principal police of the city was by federal soldiers, the public offices and property in the city were all guarded by soldiers, and the President's house and person were, or should have been, under the guard of soldiers. Martial law had been declared in the District of Columbia, but the civil courts were open and held their regular sessions, and transacted business as in times of peace. Such being the facts, the question is one of great importance, — important because it involves the constitutional guarantees thrown about the rights of the citizen, and because the security of the army and government in time of war is involved; important, as it involves a seeming conflict between the laws of peace and war. Having given the question propounded the patient and earnest consideration its magnitude and importance require, I will proceed to give the reasons why I am of the opinion that the conspirators not only may but ought to be tried by a military tribunal. A civil court of the United States is created by a law of Congress, under and according to the Constitution. To the Constitution and the law we must look to ascertain how the court is constituted, the limits of its jurisdiction, and what its mode of procedure. A military tribunal exists under and according to the Constitution in time of war. Congress may prescribe how all such tribunals are to be constituted, what shall be their jurisdiction and mode of procedure. Should Congress fail to create such tribunals, then, under the Constitution, they must be constituted according to the laws and usages of civilized warfare. They may take cognizance of such offences as the laws of war permit; they must proceed according to the customary usages of such tribunals in time of war, and inflict such punishments as are sanctioned by the practice of civilized nations in time of war. In time of peace, neither Congress nor the military can create any military tribunals, except such as are made in pursuance of that clause of the Constitution which gives to Congress the power "to make rules for the government of the land and naval forces." I do not think that Congress can, in time of war or peace, under this clause of the Constitution, create military tribunals for the adjudication of offenses committed by persons not engaged in, or belonging to, such forces.

This is a proposition too plain for argument. But it does not follow that because such military tribunals cannot be created by Congress under this clause that they cannot be created at all. Is there no other power conferred by the Constitution upon Congress or the military under which such tribunals may be created in time of war? That the law of nations constitutes a part of the law of the land must be admitted. The laws of nations are expressly made laws of the land by the Constitution when it says that "Congress shall have power to define and punish piracies and felonies committed on the high seas, and offences against the law of nations. To define is to give the limits or precise meaning of a word or thing in being; to make is to call into being. Congress has power to define, not to make, the laws of nations; but Congress has power to make rules for the government of the army and navy. From the very face of the Constitution, then, it is evident that the laws of nations do constitute a part of the laws of the land. But very soon after the organization of the federal government, Mr. Randolph, then attorney general, said: "The law of nations, although not specifically adopted by the Constitution, is essentially a part of the law of the land. Its obligation commences and runs with the existence of a nation, subject to some modifications on points of indifference." The framers of the Constitution knew that a nation could not maintain an honorable place among the nations of the world that does not regard the great and essential principles of the law of nations as a part of the law of the land. Hence Congress may define those laws but cannot abrogate them, or, as Mr. Randolph says, may "modify on some points of indifference."

That the laws of nations constitute a part of the laws of the land, is established from the face of the Constitution upon principle and by authority. But the laws of war constitute much the greater part of the law of nations. Like the other laws of nations, they exist and are of binding force upon the departments and citizens of the government, though not defined by any law of Congress. No one that has ever glanced at the many treatises that have been published in different ages of the world by great, good, and learned men, can fail to know that the laws of war constitute a part of the law of nations, and that those laws have been prescribed with tolerable accuracy. Congress can declare war. When war is declared it must be under the Constitution, carried on according to the known usages and laws of war among civilized nations. Under the power to define these laws, Congress cannot abrogate them, or authorize their infraction.

The Constitution does not permit this government to prosecute a war as an uncivilized and barbarous people. As war is required by the frame-work of our government to be prosecuted according to the known usages of war among the civilized nations of the earth, it is important to understand what are the obligations, duties, and responsibilities imposed by war upon the military. Congress, not having defined, as under the Constitution it might have done, the laws of war, we must look to the usage of nations to ascertain the powers conferred in war, on whom the exercise of these powers devolve, over whom, and to what extent do these powers reach, and in how far the citizen and the soldier are bound by the legitimate use thereof. The power conferred by war is, of course, adequate to the end to be accomplished, and not greater than what is necessary to be accomplished. The law of war, like every other code of laws, declares what shall not be done, and does not say what may be done.

The legitimate use of the great power of war, or rather the prohibitions upon the use of that power, increase or diminish as the necessity of the case demands. When a city is besieged and hard pressed the commander may exert an authority over the non-combatants which he may not when no enemy is near. All wars against a domestic enemy, or to repel invasions, are prosecuted to preserve the government. If the invading force can be overcome by the ordinary civil police of a country, it should be done without bringing upon the country the terrible scourge of war; if a commotion or insurrection can be put down by the ordinary process of law, the military should not be called out. A defensive foreign war is declared and carried on because the civil police is inadequate to repel it; a civil war is waged because the laws cannot be peacefully enforced by the ordinary tribunals of the country through civil process and by civil officers. Because of the utter inability to keep the peace and maintain order by customary officers and agencies in time of peace, armies are organized and put into the field. They are called out and invested with the powers of war to prevent total anarchy and to preserve the government.

Peace is the normal condition of a country, and war abnormal, neither being without law, but each having laws appropriate to the condition of society. The maxim *enter arma silent leges* is never wholly true. The object of war is to bring society out of its abnormal condition; and the laws of war aim to have that done with the least possible injury to persons and property. Anciently, when two nations were at war the conqueror had, or asserted, the right to take from his enemy his life, liberty, and property; if either was spared it was a favor, or act of mercy. By the laws of nations, and of war as a part thereof, the conqueror was deprived of this right.

When two governments, foreign to each other, are at war, or when a civil war becomes territorial, all of the people of the respective belligerents become by the law of nations the enemies of each other. As enemies they cannot hold intercourse, but neither can kill or injure the other except under a commission from their respective governments. So humanizing have been, and are, the laws of war, that it is a high offense against them to kill an enemy without such commission. The laws of war demand that a man shall not take human life except under a license from his government; and under the Constitution of the United States no license can be given by any department of the government to take human life in war, except according to the law and usages of war. Soldiers regularly in the service have the license of the government to deprive men, the active enemies of their government, of their liberty and lives; their commission so to act is as perfect and as legal as that of a judge to adjudicate; but the soldier must act in obedience to the laws of war, as the judge must in obedience to the civil law. A civil judge must try criminals in the mode prescribed in the Constitution and the law; so, soldiers must kill or capture according to the laws of war. Non-combatants are not to be disturbed or interfered with by the armies of either party except in extreme cases.

Armies are called out and organized to meet and overcome the active acting public enemies. But enemies with which armies have to deal are of two classes. 1. Open, active participants in hostilities, as soldiers who wear the uniform, move under the flag, and hold the appropriate commission from their government, openly assuming to discharge the duties and meet the responsibilities and dangers of soldiers, they are entitled to all belligerent rights, and should receive all the courtesies due to soldiers. The true soldier is proud to acknowledge and respect those rights, and ever cheerfully extends these courtesies. 2. Secret, but active participants, as spies, brigands, bushwhackers, jayhawkers, war-rebels, and assassins. In all wars, and especially civil wars, such secret, active enemies rise up to annoy and attack an army, and must be met and put down by the army. When lawless wretches become so impudent and powerful as not to be controlled and governed by the ordinary tribunals of a country, armies are called out and the laws of war invoked. War has never been and can never be conducted on the principle that an army is but a *posse comitatus* of a civil magistrate. An army, like all other organized bodies, has a right, and its first duty is to protect its own existence, and the existence of all its parts, by the means and in the mode usual among civilized nations when at war. The question arises, then, do the laws of war authorize a different mode of proceeding and the use of different means against secret active enemies from those used against open active enemies? As has been said, the open enemy or soldier in time of war may be met in battle and killed, wounded, or taken prisoner, or so placed by the lawful strategy of war as that he is powerless. Unless the law of self-preservation absolutely demands it, the life of a wounded enemy or a prisoner must be spared.

Unless pressed thereto by the extremest necessity, the laws of war condemn and punish with great severity harsh or cruel treatment to a wounded enemy or a prisoner. Certain stipulations and agreements, tacit or express, betwixt the open belligerent parties are permitted by the laws of war, and are held to be of a very high and sacred character. Such is the tacit understanding, or it may be usage of war, in regard to flags of truce. Flags of truce are resorted to as a means of saving human life, or alleviating human suffering. When not used with perfidy, the laws of war require that they should be respected. The Romans regarded embassadors betwixt belligerents as persons to be treated with consideration and respect. Plutarch, in his life of Cæsar, tells us that the barbarians in Gaul, having sent some embassadors to Cæsar, he detained them, charging fraudulent practices, and led his army to battle, obtaining a great victory. When the senate decreed festivals and sacrifices for the victory, Cato declared it to be his opinion that Cæsar ought to be given into the hands of the barbarians, that so the guilt which this breach of faith might otherwise bring upon the state might be expiated by transferring the curse on him who was the occasion of it. Under the Constitution and laws of the United States, should a commander be guilty of such a flagrant breach of law as Cato charged upon Cæsar, he would not be delivered to the enemy, but would be punished after a military trial.

The many honorable gentlemen who hold commissions in the army of the United States, and have been deputed to conduct war according to the laws of war, would keenly feel it as an insult to their profession of arms for any one to say they could not or would not punish a fellow soldier who was wantonly guilty of cruelty to a prisoner, or perfidy towards the bearer of a flag of truce. The laws of war permit capitulations of surrender and paroles. They are agreements betwixt belligerents, and should be scrupulously observed and performed. They are contracts wholly unknown to civil tribunals. Parties to such contracts must answer any breaches thereof to the customary military tribunals in time of war. If an officer of rank, possessing the pride that becomes a soldier and a gentleman, who should capitulate to surrender his forces and property under his command and control, be charged with a fraudulent breach of the terms of surrender, the laws of war do not permit that he should be punished without a trial, or, if innocent, that he should have no means of wiping out the foul imputation. If a paroled prisoner is charged with a breach of his parole, he may be punished, if guilty, but not without a trial. He should be tried by a military tribunal, constituted and proceeding as the laws and usages of war prescribe.

The law and usage of war contemplate that soldiers have a high sense of personal honor. The true soldier is proud to feel and know that his enemy possesses personal honor, and will conform and be obedient to the laws of war. In a spirit of justice, and with a wise appreciation of such feelings, the laws of war protect the honor and character of an open enemy. When, by the fortunes of war, one open enemy is thrown into the hands and power of another, and is charged with dishonorable conduct and a breach of the laws of war, he must be tried according to the usages of war. Justice and fairness say that an open enemy to whom dishonorable conduct is imputed has a right to demand a trial. If such a demand can be rightfully made, surely it cannot be rightfully refused. It is to be hoped that the military authorities of this country will never refuse such a demand because there is no act of Congress that authorizes it. In time of war the law and usages of war authorize it, and they are a part of the law of the land. One belligerent may request the other to punish for breaches of the laws of war, and, regularly, such a request should be made before retaliatory measures are taken. Whether the laws of war have been infringed or not is, of necessity, a question to be decided by the laws and usages of war, and is cognizable before a military tribunal. When prisoners of war conspire to escape, or are guilty of a breach of appropriate and necessary rules of prison discipline, they may be punished, but not without trial. The commander who should order every prisoner charged with improper conduct to be shot or hung would be guilty of a high offense against the laws of war, and should be punished therefor after a military trial. If the culprit should be condemned and executed, the commander would be as free from guilt as if the man had been killed in battle. It is manifest from what has been said, that military tribunals exist under and according to the laws of war, in the interest of justice and mercy. They are established to save human life and to prevent cruelty as far as possible. The commander of an army in time of war has the same power to organize military tribunals and to execute their judgments that he has to set his squadrons in the field and fight battles. His authority in each case is from the laws and usages of war. Having seen that there must be military tribunals to decide questions arising in time of war betwixt belligerents who are open and active enemies, let us next see whether the laws of war do not authorize such tribunals to determine the fate of those who are active but secret participants in the hostilities. In Mr. Wharton's " Elements of International Law," he says: " The effect of a state of war, lawfully declared to exist, is to place all the subjects of each belligerent power in a state of natural hostility. The usage of nations has modified this maxim by legalizing such acts of hostility only as are committed by those who are authorized by the express or implied command of the State, such as the regularly commissioned naval and military forces of the nation, and all others called out in its defense, or spontaneously defending themselves in case of necessity, without any express authority for that purpose." Cicero tells us in his offices, that by the Roman feudal law no person could lawfully engage in battle with the public enemy without being regularly enrolled, and taking the military oath. This was a regulation sanctioned both by policy and religion. The horrors of war would indeed be greatly aggravated if every individual of the belligerent States were allowed to plunder and slay indiscriminately the enemies' subjects without being in any manner accountable for his conduct. *Hence, it is in land-wars irregular bands of marauders are liable to be treated as lawless banditti, not entitled to the protection of the mitigated usages of war as practiced by civilized nations.*

In speaking upon the subject of banditti, Patrick Henry said in the Virginia Convention: "The honorable gentleman has given you an elaborate account of what he judges tyrannical legislation, and an *ex-post facto* law (in the case of Josiah Philips); he has misinterpreted the facts. That man was not executed by a tyrannical stroke of power, nor was he a Socrates; he was a fugitive murderer and an outlaw; a man who commanded an *infamous banditti*, and *at a time when the war was at the most perilous stage* he committed the most cruel and shocking barbarities; he was an enemy to the human name. Those who declare war against the human race may be struck out of existence as soon as apprehended. He was not executed according to those beautiful legal ceremonies which are pointed out by the law in criminal cases. The enormity of his crime did not entitle him to it. I am truly a friend to legal forms and methods; but, sir, the occasion warranted the measure. A pirate, an outlaw, or a common enemy to all mankind may be put to death at any time. It is justified by the law of war and of nations." No reader, not to say student, of the law of nations can doubt that Mr. Wheaton and Mr. Henry have fairly stated the laws of war. Let it be constantly borne in mind that they are talking of the law in a state of war. These banditti that spring up in time of war are respecters of no law, human or divine, of peace or of war, are *hostes humani generis*, and may be hunted down like wolves. Thoroughly desperate and perfectly lawless, no man can be required to peril his life in venturing to take them prisoners; as prisoners no trust can be reposed in them. But they are occasionally made prisoners. Being prisoners, what is to be done with them? If they are public enemies, assuming and exercising the right to kill, and are not regularly authorized to do so, they must be apprehended and dealt with by the military. No man can doubt the right and duty of the military to make prisoners of them, and being public enemies it is the duty of the military to punish them for any infractions of the laws of war.

But the military cannot ascertain whether they are guilty or not without the aid of a military tribunal. In all wars, and especially in civil wars, secret but active enemies are almost as numerous as open ones. That fact has contributed to make civil wars such scourges to the countries in which they rage. In nearly all foreign wars the contending parties speak different languages and have different habits and manners, but in most civil wars that is not the case; hence there is a security in participating secretly in hostilities that induces many to thus engage. War prosecuted according to the most civilized usage is horrible, but its horrors are greatly aggravated by the immemorial habits of plunder, rape, and murder practiced by secret but active participants. Certain laws and usages have been adopted by the civilized world in wars between nations that are not of kin to one another, for the purpose and to the effect of arresting or softening many of the necessary cruel consequences of war. How strongly bound are we, then, in the midst of a great war where brother and personal friend are fighting against brother and friend, to adopt and be governed by these usages. A public enemy must or should be dealt with in all wars by the same laws. The fact they are public enemies being the same, they should deal with each other according to those laws of war that are contemplated by the Constitution.

Whatever rules have been adopted and practiced by the civilized nations of the world in war to soften its hardships and severity should be adopted and practiced by us in this war. That the laws of war authorize commanders to create and establish military commissions, courts or tribunals for the trial of offenders against the laws of war, whether they be open or secret participants in the hostilities, cannot be denied. That the judgments of such tribunals may have been sometimes harsh, and sometimes even tyrannical, does not prove that they ought not to exist, nor does it prove that they are not constituted in the interest of justice and mercy. Considering the power that the laws of war give over secret participants in hostilities, such as banditti, guerillas, spies, etc., the position of a commander would be miserable indeed if he could not call to his aid the judgments of such tribunals; he would become a mere butcher of men without the power to ascertain justice, and there can be no mercy where there is no justice. War in its mildest form is horrible; but take away from the contending armies the ability and right to organize what is now known as a Bureau of Military Justice, they would soon become monster savages unrestrained by any and all ideas of law and justice. Surely no lover of mankind, no one that respects law and order, no one that has the instinct of justice or that can be softened by mercy, would in time of war take away from the commanders the right to organize military tribunals of justice, and especially such tribunals for the protection of persons charged or suspected of being secret foes and participants in hostilities. It would be a miracle if the records and history of this war do not show occasional cases in which those tribunals have erred; but they will show many, very many cases in which human life would have been taken but for the interposition and judgments of these tribunals. Every student of the laws of war must acknowledge that such tribunals exert a kindly and benign influence in time of war. Impartial history will record the fact that the Bureau of Military Justice, regularly organized during this war, has saved human life and prevented human suffering. The greatest suffering patiently endured by soldiers, and the hardest battles gallantly fought during this protracted struggle, are not more creditable to the American character than the establishment of this bureau.

This people have such an educated and profound respect for law and justice, such a love of mercy, that they have in the midst of this greatest of civil wars systematized and brought into regular order tribunals that before this war existed under the law of war, but without general rule. To condemn the tribunals that have been established under this bureau is to condemn and denounce the war itself, or, justifying the war, to insist that it shall be prosecuted according to the harshest rules, and without the aid of laws, usages, and customary agencies for mitigating those rules. If such tribunals had not existed before, under the laws and usages of war, the American citizen might as proudly point to their establishment as to our inimitable and inestimable Constitutions. It must be constantly borne in mind that such tribunals and such a bureau cannot exist except in time of war, and cannot then take cognizance of offenders and offenses where the civil courts are open, except offenders and offenses against the laws of war. But it is insisted by some, and doubtless with honesty, and with a zeal commensurate with their honesty, that such tribunals can have no constitutional existence. The argument against their constitutionality may be shortly, and I think, fairly stated thus: Congress alone can establish military or civil judicial tribunals. As Congress has not established military tribunals, except such as have been created under the articles of war, and which articles are made in pursuance of that clause in the Constitution which gives to Congress the power to make rules for the government of the army and navy, any other tribunal is and must be plainly unconstitutional, and all its acts void. This objection, thus stated, or stated in any form, begs the question. It assumes that Congress alone can establish military judicial tribunals. Is that assumption true?

We have seen that when war comes, the laws and usages of war come with it, and that during the war they are a part of the laws of the land. Under the Constitution, Congress may define and punish offenses against those laws, but in default of Congress defining those laws and prescribing punishment for their infraction, and the mode of proceeding to ascertain whether an offense has been committed, and what punishment is to be inflicted, the army must be governed by the laws and usages of war as understood and practiced by the civilized nations of the world. It has been abundantly shown that these tribunals are constituted by the army in the interest of justice and mercy, and for the purpose and to the effect of mitigating the horrors of war.

But it may be insisted that though the law of war, being part of the law of nations, constitute a part of the laws of the land, that those laws must be regarded as modified so far, and whenever they come in direct conflict with plain constitutional provisions. The following clauses of the constitution are principally relied upon to show the conflict betwixt the laws of war and the Constitution. " The trial of all crimes, except in cases of impeachment, shall be by the jury, and such trial shall be held in the State where the said crime shall have been committed; but when not committed within any State, the trial shall be at such place or places as the Congress may by law have directed." " No person shall be held to answer for a capital, or otherwise infamous crime, unless on a presentment or indictment of a grand jury, except in cases arising in the land or naval forces, or in the militia when in actual service, in time of war or public danger; nor shall any person be subject for the same offense to be twice put in jeopardy of life or limb; nor shall be compelled in any criminal case to be witness against himself, nor be deprived of life, liberty or property without due process of law, nor shall private property be taken for public use without just compensation " (Article V. of the amendments). In all criminal prosecutions the accused shall enjoy the right of a speedy and public trial by an impartial jury of the State and district wherein the crime shall have been committed, which district shall have prievously been ascertained by law, and be informed of the nature and cause of the accusation; to be confronted with witnesses against him, to have compulsory process for obtaining witnesses in his favor, and to have the assistance of counsel for his defense " (Article VI. of the amendments). These provisions of the Constitution are intended to fling around the life, liberty and property of a citizen all the guarantees of a jury trial.

These constitutional guarantees cannot be estimated too highly, or protected too sacredly. The reader of history knows that for many weary ages the people suffered for the want of them; it would not only be stupidity but madness in us not to preserve them. No man has a deeper conviction of their value, or a more sincere desire to preserve and perpetuate them, than I have. Nevertheless, these sacred and exalted provisions of the Constitution must not be read alone and by themselves, but must be read and taken in connection with other provisions. The Constitution was framed by great men — men of learning and large experience, and it is a wonderful monument of their wisdom. Well versed in the history of the world, they knew that the nation for which they were framing a government would, unless all history were false, have wars foreign and domestic. Hence the government framed by them is clothed with the power to make and carry on a war. As has been shown, when war comes the laws of war come with it. Infractions of the laws of nations are not denominated *crimes*, but *offenses*. Hence the expression in the Constitution that Congress shall have power to define and punish offenses against the law of nations. Many of the *offenses* against the law of nations for which a man may lose his life, his liberty, or his property are not crimes. It is an offense against the law of nations to break a lawful blockade, and for which a forfeiture of the property is the penalty, and yet the running of a blockade has never been considered a crime; to hold communication or intercourse with the enemy is a high offense against the laws of war, and for which those laws prescribe punishment, and yet it is not a *crime*; to act as a spy is an offense against the laws of war, and the penalty for which, in all ages, has been death, and yet it is not a crime; to violate a flag of truce is an offense against the laws of war, and yet it is not a crime of which a civil court can take cognizance; to unite with banditti, jayhawkers, guerrillas, or any other unauthorized marauders is a high offense against the laws of war; the offense is complete when the band is organized or joined. The atrocities committed by such a band do not constitute the offenses, but make the reasons, and sufficient reasons they are, why such banditti are denounced by the laws of war. Some of the offenses against the laws of war are crimes, and some are not. Because they are crimes they do not cease to be offenses against the laws of war; nor because they are not crimes or misdemeanors do they fail to be offenses against the laws of war. Murder is a crime, and the murderer, as such, must be proceeded against in the form and manner prescribed by the Constitution. In committing the murder an offense may also have been committed against the laws of war; for that offense he must answer to the laws of war, and the tribunals legalized by that law. There is, then, an apparent but no real conflict in the constitutional provisions.

Offenses against the laws of war must be dealt with and punished under the Constitution, as the laws of war, they being a part of the law of nations, direct; crimes must be dealt with and punished as the Constitution, and laws made in pursuance thereof, may direct. Congress has not undertaken to define the code of war nor to punish offenses against it. In the case of a spy, Congress has undertaken to say who shall be deemed a spy and how he shall be punished. But every lawyer knows that a spy was a well known offender under the laws of war, and that under, and according, to these laws he could have been tried and punished without an act of Congress. This is admitted by the act of Congress when it says that he shall suffer death " according to the laws and usuages of war," The act is simply declaratory of the law. That portion of the Constitution which declares that no " person shall be deprived of his life, liberty or property without due process of law " has such direct reference to and connection with trials for *crime* and *criminal* prosecutions, that comment upon it would seem to be unnecessary. Trials for offenses against the laws of war are not embraced nor intended to be embraced in these provisions. If this is not so, then every man who kills another in battle is a murderer, for he deprived a " person of life without that due process of law " contemplated by this provision; every soldier that marches across a field in battle array is liable to an action for trespass, because he does so without that due process of law. The argument that flings around offenders against the laws of war these guarantees of the Constitution would convict all the soldiers of our army of murder; no prisoners could be taken and held; the army could not move.

The absurd consequences that would of necessity flow from such an argument show that it cannot be the true construction — it cannot be what was intended by the framers of that instrument. One of the prime motives for the Union and a federal government was to confer the powers of war. If any provisions of the Constitution are so in conflict with the power to carry on war as to destroy and make it valueless, then the instrument, instead of being a great and wise one, is a miserable failure, a *felo de se*. If any man should sue out a writ of *habeas corpus*, and the returns show that he belonged to the army or navy, and was held to be tried for some offense against the rules and articles of war, the writ should be dismissed, and the party remanded to answer to the charges. So, in time of war, if a man should sue out a writ of *habeas corpus*, and it is made appear that he is in the hands of the military as a prisoner of war, the writ should be dismissed, and the prisoner remanded to be disposed of as the laws and usages of war require. If the prisoner be a regular unoffending soldier of the opposing party to the war, he should be treated with all the courtesy and kindness consistent with safe custody; if he has offended against the laws of war he should have such a trial, and be punished as the laws of war require. A spy, though a prisoner of war, may be tried, condemned, and executed by a military tribunal without a breach of the Constitution. A bushwhacker, a jayhawker, a bandit, a war rebel, an assassin, being public enemies, may be tried, condemned, and executed as offenders against the laws of war.

The soldier that would fail to try a spy or a bandit after his capture would be as derelict in duty as if he were to fail to capture; he is as much bound to try and execute, if guilty, as he is to arrest; the same law that makes it his duty to pursue and kill or capture makes it his duty to try according to the usages of war. The judge of a civil court is not more strongly bound, under the Constitution and the law, to try a criminal, than is the military to try an offender against the laws of war. The fact that the civil courts are open does not affect the right of the military tribunal to hold as a prisoner and to try. The civil courts have no more right to prevent the military, in time of war, from trying an offender against the laws of war than they have a right to interfere and prevent a battle. A battle may be lawfully fought in the very presence of the court; so a spy, a bandit, or other offender against the law of war, may be tried, and tried lawfully, when and where the civil courts are open and transacting business. The law of war authorizes human life to be taken without legal process; or that legal process contemplated by those provisions of the Constitution that are relied upon to show that military judicial tribunals are unconstitutional.

Wars should be prosecuted justly as well as bravely. One enemy in the power of another, whether he be an open or a secret one, should not be punished or executed without a trial. If the question be one concerning the laws of war, he should be tried by those engaged in the war; they, and they only, are his peers. The military must decide whether he is, or is not, an active participant in hostilities. If he is an active participant in the hostilities it is the duty of the military to take him, without warrant or other judicial process, and dispose of him as the laws of war direct. It is curious to see one and the same mind justify the killing of thousands of men in battle because it is done according to the laws of war, and yet condemning that same law when, out of regard for justice, and with the hope of saving life, it orders a military trial before the enemy are killed. The love of law, of justice, and the wish to save life and suffering should impel all good men in time of war to uphold and sustain the existence and actions of such tribunals. The object of such tribunals is obviously intended to save life, and when their jurisdiction is confined to offenses against the laws of war, that is their effect. They prevent indiscriminate slaughter; they prevent men from being punished or killed on mere suspicion. The law of nations, which is the result of the wisdom and experience of ages, has decided that jayhawkers, banditti, etc., are offenders against the laws of nature and of war, and as such amenable to the military. Our Constitution has made those laws a part of the law of the land. Obedience to the Constitution and the law, then, requires that the military should do their whole duty; they must not only meet and fight the enemies of the country in open battle, but they must kill or take the secret enemies of the country and try and execute them according to the laws of war.

The civil tribunals of the country cannot rightfully interfere with the military in the performance of their high, arduous, and perilous but lawful duties. That Booth and his associates were secret active public enemies no mind that contemplates the facts can doubt. The exclamation used by him when he escaped from the box onto the stage, after he fired the fatal shot, *sic semper tyrannis*, and his dying message, "Say to my mother that I died for my country," show that he was not an assassin from private malice, but that he acted as a public foe. Such a deed is expressly laid down in Vattel, in his work on the law of nations, as an offense against the laws of war and a great crime: "I give then the name of assassination to a treacherous murder, whether the perpetrators of the deed be the subjects of the party whom we cause to be assassinated or of our own sovereign, or that it be executed by any other emissary introducing himself as a suppliant, a refugee, or a deserter, or in fine as a stranger" (Vattel, 339.) Neither the civil nor the military department of the government should regard itself as wiser and better than the Constitution and the laws that exist under or are made in pursuance thereof. Each department should, in peace and in war, confining itself to its own proper sphere of action, diligently and fearlessly perform its legitimate functions, and in the mode prescribed by the Constitution and the law. Such obedience to and observance of law will maintain peace when it exists, and will soonest relieve the country from the abnormal state of war.

My conclusion, therefore, is, that if the persons who are charged with the assassination of the President committed the deed as public enemies, as I believe they did, and whether they did or not is a question to be decided by the tribunal before which they are tried, they not only can, but ought to be tried before a military tribunal. If the persons charged have offended against the laws of war, it would be especially wrong for the military to hand them over to the civil courts, as it would be wrong in a civil court to convict a man of murder who had in time of war killed another in battle.

JAMES SPEED,
Attorney General.

The foregoing discussion of the constitutional aspects of the question will no doubt be regarded by most people as somewhat tedious, and perhaps outside of the legal profession will be read, much less carefully studied, by but few. Yet by those who study it, it will be found to be a most profound and masterly analysis of the questions involved, viz., those of military and civil jusridiction as provided for in the Constitution, and to fully justify the opinion given as the conclusion of the argument.

We cannot too highly revere the Constitution, as it is that which gives permanence, security, and prosperity to our national life; yet there is a power greater than the Constitution — a power that by authority expressed or understood reserves the right to amend, alter, or abolish its provisions. That power is the sovereignty that resides in the people. Self preservation is a national, as much as an individual instinct, and self preservation is the first law of nature.

A government that has a right to live has a right to the use of all the means that may be found indispensable to the perpetuation of its existence. When war comes the laws of war come with it as a matter of necessity; because war, being an abnormal state of society, brings with it conditions that render inoperative and useless the means provided for the safety and security of the life, liberty, and property of the citizen, as guaranteed by the Constitution and laws. These interests are too sacred to be left wholly unprotected; and so the civilized nations of the world have adopted those rules which the wisdom and experience of mankind have found necessary for their protection in time of war. These rules, or laws, we denominate the laws of war. If the experience of mankind should dictate modifications of, or additions to, those rules for the better protection of these sacred interests of life, liberty, and property, it would be as proper to amend these as it is proper and competent to amend statute law, or to alter, amend, or abolish constitutions. Such additions or alterations, if wisely made, receive the sanction of mankind, and thus become a part of the unwritten law, having in them the authority of this sanction.

In dealing with this question, however, it was not found necessary that anything new should be devised, as the laws of war were found to authorize all that was necessary to the adjudication of the question, and to furnish the means and appliances for securing the ends of justice.

The nature of the offense charged against these prisoners placed them under the domain of martial law, as they were shown by their own acts and declarations to be secret, active enemies of the government, the purpose of their crime being to give aid to the existing rebellion. For this reason the government left them in the hands of the military to be dealt with according to the laws of war; and the President, being *ex-officio* Commander-in-Chief of the army and navy, ordered the Assistant Adjutant General of the army to detail a military commission, and send the accuse before it for a speedy trial.

CHAPTER VIII.

A MILITARY COMMISSION — ITS NATURE, CONSTITUTION, DUTIES, AND JURISDICTION.

A MILITARY commission, as we have seen, is a judicial tribunal authorized by and constituted under the laws of war during a state of war. It consists of a definite number of commissioned officers designated by the order of detail. Its jurisdiction is limited, and its duties are also prescribed by that order. It is a military court detailed to try offenders against the laws of war, and clothed with power to decide both on the law and evidence in the case, and to prescribe the punishment due to the offense. It is constituted to act under a presiding officer, who is also designated in the order of detail. It has the assistance of a judge advocate with whom it consults in regard to any questions of law or of evidence that may arise.

The office of a judge advocate does not exactly correspond with that of a states attorney in a civil court, for at the same time that it is his duty to see that the case of the government and the evidence are fairly presented, it is as much his duty to see that the accused shall have a fair and impartial trial. The party on trial has the right to have counsel of his own choice, and the government must secure the attendance of such witnesses in his defense as he may designate. The rules of law and of evidence are very nearly the same as those which prevail in the civil courts. A military commission combines, to a great extent, the functions of both court and jury, as it has to decide on questions of law and evidence as a court, and on the guilt or innocence of the accused, in the light of law and evidence, as a jury. Again, in rendering a sentence, in case of conviction, it exercises the functions of a court. The oath taken by the members of the detail, and which constitutes it a court, requires them to diligently try the case and judge and decide impartially, according to the law and evidence. Thus it will be seen that the rights of the accused are carefully guarded, and every precaution taken to make it certain that justice shall be done. This is the purpose as much in the constitution of a military as of a civil court. The only object of its constitution is to protect the innocent and condemn and punish the guilty, and thus secure the ends of justice and mercy. It is a benign provision of military law, and entitled to the highest respect and honor. Its decisions and sentences, however, must have the approval of the President of the United States to give them validity.

CHAPTER IX.

CONSTITUTION OF THE COMMISSION, AND TRIAL.

THE order of the President required the Assistant Adjutant General of the army to detail nine competent military officers to serve as a commission for the trial of the parties in custody, and also that the Judge Advocate General should proceed to prefer charges against them for their alleged offenses, and bring them to trial before the Commission, under the conduct of the Judge Advocate General as the recorder thereof, in person, and assisted by such assistant, or special judge advocates as he might select, and that the trial should be conducted with all diligence, consistent with the ends of justice. Brevet Major General Hartranft was assigned to duty, by the President's order, as Special Provost Martial General for the occasion. The following officers were designated by the Assistant Adjutant General as the detail for the court: —

Major General David H. Hunter, U.S.V., to preside over the Commission.

Major General Lewis Wallace, U.S.V.

Brevet Major General August V. Kautz, U.S.V.

Brigadier General Albion P. Howe, U.S.V.

Brigadier General Robert S. Foster, U.S.V.

Brevet Brigadier General Cyrus Comstock, U.S.V.

Brigadier General T. M. Harris, U.S.V.

Brevet Colonel Horace Porter, Aide-de-Camp.

Lieutenant Colonel David R. Clendennin, Eighth Illinois Cavalry.

Brigadier General Joseph Holt, Judge Advocate General United States Army, Judge Advocate and Recorder of the Commission, aided by such special or assistant judge advocates as he might designate.

T. M. Harris. August V. Kautz. J. A. Ekin. Hon. Jno. A. Bingham. Chas. H Tompkins. R. S. Foster. D. R. Clendenin.
D. Hunter. Lew Wallace. A. D. Howe. Hon J. Holt. H. L. Burnett
MEMBERS OF THE MILITARY COMMISSION.

The details for the Commission were made on the 6th of May, 1865, and it was ordered to meet at Washington City on the 8th of May, or as soon thereafter as possible. The Commission held its first meeting on the 9th of May, at ten o'clock A.M., all the members being present, also the Judge Advocate General.

The Hon. John A. Bingham, and Brevet Colonel H. L. Burnett, Judge Advocate, were introduced by the Judge Advocate General as assistant or special judge advocates. The accused, David E. Herold, George A. Atzerodt, Samuel Arnold, Lewis Payne, Michael O'Laughlin, Edward Spangler, Mary E. Surratt, and Samuel A. Mudd were brought into court, and being asked whether they desired to employ counsel replied in the affirmative. To afford them an opportunity to do so, the court adjourned to meet on the 10th day of May, at ten o'clock A.M. At the assembling of the court on the 10th, the Judge Advocate read a special order from the Assistant Adjutant General, E. D. Townsend, relieving General Comstock and Brevet Colonel Porter from service on the Commission, and substituting for them Brevet Brigadier General James A. Ekin, U. S. V., and Brevet Colonel C. H. Tompkins, U. S. A.

All the members being present, the Commission proceeded to the trial of the parties accused as above named, who were brought into court, and having the order detailing the Commission read to them, they were asked if they had any objection to any member named therein, to which they all replied, severally, that they had not. The members of the Commission were then duly sworn by the Judge Advocate General in the presence of the accused. The Judge Advocate General and the assistant judge advocates were then duly sworn by the president of the court in the presence of the accused.

Ben Pittman, R. Sutton, D. F. Murphy, R. R. Hitt, J. J. Murphy, and Edward V. Murphy were sworn by the Judge Advocate General, in the presence of the accused, as reporters to the Commission. The accused were then severally arraigned on the following charge and specifications: —

Charge and Specifications against David E. Herold, George A. Atzerodt, Lewis Payne, Michael O'Laughlin, Edward Spangler, Samuel Arnold, Mary E. Surratt, and Samuel A. Mudd.

Charge. — For maliciously, unlawfully, and traitorously, and in aid of the existing armed rebellion against the United States of America, on or before the 6th day of March, A.D. 1865, and on divers other days between that day and the 15th day of April, A.D. 1865, combining, confederating, and conspiring together with one John H. Surratt, John Wilkes Booth, Jefferson Davis, George N. Sanders, Beverly Tucker, Jacob Thompson, William C. Cleary, Clement C. Clay, George Harper, George Young, and others unknown, to kill and murder within the military department of Washington, and within the fortified and intrenched lines thereof, Abraham Lincoln, late, at the time of said combining, confederating, and conspiring President of the United States of America and Commander-in-Chief of the army and navy thereof; Andrew Johnson, now Vice-President of the United States aforesaid; William H. Seward, Secretary of State of the United States aforesaid; and Ulysses S. Grant, Lieutenant General of the army of the United States aforesaid, then in command of the armies of the United States under the direction of the said Abraham Lincoln; and in pursuance of, and in prosecuting said malicious, unlawful, and traitorous conspiracy aforesaid, and in aid of said rebellion, afterwards, to wit, on the 14th day of April, A.D. 1865, within the military department at Washington aforesaid, and within the fortified and intrenched lines of said military department, together with said John Wilkes Booth and John H. Surratt, maliciously, unlawfully, and traitorously murdering the said Abraham Lincoln, then President of the United States and Commander-in-Chief of the army and navy of the United States as aforesaid; and maliciously, unlawfully, and traitorously assaulting with intent to kill and murder the said William H. Seward, then Secretary of State of the United States as aforesaid; and lying in wait with intent maliciously, unlawfully, and traitorously to kill and murder Andrew Johnson, then being Vice-President of the United States; and the said Ulysses S. Grant, then being Lieutenant General, and in command of the armies of the United States as aforesaid.

Specifications.—In this, that they, the said David E. Herold, Edward Spangler, Lewis Payne, Michael O'Laughlin, Samuel Arnold, Mary E. Surratt, George A. Atzerodt, and Samuel A. Mudd, together with the said John H. Surratt and John Wilkes Booth, incited and encouraged thereunto by Jefferson Davis, George N. Sanders, Beverly Tucker, Jacob Thompson, William C. Cleary, Clement C. Clay, George Harper, George Young, and others unknown, citizens of the United States aforesaid, and who were then engaged in armed rebellion against the United States of America, within the limits thereof, did, in aid of said armed rebellion, on or before the 6th day of March, A.D. 1865, and on divers other days and times between that day and the 15th day of April, A.D. 1865, combine, confederate, and conspire together at Washington City, within the military department of Washington, and within the intrenched fortifications and military lines of the said United States, there being unlawfully, maliciously, and traitorously to kill and murder Abraham Lincoln, then President of the United States aforesaid, and Commander-in-Chief of the army and navy thereof; and unlawfully, maliciously, and traitorously to kill and murder Andrew Johnson, now Vice-President of the said United States, upon whom, on the death of the said Abraham Lincoln, after the 4th day of March, A.D. 1865, the office of President of the said United States and Commander-in-Chief of the army and navy thereof would devolve; and to unlawfully, maliciously, and traitorously kill and murder Ulysses S. Grant, then Lieutenant General, and under the direction of Abraham Lincoln, in command of the armies of the United States aforesaid; and unlawfully, maliciously, and traitorously to kill and murder William H. Seward, then Secretary of State of the United States aforesaid, whose duty it was by law, upon the death of the said President and Vice-President of the United States aforesaid, to cause an election to be held for electors of President of the United States; the conspirators aforesaid, designing and intending by the killing and murder of the said Abraham Lincoln, Andrew Johnson, Ulysses S. Grant, and William H. Seward, as aforesaid, to deprive the army and navy of the said United States of a constitutional commander-in-chief; and to deprive the armies of the United States of their lawful commander; and to prevent a lawful election of President and Vice-President of the United States aforesaid; and by the means aforesaid to aid and comfort the insurgents engaged in armed rebellion against the said United States as aforesaid, and thereby to aid in the subversion and overthrow of the Constitution and laws of the said United States.

And being so combined, confederated and conspiring together in the prosecution of said unlawful and traitorous conspiracy, on the night of the 14th day of April, A.D. 1865, at the hour of about ten o'clock and fifteen minutes P.M., at Ford's Theatre on Tenth Street, in the City of Washington, and within the military department and military lines aforesaid, John Wilkes Booth, one of the conspirators aforesaid, in pursuance of said unlawful and traitorous conspiracy, did then and there unlawfully, maliciously, and traitorously, and with intent to kill and murder the said Abraham Lincoln, discharge a pistol then held in the hands of him, the said John Wilkes Booth, the same being then loaded with powder and a leaden ball, against and upon the left and posterior side of the head of the said Abraham Lincoln; and did thereby then and there inflict upon him, the said Abraham Lincoln, then President of the United States and Commander-in-Chief of the army and navy thereof, a mortal wound whereof afterwards, to wit, on the 15th day of April, A.D. 1865, at Washington City aforesaid, the said Abraham Lincoln died; and thereby, then and there, and in pursuance of said conspiracy, the said defendants, and the said John Wilkes Booth and John H. Surratt did, unlawfully, traitorously and maliciously, and with intent to aid the rebellion as aforesaid, kill and murder the said Abraham Lincoln, President of the United States, as aforesaid. And in further prosecution of the unlawful, and traitorous conspiracy aforesaid, and of the murderous and traitorous intent of said conspiracy, the said Edward Spangler, on the said 14th day of April, A.D. 1865, at about the same hour of that day as aforesaid, within the said military department and military lines aforesaid, did aid and assist the said John Wilkes Booth to obtain entrance to the box in the said theatre, in which said Abraham Lincoln was sitting at the time he was assaulted and shot as aforesaid by John Wilkes Booth; and also did, then and there, aid said Booth in barring and obstructing the door of the box of said theatre, so as to hinder and prevent any assistance to, or rescue of, the said Abraham Lincoln against the murderous assault of the said John Wilkes Booth; and did aid and abet him in making his escape after the said Abraham Lincoln had been murdered in manner aforesaid.

And in further prosecution of said unlawful, murderous, and traitorous conspiracy, and in pursuance thereof, and with the intent as aforesaid, the said David E. Herold did, on the night of the 14th day of April, A.D. 1865, within the military department and military lines aforesaid, aid, abet, and assist the said John Wilkes Booth in the killing and murder of the said Abraham Lincoln, and did, then and there, aid, abet, and assist him, the said John Wilkes Booth, in attempting to escape through the military lines aforesaid, and did accompany and assist the said John Wilkes Booth in attempting to conceal himself and escape from justice after killing and murdering said Abraham Lincoln as aforesaid.

And in further prosecution of said unlawful and traitorous conspiracy, and of the intent thereof, as aforesaid, the said Lewis Payne did, on the same night of the 14th day of April, A.D. 1865, about the same hour of ten o'clock and fifteen minutes P.M., at the city of Washington, and within the military department and military lines aforesaid, unlawfully and maliciously make an assault upon the said William H. Seward, Secretary of State, as aforesaid, in the dwelling house and bed-chamber of him, the said William H. Seward, and the said Payne did, then and there, with a large knife held in his hand, unlawfully, traitorously, and in pursuance of said conspiracy, strike, stab, cut, and attempt to kill and murder the said William H. Seward, and did thereby, then and there, and with the intent aforesaid, with said knife inflict upon the face and throat of the said William H. Seward divers grievous wounds. And the said Lewis Payne, in further prosecution of said conspiracy, at the same time and place last aforesaid, did attempt, with the knife aforesaid, and a pistol held in his hand, to kill and murder Frederick W. Seward, Augustus H. Seward, Emrick W. Hansel and George F. Robinson, who were striving to protect and rescue the said William H. Seward from murder by the said Lewis Payne, and did, then and there, with said knife and pistol held in his hands, inflict upon the head of the said Frederick W. Seward, and upon the persons of said Augustus H. Seward, Emrick W. Hansel, and George F. Robinson, divers grievous and dangerous wounds, with intent then and there to kill and murder the said Frederick W. Seward, Augustus H. Seward, Emrick W. Hansel, and George F. Robinson.

And in further prosecution of said conspiracy and its traitorous and murderous designs, the said George A. Atzerodt did, on the night of the 14th of April, A.D. 1865, and about the same hour of the night aforesaid, within the military department and military lines aforesaid, lie in wait for Andrew Johnson, then Vice-President of the United States aforesaid, with the intent unlawfully and maliciously to kill and murder him, the said Andrew Johnson.

And in further prosecution of the conspiracy aforesaid, and of its murderous and treasonable purposes aforesaid, on the nights of the 13th and 14th of April, A.D. 1865, at Washington City, and within the military department and military lines aforesaid, the said Michael O'Laughlin did, then and there, lie in wait for Ulysses S. Grant, then lieutenant general and commander of the armies of the United States as aforesaid, with intent then and there to kill and murder the said Ulysses S. Grant.

And in further prosecution of said conspiracy, the said Samuel Arnold did, within the military department and the military lines aforesaid, on or before the 6th day of March, A.D. 1865, and on divers other days and times between that day and the 15th day of April, A.D. 1865, combine, conspire with, and aid, counsel, abet, comfort, and support the said John Wilkes Booth, Lewis Payne, George A. Atzerodt, Michael O'Laughlin, and their confederates in said unlawful, murderous and traitorous conspiracy, and in the execution thereof aforesaid.

And in further prosecution of said conspiracy, Mary E. Surratt did, at Washington City and within the military department and military lines aforesaid, on or before the 6th day of March, A.D. 1865, and on divers other days and times between that day and the 20th day of April, A.D. 1865, receive, entertain, harbor, and conceal, aid and assist the said John Wilkes Booth, David E. Herold, Lewis Payne, John H. Surratt, Michael O'Laughlin, George A. Atzerodt, Samuel Arnold, and their confederates, with knowledge of the murderous and traitorous conspiracy aforesaid, and with the intent to aid, abet, and assist them in the execution thereof, and in escaping from justice after the murder of the said Abraham Lincoln as aforesaid.

And in further prosecution of said conspiracy the said Samuel A. Mudd did at Washington City and within the military department and military lines aforesaid, on or before the 6th day of March, A. D. 1865, and on divers other days and times between that day and the 20th day of April, A.D. 1865, advise, encourage, receive, entertain, harbor and conceal, aid and assist the said John Wilkes Booth, David E. Herold, Lewis Payne, John H. Surratt, Michael O'Laughlin, George A. Atzerodt, Mary E. Surratt, and Samuel Arnold, and their confederates, with knowledge of the murderous and traitorous conspiracy aforesaid, and with the intent to aid, abet, and assist them in the execution thereof and in escaping from justice after the murder of the said Abraham Lincoln, in pursuance of said conspiracy in manner aforesaid. By order of the President of the United States.

J. HOLT,
Judge Advocate General.

Charge and Specifications Indorsed.

"Copy of the within charge and specification delivered to David E. Herold, George A. Atzerodt, Lewis Payne, Edward Spangler, Michael O'Laughlin, Samuel Arnold, Mary E. Surratt, and Samuel A. Mudd, on the 8th day of May, 1865.

[Signed] "J. F. HARTRANFT,
"*Brevet Major General and Special Provost Marshal General.*"

The accused severally plead as follows: —
To the specification, "Not guilty."
To the charge, "Not guilty."

The Commission then proceeded to consider the rules and regulations by which its proceedings should be governed or conducted. The prisoners were served, as we have seen, with a due notice of the offenses with which they were charged, and required to be confronted with the witnesses against them. They were allowed the benefit of counsel of their own choice and compulsory attendance of witnesses in their defense. In short, they were accorded every condition that was necessary to a fair and impartial trial. In this case the only qualification required of the counsel selected or employed by the accused in their defense was, that they should submit or file evidence of having taken the oath required by an act of Congress, or should take said oath before being permitted to appear in the case.

The examination of witnesses was conducted on the part of the government by the Judge Advocate and by counsel on the part of the accused. The evidence was taken down by short-hand reporters who were sworn to record the evidence faithfully and truly, and not to communicate the same, or any part of the proceedings on the trial, except by authority of the presiding officer. They were required to furnish a copy of the evidence taken each day to the Judge Advocate, and also a copy to prisoners' counsel. No reporters except the official reporters were allowed access to the courtroom. The Judge Advocate, however, was allowed to furnish to the agent of the Associated Press, at his discretion, a copy of such testimony and proceedings as might be published during the trial without injury to the public and to the ends of justice. All other publication of the evidence and of the proceedings during the trial was forbidden, and was to be dealt with as a contempt of court. The testimony being closed, the case was to be immediately summed up by one judge advocate, selected by the Judge Advocate General, to be followed or opened, if the Judge Advocate General so selected, by counsel for the prisoners, and the argument closed by one judge advocate.

The argument being closed, the court was to proceed immediately to deliberate and make its determination. The provost marshal was required to have the prisoners present during the trial, and was held responsible for their safe keeping. Their counsel was permitted to hold communication with them in the presence, but not in the hearing, of the guard. Counsel for the prisoners were required to furnish immediately a list of witnesses required for the defense of their respective clients to the Judge Advocate General, who procured their attendance in the usual manner. At the meeting of the Commission on May the 11th, Samuel A. Mudd asked permission to introduce Frederick Stone, Esq., and Thomas Ewing, Jr., Esq., as his counsel. Mary E. Surratt asked to introduce Frederick Aiken, Esq., and John W. Clampitt, Esq., as her counsel, which applications were granted by the court. At its meeting on May 12th, David E. Herold asked to introduce Frederick Stone, Esq., as his counsel; Samuel Arnold asked to introduce Thomas Ewing, Jr., Esq., as his counsel; George A. Atzerodt asked to introduce William E. Doster, Esq., as his counsel; Michael O'Laughlin applied for permission to introduce Walter S. Cox, Esq., as his counsel; Lewis Payne asked to introduce William E. Doster, Esq., as his counsel; Edward Spangler applied for permission to introduce Thomas Ewing, Jr., Esq., as his counsel; which applications were granted, and Messrs. Doster and Cox, having first taken the oath prescribed by act of Congress approved July 2d, 1862, in open court, appeared accordingly. The accused, Mary E. Surratt, applied for permission to introduce Hon. Reverdy Johnson as additional counsel for her, and permission being granted, he appeared accordingly. The admission of Mr. Johnson was objected to by the author, a member of the court, on the ground that he had very light views of the obligations of an oath, and in proof of this, reference was made to an open letter to the people of Maryland, written a few months previously by the honorable gentleman, in which he advised them to take the oath prescribed by the late Constitutional Convention of that State as a qualification for the exercise of the right of suffrage in the adoption or rejection of the amended Constitution, in which letter he took the ground that as the convention had transcended its power in prescribing such an oath, which in effect was intended to exclude all disloyal persons from participation in this right of citizenship, it carried in it no moral obligation; and that they might therefore take it as a matter of indifference, even though they were disloyal. The honorable gentleman at first treated this objection to his appearance with great *hauteur* of manner, and appeared to be astonished that an obscure officer in the army, whom nobody knew, should presume to arraign a man in his position as incompetent to appear before such a court. He was answered by the president of the Commission, who said, that had not General Harris raised this objection he had intended doing so himself. The honorable gentleman, seeing that there was danger of his exclusion from the court, and that it could not be bluffed, immediately came down from his high horse, and in a very respectful manner entered into a lengthy explanation of the letter referred to, which explanation did not put a better face on the matter, but as he in closing emphatically declared that he did recognize the moral obligation of an oath, the objection was withdrawn, and he was admitted and appeared accordingly. The accused severally then asked, for the time, to withdraw their plea of "Not guilty," heretofore filed, so that they might plead to the jurisdiction of the court.

This being granted, they offered the following plea to the jurisdiction of the court: —

"——— ———, one of the accused, for plea says that this court has no jurisdiction in the proceedings against him, because he says he is not, and has not been, in the military service of the United States.

"And for further plea, the said ——— ——— says that loyal civil courts, in which all the offenses charged are triable, exist, and are in full and free operation in all the places where the several offenses charged are alleged to have been committed.

"And for further plea, the said ——— ——— says that the court has no jurisdiction in the matter of the alleged conspiracy, so far as it is charged to have been a conspiracy to murder Abraham Lincoln, late President of the United States, and William H. Seward, Secretary of State, because he says said alleged conspiracy, and all acts alleged to have been done in the formation and in the execution thereof, are in the charge and specifications alleged to have been committed in the City of Washington, in which city are loyal civil courts in full operation, in which all said offenses charged are triable.

"And the said —— —— for further plea says this court has no jurisdiction in the matter of the crime of murdering Abraham Lincoln, late President of the United States, and William H. Seward, Secretary of State, because he says said crimes and acts done in execution thereof are, in the charge and specifications, alleged to have been committed in the City of Washington, in which city are loyal civil courts, in full operation, in which said crimes are triable."

In answer to this plea the judge advocate presented the following replication: —

"Now come the United States, and for answer to the special plea by one of the defendants, —— ——, plead to the jurisdiction of the Commission in this case, say that this Commission has jurisdiction in the premises to try and determine the matters in the charge and specifications alleged and set forth against the said defendant, —— ——.

"J. HOLT,
"Judge Advocate General."

The court was then cleared for deliberation, and on being reopened the Judge Advocate announced that the pleas of the accused had been overruled by the Commission. The accused then made application for severance as follows: —

"—— ——, one of the accused, asks that he be tried separate from those who are charged with him, for the reason that he believes his defense will be greatly prejudiced by a joint trial."

The Commission overruled the application for severance. The accused then severally plead: —

To the specifications, "Not guilty."

To the charge, "Not guilty."

The considerations on which the motion for severance was overruled were, that the charge alleged a conspiracy on the part of the persons accused and on trial, with others unknown, unlawfully, maliciously, and traitorously to kill and murder the President and others. The fact of entering into a conspiracy to do unlawful acts gives to the associated body, in law, an individuality; personality is merged in the common purpose of those thus combining themselves together, and so the declaration or act of any one of them, touching the accomplishment of the common purpose, becomes the declaration or act of all. The guilt is equally shared by all. If the government could not sustain the charge of a conspiracy, then none of the accused could be found guilty of entering into a conspiracy as alleged. The fact of a conspiracy being established, it only remained to be shown in each case that the accused was a member of it; proving this, he would be held to be a sharer in the guilt, although not present at the commission of the crime; but failing to establish the fact of his belonging to the conspiracy, his innocence must be legally admitted. In other words he could not be found guilty. There can in law be no severance of an individuality; and so the application for a separate trial was denied, or overruled.

On the demurrer to the jurisdiction of the court, the Commission held that it could not admit this to be a question that it could properly take under its consideration. To the executive department of the government alone belonged the decision of this question as to the kind of trial that the accused should have; and the President, after maturely considering it in the light of the Constitution and the related facts, and after having submitted it to his Attorney General for his opinion, accepting that opinion as the correct conclusion of his very exhaustive argument, embracing all the Constitutional questions involved, had determined that these parties were offenders against the laws of war, as their offense was the act of secret, active participants in the existing hostilities, and committed with a deep political intent, the purpose of which was to give aid to the existing rebellion, and so, justly, under the Constitution, subjecting them to *law martial*, and trial by a military commission. The President, being *ex-officio* Commander-in-Chief of the armies of the United States, had the right to order a detail of officers to constitute such court, and by order to specify the duties required of them. Their duty as officers of the army required of them simply obedience to the orders of the President of the United States and to those over them in the organization of the military arm of the government. To this they were bound by the solemn obligations of their official oath. To have entertained this question would have been an act of disobedience, subjecting them to discipline; to have refused to serve would have been an act of mutiny. The officers composing this court were, according to the biographers of President Lincoln (Nicolay and Hay) "not only officers high in rank, but of unusual weight of character"; they had been thoroughly schooled in military discipline, and so recognized the duty of obedience to orders as the first duty of a soldier. It was not any part of their duty to discuss the wisdom, propriety, or legality of an order before entering upon the act of obedience. Their duty was simply to obey, and for this they were properly held responsible. The order of detail assigned to them the specific duty of trying the accused under the charge and specifications prepared against them by the government, and so, as loyal, obedient soldiers, loving their country and having faith in its government, they had nothing to do but to enter upon and discharge the duties for which they had been detailed.

As before stated, the Hon. Reverdy Johnson, a United States Senator from Maryland, volunteered to defend Mrs. Mary E. Surratt, selecting her for his client that he might have the benefit, for the purpose of his argument, of the sympathy which we all naturally feel for her sex. It was not his purpose to defend her any more than any other one or all of the prisoners, as he addressed himself simply to the task of arguing the question of jurisdiction. His real object was, evidently, to get himself before the Commission, that he might arraign the martyred President before the country and before the world, and denounce his acts for the prosecution of the war as unconstitutional and tyrannical usurpations of power. He made a lengthy, and from the stand-point of the right of secession, able argument against the right to try these cases before a military tribunal. The Commission was made up largely of men sufficiently versed in constitutional law, as well as the laws of nations and of war, to be little influenced by his sophistries. Their position towards the government on these questions had placed them where they were, as officers in its military service, and they could not be swerved from the loyal discharge of their duty. The reply of the Hon. John A. Bingham to the sophistries of the honorable senator, is a masterpiece of logical reasoning, as also of forensic eloquence and legal acumen, and will well repay the careful study, not only of every student of law, but of every young man who has an ambition to become intelligent in matters of public interest, involving the rights, duties, and privileges of the citizen in time of peace and in time of war.

It will be found not only thoroughly learned and exhaustive of all questions involved, as a legal argument, but also the very embodiment of patriotic devotion to our free institutions of government, and to the cause of civil liberty, justice, humanity, and moral progress.

The Commission was diligently engaged in the trial of the prisoners from the 11th day of May until the 30th day of June, a period of about seven weeks being consumed in hearing the testimony and the motions and arguments of counsel. As I have given, in narrative form, the facts proven against each of the accused, as they stood unimpeached and uncontroverted by testimony given in defense, in giving the history of their arrest, it is unnecessary that I should give it formally, as it appears upon the record of the trial.

After maturely deliberating on the evidence adduced in the case of each of the accused, the findings of the Commission were as follows: —

In the case of David E. Herold: Of the specification guilty; except " combining, confederating, and conspiring with Edward Spangler," as to which part thereof not guilty. Of the charge guilty; except the words of the charge, " combining, confederating, and conspiring with Edward Spangler," as to which not guilty. And the Commission did, therefore, sentence him, the said David E. Herold, to be hanged by the neck until he be dead, at such time and place as the President of the United States should direct, two-thirds of the Commission concurring therein.

In the case of George A. Atzerodt: After mature consideration of the evidence adduced, the Commission found the accused, of the specification guilty; except " combining, confederating, and conspiring with Edward Spangler," of this not guilty. Of the charge guilty; except " combining, confederating, and conspiring with Edward Spangler," of this not guilty. And the sentence of the Commission was that he be hanged by the neck until he be dead, at such time and place as the President of the United States might direct, two-thirds of the Commission concurring therein.

In the case of Lewis Payne, the Commission found him, of the specifications guilty; of the charge guilty; with the same exceptions as in the case of Atzerodt; and sentenced him to be hung as above, two-thirds of the Commission concurring therein.

In the case of Mary E. Surratt, the Commission found her, of the specifications guilty, and of the charge guilty; except as to "receiving, sustaining, harboring, and concealing Samuel Arnold and Michael O'Laughlin"; and except as to " combining, confederating, and conspiring with Edward Spangler," and of this not guilty; and sentenced her to be hanged by the neck until she be dead, at such time and place as the President of the United States should direct, two-thirds of the Commission concurring therein.

In the case of Michael O'Laughlin, the Commission found him guilty of the specifications, except the words thereof, " And in further prosecution of the conspiracy aforesaid, and of its murderous and treasonable purposes aforesaid, on the night of the 13th of April, A.D. 1865, at Washington City, and within the military department and military lines aforesaid, the said Michael O'Laughlin did, then and there, lie in wait for Ulysses S. Grant, then Lieutenant General and commander of the armies of the United States, with intent, then and there, to kill and murder the said Ulysses S. Grant"; of said words not guilty. Of the charge guilty, except "combining, confederating, and conspiring with Edward Spangler"; of this not guilty. O'Laughlin was sentenced by the Commission to be imprisoned at hard labor for life, at such place as the President might direct, two-thirds of the Commission concurring therein. In the case of Edward Spangler, the Commission found him guilty of the charge and specifications, with exceptions similar to the above, and sentenced him to be imprisoned at hard labor for the term of six years, at such place as the President might direct, two-thirds concurring therein.

In the case of Samuel Arnold, the decision of the Commission was, that he was guilty of the charge and specifications, with exceptions similar to the above, and that he should be imprisoned for life at hard labor at such place as the President should direct, two-thirds concurring.

In the case of Samuel A. Mudd, the Commission found him guilty of the charge and specifications, with similar exceptions, as the evidence required, and sentenced him to be imprisoned at hard labor for life, as above.

The findings and sentences of the Commission were approved by the President, and those of the accused who were sentenced to imprisonment at hard labor were ordered by him to be sent to the military prison at the Dry Tortugas, and they were transported there accordingly.

In the case of those who were sentenced to death, the President ordered their execution to take place on the 7th day of July, one week after they were convicted and sentenced by the court, and they were accordingly executed.

After the conviction and sentence of Mrs. Surratt, Judge Bingham, at the request of a member of the court, drew up the following petition: "To the President: The undersigned, members of the military commission appointed to try the persons charged with the murder of Abraham Lincoln, etc., respectfully represent that the Commission have been constrained to find Mary E. Surratt guilty upon the testimony of the assassination of Abraham Lincoln, late President of the United States, and to pronounce upon her, as required by law, the sentence of death; but in consideration of her age and sex, the undersigned pray your Excellency, if it is consistent with your sense of duty, to commute her sentence to imprisonment for life in the penitentiary."

This petition was signed by five members (a majority) of the court, and although not constituting a part of the record, was presented along with the record by the Judge Advocate General to the President. The record was carefully considered and discussed by the President and a full cabinet, when, without a dissenting voice, the sentences of the Commission were confirmed, and the prayer of the petition was rejected.

Mrs. Surratt's counsel then sued out a writ of *habeas corpus* to take her out of the hands of the military authorities, and thus to secure for her a civil trial, or perhaps an entire release, after the President had approved the findings and sentence of the court.

The President had set the 7th day of July, 1865, as the day for the execution of those who had been sentenced to death, and had given orders accordingly to the military officer under whose charge they had been placed. On the forenoon of that day, on the application of Mrs. Surratt's counsel, Judge Wylie, of the Supreme Court of the District of Columbia, endorsed on her application : —

"Let the writ issue as prayed, returnable before the criminal court of the District of Columbia, now sitting at the hour of ten o'clock A.M., this 7th day of July, 1865."

[Signed] "ANDREW WYLIE,
"*A Justice of the Supreme Court of the District of Columbia.*
"July 7th, 1865."

This writ was served on General Hancock, who had custody of, and was charged with the execution of the prisoners, and who, accompanied by Attorney General Speed, appeared before Judge Wylie in obedience to the writ, on which the following return was made : —

HEADQUARTERS MIDDLE MILITARY DIVISION,
WASHINGTON, D. C., July 7th, 1865.

To Hon. ANDREW WYLIE, *Justice of the Supreme Court of the District of Columbia:* —

I hereby acknowledge the service of the writ hereto attached and return the same, and respectfully say that the body of Mary E. Surratt is in my possession under and by virtue of an order of Andrew Johnson, President of the United States, and Commander-in-Chief of the army and navy, for the purposes in said order expressed, a copy of which is hereto attached and made part of this return; and that I do not produce said body by reason of the order of the President of the United States, indorsed upon said writ, to which reference is hereby respectfully made, dated July 7th, 1865.

The order of the President, made a part of the above return, is as follows: —

EXECUTIVE OFFICE, July 7th, 1865, 10 o'clock A.M.

To Major General W. S. HANCOCK, *Commander, etc.:* —

I, ANDREW JOHNSON, President of the United States, do hereby declare that the writ of *habeas corpus* has been heretofore suspended in such cases as this, and I do hereby especially suspend this writ, and direct that you proceed to execute the order heretofore given upon the judgment of the military commission, and you will give this order in return to the writ.

ANDREW JOHNSON, *President.*

The court ruled that it yielded to the suspension of the writ of *habeas corpus* by the President of the United States.

Thus ended the contest over the jurisdiction of the military commission. It has never been revived with success and never will be, as the sound sense of every patriotic American, whose heart beats true to the cause of liberty, justice, good morals, and good government, rests on the arguments that determined this trial by a military commission as its sanction, both by our inimitable Constitution and by the laws of war. In the light of these arguments, this trial will ever hereafter have the authority of a precedent, should another crisis arise involving the principles on which it rests. It was only those whose sympathies were with the rebellion who demurred to it at the time, and whose yelp is occasionally heard, even at this late day, but on a very cold trail.

The sentence of the Commission was executed on the 7th day of July, 1865, in accordance with the President's order, by General Hancock, in the yard of the old Capitol prison. Thus the trial and the execution were alike at the hands of the military; and thus the authority and justice of the government were vindicated, and a solemn warning was given to all traitors to desist from schemes of assassination; a warning which, as we shall yet see, taught them a salutary lesson, and in some measure brought them to their senses.

We shall now turn our attention to the persons just now referred to, some of whom were known, but many were unknown. Before doing this, however, it seems due to our history at this point to say a word about Booth's co-conspirator, John H. Surratt, who would seem to have dropped out of sight in the narrative I have given of the arrest and trial of the conspirators.

It will be remembered that he carried the dispatches from the Richmond government to the Canada conspirators, sanctioning the arrangements that had been made by them to secure the assassinations they had planned; that he arrived with these dispatches at Montreal on the 6th of April; and that the execution of the plot was at once entered upon, those of the conspirators who were to take an active part preparing immediately and starting for Washington, boasting openly of what they would do when they should have reached their destination. Some of these were known, and will be hereafter referred to by name; but there would seem to have been a number of them whose names were never learned. John H. Surratt came back, either alone or in company with some of them. That he was in Washington, aiding and abetting, on the day and night of the assassination, was positively sworn to by one of the witnesses who was well acquainted with him; and from the concurrence of testimony, there is good reason to believe that he was one of the two parties with whom Booth was in communication on the sidewalk in front of the theatre, as heretofore narrated, and that he acted as monitor, calling the time for Booth. He seems, however, to have had the bumps both of cautiousness and secretiveness largely developed, and so kept himself as much as possible out of sight in the transaction in which he was no doubt, at the same time, an active participant. He most probably left Washington on the first train after the work was done, as we have no trace of him again until we find him at Burlington, Vt., on his way to Canada, on the 18th of April. As it is my purpose to devote a chapter or two to his case especially, I shall not, at this time, pursue it any further; but as he was undoubtedly a very active and important factor in the conspiracy, and escaped justice merely by escaping capture at the time, and so securing a civil trial after the war was over, a history of his case naturally comes within the scope of my plan, and will serve to illustrate what I have already said in relation to the existing facts in regard to the population of the District of Columbia that would have rendered a civil trial futile in the cases brought before the Commission.

CHAPTER X.

EVIDENCE IN REGARD TO ATROCITIES NOT EMBRACED IN THE CHARGE AND SPECIFICATIONS, FOR WHICH DAVIS AND HIS CANADA CABINET WERE RESPONSIBLE.

IT will have been noticed that in its charge and specifications against the prisoners on trial the government charged Jefferson Davis, George N. Sanders, Beverly Tucker, Jacob Thompson, William C. Cleary, Clement C. Clay, George Harper, George Young, and others unknown, with combining, confederating, and conspiring together with one John H. Surratt and John Wilkes Booth to kill and murder Abraham Lincoln, Andrew Johnson, William H. Seward, and Ulysses S. Grant; and in the specifications it is alleged that David E. Herold, Edward Spangler, Lewis Payne, Michael O'Laughlin, Samuel Arnold, Mary E. Surratt, George Atzerodt, and Samuel A. Mudd, together with the said John H. Surratt and John Wilkes Booth, incited and encouraged thereunto by Jefferson Davis, George N. Sanders, Beverly Tucker, Jacob Thompson, William C. Cleary, Clement C. Clay, George Harper, George Young, and others unknown, did kill and murder Abraham Lincoln, and assault violently with intent to kill William H. Seward. In this the government distinctly and unequivocally charged Jefferson Davis and his allies with inciting and encouraging the prisoners on trial to the commission of this great crime, with the political intent of giving aid to their sinking cause. They were not arraigned before the Commission, for they were not in custody; but they were arraigned before the world. The Commission was then not called upon to render a finding in their case; but the government was called upon to present to the world through the Commission the evidence on which its grave charge against these men, who had rendered themselves conspicuous before the world, was founded. Its honor and dignity made this obligatory upon it. A careful reading of the charge and specifications on which the assassins were arraigned and tried will show that it was competent for the government to present, on that trial, the evidence in its possession on which it charged Jefferson Davis, Jacob Thompson, Clement C. Clay, Beverly Tucker, George N. Sanders, William C. Cleary, George Young, George Harper, and others, as being inciters to this crime. This evidence was so conclusive of their guilt as charged, that had they been before the Commission they could only have escaped conviction by impeaching the government's witnesses.

Before entering upon the consideration of the evidence a few prefatory remarks seem to be necessary. At an early period of the rebellion Jefferson Davis and his cabinet felt the necessity of sending some of the strongest men of the Confederacy to establish their headquarters in Canada, to look after the interests of the rebel cause, both at home and abroad, and to render assistance to that cause in every way that they could. Amongst its agents thus sent to Canada we find Jacob Thompson of Mississippi, who had been Secretary of the Interior during Buchanan's administration; Clement C. Clay, who had been a United States Senator from Alabama; Beverly Tucker, who had been a circuit judge in Virginia; George N. Sanders, William C. Cleary, George Young, George Harper, and others of less note, acting in subordinate capacities under the above conspicuous leaders and agents.

These agents had been domiciled within the territory of a neutral government to carry on belligerent operations, contrary to the laws of nations and also of war; and the operations planned by them from time to time, and sometimes executed, were of the highest moral turpitude. The fact that, although the government of Canada held the position of a neutral power as between the belligerents, yet its people, in the proportion of five to one, sympathized with the rebellion, made it very favorable to the execution of the schemes of these Southern emissaries. They also occupied a position that geographically was most favorable to their purposes. They were within easy and constant communication with the enemies of the government that were to be found in every Northern State, and at the same time were able to afford a place of refuge for rebel prisoners who were able to find means of escape from Northern prisons. Canada was a place where disloyal refugees and persons accused of offenses against the government congregated all through the war; and so Jefferson Davis's Canada Cabinet was never at a loss for material for carrying out its plans without regard to their character. They were constantly surrounded by desperate and reckless men, who were in deep sympathy with them in their desperate purpose to overthrow the government, and like them, ready to engage in anything that might give aid in carrying out that purpose. From the head of the rebel government on down through the ranks of this class of its agents, there appears to have been no restraint from any moral consideration. The honorable men of the Confederacy were found, to a large extent, in the ranks of its soldiers engaged in open warfare. he assassination plot was the last card of these desperate men; it was preceded by many others in which the laws of war and the laws of morals were utterly ignored. We will, therefore, in the first place, present some of the most flagrant of these, in regard to which the evidence makes Jefferson Davis and his Canada Cabinet responsible, in order that from these revelations we may be thoroughly informed of their utter disregard of every moral consideration, and that we may thus be prepared for the conclusions to which the evidence of their complicity in, and responsibility for, the assassination plot point.

To show the utter lack of moral appreciation, the entire disregard of all moral requirements, and contempt for the enlightened Christian sentiment of the world as embodied in the accepted codes of martial and international law, and that the assassination plot was only in keeping with their other schemes to aid the rebel cause, I deem it necessary to dwell at some length on the statement of these schemes, as shown by the testimony before the Commission. The St. Albans raid, under the lead of Lieutenant Bennett H. Young (made a lieutenant for this occasion only, and that by the filling up for him of a Commission that was sent to Clay, in blank, by the rebel secretary of war, and to be thus conferred by him, at his discretion, on the persons he engaged in such expeditions, as a protection in case of a trial for extradition), was simply a hostile expedition planned by these conspirators, who organized a squad of about twenty escaped Confederate soldiers from the prisons in which they had been confined, and placed them under command of Young, armed with one of these commissions for his protection. This bogus lieutenant was instructed to pass through the New England States with his command, and escape by the way of Halifax, burning towns and farm-houses as he went; and by robbing and plundering to secure all the money he could, and whatever else he could convert to the use of the Confederate government. He made a foray into Vermont; set fire to the town of St. Albans; robbed two banks, securing about two hundred thousand dollars; and then, finding himself confronted by such opposition that he was unable to proceed, was compelled to retreat into Canada, being so closely pursued that he and a good part of his command were made prisoners. They were committed to jail to await a trial for extradition.

This was simply a guerilla raid, organized on neutral territory, not for the purpose of engaging in open and honorable warfare against an armed foe, but to burn and plunder the property of unarmed people, who were non-combatants engaged in the pursuits of peaceful life. Young's commission, however, enabled him to defeat the demand for his extradition, as he was not captured until he had regained that neutral territory on which, in violation of the law of nations, his expedition had been organized. It is easy to see from this where the sympathies of the Canadian court that tried this case lay. Pending this trial for extradition, Clay became very uneasy for fear the commission conferred by him on Young might not prove a sufficient protection, and so he sent Richard Montgomery, who was in the employ of the United States in its department of secret service, and who had so well wormed himself into the confidence of the Canada Cabinet as to be employed by them on this mission, with a letter to James A. Seddon, the rebel secretary of war, urging him by every consideration he could think of to give a direct sanction to Young's act, and to demand in the name of the Confederate government that he should be released.

This letter was carried to Richmond by Montgomery, after having been exhibited to the Secretary of War of the United States. I refer to this as showing the status of Montgomery with these agents of the Confederate government in Canada, and as evidence of his having gained their entire confidence; and so he was in a position to be a witness, before the Commission, as being informed of their plans and of their doings. In response to this argument and earnest appeal of Clay, the rebel government shouldered the responsibility of the St. Albans raid, and shielded the raiders against extradition. The following is a copy of Lieutenaut Young's instructions from the rebel government: —

CONFEDERATE STATES OF AMERICA,
WAR DEPARTMENT,
RICHMOND, VA., June 16th, 1864.

To Lieutenant BENNETT H. YOUNG: —

LIEUTENANT: — You have been temporarily appointed first lieutenant in the provisional army for special service. You will proceed without delay to the British Provinces, where you will report to Messrs. Thompson and Clay for instructions.

You will, under their direction, collect together such Confederate soldiers who have escaped from the enemy, not exceeding twenty in number, as you may deem suitable for the purpose, and will execute such enterprises as may be entrusted to you.

You will take care to commit no violation of the local law, and to obey implicitly their instructions.

You and your men will receive from these gentlemen transportation and the customary rations and clothing, or commutation therefor.

JAMES A. SEDDON,
VA. June 16th.   Secretary of War.

Here we have the response to Clay's letter, and everything fixed up for the defense of Young and his men after the act had been committed, the papers being antedated to meet the requirements of the case.

During the progress of this trial for the extradition of the raiders, Thompson, Clay, Tucker, and Sanders necessarily held a kind of professional intercourse with the counsel representing the United States. Sanders, on one occasion, became full of self-importance, as also, probably, of whiskey, when his discretion forsook him, and he gave vent to the vaunting and boasting of a braggadocio. He said this raid was not the last that would occur, but it would be followed by the depleting of many other banks and the burning of other towns on the frontier, and that many

Yankee sons of —— (using a coarse and vulgar expression) would be killed. He said they had their plans perfectly organized, and men ready to sack and burn Buffalo, Detroit, New York, and other places, and had deferred them for a time, but would soon see the plans wholly executed; and any preparations that could be made by the government to prevent them, would not, though they might delay them for a time. He claimed to be acting as the agent of the Confederate government, and we have seen that it assumed the responsibility. Several other raids of like character were planned, but were prevented by preparations which the government was enabled to make by being informed of them in advance by persons engaged in its secret service, or by other friends in Canada, who, being in the confidence of the conspirators, became informed as to their plans.

These plans involved a warfare against non-combatants; a war, as we shall see, of poisoning reservoirs, of burning towns and cities by wholesale; a war of the destruction of men, women, and children; burning of hospitals, churches, and private dwellings; a war for the destruction of life and property; in short, a war against humanity. The City of New York came in for a large share of their consideration. The destruction of the Croton dam was an enterprise that seemed very desirable to them, and for which they planned; and had the rebel armies been able to keep the field a little while longer, this would no doubt have been attempted and perhaps accomplished. The poisoning of the reservoirs supplying the city with water seemed very desirable to them, and was much discussed. This was one of the hobbies of the infamous Dr. Blackburn and a Mr. M. A. Pallen of Mississippi, who had been a surgeon in the rebel army. They had made a calculation of the capacity of the reservoirs supplying the city, and had calculated the amount of poison required to make an ordinary draught of water fatal to life. Amongst the poisons they had considered arsenic, strychnine, and prussic acid as available. Blackburn thought the project feasible. Thompson feared it would be impossible to collect so large a quantity of poisonous matter without exciting suspicion and leading to the detection of the parties engaged in it. Pallen and others thought it could be managed in Europe. This matter was fully and freely discussed in June, 1864, by Blackburn, Pallen, Thompson, Sanders, and Cleary.

The moral question involved in the destruction, by poison, of the entire population of the American commercial metropolis, — men, women, and children, — did not enter into their thoughts; it was, in fact, a scheme dear to their hearts; the difficulties attending its accomplishment were the only things that gave them any trouble.

This is that same Dr. Blackburn who, with the approbation of Thompson and his gang, made an effort in the summer of 1864 to spread pestilence in Washington City, and in other cities occupied by federal troops, as far south as could be reached, by means of clothing infected with yellow fever and with small-pox.

Conover testified to this positively and circumstantially as one of their many wicked schemes to spread consternation over the North, and so demoralize the people that they would be willing to make peace on any terms.

As this last scheme is so monstrous in character that it can only be believed on the fullest proof, I give the testimony of Godfrey Joseph Hyams before the Commission, in full.

"I am a native of London, Eng., but have lived south nine or ten years. During the past year I have resided in Toronto, Can. About the middle of December, 1863, I made the acquaintance of Dr. Blackburn. I was introduced to him by the Rev. Stewart Robinson at the Queen's Hotel in Toronto. I knew him by sight previously, but before that had no conversation with him. I knew that he was a Confederate and was working for the rebellion. Dr. Blackburn was then about to take south some men who had escaped from the federal service, and I asked to go with him. He asked me if I wanted to go south and serve the Confederacy. I said I did. He then told me to come upstairs to a private room, as he wanted to speak to me. He took me upstairs, and after we had entered his room he pledged his word as a freemason, and offered his hand in friendship, that he would never deceive me. He said he wanted to confide to me an expedition. I told him I would not care if I did. He said I would make an independent fortune by it, at least one hundred thousand dollars, and get more honor and glory to my name than General Lee, and be of more assistance to the Confederate government than if I was to take one hundred thousand soldiers to reinforce General Lee. I pledged my word that I would go if I could do any good. He then told me he wanted me to take a certain quantity of clothing, consisting of shirts, coats, and underclothing, into the States, and dispose of them by auction. I was to take them to Washington City, to Norfolk, and as far south as I could possibly go, where the federal government held possession and had the most troops, and to sell them on a hot day or of a night; that it did not matter what money I got for the clothing, I had just to dispose of them in the best market where there were the most troops, and where they would be most effective, and then come away. He told me I should have one hundred thousand dollars for my services, sixty thousand dollars of it directly after I returned to Toronto; but he said that would not be a circumstance to what I should get. He said I might make ten times one hundred thousand dollars. I was to stay in Toronto, and go on with my legitimate business until I heard from him. He told me to keep quiet, and if I moved anywhere I was to inform Dr. Stewart Robinson where I went to, and he would telegraph for me, or write to me through him. Sometime in the month of May, 1864, I went to my work and worked on until the 8th day of June, '64; it was on a Saturday night; I had been out to take a pair of boots home to a customer of mine; when I returned home my wife had a letter for me from Dr. Blackburn, which Dr. Stewart Robinson had left in passing there. I read the letter, and went out to see Dr. Robinson. I asked him what I was to do about it. He said he did not know anything about it; that he did not want to furnish any means to commit an overt act against the United States government. He advised me to borrow from Mr. Preston, who keeps a tobacco manufactory in Toronto, enough money to take me to Montreal, and there get money from Mr. Slaughter, according to the directions contained in Dr. Blackburn's letter. This letter instructed me to proceed from Montreal to Halifax to meet Dr. Blackburn; it was dated Havana, May 10th, 1864. I went to Halifax to a gentleman by the name of Alexander H.

Keith, Jr., and remained under his care until Dr. Blackburn arrived in the steamer 'Alpha,' on the 12th of July, 1864. When Dr. Blackburn arrived he sent to the Farmer's Hotel, where I was staying, for me. I went to see him, and he told me that the goods were on board the steamer 'Alpha,' and that the second officer on the steamer would go with me and get the goods off, as they had been smuggled in from Bermuda. Mr. Hill, the second officer, told me to get an express wagon and take it down to Cunard's steamboat wharf. I did so, and there got eight trunks and a valise. I was directed to take them to my hotel, and put them in a private room. I put them in Mr. Doran's private sitting-room. I then went around to Dr. Blackburn, and told him I had got the goods off the steamer. He told me that the five trunks tied up with ropes were the ones for me to take, and asked me if I would take the valise into the States and send it by express, with an accompanying letter, as a donation to President Lincoln. I objected to taking it, and refused to do so. I then took three of the trunks and the valise around to the hotel. He was then staying at the Halifax Hotel. The trunks had Spanish marks upon them, and he told me to scrape them off, and that Mr. Hill would go with me the next morning and make arrangements with some captain of a vessel to take them. There were two vessels there running to Boston, and I was to make an arrangement with either of them to smuggle the trunks through to Boston. The next morning I went down with Mr. Hill to the vessels. Mr. Hill had a private conversation with Captain McGregor, the captain of the first vessel, to whom we applied to take the goods, and he refused.

"We then went to see Captain O'Brien of the bark 'Halifax.' Hill told him that I had some presents in my trunks, consisting of silks, satin dresses, etc., that I wanted to take to my friends. The Captain and Mr. Hill had a private conversation, and when the Captain came out he consented to take them. I was to give him a twenty-dollar gold piece for smuggling them in. I put them on board the vessel that day and he stowed them away. The vessel lay five days at Boston before he could get a chance to get them off, but finally he succeeded in getting them off, and expressed them to Philadelphia, where I received them and brought them to Baltimore. I then took out the goods, which were very much rumpled, and smoothed them out and arranged them, bought some new trunks, and repacked them and brought them to this city. Dr. Blackburn, by way of caution, asked me before leaving if I had had the yellow fever, and on my saying 'no,' he said, 'You must have a preventive against taking it. You must get some camphor and chew it, and get some strong cigars, the strongest you can get; and be sure to keep gloves on your hands when handling the things.' He gave me some cigars that he said he had brought from Havana, which he said were strong enough for anything. When I arrived in this city, I turned over five of the trunks to Messrs. W. L. Wall & Company, commission merchants in this city, and four to a man by the name of Myers, from Boston, a sutler for Siegel's or Weitzel's division. He said he had some goods which he was going to take to New Berne, N.C., and I told him that I had a lot of goods that I wanted to sell, and, to make the best market I could for them, I would turn them over to him on commission. I also told him I would shortly have more, and mentioned that I had disposed of some to Wall & Company, of this city. Dr. Blackburn told me, when I was making arrangements, that I should let the parties to whom I disposed of my goods know that I would have a big lot to sell, as it was in contemplation to get together about a million dollars' worth of goods and dispose of them in that way. Dr. Blackburn stated that his object in having these goods disposed of in different cities was to destroy the armies, or anybody that they came in contact with. All these goods, he told me, had been carefully infected in Bermuda with yellow fever, small-pox, and other contagious diseases.

"The goods in the valise, which were intended for President Lincoln, I understood him to say had been infected with yellow fever and small-pox. This valise I declined taking charge of and turned it over to him at Halifax Hotel, and I afterwards heard that it had been sent to the President. On the five trunks that I turned over to Wall & Company I got an advance of one hundred dollars. Among these five trunks there was one that was always spoken of by Blackburn to me as 'Big No. 2,' which he said I must be sure to have sold in Washington. On disposing of the trunks I immediately left Washington, and went straight through until I got to Hamilton, Canada. In the waiting-room there I met Mr. Holcomb and Clement C. Clay. They both rose, shook hands with me, and congratulated me upon my safe return, and upon my making a fortune. They told me I should be a gentleman for the future, instead of a working man and a mechanic. They seemed perfectly to understand the business in which I had been engaged.

"Mr. Holcomb told me that Dr. Blackburn was at the Donegan Hotel, in Montreal, and that I had better telegraph to him stating that I had returned. As Dr. Blackburn had requested me to telegraph to him as soon as I got into Canada, I did so, and the next night, between eleven and twelve o'clock, Dr. Blackburn came up and knocked at the door of my house. I was in bed at the time. I looked out of the window, and saw Dr. Blackburn there. Said he, 'Come down, Hyams, and open the door; you are like all damned rascals who have been doing something wrong — you're afraid that the devil is after you.' He was in company with Bennett H. Young. I came down and let him in. He asked me how I had disposed of the goods and I told him. 'Well,' said he 'that is all right as long as "Big No. 2" went into Washington; it will kill them at sixty yards distance.' I then told the doctor that everything had gone wrong at my home in my absence; that I needed some funds; that my family needed money. He said he would go to Colonel Jacob Thompson and make arrangements for me to draw upon him for any amount of money that I required. He then said that the British authorities had solicited his services in attending the yellow fever that was then raging in Bermuda; that he was going on there; and that as soon as he came back he would see me. I went up to Jacob Thompson the next morning, and told him what Dr. Blackburn had said. He said 'Yes'; Dr. Blackburn had been there and had made arrangements for me to draw one hundred dollars whenever it was shown that I had made disposition of the goods according to his directions. I told him I needed money; that I had been so long away from home that everything I had was gone, and I wanted money to pay my rent, etc. He said, 'I will give you fifty dollars now, but it is against Dr. Blackburn's request; when you show me that you have sold the goods, I will give you the balance.' He asked me to give him a receipt, which I did: 'Received of Jacob Thompson the sum of fifty dollars on account of Dr. Blackburn.' That was about the 11th or 12th of August last. The next day I wrote to Messrs. Wall & Company, of Washington, desiring them to send me an account of the sales, and the balance due me. When I received their answer, I took it to Colonel Thompson. He then said he was perfectly satisfied I had done my part, and gave me a check for fifty dollars on the Ontario Bank. I gave him a receipt: 'Received of Jacob Thompson one hundred dollars in full on account of Dr. Luke P. Blackburn.' I told Thompson of the large sum which Dr. Blackburn had promised me for my services and that he and Mr. Holcomb had both told me that the Confederate government had appropriated two million dollars for the purpose of carrying it out; but he would not pay me any more. When Dr. Blackburn returned from Bermuda, I wrote to him at Monttreal, and told him I wanted some money, and that he ought to send me some; but he made no reply to my letter. I was then sent down to Montreal with a commission for Bennett H. Young, to be used in his defense it the St. Albans raid case. I there met Dr. Blackburn. He said I had written some hard letters to him, abusing him, and that he had no money to give me. He then got into his carriage at the door and rode off to some races, I think, and never gave me any more satisfaction. As I wanted money before leaving for the States, I went to the Clifton House, Niagara. Dr. Blackburn told me he had no money with him then, but that he would go to Mr. Holcomb and get some, as he had Confederate funds with him. Blackburn said that when I returned he would get the money for the expedition from either Holcomb or Thompson, it did not matter which. From this, and from Holcomb and Clay both shaking hands with me and congratulating me at Hamilton upon my safe return, I thought, of course, they knew all about it. I do not know that Dr. Stewart Robinson knew of the business in which I was engaged, but he took good care of me while

I was at Toronto, in the fall, and until Dr. Blackburn wrote for me in the spring; and when he gave me Dr. Blackburn's letter, he told me to borrow the money from Mr. Preston to take me to Montreal, as he said he did not want to commit an overt act against the Government of the United States himself. Mr. Preston lent me ten dollars to go to Montreal. On arriving at that place, according to the directions of Dr. Blackburn's letter, I went to Mr. Slaughter to get the means to take me to Halifax. Mr. Slaughter was short of funds, and had only twenty dollars that he could give me. He said that I had better go to Mr. Holcomb, who was staying at the Donegan Hotel, and he would give me the balance. I went to the Hotel and sent up my name, and he sent for me to come up. I told him I wanted some money to take me to Halifax; he asked me how much I wanted; I told him as much as would make up forty dollars; he said 'You had better take fifty dollars,' but as I did not want that much I only took enough to make forty dollars. When I came to Washington to dispose of my goods, which was on the 5th of August, 1864, I put up at the National Hotel, registered my name as J. W. Harris, under which name I did business with Wall & Company."

Here we have a straightforward, circumstantial account of the efforts made and the means used to spread pestilence and death amongst citizens and soldiers alike, in the capital of the nation, and in other cities and camps, a special consignment, supposed to contain the contagion of yellow fever and small-pox, being sent as "a donation to President Lincoln." This was for the purpose of taking his life, and at the risk of the lives of his household. Blackburn, Clay, Thompson, and Holcomb were the originators of the plan, and as guilty as the infamous scoundrel, Hyams, who, to gratify his desire for revenge on them for their perfidy in putting him off with a mere pittance of the promised reward for his services in the matter, comes before the Commission and reveals the whole history of their infamy. No one who reads his story will doubt that he was a conscienceless scoundrel, who, for the hope of obtaining a large sum of money, according to their promise, was willing to make himself an instrument in the wholesale and indiscriminate destruction of human life. But monster as he was, he was not more a monster than was each one of his employers. He was evidently a man well qualified for the task in which he was employed; in the first place destitute of conscience, and then a man of a good degree of intelligence, shrewdness, and knowledge of affairs. Granting that he was selected by Dr. Robinson, and recommended by him to Dr. Blackburn, he could not have made a better selection had he had full knowledge of the work cut out for him to do. And when we consider Blackburn's perfidy in his dealings with him, pledging his faith as a freemason and giving him his hand in friendship, assuring him that he would never deceive him; then building him up in the idea that he would receive one hundred thousand dollars, and perhaps ten times that amount as his reward; and then, after he had performed a service that put his own life in jeopardy, to put him off with a mere pittance of the amount promised, we cannot wonder that a man constituted as Hyams was should divulge the terrible secret in revenge for the shabby treatment he had received at their hands.

See how Clay and Holcomb meet him on his return! They understand all about the character of his mission, congratulate him on his safe return, and on the fact that from thenceforth he was not to be known as a laboring man and a mechanic, but as a gentleman.

No wonder that he, when for the pitiful sum of one hundred dollars he had signed for Thompson a receipt in full on account of Dr. Blackburn, vowed to have revenge. How true it is that there must be honor even amongst the worst of villains, in order that they may hang together. They broke faith with Hyams, and Hyams revealed circumstantially, and fully, their great crime against humanity. We have now seen these men planning to poison the water supply of New York City to the extent of fatality to its whole population, men, women, and children,—helpless age, and more helpless infancy doomed to death by the scope of their plan; and now, we have found them engaged in an effort to spread pestilence with the same purpose of the indiscriminate destruction of human life. What worse can they do? Can we after this be surprised at anything they may undertake? It will not avail to say that a man who could be hired to do such a thing as this is unworthy of credence, even under oath, and so that his testimony is not to be received. Hyams' story bears on its face the marks of a truthful narrative of the facts, just as they occurred, and it does not follow that because a man is a confessed scoundrel he is incapable of telling the truth. No adequate motive for falsehood in this case can be assigned. Had his employers kept faith with him, he would no doubt have kept their terrible secret, and it would have been buried with him. That they did not, only becomes a reason for his disclosure of the facts, not for his fabrication of falsehoods. But then his statement as to how he disposed of the goods in Washington City is fully confirmed by the testimony of Wall & Company, who produced an account of the transaction agreeing exactly, in date and amount, with that given by Hyams, and also in regard to his *alias* of J. W. Harris. It was also corroborated by the National Hotel register of that date.

Conover testified to this as one of the schemes planned by Thompson and his gang, and Hyams gives a full account of the manner of its execution. For some reason the infection was a failure in Washington City; but not so with the goods sent by Myers, the sutler, to New Berne, N.C. It will be recollected that an epidemic of yellow fever broke out there in the latter part of the summer of 1864, that swept away large numbers of people, both citizens and soldiers. No doubt this epidemic was due to the infection carried in the clothing that Myers received from Hyams, to be sold on commission; and that in the great day of final account these men will find themselves arraigned as the murderers of all those who fell as the victims of their hellish plot, before a tribunal that is infinitely perfect in its knowledge and just in its decisions.

Plot to Burn New York City and its Attempted Execution.

The plot to burn the city of New York was attempted to be carried out on the 25th of November, 1864. I will give the history of this attempt as narrated in his confession, by Robert C. Kennedy, one of the gang of incendiaries sent there for that purpose, who was arrested, tried, found guilty, condemned, and hanged for his crime. Before his execution he made a full confession as follows:—

"After my escape from Johnson's Island I went to Canada, where I met a number of Confederates. They asked me if I was willing to go on an expedition. I replied: 'Yes, if it is in the service of my country.' They said: 'It is all right,' but gave me no intimation of its nature, nor did I ask for any. I was then sent to New York, where I stayed some time. There were eight men of our party, of whom two fled to Canada. After we had been in New York three weeks we were told that the object of our expedition was to retaliate on the North for the atrocities in the Shenandoah Valley. It was designed to set fire to the city on the night of the Presidential election; but the phosphorus was not ready, and it was put off until the 25th of November. I was stopping at the Belmont House, but moved into Prince Street. I set fire to four places — in Barnum's Museum, Lovejoy's Hotel, Tammany Hotel, and the New England House. The others merely started fires in the house where each one was lodging, and then ran off. Had they all done as I did, we would have had thirty-two fires and played a huge joke on the fire department. I know that I am to be hung for setting fire to Barnum's Museum, but that was only a joke. I had no idea of doing it. I had been drinking and went in there with a friend, and, just to scare the people, I emptied a bottle of phosphorus on the floor. We knew it would not set fire to the wood, for we had tried it before, and at one time had concluded to give the thing up. There was no fiendishness about it. After setting fire to my four places, I walked the streets all night, and went to the Exchange Hotel early in the morning. We all met there that morning and the next night. My friend and I had rooms there, but we sat in the office nearly all the time reading the papers, while we were watched by the detectives, of whom the hotel was full. I expected to die there, and if I had it would have been all right; but now it seems rather hard. I escaped to Canada and was glad enough when I crossed the bridge in safety. I desired, however, to return to my command, and started with my friend for the Confederacy *via* Detroit. Just before entering the city he received an intimation that the detectives were on the look-out for us, and giving me the signal he jumped from the cars. I did not notice the signal, but kept on and was arrested in the depot. I wish to say that the killing of women and children was the last thing thought of. We wanted to let the people of the North understand that there were two sides to this war, and that they could not be rolling in wealth and comfort while we at the South were bearing all the hardships and privations. In retaliation for Sheridan's atrocities in the Shenandoah Valley, we desired to destroy property; not the lives of women and children, although that would, of course, have followed in its train."

Done in the presence of   LIEUT. COL. MARTIN BURKE and
                                             J. HOWARD, JR.

arch 24th, 1865, 10.30 P.M.

Kennedy, in the presence of death, made this free and full confession, carefully confining himself to the narration of his own and the acts of his fellow incendiaries. He does not tell who planned this enterprise of death and destruction for the great metropolis of the country, and whilst honestly confessing his own part in it, is very careful not to compromise anybody else. But we are not left without information as to who were the employers of him and his gang; and here again Thompson and his fellow agents of the rebel government in Canada are made to appear as its originators, and must be held responsible, not only for the attempt thus made to destroy New York by fire, but also for the worst consequences that could have happened had their attempt proven successful.[1] Kennedy says they did not desire to destroy the lives of women and children, although that would of course have followed in its train. Thompson, Clay, Cleary, Sanders, and any others that had any hand in setting this expedition on foot, could not fail to know what would necessarily follow in its train if successful, but were not deterred by the knowledge of the fact that it involved not merely the destruction of property, but of necessity also the destruction of women and children; for the firing of a city like New York in many places, simultaneously, if successful in its object, the destruction of the city, must necessarily result in the same kind of indiscriminate destruction of human life that resulted at New Berne, from the dissemination of pestilence sent there in the clothing that that inhuman fiend, Dr. Blackburn, had carefully infected and sent there for that very purpose. In the early ages of the world war meant the indiscriminate destruction of all that belonged to the enemy. The spirit of war then was to exterminate the foe. Prisoners of war were slaughtered after the battle was ended. Women and children were killed or carried into slavery. Men had not learned to exercise mercy in war. It meant universal destruction of life, and confiscation of the property of the enemy. It meant even the confiscation of the territory or country in which he lived. It is so yet among the savage tribes of the earth. With them the murder of a woman about to become a mother is nothing, and the dashing out of the brains of her children against a stone or a tree, before her eyes, yields to them a fiendish satisfaction. Civilized nations, however, do not so carry on war, and the laws of war do not permit this mode of warfare. The annals of no age of the world, or of the

[1] Conspiracy Trial, pp. 29, 30, testimony of Conover; also p. 36, testimony of Dr. Merritt; also p. 25, testimony of Montgomery.

most rude and savage people of the earth, afford examples more atrocious than those planned and executed, or attempted to be executed, by these agents of Jefferson Davis in Canada, and by other agents, as we shall see, whose deeds were sanctioned and paid for by Davis and his Secretary of State Benjamin.

The prison-pen at Andersonville was evidently planned for the destruction of the lives of the prisoners of war that were sent there; and if any escaped death, it was intended that they should be so physically injured that they could never again render any service to the Union cause. In a country abounding in forest shade and pure water, there can be no excuse given for locating a prison-pen in a little intervale, wholly destitue of shade, where men without tents or shelter of any kind were huddled together by the thousands, with a very meagre supply of water, for a long time, even for quenching thirst, and none at all for the purposes of cleanliness, and what they had for the former purpose being contaminated with all the filth from the drainage of the town just above.

It is evident that this location was made with a view to the destruction of life and the ruin of health. Then, for the further carrying out of this purpose, the rations supplied were not only wholly insufficient in quantity, but most unwholesome in quality, exactly adapted to aid the effects of miasmatic exposure, and foul water, in bringing on stomach and bowel troubles and low forms of fever, which were kept up until life was literally drained out, and death from exhaustion ensued. Here, without any sympathetic medical assistance or proper medicine, men were dying daily by the fifties and the hundreds, and the survivors becoming mere ghostly spectres; whilst the inhuman monster, Wirtz, stood gloating over the scene in devilish glee, and his inhuman guards were constantly on the lookout for pretexts to shoot down their fellowmen, as though the terrible harvest of death, secured by their arrangements and management of this graveyard of the living, was too meagre, and required their bullets to enrich it. Such was Andersonville. The purpose of its location and management are too obvious to need remark; and for all this, Jefferson Davis and his Secretary of War are to be held responsible. Far be it from me to bring up this matter for the purpose of giving a fresh impulse to sectional enmity. I only do it to show the low moral status of those who were responsible for the conduct of the war on the side of the rebellion, in order that from all this we may be prepared for the evidence presented to the world through the Commission, sustaining the grave charges of the government.

There was no doubt an element, perhaps a large element of the population of the Southern States, that was in full sympathy with this policy; but such a policy could only have been abhorrent to the honorable foe who bravely confronted us on the field of conflict. It was the stay-at-home-and-fight element that sanctioned these atrocities. War is cruel when conducted on the strictest rules of civilized warfare. War is destructive; it is harsh and unrelenting. Foeman must meet foeman with his steel. It is a game in which human life is always the price of success and the cost of failure. The enemy must be met and overcome; his resources must be reached and cut off if it can be done, thus starving him into submission, as a more humane way of getting the victory over him than by taking his life. But amongst civilized people no enemy is to be deprived of life but the armed and active foe in the field, in honorable and open combat, except for crime. The lives of women, children, prisoners of war, and of non-combatants generally, must be held sacred. Thus we see how much the horrors of war have been mitigated by the more enlightened sentiments and Christian morality of the world's present state of civilization. When these shall have done their perfect work, wars will cease. The time will yet come when men shall learn war no more. May God hasten the day.

In charging Jefferson Davis, and those associated with him in the conduct of the war with an utter disregard of the laws of war, and of being guilty of atrocities that are only matched in savage life, I wish again to make a distinct disclaimer in behalf of those who fought, and of those who conducted his operations in the field. Whilst I abhor their construction of the Constitution and theory of the union of the States as destructive of the hopes of liberty and of free government, tending continually to disintegration, and making the idea of a nation an impossibility, I admire and honor the courage and bravery with which they maintained their theory, and accord to them the honor, as well as the courage of true soldiers.

To them the idea of winning success by the means we have had under consideration, and for which we have found the political leaders of the rebellion responsible, including the highest officer of the Confederacy, would have been as abhorrent as to myself. Not a word that I have written can tarnish the fame of the true soldier; and I have carefully avoided charging anything against even the politicians of the Confederacy that is not sustained by indisputable evidence. Considered morally, their methods can never be justified; yet it was by these methods, with assassination added, that the political leaders of the rebellion sought to obtain success, and because of this, must for all time in history fall under the condemnation of the enlightened Christian conscience of the world. That they were guilty of all these things has been abundantly proven; but as we shall see, the evidence has not yet been exhausted. They attempt to shield themselves under the claim of justifiable retaliation. Retaliation for what? They answer, "The atrocities committed by Sheridan in the Shenandoah Valley." Let us consider this question for a moment. It was the fortune of the writer to be serving under Sheridan at the time these alleged atrocities were committed, and to be an eye-witness of them. What did Sheridan do? He burnt all the stack-yards and barns containing grain and hay, and all the mills and factories found in the valley from above Harrisonburg on down to near Winchester, or perhaps lower down than that. He also appropriated all the horses, cattle, sheep, etc., that could have been made available for the support and aid of an enemy. He dealt merely with property, and that such property alone as would have enabled General Lee again to have threatened the national capital by an invading foe by this route, as he had twice, or oftener, done before, thus making it necessary to employ a large force from our army in guarding this route. General Grant determined to render this division of his forces unnecessary, by rendering the valley impracticable to Lee by this destruction of the abundant supplies that it furnished, in order that he might have the benefit of Sheridan's forces in his investment of Richmond.

It was simply the destruction of property by which the rebellion could sustain itself, and thus prolong its existence, in order to shorten the war, and thus save the expenditure of human life. There was no property destroyed or confiscated but such as could be used for the subsistence and movements of an army. It was simply a question of shortening the war, and thus economizing human life by the destruction of property, and so was a measure fully justified by the laws and usages of war. Sheridan acted under Grant's orders in this matter, and his acts were only atrocious as war itself is atrocious, and can never serve as a justification of schemes that in every instance involved the lives of non-combatants, and even of women and children. All of this destruction of property in the Shenandoah Valley by Sheridan was done, and accounted for, strictly in accordance with the laws and usages of war, and has never been challenged by the civilized nations of the world as an unwarranted atrocity. It was harsh in the extreme; but as a military necessity it was justifiable. It included in its object mercy towards the lives of men.

As the cause of the Confederacy began to lose ground in the summer of 1864, and the signal success of our arms made it clear that it would not be able to maintain the fight to a successful close, the political leaders became desperate and reckless as to the means to which they resorted. The City Point explosion, the burning of a number of steamboats on the Ohio and Mississippi rivers, and the burning of a soldiers', or United States, hospital at Louisville, Ky., were amongst the occurrences of that eventful summer. The following extract from the report of John Maxwell to Captain Z. McDaniel, commanding Torpedo Company, explains the City Point explosion:—

"Captain: I have the honor to report that in obedience to your order, and with the means and equipments furnished me by you, I left this city (Richmond) 26th July last for the line of the James River, to operate with the 'hozological torpedo' against the enemy's vessels navigating that river. I had with me Mr. R. K. Dillard, who was well acquainted with the localities, and whose services I engaged for the expedition.

"On arriving in Isle of Wight County, on the 2d of August,

we learned of immense supplies of stores being landed at City Point; and for the purpose, by stratagem, of introducing our machine upon the vessels there discharging stores, started for that point. We reached there before day-break on the 9th of August last, having travelled mostly by night, and crawled upon our knees to pass the east picket line. Requesting my companion to remain behind about half a mile, I approached cautiously the wharf, with my machine and powder covered by a small box. Finding the captain had come ashore from a barge then at the wharf, I seized the occasion to hurry forward with my box. Being halted by one of the wharf sentinels, I succeeded in passing him by representing that the captain had ordered me to convey the box on board. Hailing a man from the barge, I put the machine in motion, and gave it in his charge. He carried it aboard. The machine contained about twelve pounds of powder. Rejoining my companion we retired to a safe distance to witness the effect of our effort.

"In about an hour the explosion took place. Its effect was communicated to another barge beyond the one operated upon, and also to a large wharf building containing their stores (enemy's), which was totally destroyed. The scene was terriffic, and the effect deafened my companion to an extent from which he has not recovered. My own person was severely shocked, but I am thankful to Providence that we have both escaped without injury. We obtained and enclose slips from the enemy's newspapers, which afford their testimony of the terrible effects of the blow. The enemy estimate the loss of life at fifty-eight killed and one hundred and twenty-six wounded, but we have reason to believe it greatly exceeded that.

"The pecuniary damage we heard estimated at four millions of dollars; but of course we can give you no account of the extent of it exactly. I may be permitted, Captain, here to remark *that a party of ladies*, it seems, were killed by this explosion. It is saddening to me to realize the fact that the terrible effects of war [he should have added as thus conducted] induce such consequences; but when I remember the ordeal to which our own women have been submitted, and the barbarities of the enemy's crusade against us and them, my feelings are relieved by the reflection that whilst this catastrophe was not *intended* by us, it amounts only, in the providence of God, to *just retribution.*"

Hear the pious scoundrel salving his conscience with the old cry of " just retribution ! "

The following will explain the agency by which boats on the Ohio and Mississippi rivers, and the United States Hospital at Louisville, Ky., were burned. It is the testimony of Edward Frazier before the Commission :—

" I am a steamboat man, and have been making St. Louis my home for the last nine or ten years. During 1864 I knew of the operations of Tucker, Minor Majors, Thomas L. Clark, and Colonel Barrett, of Missouri, for burning boats carrying government freight, transports, and other vessels on the Ohio and Mississippi and other rivers. These men were in the service of the Confederate Government. I knew of the following steamboats having been burned by the operations of these parties: the ' Imperial,' ' Hiawatha,' the ' Robert Campbell,' the ' Louisville,' the ' Daniel G. Taylor,' and others, besides some in New Orleans that I do not know the names of. The ' Imperial ' was one of the largest and finest transports on the western waters. In the case of the burning of the ' Robert Campbell,' which was destroyed in the stream when under way, at Milikin's Bend, twenty-five miles above Vicksburg, there was a considerable loss of life. The agent who destroyed this boat was on board. These boats were all owned by private individuals. The operations of these men were to include government hospitals, store-houses, and everything appertaining to the enemy. A United States hospital at Louisville was burned in June or July of 1864. I do not know who burned it, but a man named Dillingham claimed compensation for it. I was in Richmond from the 20th to the 25th or 26th of August last, when I had an interview with the rebel Secretary of War, the Secretary of State, and Mr. Jefferson Davis. Thomas L. Clark, Dillingham, and myself, called there in connection with the boat burning, and put in claims to Mr. James A. Seddon, the rebel Secretary of War. Mr. Clark introduced me to Mr. Seddon. He told me that he had thrown up that business, that it was now in the hands of Mr. Benjamin. We went to him, and Mr. Benjamin looked at the papers we brought him, and asked me if I knew anything about them. I told him that I did, and that I believed they were all right. He asked me if I was from St. Louis. I told him I was. He then asked Mr. Clark if he knew me to be all right, and he said I had been represented to him by Mr. Majors as being all right. Mr. Benjamin told us all three to call the next day. We did so, when he said he had shown these papers to Jefferson Davis, and he (Benjamin) wanted to know if we would not take thirty thousand dollars and sign receipts in full. We told him we would not. Mr. Benjamin then said that if Dillingham was to claim this in Louisville, he wanted a statement of it. We went back to the hotel, and I wrote the statement myself. It read that Mr. Dillingham had been hired by General Polk, and that he had been sent to Louisville expressly to do that work; namely, to burn the hospital. It was then talked over with Mr. Benjamin, and we made a settlement with him for fifty thousand dollars; thirty-five thousand dollars down in gold, and fifteen thousand dollars on deposits, to be paid in four months, provided the claims proved correct. The money was paid by a draft on Columbia for thirty-four thousand, eight hundred dollars, in gold, and two hundred dollars in gold we got in Richmond. We received the gold on the draft at Columbia. Whilst in Richmond, Mr. Benjamin told me that Mr. Davis wanted to see me. I went in with Mr. Benjamin to see Mr. Davis, and we sat and talked. The conversation first was about what was called the Long Bridge, between Nashville and Chattanooga. Mr. Davis wanted to know what I thought about destroying it. He said they had been thinking of it, and of sending some one to have it done. I told him I knew of the bridge, though I did not, for I had never been there, but did not know what to think about destroying it. He said I had better study it over. Finally I told him I thought it could be done. Mr. Benjamin, I believe it was, first remarked that he would give four hundred thousand dollars if that bridge was destroyed, and asked me if I would take charge of it. I told him I would not unless the passes were taken away from those men that were now down there, and

Mr. Davis said it should be done. The conversation then turned on the burning of the steamboats. I told Mr. Davis that I did not think it was any use burning steamboats, and he said no, he was going to have that stopped. The next day I saw an order taking away passes issued on or before the 23d of August. These passes were permits to do this kind of work. I presume Mr. Davis knew that the money I received was for the work that I had done; he knew that I had received money there. Mr. Davis seemed fully aware of what we had done, and he did not condemn it. Mr. Majors and Barrett belonged to an organization known as the 'O. A. K.', or 'Order of American Knights.'" The witness was asked to state, if he thought proper to do so, whether he was also a member of that order; but he declined to say. 'I understood' (said the witness) 'that Colonel Barrett held the position of adjutant general of this organization, of the Sons of Liberty, for the State of Illinois. I do not know that Majors and Barrett were in Chicago in July last, but Mr. Majors left St. Louis either in June or July, to go to Canada, and I presume went there by way of Chicago."

Here again, we see the moral plane on which Davis and Benjamin worked for the success of the Confederacy. We find them employing and paying agents for burning boats, midstream, regardless of the destruction of the lives of non-combatants, including, most likely, women and children amongst the passengers aboard; burning a hospital filled with sick, wounded, and dying soldiers, who, according to the laws of civilized warfare, are entitled to the sacred protection of even the enemy, whether in or out of their territory and possession. We have now found Davis and his agents in Canada planning and carrying out schemes for assassination or murder by wholesale, by spreading pestilence, poisoning of reservoirs, burning cities, hospitals, and boats on their way loaded with passengers, and by the use of explosives murdering women. Human life, under any imaginable conditions of existence, received no consideration at their hands if its sacrifice held out to them any prospect of advancing their cause.

Another foul plot to murder prisoners of war held in Libby Prison, right under the eyes of Davis and his Cabinet, is detailed as follows by Erastus W. Ross, a witness before the Commission: —

"I was in the service of the rebel government. I was conscripted and detailed as a clerk at Libby Prison, and never served in the army. In March, 1864, General Kilpatrick was making a raid in the direction of Richmond. About that time the prison was mined. I saw the place where I was told the powder was buried under the prison; it was in the middle of the building. The powder was put there secretly in the night. I never saw it, but I saw the fuse. It was put in the office. I was away at my uncle's the night that the powder was put there, and was told of it the next morning by one of the colored men at the prison. There were two sentinels near the place to prevent any person approaching it. The excavation made was about the size of a barrel head, and the earth was thrown up loosely over it. Major Turner, the commandant of the prison, had charge of the fuse. He told me that the powder was there, and that the fuse was to set it off; that it was put there for the security of the prisoners, and if the army got in it was to be set off for the purpose of blowing up the prison and the prisoners. The powder was secretly taken out in May, and the whole building was then shut up. The prisoners had all been sent to Macon, Ga. I suppose the powder was placed there by the authority of General Winder or the Secretary of War. Major Turner said he was acting under the authority of the rebel war department, though I never saw any written orders about it."

John Latouche testified as follows: "I was first lieutenant in Company B, Twenty-fifth Virginia Battallion, C. S. A. I was detailed to post duty in Richmond to regulate the details of the guards of the military prisons there, and in March, 1864, I was on duty at Libby Prison. Major Turner, the keeper of the prison, told me that he was going to see General Winder about the guard. On his return he told me that General Winder himself had been to see the Secretary of War, and that they were going to put powder under the prison. In the morning of the same day the powder was brought. There were two kegs of about twenty-five pounds each, and a box which contained about as much as the kegs. A hole was dug in the centre of the middle basement, and the powder was put down there. The box when put in just came level with the ground, and the place was covered over with gravel. I did not see any fuse to it then. I placed a sentry over this powder so that no accident might occur, and the next day Major Turner, who had charge of the fuse, showed it to us in his office; he showed it to everybody there. It was a long fuse made of gutta-percha, such a one as I had never seen before. In May, I think it was, Major Turner went South, and all of the prisoners were sent out of the Libby building proper to the south; and General Winder sent a note down to the office with directions to take up the powder as privately or as secretly as possible. I forget his exact words. The note was delivered into my hands for the inspector of the prison, to whom I either gave or sent it. I afterward heard Major Turner say that in the event of the raiders coming into Richmond he would have blown up the prison. I understood him to say those were his orders."

We are not left, however, to infer that this gunpowder plot, by which the lives of twelve hundred Union officers held as prisoners of war were to have been sacrificed in case Colonel Dahlgren should have gotten into the city for the purpose of their liberation, was authorized by the head of the rebel government.

The box turned over by General Johnson to General Schofield, containing the archives of the Confederate government, contained the proof that Jefferson Davis ordered these preparations to be made, and that his subordinates had orders to carry the plot into execution in the event of the contingency above referred to. These archives also showed that in this he was sustained by the committee of the rebel congress on the conduct of the war. Pollard, also, in his history of the "Lost Cause," attempts to justify this plot. In all this we see the debasing influence of human bondage on the moral sense of a people. Who, except under the influence of such a demoralization, could have planned for the wholesale sacrifice of their prisoners of war?

Here we have Mr. Seddon, the rebel Secretary of War, of course not on his own responsibility, but under the orders of his superior, Jefferson Davis, ordering the officer in charge of the prisoners of war in their possession to mine the building in which they were confined, and in the event of a Yankee raid entering the city, to blow up the building, and thus murder, at one fell swoop, all the prisoners in it to prevent their being rescued and taken back into the service. Need we wonder that an administration that could deliberately prepare to murder its prisoners of war rather than suffer their liberation under the fortunes of war, should have deliberately planned for the destruction of its prisoners by the starvation and cruelties of Andersonville?

It gives me no pleasure to rehearse these things, but it is due to the truth of history that they should be known. I desire to see a speedy and complete reconciliation of these two sections of our country; and I have always rejoiced that we who faced each other on the fields of deadly conflict, have, from the time of the surrender of Lee's army, been ready to meet each other as friends and brothers and fellow citizens of a common country. The sight witnessed at Appomattox of the soldiers of our army emptying their haversacks to satisfy the wants of men who but the hour before stood confronting them as foes, but who now had laid down their arms, worn out and famishing, was a glorious exhibition of the best side of our nature, and plainly said that though we had been enemies in war in peace we would be friends, and foreshadowed the speedy reconciliation that has followed our terrible strife, so far as the soldiers of the two armies are concerned. I charge none of these things on these men. I fix the responsibility for these things on the political leaders of the rebellion, and not even on them indiscriminately but only on such of them as are named in the charge and specifications under which, through the medium of the Commission, they were arraigned before the world, and the evidence of their guilt was produced. It is to show that the government in so doing completely vindicated its dignity and honor that I write.

If the acts of public men render them infamous in history, the responsibility rests in their bad exercise of that freedom of will that makes us responsible beings.[1] And in human affairs, bad

---

[1] The archives of the rebel war department reveal the fact that the powder was placed under the Libby Prison by order of Davis and Seddon, sanctioned by a committee of the rebel congress.

examples should be held up as warnings, just as good examples should be held up for imitation and encouragement.

We shall now approach a little more closely to the consideration of the responsibility of Jefferson Davis and his Canada Cabinet for the assassination of Abraham Lincoln; and will show, we think, by incontestible evidence, that they were co-conspirators with Booth and his gang, or rather, that they originated and concocted the plan, and that Booth and his followers were merely their hired assassins for the accomplishment of their purposes.

CHAPTER XI.

EVIDENCE PRESENTED BY THE GOVERNMENT TO SUSTAIN ITS CHARGE AND SPECIFICATIONS.

THE following letter was found in the box turned over by General Joseph A. Johnson, at Charlotte, N.C., to General Schofield, and said to contain the archives of the Confederate government: —

MONTGOMERY, WHITE SULPHUR SPRINGS, VA.

To HIS EXCELLENCY, *the President of the Confederate States of America*:—

DEAR SIR:— I have been thinking for some time that I would make this communication to you, but have been deterred from doing so on account of ill health. I now offer you my services, and if you will favor me in my designs, I will proceed, as soon as my health will permit, to rid my country of some of her deadliest enemies, by striking at the very heart's blood of those who seek to enchain her in slavery. I consider nothing dishonorable having such a tendency. All I ask of you is to favor me by granting me the necessary passes, etc., on which to travel while in the jurisdiction of the Confederate government. I am perfectly familiar with the North, and feel confident I can execute anything I undertake. I am just returned from within their lines. I am a lieutenant in General Duke's command, and I was on the raid last June in Kentucky under General John H. Morgan. I and all of my command excepting about three or four, and two commissioned officers, were taken prisoners; but finding a good opportunity, while being taken to prison, I made my escape from them. Dressing myself in the garb of a citizen, I attempted to pass through the mountains, but finding that impossible, narrowly escaping two or three times from being retaken, I shaped my course north, and went through to the Canadas, from where, by the assistance of Colonel Holcomb, I succeeded in making my way around and through the blockade; but having yellow fever, etc., at Bermuda, I have been rendered unfit for service since my arrival. I was reared up in the State of Alabama, and educated in its university. Both the Secretary of War and his assistant, Judge Campbell, are personally acquainted with my father, William J. Alston, of the fifth Congressional District of Alabama, having served in the time of the old Congress, in the years 1849-50 and 1851. If I do anything for you, I shall expect your full confidence in return. If you do this, I can render you and my country very important service. Let me hear from you soon. I am anxious to be doing something, and having no command at present, all, or nearly all, being in garrison, I desire that you favor me in this a short time. I would like to have a personal interview with you, in order to perfect the arrangements before starting.

I am, very respectfully,
Your obedient servant,
LIEUTENANT W. ALSTON.

This letter, it will be observed, is without date; but the box in which it was found was marked, "Adjutant and Inspector General's Office; letters received July to December, 1864." Lieutenant Alston was captured in Kentucky in June, 1864, and so, in making his escape through Canada, made the acquaintance of the rebel agents there, just at the time that they were full of the assassination scheme. It was probably from his intercourse with them that he became infatuated with this idea, although he does not give them the credit of it. He seems to have been an ambitious youth who desired to impress the rebel President with the idea that this was an original scheme of his own. Mark how unblushingly he opens his mind to Davis in presenting his plot! It is nothing less than "striking at the heart's blood of some of his country's deadliest foes," of whom everybody then knew that Abraham Lincoln was universally regarded in the South as chief. It is a plain offer to aid his country's cause by entering upon the policy of assassinating the loyal men of the country whose official duty required them to put down the rebellion. He considers nothing dishonorable that tends to accomplish this. He does not merely propose to strike at the heart's blood of Abraham Lincoln. No; like the Canada conspirators, he has a more comprehensive scheme. Did Jefferson Davis feel insulted by being thought capable of giving his sanction to such a foul and dishonorable proposition? Let us see.

The following is his endorsement put upon it: —

INDORSEMENT.

A. I. 390. Lieut. W. Alston, Montgomery, Sulphur Springs, Va. (no date). Is Lieutenant in General Duke's command. Accompanied raid into Kentucky and was captured, but escaped into Canada, from whence he found his way back. Been in bad health. Now offers his services to rid the country of some of its deadliest enemies. Asks for papers to permit him to travel within the jurisdiction of this government.

Would like to have an interview and explain. Respectfully referred, by direction of the President, to the Honorable Secretary of War.

BURTON N. HARRISON,
Private Secretary.

Received November 19th, 1864.
Recorded book A.A.G.O., December 16th, 1864.
A.G. for attention.
By order of J. A. CAMPBELL, A.S.W.

The handwriting of the private secretary of Jefferson Davis, Burton N. Harrison, and of the Assistant Secretary of War, J. A. Campbell, in the endorsements, was verified before the Commission by Lewis W. Chamberlain, who had been a clerk in the war department at Richmond, and was well acquainted with the handwriting of both of these gentlemen.

From the consideration given by the rebel President, as shown by these careful and favorable endorsements, would it be unreasonable to conclude that Lieutenant Alston was granted the interview that he desired, and that, armed with the permission and authority of the rebel chief, he became one of the active participants in the closing scenes of the drama?

We have other evidence that at this very time the mind of Jefferson Davis was turned in this direction, and that he was inciting his agents in Canada to turn their attention to a grand political scheme of wholesale assassinations.

To show the moral obtundity of the political stay-at-home-and-fight rebels about this time, I will reproduce an advertisement of this proposition to assassinate President Lincoln and the other civil officers of the government, that was published in the *Selma* (Alabama) *Dispatch*, in December, 1864, under the caption —

"MILLION DOLLARS FOR ASSASSINATION

"One million dollars wanted to have peace by the 1st of March. If the citizens of the Southern Confederacy will furnish me with the cash, or good securities for the sum of one million dollars, I will cause the lives of Abraham Lincoln, William H. Seward, and Andrew Johnson to be taken by the 1st of March next. This will give us peace, and satisfy the world that cruel tyrants cannot live in a land of liberty. If this is not accomplished, nothing will be claimed beyond the sum of fifty thousand dollars in advance, which is supposed to be necessary to reach and slaughter the three villains. I will give, myself, one thousand dollars towards this patriotic purpose. Every one wishing to contribute will address Box X, Cahawba, Alabama. December 1st, 1864."

This advertisement was proven by compositors in the *Dispatch* office to have been put in that paper by Mr. G. W. Gale, a lawyer of considerable reputation, and that the copy was in his handwriting, which was well known at that office. My impression is that several of the Richmond papers reproduced this advertisement, as also many other papers in the Confederacy. The treasonable purpose to overthrow the Constitution by the assassination of the President, Vice-President, and Secretary of State shows that the plan had been maturely considered in the light of the conditions that would render it most effective in securing the object in view, and that it was a deep political scheme to give the rebellion a new lease of life, and put it on its feet again under more favorable conditions for success. I have already given incidentally, and in a fragmentary way, glimpses of the testimony on which the charges of the government were founded. I will now present in a connected form the testimony bearing on the question.

Richard Montgomery testified before the Commission that Thompson said to him in the summer of 1864 that he had his friends all over the North, and that he could have anybody put out of his way that he chose; that he would only have to point out the man that he considered in his way, and his friends would remove him, and would consider it no crime when done for the cause of the Confederacy. Clay also, on being told by Montgomery what Thompson had said, replied, " That is so; we are all devoted to our cause and ready to go any lengths — to do anything in the world to serve our cause." Thompson said his friends would do this and not let him know anything about it if necessary. That this was not mere bragadocio is evident from the fact that Montgomery was accepted by Thompson as a confederate in full sympathy with himself, and entitled to his fullest confidence.

Merritt testified that he first heard of the assassination plot in October or November, 1864, when he was told by Young, in reply to an inquiry of Merritt in regard to a contemplated raid : " We have something on the *tapis* of much more importance than any raids we have made, or can make." He said, " It was determined that Old Abe should never be inaugurated." He said they had plenty of friends in Washington; and speaking of Mr. Lincoln, he called him a damned old tyrant. Merritt was afterwards introduced to George N. Sanders by Colonel Steele, and in the course of the conversation that ensued, Steele said, "the damned old tyrant will never serve another term if he is elected." Sanders replied, "he (Lincoln) would have to keep himself mighty close if he did serve another term." In January, 1865, Thompson told Montgomery that a proposition had been made to him to rid the world of the tyrant Lincoln, Stanton, Grant, and some others. He said he knew the men that made the proposition to be bold, daring men, and able to execute anything they would undertake without regard to cost. He said he was in favor of the proposition, but had concluded to defer giving his answer until he should have consulted with his government at Richmond; and that he was only waiting for their approval; adding that he thought it would be a great blessing to the people, both North and South, to have these men killed. Beverly Tucker, in a conversation with Montgomery after the assassination, recounting the many wrongs the South had received at the hands of Mr. Lincoln, said, "that he deserved his death, and it was a pity he had not met it long ago; that it was too bad that the boys had not been allowed to act when they wanted to."

Conover testified that he saw Booth in Montreal about the latter part of October, 1864. He was strutting about the St. Lawrence Hall, playing billiards, etc., but occasionally was to be seen in confidential intercourse with Sanders and Thompson.

Whilst in Canada at this time the plot to assassinate was fully decided upon, as will be shown by the "Selby letter" subjoined. This letter was picked up in a street car in New York by a couple of ladies, one of whom, Mrs. Mary Hudspeth, testified before the Commission as follows: "In November last, after the presidential election, and on the day that General Butler left New York, as I was riding on the Third Avenue cars in New York City, I overheard a conversation of two men. They were talking most earnestly. One of them said he would leave for Washington day after to-morrow. The other was going to Newburg or New Berne that night. One of the two was a young man with false whiskers. This I observed when a jolt of the car pushed his hat forward and at the same time pushed his whiskers, by which I observed that the front face was darker than it was under the whiskers. Judging by his conversation, he was a young man of education. The other, whose name was Johnson, was not. I noticed that the hand of the younger man was very beautiful, and showed that he had led a life of ease and not of labor.

"They exchanged letters whilst in the car. When the one who had the false whiskers put back the letters in his pocket, I saw a pistol in his belt. I overheard the younger one say that he would leave for Washington the day after to-morrow. The other was very angry because it had not fallen on him to go to Washington. Both left the cars before I did. After they had left, my daughter, who was with me, picked up a letter which was lying on the floor of the car, immediately under where they sat, and gave it to me, and I, thinking it was mine, as I had letters of my own to post at the Nassau Street Post-office, took it without noticing that it was not one of my own. When I got to the brokers, where I was going with some gold, I noticed an envelope with two letters in it. These are the letters, and both were contained in one envelope. After I examined the letters and found their character, I took them first to General Scott, who asked me to read them to him. He said he thought they were of great importance, and asked me to take them to General Dix. I did so. The letters are as follows: —

"DEAR LOUIS: — The time has at last come that we have all so wished for, and upon you everything depends. As it was decided before you left, we were to cast lots. Accordingly we did so, and you are to be the Charlotte Corday of the nineteenth century. When you remember the fearful, solemn vow that was taken by us you will feel there is no drawback — *Abe* must *die*, and *now*. You can choose your weapons — the cup, the *knife*, the *bullet*. The cup failed us once, and might again. Johnson, who will give *this*, has been like an enraged demon since the meeting because it has not fallen upon him to rid the world of the monster. He says the blood of his gray-haired father and his noble brother call on him for revenge, and revenge he will have; if he cannot wreak it upon the fountain head, he will upon some of the blood-thirsty generals. Butler would suit him. As our plans were all concocted and well arranged, we separated; and as I am writing on my way to Detroit, I will only say that all rests upon you. You know where to find your friends. Your disguises are so perfect and complete, that without *one* knew *your face* no police telegraphic despatch would catch you. The English gentleman, Harcourt, must not act hastily. Remember he has ten days. Strike for your home, strike for your country; bide your time, but strike sure. Get introduced, congratulate him, listen to his stories — not many more will the brute tell to earthly friends. Do anything but fail, and meet us at the appointed place within the fortnight. Inclose this note, together with one of poor Leenea. I will give the reason for this when we meet. Return by Johnson. I wish I could go to you, but duty calls me to the West; you will probably hear from me in Washington. Sanders is doing us no good in Canada.

"Believe me your brother in love,
"CHARLES SELBY."

"ST. LOUIS, October 21st, 1864.

"DEAREST HUSBAND: — Why do you not come home? You left me for ten days only, and now you have been from home more than two weeks. In that long time, only sent me one short note — a few cold words — and a check for money, which I did not require. What has come over you? Have you forgotten your wife and child? Baby calls for papa until my heart aches. We are *so lonely without you.* I have written to you again and again, and, as a last resource, yesterday wrote to Charlie, begging him to see you and tell you to come home. I am so ill — not able to leave my room; if I was, I would go to you wherever you were, if in *this world.* Mamma says I must not write any more, as I am too weak. Louis, darling, do not stay away any longer from your heart-broken wife,

"LEENEA."

General Dix sent these letters to the War Department at Washington. They were given to President Lincoln, who put them in an envelope, marked it "Assassination," and laid it away in his desk, where it was found after his death. Mrs. Hudspeth testified that she picked these letters up on the day that General Butler left New York. General Butler had orders to leave on the 11th of November, but upon application got permission to remain until the 14th. Booth left Washington on the early morning train on November 11th, which would put him into New York on the afternoon of that day. Here he met his co-conspirator, Johnson, on the cars, and in exchanging letters with him, dropped these letters without noticing it. The Leenea letter was to have been returned by Johnson. He was to leave for Washington on the day after to-morrow, which, reckoning from the 11th, would be the 13th. The hotel register accounts for him again at Washington on the 14th in the early part of the evening. That the young man described by Mrs. Hudspeth was John Wilkes Booth was shown by her recognition of his photograph, shown to her in the presence of the Commission, when she declared that that was the same face.[1]

[1] The Charles Selby letter was proven to be in the handwriting of John Wilkes Booth by experts, on comparison, on the trial of John H. Surratt.

It was also shown by the testimony of Samuel Knapp Chester, the actor, that Booth was in New York about this time, laboring with Chester in the most urgent manner to draw him into the conspiracy. It is true he represented to him that the purpose was to capture the President, and carry him a prisoner to Richmond; that this feat was to be performed at Ford's Theatre in Washington, and that Chester's part in it would be the easy one of simply opening the door of exit on a given signal; but can any sane man believe that this was his purpose? The impracticability of this proposition could not but have been as apparent to Booth as it was to Chester, who begged Booth, finally, to never mention the subject to him again. It is evident Booth intended to withhold from Chester his real purpose until he could get him irrevocably committed to the conspiracy. The letter which he had dropped, and which I have given above, reveals the real purpose of the conspiracy. It will be seen by this letter that it was in contemplation at that time to act at once, or at least as soon as a good opportunity should be found, or could be made. He who was "to be the Charlotte Corday of the nineteenth century" had his choice as to the weapons he should use; but whether it should be the cup, the knife, or the bullet, it simply meant death. Why was not the purpose carried out at that time as arranged for at the meeting to which the letter refers? As will be shown by the subsequent testimony, the assassins were restrained from present action by the agents of the rebel government in Canada, who desired to have explicit sanction to the arrangements they had made as to the compensation, and authority for the expenditure it involved.

Let us see now how the testimony connects the rebel agents in Canada with this meeting that was held in the latter part of October, or first of November, 1864, and with its conclusions, which resulted in arrangements for these assassinations. Montgomery testified that in January, 1865, Jacob Thompson told him that a proposition had been made to him to rid the world of the tyrant Lincoln, Stanton, Grant, and some others. The men who had made the proposition, he said, he knew to be bold, daring men, and able to execute anything they would undertake without regard to cost. He said he was in favor of the proposition but had determined to defer his answer until he had consulted with his government at Richmond, and he was then only waiting their approval, adding that he thought it would be a blessing to the people, both North and South, to have these men killed. A few days after the assassination, Montgomery had a conversation with Beverly Tucker in Montreal. He said a great deal about the wrongs the South had received at the hands of Mr. Lincoln, and that he deserved his death, and it was a pity he had not met with it long ago. He said "It was too bad that the boys had not been allowed to act when they wanted to." Thus we see that "the boys" were kept back from the execution of the plot for which they had made ready late in October, or early in November, at the meeting referred to in the Selby letter, by Thompson and his clique, who had concluded to defer it until they should have obtained the sanction of their government at Richmond to their arrangements, which no doubt involved the expenditure of a large sum of money. Montgomery at this time related a portion of the conversation with Thompson, given above, to William C. Cleary, who was Thompson's confidential secretary, when Cleary told him that Booth was one of the men to whom Thompson referred; and speaking of the assassination, he said "It was too bad that the whole work had not been done," adding, "They had better look out; we have not done yet." Cleary told Montgomery during this conversation that Booth had been there visiting Thompson twice in the winter; the last time he thought was in December.

That Cleary was well acquainted with all that Thompson, Tucker, and Clay were doing is clear from the relation he sustained to Thompson; and Thompson himself told Montgomery that Cleary was posted in all his affairs, and that if he (Montgomery) sought him at any time when he was absent, he could confide his business to Cleary.

Conover testified that he called on Thompson, in the early part of February, 1865, to make some inquiry about the intended raid on Ogdensburg, when Thompson said to him, "There is a better opportunity, a better chance to immortalize yourself and save your country." Conover replied that he was willing to do anything to save the country. Thompson then said, "Some of our boys are going to play a grand joke on Abe and Andy." Upon Conover asking him for a further explanation, he said, "It was to kill them, or, rather, to remove them from office." He said, "it was only removing them from office; that the killing of a tyrant was no murder." He told Conover then, or subsequently, that he had conferred a commission on Booth for this purpose, and would commission all who engaged in it, so that whether it succeeded or failed, if they escaped to Canada, they could not be claimed under the extradition treaty. The Confederate government kept these Canada agents supplied with commissions in blank, to be filled up by them at their pleasure, to cover cases like these. In this conversation of Thompson with Conover, in February, in which he was endeavoring to enlist Conover in the plot, he argued that killing a tyrant in such a case was no murder, and asked him if he had ever read the work entitled, "Killing no Murder," a letter addressed by Colonel Titus to Oliver Cromwell. Mr. Hamlin was to have been included in the scheme, had it been put into execution before the 4th of March. In a subsequent conversation in April, Mr. Hamlin was omitted, and Vice-President Johnson put in his place. We here again see the political intent of this scheme, in that it was the office, not the man, that was really the subject of the blow.

Merritt testified to an interview he had with Harper, Caldwell, Randall, Charles Holt, and a man called "Texas," at the Queen's Hotel, in Toronto, on the 6th of April, 1865. Harper said they were "going to the States, and were going to kick up the damnedest row that had ever been heard of." He said to Merritt, an hour or two afterwards, that "if he (Merritt) did not hear of the death of Old Abe, and the Vice-President, and General Dix in less than ten days he might put him down as a damned fool. We have now had abundant proof that Thompson, Clay, Tucker, Sanders, Cleary, etc., were guilty of combining, confederating, and conspiring with Booth, and the others, to assassinate Abraham Lincoln, Andrew Johnson, William H. Seward, etc.; that this plot originated with them, and that they diligently prosecuted the work of preparation for it from October, 1864, until its denouement, in April, 1865. It appears to have engrossed their minds;

it was the great subject of conversation in all of their secret conclaves, the great burden of all their thoughts, the very height of their ambition.

Let us next see to what extent the head of the rebel Confederacy, Jefferson Davis, is implicated in it by the evidence. We have already seen by his favorable reception of the Alston letter and the endorsement he put upon it, that there was nothing in his mind or moral nature that revolted at its base, cowardly, and dishonorable proposition to "strike at the very heart's blood of some of our country's deadliest foes." On the contrary, he refers it to his Assistant Secretary of War, marked "For attention."

Having obtained this index to the state of his mind, we find ourselves prepared to receive the testimony of Dr. J. B. Merritt as to a letter read by Sanders in a meeting of rebels in Montreal, about the middle of February, 1865, at which ten or fifteen persons were present, amongst whom were Sanders, Colonel Steele, Captain Scott, George Young, Byron Hill, Caldwell, Ford, Benedict, Kirk, and Merritt. Sanders said he had received the letter from "the President of our Confederacy" (meaning Jefferson Davis). The substance of this letter was, that if the confederates in Canada and in the States were willing to submit to be governed by such a tyrant as Lincoln he did not wish to recognize them as friends and associates, and he expressed his approbation of any measures they might take to accomplish this object. It is true Dr. Merritt did not see Davis's signature to the letter, and would not have known it had he seen it, but the letter was first read openly by Sanders, and then handed to the others, several of whom read it, and none questioned either its author or authenticity. Colonel Steele, Young, Hill, and Captain Scott read it, and no objection was raised. After reading this letter, Sanders went on to name a number of persons who were ready and willing, as he said, to engage in the undertaking to remove the President, Vice-President, the cabinet, and some of the leading generals, and said there was any amount of money to accomplish the purpose. Amongst the persons whom he said thus stood ready to engage in this work, he named Booth, George Harper, Charles Caldwell, one Randall, and Harrison (by which name Surratt was known), and one or two others, one of whom they called "Plug Tobacco," or "Port Tobacco." I will here remark that Atzerodt was sometimes called by this latter name. Sanders said that Booth was heart and soul in this project of assassination, and felt as much as any person could feel, for the reason that he was a cousin to Beall, who was hung in New York. He said that if they could dispose of Mr. Lincoln it would be an easy matter to dispose of Mr. Johnson; he was such a drunken sot it would be an easy matter to dispose of him in some of his drunken revelries.

When Sanders read the letter he also spoke of Mr. Seward. "I inferred," says Dr. Merritt, "it was partially the language of the letter. It was, I think, that if the President, Vice-President, and Mr. Seward could be disposed of, it would be satisfying the people of the North that they (the Southerners) had friends in the North, and that peace could be obtained on better terms than could be otherwise obtained."

It will be remembered that Booth sent to Chester fifty dollars in a letter when trying to get him into the conspiracy, and that at their final interview in February, Chester positively refused to have anything to do with it, and returned to Booth the fifty dollars he had received. Booth took the money, saying at the same time he would not do so only he was short of funds. He had told Chester that there was plenty of money in the affair, and that if he would join he would never want for money again as long as he lived. He said, however, as an excuse for taking back the fifty dollars he had sent him, that he was very short of funds, and that he, or some one, would have to go to Richmond to replenish. Wiechmann testified that John H. Surratt left Washington for Richmond on the 27th of March, and returned on the 3d of April; that on his return he showed him nine, or eleven, twenty-dollar gold pieces and sixty dollars in currency. Wiechmann was on intimate terms of personal intercourse with Surratt, lived in the same house with him, and was with him daily when at home, and expressed himself as quite certain that he had no gold when he left Washington. He was not engaged in any business by which he could make money. His mother had a very limited income from the rent of her farm and tavern, and kept boarders to enable her to make ends meet; yet her son was constantly spending money in traveling about, and so must have been supplied by his Canada friends, whom he visited occasionally; and the chief calls he had for expenditure appear to have arisen from his prosecution of their schemes. Returning thus from Richmond to Washington on the 3d of April, he left the same evening, according to Wiechmann, for Canada.

Conover testified that he saw him in Montreal on the 6th or 7th of April, in Mr. Thompson's room, and he learned from their conversation that Surratt had just brought despatches from Richmond to Mr. Thompson. One despatch was from Mr. Benjamin, the rebel Secretary of State, and one, which Conover thought was a cipher despatch, from Jefferson Davis. Conover had previously been solicited by Thompson to participate in this work of assassination, and so was freely admitted to their secret councils. After reading these letters from Davis and Benjamin, Thompson, laying his hands on them, said, "This makes the thing all right," referring to the assent of the rebel authorities. Mr. Lincoln, Mr. Johnson, the Secretary of War, Mr. Stanton, and the Secretary of State, Mr. Seward, Judge Chase, and General Grant were to be the victims. Mr. Thompson said this would leave the government entirely without a head; that there was no provision in the Constitution of the United States by which they could elect another President if these men were removed. The long waited for authority to use funds which the rebel government had placed to the credit of Mr. Thompson having been now secured in the despatch from Mr. Benjamin, and his chief, Jefferson Davis, no time was lost in putting the ball in motion. Mr. Thompson had over six hundred thousand dollars to his credit in the Ontario Bank of Montreal, and within two days after receiving these letters, he drew on his deposit for over two hundred thousand dollars. Conover saw Surratt in Montreal from the 6th or 7th to the 9th of April, and having been admitted to their confidence by Thompson, on his receiving the despatches, was accepted by Surratt as being one of themselves, and so he was under no restraint in conversing with Conover. From the whole of his conversation Conover inferred that he was to take his part, whatever that might be, in the conspiracy. We have already learned from Merritt's testimony, that after Surratt's return to Canada on the 6th of April there was an immediate bustle amongst those in Canada who were to go to Washington to take part in the plot, and that they began to leave on the 8th. The sinews of war having been furnished, there was great eagerness, expressed and apparent, to be off for the execution of the plot, and great boasting on the part of those who went as to what they were going to do. Having set their hired assassins in motion, Thompson and his gang stood waiting in a great state of expectancy for the result. Conover testified that on the day before, or the very day of the assassination, he had a conversation with William C. Cleary about the rejoicing in the States over the surrender of Lee and the capture of Richmond. Cleary remarked that they "would put the laugh on the other side of their mouths in a day or two." "The conspiracy was at that time talked of amongst them about as freely as one would speak of the weather."

Jefferson Davis received his first intelligence of the assassination at Charlotte, N.C., on the 19th of April, in a telegram from General Breckinridge, as follows: —

"GREENSBORO', April 19, 1865.

"*His Excellency President Davis:* —

"President Lincoln was assassinated in the theatre at Washington on the night of the 11th inst. Seward's house was entered on the same night and he was repeatedly stabbed, and is probably mortally wounded.
[Signed] "JOHN C. BRECKINRIDGE."

Davis received this telegram whilst harranguing in his grandiloquent style the crowd that had gathered about him, trying to convince them that they were not whipped, and would yet succeed. At the conclusion of his speech, he read the telegram to his auditors; and after the manifestations of delight at the news had subsided, he made this comment: "Well, if it were done, it were better it were well done."

On the following day, when dining at the house of the witness, Mr. Lewis F. Bates, with General Breckinridge, who had come to pay him a visit, upon General Breckinridge saying in regard to the assassination that he regretted it very much — that it was very unfortunate for the people of the South at that time — Davis replied, "Well, General, I don't know; if it were done at all, it were better that it were well done; and if the same had been done to Andy Johnson, the beast, and Secretary Stanton the job would then be complete." Mark the disappointment of the man, and his bitter dissatisfaction with the result of the plot to which he had so recently given his sanction! The telegram informed him of the death of President Lincoln at the hands of an assassin, and gave him strong grounds to conclude that Secretary Seward had been put out of the way in the same way, and was dead; but this does not satisfy him. The work had not been well done because "Andy Johnson" still lived, and so they had failed in their purpose to subvert the government. Hear him growl, "It were better it were well done; and if the same had only been done to Andy Johnson, the beast, and to Secretary Stanton, the job would then have been complete," and we might have taken fresh courage. His co-conspirators in Canada, when informed of the result, gnashed their teeth in rage and disappointment. They expressed their regret that "the boys had not been allowed to act when they wanted to," and swore "they were not done with them yet." At first their attitude was that of defiance, and their expressions of regret at their failure to completely carry out their plot were mingled with threatenings as to what they would yet do. They boasted while the trial was going on that they had their friends at court, and were kept posted from day to day as to what was going on. The promptness of the government in bringing its prisoners before a military commission for trial, making it obvious that there was to be no fooling in the case, together with their continued disasters in the field, ending in the speedy collapse of the rebellion and the capture of Jefferson Davis, brought them to their senses, and to a realization of their own danger; and so they at once commenced to destroy all documentary evidence of their guilt. They declared in the presence of Montgomery, and also of Merritt, that they had destroyed all their papers, lest some Yankee should steal them and they should be brought up in a possible future trial as evidence against them.

Now, let us consider what is lacking in this testimony to make the evidence of Davis's complicity in this crime complete. Nothing, manifestly, but the letters referred to in the testimony; the first, that read by Sanders, and credited by him to Davis, inciting his friends in Canada to the commission of this crime, and pointing out specifically whom he would have them put out of the way; and the second, carried by Surratt to Thompson, on which Thompson laid his hand and exclaimed, "This makes the thing all right!" But the absence of this missing link in the chain of evidence against him is accounted for, and that in a way that makes the chain even stronger, if possible, than if we were able to produce these documents.

His co-conspirators in Canada declare to two witnesses and in the presence of a third, George B. Hutchinson, that they have destroyed all their papers; giving as the reason for so doing, the fear that some "Yankee son of a b—h" might steal them, and they should be used as evidence against them.

They burn their papers and then silently steal away. *Exeunt omnes.*

CHAPTER XII.

THE GOVERNMENT WITNESSES AGAINST DAVIS AND HIS ASSOCIATES IN THIS CRIME.

INASMUCH as the testimony given above so completely sustains the charge and specifications made by the government against Jefferson Davis, George N. Sanders, Jacob Thompson, Beverly Tucker, Clement C. Clay, William C. Cleary, *et al*, that had they been before the Commission their successful defense could only have been made by impeachment of the witnesses against them, I will now show that this could not have been done. The principal witnesses in this department of the trial, in which the Commission was only used as a medium through which to present to the world, before whom the charges were made, the evidence on which they rested, were Richard Montgomery, Sanford Conover, and Dr. James B. Merritt. Richard Montgomery was originally a citizen of the city of New York, and was in the employ of the government in its department of secret service. He was sent to Canada, in the summer of 1864, to acquire information of the plans and purposes of the rebels assembled in Canada.

He acted faithfully toward the government in this service, imparting to it all the information he obtained from time to time that was of any importance.

He was a man of intelligence, good character, and was trusted by the government. There was no attempt made before the Commission to impeach his character for credibility. Of course the purpose of his mission to Canada required him to gain the confidence of the men whose movements he had been sent to watch, and a knowledge of whose plans and purposes it was his duty to obtain. To do this it was necessary not only that he should conceal from them his real character and mission, but that he should be known to them as a man holding the same opinions and actuated by the same purposes as themselves. To gain fully their confidence was necessary to the success and usefulness of his mission. This he could only do by making them believe that his sentiments and purposes were in unison with their own. Of course this involved duplicity and falsehood, yet it is held to be allowable in war, because it may be made to contribute to success. A great deal of the strategy in war consists in deceiving the enemy; and if it is ever allowable by falsehood to deceive, it was certainly allowable by falsehood to deceive those who were playing false to their government to accomplish its overthrow. They were secretly concocting their schemes for the accomplishment of this purpose; and to be forearmed against them, it was necessary to be forewarned of them. This could only be done by this kind of deception, which is the same in its nature as that practiced by every spy. But spies are used by both parties to the conflict in every war. War is in its very nature atrociously wicked; and so, its ethics cannot be made to conform to the accepted morality that ought to govern peaceful life. But whilst war is wicked and ought never to be provoked, it is yet justifiable when it becomes necessary to the preservation of the life of a nation. Upon the aggressor in this case the responsibility belongs. On him the guilt falls. A defensive war is always justifiable; and so, according to the code of military ethics, everything that is necessary to its successful prosecution is also justifiable. This secret service department has always been considered one of these indispensable necessities; and it has never been regarded as a just ground of impeachment of a man's character for truthfulness and honesty that he has been found engaged in this kind of service. Indeed the very nature of the duties of this service call for a man of sterling integrity, in order that the information obtained through him may have the quality of reliability.

That Richard Montgomery succeeded fully in gaining the confidence of these Canada rebels is shown by the fact that they made him a medium of communication between themselves and the Richmond government. His character is further shown by the fact that when they paid him one hundred and fifty dollars for carrying despatches to Richmond he credited the government with it on his expense account. And that he acted faithfully in the discharge of his duties to his government is shown by the fact that he always submitted the despatches sent by him to the authorities at Washington, where copies of them were kept when they were allowed to pass. This is sufficient evidence that he was in a position to learn the facts to which he testified, and also presumptive evidence of the credibility of his statements. The force of his evidence could only have been broken by undoubted proof that he was a man that could not be believed under oath.

Dr. James B. Merritt was a native of Canada by accident, having been born there whilst his parents were there on a visit, but had been all his life a citizen of the State of New York. He went to Canada in the spring of 1864, and practiced his profession at Windsor and Dumfries. He passed amongst the rebels in Canada as a sympathizer of the Southern cause, and was accepted by them as a good rebel, and was fully taken into their confidences. They talked freely to him, and revealed their plans to him without hesitation or reserve. His testimony, as we have seen, is very specific, and relates to facts of the greatest importance. He testified that his sympathies had always been with his government, and that his object in dissembling in his intercourse with the Canada rebels was to be able to impart information to the United States government when he deemed it of sufficient importance to justify or require its communication.

That he did thus voluntarily, and without compensation, furnish valuable information to the government was shown. He had thus communicated to the Provost Marshal at Detroit the plot to burn New York City. It was also shown that he had made an effort to communicate the knowledge he had obtained, after the meeting of the 6th of April, at which John H. Surratt delivered to Thompson the despatches he had brought from Richmond, as to the parties starting from Canada to Washington to assist in the work of assassination. There was sufficient evidence of his loyalty and usefulness to the government, and his credibility was not assailed. He was a self-constituted secret service man, working without compensation, and so entitled to all the more honor.

Sanford Conover, known to the conspirators as James Watson Wallace, was born and educated in New York City. He had been living in the South for five or six years when the rebellion broke out, and was conscripted into the rebel service from near Columbia, S.C., early in 1863, but was detailed and served as a clerk in the rebel war department at Richmond for six months. His sympathies being on the side of the Union, he embraced the first good opportunity he could find to desert, and ran the blockade from Richmond, walking most of the way. He rode on the cars as far as Hanover Junction, and then walked up through Snickersville to Charlestown, and from there to Harper's Ferry, and so on to Washington, reaching there in the latter part of December, 1863. Whilst in Washington he became a correspondent of the New York *Tribune*, and went to Canada in that capacity in October, 1864. He testified that he received compensation from the *Tribune* for his services as correspondent, but had never received anything from either the United States or the Confederate government, and that his sympathies had always been with the Union cause. The fact that he was not willing to remain in the safe and easy position of a clerk in the rebel war department, but chose rather to take the hazard of deserting, fully confirms his sworn statements as to his political sympathies. He also was a self-constituted secret service agent of the United States, serving without pay. He seems to have been peculiarly successful in working himself into the confidence of Davis's agents in Canada, who admitted him to their conferences and revealed fully and freely to him all of their plans. His testimony is specific and conclusive as to their guilt. After he had testified before the Commission he was sent back to Canada by the Judge Advocate General to get the official report of the St. Albans trial, to be used in evidence. Arriving in Montreal, he was received in the most friendly manner by the conspirators, who had not the least idea that he had been a witness before the Commission, and so they went on with their confidences as to what they would yet do, declaring they were not done yet, etc. But after he had been there a day or two, his testimony, which had hitherto been withheld, was published in the New York papers, and this revealed to them the fact that Sanford Conover was their James Watson Wallace.

Of course they were like demons in their rage when they saw that he had revealed all of their doings. He was at once virtually made a prisoner by twelve or fifteen men armed to the teeth, who confronted him with his testimony before the Commission. Conover found himself suddenly and unexpectedly placed in a situation of great difficulty and danger, escape being impossible, and so he denied that he had been before the Commission as a witness.

They then required him to make a denial under oath, and set a lawyer at work to put this disavowal in the most imposing shape, whilst they sent for an officer to administer the oath, informing Conover that he must appear to the officer not only to be willing, but anxious to swear to this disclaimer, in which they make him say he had been personated before the Commission by some infamous scoundrel, who had sworn to a tissue of falsehoods, and telling him that if he manifested the least hesitation or unwillingness his life would pay the forfeit. He at first, in order to get away from them, proposed that he would go to the hotel and prepare the paper that they required. O'Donnell told him that would not do, and that he would shoot him down like a dog if he did not do as they required. Conover still declining, Sanders said to him, "Wallace, you see what kind of hands you are in; I hope you will not be so foolish as to refuse." Seeing there was no other way of escape from them, Conover finally did what they required. They then had a lawyer, by the name of Kerr, to write out and sign and be qualified to a very formal affidavit covering the whole case, to the effect that he was present and saw Conover swear to the disavowal referred to, and that he did it willingly, and appeared anxious to do so, in justice to his own character. These affidavits they at once published to the world through the Canada papers, and with them also published the following advertisement, as if from Conover: —

> Five hundred dollars reward will be given for the arrest, so that I can bring to punishment, in Canada, of the infamous and perjured scoundrel who recently personated me under the name of Sanford Conover, and deposed to a tissue of falsehoods before the Military Commission at Washington.
> JAMES W. WALLACE.

They also wrote and published over his name, as if from him, the following letter: —

To the Editor of the Evening Telegraph : —

Sir : — Please publish my affidavit now handed you, and the subjoined advertisement. I will obtain and furnish others for publication hereafter. I will add that if President Johnson will send me a safe conduct to go to Washington and return here, I will proceed thither and go before the military court and make *profert* of myself, in order that they may see whether or not I am the Sanford Conover who swore as stated.

MONTREAL, June 8th, 1865.   JAMES W. WALLACE.

Conover not returning to Washington at the time he was expected, it was realized that he had been put in jeopardy by the premature publication of his testimony, and so it became the duty of the United States to follow him with its protecting arm, and he was rescued through the intervention of General Dix.

Being thus rescued, he came again before the Commission and testified circumstantially to all of the above facts, and thus exposed the effort of the conspirators to break the force of his testimony by an affidavit extorted by violence whilst he was virtually a prisoner, and supported by that of Kerr, who may not have known that he testified to a falsehood, as the coercion was used before he was sent for, and still held over the head of Conover by the threat that if he manifested the least hesitation or unwillingness before Kerr his life would pay the forfeit. The testimony of Conover as to the circumstances under which this affidavit was extorted from him, was substantiated, as also his character, by Nathan Auser, who testified as follows : —

"I reside in New York, and am acquainted with Sanford Conover, who has just testified. I have known him eight or ten years; his character for integrity and usefulness is good as far as I know. I recently accompanied him to Montreal, in Canada, and was present at an interview which he had with Beverly Tucker, George N. Sanders, and that clique of rebel conspirators.

"After we went into O'Donnell's room, at Montreal, Mr. Cameron gave each of us a paper containing the evidence Mr. Conover gave here in Washington before the Commission, when he denied it. They told him he must sign a written paper to that effect, and if he did not he would not leave the room alive. O'Donnell said that he would shoot him like a dog if he did not. Mr. Conover was first going to his hotel to write the paper; at first they agreeed to this, but when they got as far as St. Lawrence Hall they made up their minds they would not let him do this himself, and when they went upstairs at St. Lawrence Hall they would not let me go up. There were, I think, twelve or fifteen of the conspirators together; among them Sanders, Tucker, O'Donnell, General Carroll, Pallen, and Cameron. They all accompanied him for the purpose of preventing his escape and obliging him to do what they required."

Thus was their attempt to break the force of Conover's testimony by fraud and violence exposed, and they were left in a more pitiable condition than if they had not made the effort. Conover stands in a better light as a witness than he did before it was made.

The question will naturally suggest itself to the intelligent reader, why, if these men knew of the purpose and preparations referred to as the result of the reception of the despatches from Richmond at the hands of Surratt, did they not inform the authorities at Washington? Accepting the fact that they had all the knowledge on this subject which is implied in their testimony, and that they were loyal to the government, as they declared themselves to be under oath, this would seem plainly to have been their duty.

The counsel for the defense were not slow to perceive this fact, and sought to weaken their standing before the Commission by asking them this very question. The answers elicited, however, only served to strengthen their testimony. In answer, Dr. Merritt stated as follows: "On Saturday the 8th of April I was at Galt, five miles from which place Harper's mother lives, and I ascertained there that Harper and Caldwell had stopped there and had started for the States. When I found they had left for Washington, probably for the purpose of assassinating the President, I went to Squire Davidson, a justice of the peace, to give information and have them stopped.

"He said that the thing was too ridiculously or supremely absurd to take any notice of; it would only appear foolish to give such information and cause arrests to be made on such grounds; it was so inconsistent that no person would believe it; and he declined to issue any process. I then called upon the judge of the court of assizes, made my statement to him, and he said I should have to go to the grand jury."

In his answer it is made to appear that Dr. Merritt made an earnest effort to have this information imparted to the government, and did all that we can reasonably think that he ought to have done.

His testimony is corroborated by that of Squire Davidson, who made a statement to the government after the assassination, of this interview that Merritt had sought with him and of the purpose of it; and it was upon this information that Dr. Merritt was brought before the Commission as a witness.

In answer to this question, Conover testified as follows: " I communicated to the New York *Tribune* the contemplated assassination of the President, and the intended raid on Ogdensburg. The assassination plot they declined to publish because they had been accused of publishing sensational stories. The assassination plot I communicated in March last, and also in February, I think, — certainly before the 4th of March. My reasons for communicating the intended assassinations to the *Tribune*, and not directly to the government, was that I supposed that the relations between the editor and proprietor of the *Tribune* and the government were such that they would lose no time in giving information on the subject. In regard to the conspiracy, as well as to some other secrets of the rebels in Canada, I requested Mr. Gay, of the *Tribune*, to give information to the government, and I believe he has formerly done so."

Here again we find that the witness Conover fulfilled his duty, which, under the circumstances in which his testimony places him in regard to the matter, any reasonable man could have required of him. And his position was also strengthened before the Commission by the answer elicited.

Lewis F. Bates, who testified as to Jefferson Davis's remarks to his auditors on reading to them the telegram from General Breckinridge, informing him of the assassination of the President, etc., and of his remarks to General Breckinridge on the following day at the dinner table, was a resident of Charlotte, N.C., where he had been for a little over four years. He was superintendent of the Southern Express Company for the State of North Carolina. He was a native of Massachusetts. The responsible position in which we find him vouches for his standing as a reliable man amongst those who knew him. His character was further established before the Commission by the testimony of a witness who was acquainted with him, James E. Russell, as follows: "I reside in Springfield, Mass. I have known Lewis F. Bates for about twenty-five years. For the last five years I have not known anything of his whereabouts, until I learned from him that he had been living in Charlotte, N.C. He was in business as a baggage-master on the Western Railroad, Massachusetts, while I was conductor, and I never heard anything against his reputation for truth."

Burton N. Harrison, private secretary to Jefferson Davis, in an article entitled, "An Extract from a Narrative, written not for publication, but for the entertainment of my children only," published in the *Century Magazine*, New Series, Vol. V., pp. 136 and 137, says: "In pursuance of the scheme of Stanton and Holt to fasten upon Mr. Davis charges of a guilty foreknowledge of, and participation in, the murder of Mr. Lincoln, Bates was afterwards carried to Washington and made to testify (before the military tribunal, I believe, where the murderers were on trial) to something about that speech [referring to Davis's speech at Charlotte, N.C.]. As I recollect the reports of the testimony published at the time, they made the witness say that Mr. Davis had approved of the assassination, either explicitly or by necessary implication; and that he added, 'If it was to be done it is well it was done quickly,' or words to that effect. If any such testimony was given it is false and without foundation; no comment upon or reference to the assassination was made in that speech. I have been told the witness has always stoutly insisted he never testified to anything of the kind, but that what he said was altogether perverted in the publication made by the rascals in Washington. Col. William Preston Johnston tells me he has seen another version of the story, and thinks Bates is understood to have fathered it in a publication made in some newspaper after his visit to Washington; it represents Bates as saying that the words above mentioned as imputed to Mr. Davis were used by him, not, indeed, in the speech

I have described, but in a conversation with Johnston at Bates's house. Johnston assures me that, in that shape, too, the story is false; that Mr. Davis never used such words in his presence, or any words at all like them. He adds that Mr. Davis remarked to him at Bates's house, with reference to the assassination, that Mr. Lincoln would have been much more useful to the Southern States than Andrew Johnson, the successor, was likely to be; and I myself heard Mr. Davis express the same opinion at that period." On p. 145, same article, he says: "It was at that cavalry camp we first heard of the proclamation offering one hundred thousand dollars for the capture of Mr. Davis upon the charge, invented by Stanton and Holt, of participation in the plot to murder Mr. Lincoln. Colonel Pritchard had himself just received it, and considerately handed a printed copy of the proclamation to Mr. Davis, who read it with a composure unruffled by any feeling other than scorn. The money was several years afterwards paid to the captors. Stanton and Holt, lawyers both, very well knew that Mr. Davis could never be convicted upon an indictment for treason, but were determined to hang him anyhow, and were in search of a pretext for doing so." And again in conclusion he says, "To have been a prisoner in the hands of the government of the United States, and not to have been brought to trial upon any of the charges against him, is sufficient refutation of them all. It indicates that the people in Washington knew the accusations could not be sustained." Had Mr. Harrison adhered to his original purpose of simply entertaining his children with this article it would have been much to his credit. It seems, however, that upon reading and re-reading it he came to regard it as too clever a production, and of too much public importance, to be restricted to so narrow a sphere, and so he publishes this lengthy extract from it in the *Century*. The article, as it appears in the *Century*, is mostly devoted to an account of the flight of Mr. Davis and his family from Richmond, and their progress southward until captured.

We have simply extracted from this article that part which from the nature of the subject claims our attention, as it relates to the testimony of Lewis F. Bates before the Commission. Let us first notice Mr. Harrison's assumption that Secretary Stanton and General Holt had concocted a scheme to fasten on Jefferson Davis a guilty complicity in the murder of Mr. Lincoln. This charge Mr. Harrison makes with brazen effrontery, but does not bring a scintilla of evidence to sustain it. Here are two high officers of the government, — the Secretary of War, and the head of the Department of Military Justice, — men of unsullied personal and official reputation, charged with concocting a scheme to take the life of Jefferson Davis on a trumped-up charge, and sustained by false testimony. The Secretary of War, as was his duty, employed every agency in his power to ferret out the conspirators, and in the progress of his investigations turned over to the Judge Advocate General all the facts that came to his knowledge, together with the names of the persons by whom they could be proven. These persons were brought before the Judge Advocate and carefully examined as to what they knew, and so became witnesses before the Commission, when they were found to have knowledge of facts bearing on the great crime that had been committed.

That any witness was in any manner coerced, or required to render testimony that had been prepared for him by these officers as charged, will only be believed by those who are ignorant of the personal and official character of these noble, patriotic, men, or those who, like Mr. Harrison, are willing to thus calumniate on their own responsibility. That Mr. Bates was testifying under any manner of duress will not be believed by any member of the Commission who is yet living, and who can recall the appearance and manner of the witness in giving his testimony. He was evidently telling just what he had seen and heard, and did it willingly. The charge of Mr. Harrison, that Bates was carried to Washington and made to testify, rests simply on the authority of Mr. Burton N. Harrison, whilom private secretary to Jefferson Davis, unsustained by any evidence.

The evidence given by Bates was taken down, as delivered, by a stenographer, and read to him before he was discharged, and its correctness admitted by him, as witnessed by his signature. This testimony was published in the newspapers, and also in the official record of the trial. What excuse, then, can Mr. Harrison give for quoting it as he recollected it, and so failing to give anything like a correct version of his testimony?

The testimony of Bates was that Mr. Davis, whilst addressing the people from the steps of Bates's house, received a telegram from General Breckinridge informing him of the assassination of President Lincoln, and that an attempt had been made on the life of William H. Seward, and that he was repeatedly stabbed and probably mortally wounded, and that in concluding his speech he read the telegram aloud, and made this remark, "If it were to be done it were better it were well done." The witness added, "I am quite sure that these are the words he used." And again, "A day or two afterward Jefferson Davis and John C. Breckinridge were present at my house, when the assassination of the President was the subject of conversation. In speaking of it, John C. Breckinridge remarked to Davis that he regretted it very much, that it was very unfortunate for the people of the South at that time. Davis replied, 'Well, General, I don't know; if it were to be done at all, it were better that it were well done, and if the same had been done to Andy Johnson, the beast, and to Secretary Stanton, the job would then be complete.' No remark was made at all as to the criminality of the act, and from the expression used by John C. Breckinridge I drew the conclusion that he simply regarded it as unfortunate for the people of the South at that time." Here is Bates's testimony as it stands recorded, and was also published at the time.[1] Why did not Mr. Harrison address himself to this testimony instead of giving his version of it from memory, and confounding it with newspaper reports as to what Bates claimed to have been his testimony, and thus finding an opportunity to substitute Col. William P. Johnston for General Breckinridge, thus contradicting it through Johnston? General Breckinridge was the only man who could have contradicted Bates's testimony. If he ever did do this it has not come to the knowledge of the writer. Bates's testimony cannot be set aside in the manner attempted by Mr. Harrison.

The charge made by the government on that trial against Jefferson Davis of inciting and encouraging the assassins, implicating

---

[1] It is highly improbable that the witness would have given false testimony as to this conversation between Davis and General Breckinridge because of the certainty of its contradiction by the latter.

him thus far in the murder of Mr. Lincoln, was only made upon the evidence before it, and which we have already presented at length.

It was not a trumped-up charge for the purpose of gratifying malice, or with a view to the taking of the life of Mr. Davis unjustly in revenge, but a charge made in good faith, and sustained by evidence that has never been overthrown.

The conclusion of Mr. Harrison, that the government conceded that its charge against Mr. Davis was unfounded in that it did not prosecute it when it had him in custody as a prisoner, is a *non sequitor*.

The rebellion was declared to be at an end shortly after the trial of the assassins. The proclamation of martial law ceased with the proclamation of peace. Civil law took the place of martial law with the issuance of the proclamation that the rebellion was at an end. The work of reconstruction belonged to the political department of the government, and the benign policy of condoning the past, and only securing guarantees for the future was wisely adopted; this security is found in the fourteenth amendment to the Constitution, and illustrates the tempering of justice with mercy as had never been before done in the history of the race. It can never be claimed that the government abandoned its charge made against any of these parties because it did not bring them to trial when it had it in its power to do so. The charges as made have never been withdrawn. They stand in the records of that trial, and the evidence on which the charges were based has been presented to the world and the question of the guilt or innocence of the parties has been referred to the decision of an enlightened and impartial public sentiment and to the judgment of the world.

But we will now consider the credibility of this testimony from another standpoint. Here we have three witnesses, — Conover, Montgomery, and Merritt, — strangers to each other, testifying as to the facts known to each one separately, and they completely corroborate each other. There could have been no possible collusion, and yet their testimony is the same. It is, as it were, the continued story of one man, who is consistent with himself at every point. The purposes of the conspirators and their plans through a period of several months are the same, whether they come to us through Conover, Montgomery, or Merritt. "Out of the abundance of the heart the mouth speaketh." The assassination plot was that which engrossed their thoughts. They were continually scheming for its accomplishment; it was the thing dear to their hearts and was the constant theme of their tongues.

The witnesses corroborate each other in showing that this was the case. In regard to the fact testified to by both Montgomery and Merritt, that the conspirators stated they were destroying their papers, we have the additional testimony of George B. Hutchinson, who testified as follows: "On the 2d of June, and on the morning of the 3d, 1865, I saw Dr. Merritt in conversation with Beverly Tucker, at St. Lawrence Hall, in Montreal. I heard Beverly Tucker say in reply to a remark of Dr. Merritt, that he had burned all the letters for fear that some 'Yankee son of a b——h' might steal them out of his room and use them in testimony against him. They were at the time speaking about this trial, and the charges against them. They were talking to Dr. Merritt as to one to whom they gave their confidence."

Who, in the light of all the facts given in this testimony, which fulfills all the conditions, on down to the crucial test of credibility —that of the concurrence of three witnesses, who were entire strangers to each other, in the statement of all the essential facts — can doubt that all these men implicated in the charge and specifications preferred by the government were equally guilty with John H. Surratt and John Wilkes Booth of the assassination accomplished, and that attempted; as, also, of the others planned. It matters not that for good and sufficient reasons they were never called to account by the government, when it had it in its power to do so; they yet stand, and must forever stand, condemned by an intelligent and candid world. If their guilt is not proven I do not see how it would be possible to prove anything.

CHAPTER XIII.

A CRITICISM OF NICOLAY AND HAY.

NICOLAY and Hay in their "Life of Lincoln" (see *Century Magazine* for January, 1890, p. 439), say: "The surviving conspirators, with the exception of John H. Surratt, were tried by a military commission sitting in Washington in the months of May and June.

"The charges against them specified that they were 'incited and encouraged' to treason and murder by Jefferson Davis and the Confederate emissaries in Canada. This was not proven on the trial; the evidence bearing on the case showed frequent communication between Canada and Richmond and the Booth coterie in Washington, and some transactions in drafts at the Montreal Bank where Jacob Thompson and Booth kept their accounts. It was shown by the sworn testimony of a reputable witness that Jefferson Davis at Greensboro', on hearing of the assassination, expressed his gratification at the news; but this, so far from proving any direct complicity in the crime, would rather prove the opposite, as a conscious murderer usually conceals his malice. Against all the rest, the facts we have briefly stated were abundantly proved," etc. In a foot-note they add: "When captured by General Wilson he (Jefferson Davis) affected to think he cleared himself of suspicion in this regard by saying that Johnson was more objectionable to him than Lincoln — not noticing that the conspiracy contemplated the murder of both." From this there would seem to have been some doubt in the mind of the writer on the question of Davis's innocence. Again, they say: "Davis, in speaking to General Wilson about this charge, said that he regarded the charge of treason as likely to give him more trouble than this." Of course he relied on the sagacity of his co-conspirators in Canada for the destruction of all documentary evidence against him, and so he felt that his guilt could not be proven. The writer has the highest regard for these authors, and a very high appreciation of the manner in which they have handled their great subject. The history of several of the last years of the life of Abraham Lincoln is inseparably linked with the history of his country, and that the most momentous period of its history. To do justice to the subject of their memoir required a vast amount of the most painstaking research, and a general overhauling of the political history of the country over a period of a dozen or more years.

This was a work of great labor, involving a careful examination of a multitude of documents and records. They had that familiar, personal acquaintance with Mr. Lincoln, growing out of their official relations to him, that enables them to form a correct estimate of his intellectual and moral character, and of the innermost feelings and governing motives of his life. They have done their work faithfully and well, and have presented Mr. Lincoln in his true character, and made manifest his wonderful astuteness, his wisdom, forbearance, charity, gentleness, and toleration toward his fellowmen, as well as his *firmness* and fidelity to the right, to the gaze of an admiring world. It is with feelings of regret that faithfulness to my purpose of giving a true history of the great conspiracy which culminated in his death requires me to take issue with them in their treatment of this case. It will be evident to all my readers who have read and carefully considered the evidence presented by the government to sustain its charge against Jefferson Davis and his confederates in Canada, that authors who were familiar with it could never have come to the conclusion so confidently expressed by these authors when they say, " This was not proved on the trial." The abstract of the evidence which they then proceed to give, shows an equal degree of unfamiliarity with it. It consists merely in a confused jumbling of a few comparatively unimportant facts, leaving unnoticed and untouched the great mass of relevant and conclusive testimony that I have presented. The account which they give of the manner in which Davis received the news of the assassination does not consist at all with the testimony. They say: " It was shown by the sworn testimony of a reputable witness that Jefferson Davis at Greensboro', on hearing of the assassination, expressed his gratification at the news; but this, so far from proving any direct complicity in the crime, would rather prove the opposite, as a conscious murderer usually conceals his malice."

Jefferson Davis received the news of the assassination at Charlotte, not at Greensboro'. Breckinridge telegraphed the news to him from Greensboro'. It is the testimony of Lewis F. Bates to which they refer. But my readers, who have so lately read Mr. Bates' testimony, I am sure will not recognize it in the account which these authors give of it; and as they have failed in giving us a true account of the testimony, we cannot wonder if they draw an erroneous conclusion from it inferentially. It will be remembered that all the expressions that escaped from the rebel chief on that occasion were those of deep-felt dissatisfaction and bitter disappointment. A free rendering of his language on that occasion would amount to just this: "It might just as well not have been done at all, since the job was not thoroughly done. If Andy Johnson, the beast, and Stanton had only been included, the job would then have been complete. It would have been of some account to us." His whole speech and demeanor on that occasion show him to have been a co-conspirator, fully aware of the scope of their plot, and displeased at the incompleteness of the "job."

Again, on page 432 of the *Century* for January, 1890, we find the following: "He (Booth) was a fanatical secessionist; had assisted at the capture of John Brown, and had imbibed, at Richmond and other Southern cities where he had played, a furious spirit of partisanship against Mr. Lincoln and the Union party.

"After the re-election of Mr. Lincoln, which rung the knell of the insurrection, Booth, like many of the secessionists North and South, was stung to the quick by disappointment. He visited Canada, consorted with the rebel emissaries there, and at last — whether or not at their instigation cannot certainly be said — conceived a scheme to capture the President and take him to Richmond. He spent a great part of the autumn and winter inducing a small number of loose fish of secession sympathies to join him in this fantastic enterprise. He seemed always well supplied with money, and talked largely of his speculations in oil as a source of income; but his agent afterwards testified that he never realized a dollar from that source — that his investments, which were inconsiderable, were a total loss. The winter passed away, and nothing was accomplished. On the 4th of March, Booth was at the capitol, and created a disturbance by trying to force his way through the line of policemen who guarded the passage through which the President passed to the east front of the building. His intentions at this time are not known. He afterwards said he lost an excellent chance of killing the President that day. There are indications in the evidence given on the trial of the conspirators that they suffered some great disappointment in their schemes in the latter part of March; and a letter from Arnold to Booth, dated 27th March, showed that some of them had grown timid of the consequences of their contemplated enterprise, and were ready to give it up. He advised Booth, before going farther, to go and see how it would be taken at R——d. But timid as they might be by nature, the whole group was so completely under the ascendency of Booth that they did not dare disobey him when in his presence; and after the surrender of Lee, in an excess of malice and rage which was akin to madness, he called them together and assigned each his part in the *new crimes* [the italics are ours], the purpose of which had arisen suddenly in his mind out of the ruins of the abandoned abduction scheme. This plan was as brief and simple as it was horrible. Powell, *alias* Payne, the stalwart, brutal, simple-minded boy from Florida, was to murder Seward; Atzerodt, the comic villain of the drama, was assigned to remove Andrew Johnson; Booth reserved for himself the most difficult and most conspicuous role of the tragedy; it was Herold's duty to attend him as a page, and aid in his escape."

In this rather long extract, in which the situation is pictured with a facile pen, there are are two assumptions that are wholly irreconcilable with the evidence.

The first is, that the plot was at first to capture the President and carry him to Richmond, whether with or without the approbation of the Canada conspirators, our author's assume cannot be known.

The evidence does not show that such a plot was really entertained either by Booth or his co-conspirators in Canada. Conover testified that he heard this scheme discussed at a meeting of the latter in February; but it does not appear that it was ever considered practicable, or was really entertained by them. The proposition was too quixotic to receive the serious consideration of rational, intelligent men. All the testimony in regard to the Canada conspirators shows that they were all the time from October, 1864, devoting all their thoughts to securing the assassination, not only of the President, but also of the others named in the charge and specifications, and that by nothing but the assassination of all of these men could the political end which they sought be secured. This assumption of our authors is shown by the testimony to be wholly untenable. The next assumption to which I take exceptions is equally untenable in the light which the testimony throws on the subject. It is, that the assassination was the result of a hasty impulse of rage and disappointment, akin to madness; that a new crime was thus conceived, which grew out of the ruins of the abduction plot, which I have already sufficiently shown was never entertained by any of the parties. So far from being the result of a hasty impulse, the testimony clearly proves that it had been long entertained, and that they had all been planning, preparing, and arranging for its execution for months.

It is greatly to be regretted that such popular, and usually reliable, authors, should have allowed themselves on this occasion to write thus loosely, and express opinions and conclusions so much at variance with the testimony. It tends to obscure the truth of history, and to the formation of an erroneous public opinion.

The conclusion at which I have arrived, and expressed without hesitation, as to the guilt of Davis and his Canada Cabinet in this matter, stands untouched by that expressed by these authors, because it is manifest that they not only had never studied, but were quite unfamiliar with, the evidence on which alone a right judgment can be based.

All I ask of my readers is, that they will scan carefully what I have given as having been fairly deduced from the testimony before the Commission, or to study the testimony itself as given in Pittman's official report of the trial, and then judge between us.

CHAPTER XIV.

JACOB THOMPSON'S BANK ACCOUNT. WHAT BECAME OF THE MONEY?

THE testimony before the Commission developed the fact that the Canada Cabinet was kept well supplied with money, and that Jacob Thompson was the Judas that carried the bag.

His treasury was kept replenished by Southern bills of exchange on Liverpool. Robert Anson Campbell, first teller of the Ontario Bank of Montreal, Canada, appeared before the Commission and gave testimony as to Thompson's transactions with his bank as follows: "I know Mr. Jacob Thompson very well. His account with the Ontario Bank I hold in my hand. It commenced May 30th, 1864, and closed April 11th, 1865. Prior to May 30th, he left with us sterling exchange, drawn on the rebel agents at Liverpool, for collection. The first advice we had was May 30th, when there was placed to his credit £2,061 17s. and $1\frac{1}{2}d.$, and £20,618 11s. 4d., amounting to $109,965.63. The aggregate amount of the credits is $649,873.28, and there is a balance still left to his credit of $1,766.23; all the rest has been drawn out. Since about the 1st of March he has drawn out $300,000, in sterling exchange and deposit receipts. On the 6th of April last there is a deposit receipt for $180,000. The banks in Canada give deposit receipts, which are paid when presented, upon fifteen days notice. On the 8th of April he drew a bill of £446 12s. 1d., and on the same day £4,000, sterling. On the 24th of March he drew $100,000 in exchange; at another time, $19,000. This sterling exchange was drawn to his credit, and also the deposit receipts.

"Mr. Jacob Thompson has left Montreal since the 14th of April last. I heard him say he was going away. He used to come to the bank two or three times a week, and the last time he was in he gave a check to the hotel keeper, which I cashed, and he then left the hotel. His friends stated to me that he was going to Halifax, overland. Navigation was not open then, and I was told he was going overland to Halifax, and thence to Europe. I thought it strange at the time that he was going overland, when by waiting two weeks longer he could have taken a steamer; and it was talked of in the bank among the clerks. The account was opened with Jacob Thompson individually. The newspaper report was that he was financial agent of the Confederate States. We only knew that he brought Southern sterling exchange bills, drawn on Southern agents in the old country, and brought them to our bank for collection. How they came to him we did not know. He was not, as far as I know, engaged in any business in Canada requiring these large sums of money.

"He had other large money transactions in Canada. I knew of one transaction of $50,000, that came through the Niagara District Bank, at St. Catherines, a check drawn to the order of Mr. Clement C. Clay, and deposited by him in that bank; they sent it to us, August 16th, 1864, to put to their credit.

"Thompson has several times bought from us United States notes or greenbacks. On August 25th he bought $15,000 in greenbacks, and on July 14th, $19,125. This was the amount he paid in gold, and at that time the exchange was about 55. I could not say what the amount of greenbacks was, but that is what he paid for it in gold. On March 14th last he bought $1,000 worth of greenbacks at 44¾, for which he paid $552.20 in gold. On the 20th of March he bought £6,500 sterling at 9½. He also bought drafts on New York in several instances. J. Wilkes Booth, the actor, had a small account at our bank. I had one or two transactions with him, but do not remember more at present. He may have been in the bank a dozen times; and I distinctly remember seeing him once. He has still left to his credit $455, arising from a deposit made by him, consisting of $200, in $20 Montreal bills, and Davis's check on Merchant's Bank of $255. Davis is a broker, who kept his office opposite the St. Lawrence Hall, and is, I think, either from Richmond or Baltimore.

"When Booth came into the bank for this exchange he bought

a bill of exchange for £61 and some odd shillings, remarking, 'I am going to run the blockade, and in case I should be captured can my capturers make use of the exchange?' I told him they could not unless he endorsed the bill, which was made payable to his order. He then said he would take $300, and pulled out that amount, I think, in American gold. I figured up what $300 would come to at the rate of exchange. I think it was 9½, and gave him a bill of exchange for £61 and some odd shillings."

The bills of exchange found on Booth's body at the time of his capture were here exhibited to the witness, who said, "These are the Ontario Bank bills of exchange that were sold to Booth, bearing date October 27th, 1864."

Testimony of Daniel S. Eastwood.

THE BEN WOOD DRAFT.

The following is the testimony of Daniel S. Eastwood, in regard to Jacob Thompson's bank account, and serves to account for $25,000 of his expenditures: "I am assistant manager of the Montreal branch of the Ontario Bank, Canada. I was officially acquainted with Jacob Thompson, formerly of Mississippi, who has for some time been sojourning in Canada, and have knowledge of his account with our bank, a copy of which was presented to this Commission by Mr. Campbell, our assistant teller.

"The moneys to Mr. Thompson's credit accrued from the negotiation of bills of exchange, drawn by the secretary of the treasury of the so-called Confederate States on Frazier Trenholm & Company, of Liverpool. They were understood to be the financial agents of the Confederate States at Liverpool, and the face of the bills, I believe, bore that inscription. Among the dispositions made from that fund, by Jacob Thompson, was $25,000 paid in accordance with the following requisition: —

```
4329.                              MONTREAL, Aug. 10th, 1864.
     Wanted from the Ontario Bank, 3 days' sight,
             On New York,
                    Favor of BENJAMIN WOOD, Esq.
         $25,000
       For ——— current funds.
         $10,000
       Deliv. 60 p. c.
       Ex. $15.00
                                                  A. M.
```

"The '$10,000' underneath the $25,000 is the purchase money in gold of $25,000 worth of United States funds.

"At Mr. Thompson's request the name of Benjamin Wood was erased (the pen being just struck through it), and my name as an officer of the bank written immediately beneath it, that the draft might be negotiable without putting any other name to it.

"I have in my hand, it having been obtained from the cashier of the City Bank in New York, the original draft for the $25,000 on which that requisition was made by Mr. Thompson, in the name of Benjamin Wood. It reads:—

$25,000.   THE ONTARIO BANK.   No. 4329.

MONTREAL, 10th of August, 1864.

At three day's sight please pay to the order of D. S. EASTWOOD, in current funds, twenty-five thousand dollars value received, and charge the same to account of this branch.

| U. S. Internal Revenue 2 cent Stamp. | To Cashier City Bank, New York. | H. Y. STANUS, *Manager.* |

INDORSED.

Pay to Hon. BENJAMIN WOOD, Esq., or order.

D. S. EASTWOOD.
B. WOOD.

"I have found this draft in the hands of the payee of the City Bank in New York, and I understand from the cashier it has been paid. Mr. Thompson was frequently in the habit of drawing moneys in the name of an officer of the bank, so as to conceal the person for whom it was really intended.

"A good deal of Thompson's exchange was drawn in that way, so that there is no indication, except from the bank or the locality on which the bill was drawn, to show where use was made of the funds. Large amounts were drawn for, at his instance, on the banks of New York, but we were not acquainted with the use they were put to.

"The Ben. Wood, to whom the draft was made payable, is, I believe, the member of Congress, and the owner of the New York *News.*" Jacob Thompson's bank account, already in evidence, was handed to the witness, who said: "This is a copy of Jacob Thompson's banking account with us, as testified to by Robert Anson

Campbell. I see in the account entries of funds that were used for purpose of exchange on New York, and also on London. The item $189,999, on the 6th of April, 1865, was issued in deposit receipts, which may be paid anywhere."

In answer to a question by Mr. Aiken, counsel for defense, the witness said: "I do not remember any drafts cashed at our bank in favor of James Watson Wallace, Richard Montgomery, or James B. Merritt. I have no recollection of the names."

Evidence of George Wilkes: "I am acquainted with Benjamin Wood, of New York, and am familiar with his handwriting. The signature at the back of that bill of exchange I should take to be his. At the date of this bill Benjamin Wood was a member of Congress of the United States. He was editor and proprietor of the New York *News*, so he told me himself. The paper, I have heard, has been recently managed by John Mitchell, late editor or assistant editor of the Richmond *Examiner* and the Richmond *Enquirer*." The endorsement was further proven to be in the handwriting of Ben. Wood by the testimony of Abram D. Burrell. This testimony not only accounts for $25,000 paid to Ben. Wood, then a member of Congress from New York City, for services rendered to the rebel cause in the halls of legislation, or attempted to be there rendered, but more particularly in the management of the New York *News*. In his capacity as a legislator as well as that of editor, Ben. Wood made himself conspicuous as a traitor to his country, and thus he was rewarded by Jacob Thompson for his services to the rebel cause. The testimony also throws light on Jacob's method of doing business in a secret, underhanded manner, in order that the object and purport of his transactions being thus concealed from public knowledge he could engage in any wicked scheme without detection. Witness has drafts for $180,000 on the 6th of April, all being put in such form that they could not well be traced, and so that it could not well be ascertained who were the payees, or where paid, or whether they were ever paid at all. They were probably held by this skilfull secret financier in such shape that, upon the failure to fulfill the contract and then come forward and claim the reward, they reverted to the Hon. Jacob Thompson.

The testimony of these witnesses reveals several very important facts bearing on the subject of our investigations. First, it is shown that the rebel agents in Canada were kept well supplied with money by the Richmond government, their credits in the Canada banks arising from Southern bills of exchange on the rebel agents at Liverpool. Now the question arises, for what purpose was this money placed at their disposal? They were sent by the rebel government to Canada to work for the success of the rebellion in ways and by means which have been disclosed by the testimony. Of course, then, they were supported whilst in Canada by the Richmond government, and it is reasonable to suppose at a fixed salary that had been agreed upon in advance. Then, of course, their personal expenses had to be met, and as they were by no means parsimonious in their habits, this item alone would make a considerable draft on their treasury. Then they employed a good many men, escaped rebel soldiers and other rebel refugees at various times to execute various schemes concocted by them to aid the rebellion.

One witness stated that they said they had eight hundred men secreted in Chicago, in the summer of 1864, to aid in a plan to liberate the rebel prisoners at Camp Douglass, which plan was frustrated by the government being informed of it in advance by friends in Canada who were cognizant of the plot. Of course the expenses of all of these men had to be met, and no doubt liberal compensation made to those who were entrusted with the execution of the plot. So, also, the plot to burn the city of New York, the St. Albans raid, and various other schemes of like character cost a good deal of money. Of course they defrayed all of the expenses of the trial of the St. Albans raiders for extradition. The scheme of spreading disease and death through infected clothing, in which Dr. Blackburn was employed as their agent, no doubt cost them a good round sum. It will be remembered that Blackburn employed Godfrey Joseph Hyams as his agent to get the infected clothing sold at such places in the United States as he indicated, under the promise of one hundred thousand dollars; and although he and Thompson chiselled Hyams out of nine hundred and ninety-nine thousand nine hundred dollars of this, it is quite reasonable to suppose that Blackburn received large pay for his risk and trouble in going to Bermuda and carefully infecting this clothing.

The witness, Montgomery, testified that he heard Clay say, in speaking of these enterprises, that "they always had plenty of money to pay for anything that was worth paying for." We have seen from the testimony that Booth, and we have good reason to infer that Surratt also, were kept plentifully supplied with money from the time that a definate arrangement was made with them to take charge of the assassination job in the latter part of October, 1864, until the final accomplishment, so far as it was accomplished, of their plot. We have seen that they were both without occupation, or legitimate source of income, during all that time, and that they were actively engaged in preparation for their work, and were going in a style of prodigality in their expenditures, travelling a great deal, boarding not only themselves, but also several of the hired assistants, at hotels in Washington, without regard to cost, even stipulating in the case of Payne that his meals should be served to him in his room. Then they were every way profligate in their habits, especially in drinking and smoking — both costly vices — and also in purchasing horses and hiring them kept at livery stables; and still further in hiring horses of livery men for their excursions about the suburbs of the city in perfecting their plans for escape. Again, Booth always had money to use in drawing into the plot, and in holding assistants. No doubt the fifty dollars sent to Arnold in a letter came from Booth; and we know he sent in a letter fifty dollars to Chester to induce him to join him, and although he allowed Chester to return this money it was not until he had fully satisfied himself that it was useless to press Chester any further on the subject. They were evidently as profuse in their promises of reward to their co-conspirators whom they hired as Blackburn was to Hyams. Booth offered to deposit three thousand dollars for a retainer's fee to Chester; and, in addition to this, assured him that if he would go into the conspiracy he would never want for money as long as he lived. Even so worthless a fellow as Atzerodt had been fed with the idea that he would soon have as much gold as would keep him a gentleman the balance of his life.

Now, where was all this money to come from? Evidently from Jacob Thompson's bank account. The evidence of the bank teller shows that the bill of exchange which was found on Booth's body after his death was the same bought of him by Booth. This bill of exchange was dated Oct. 27, 1864.

It will be remembered that the Selby letter (the Selby being, no doubt, an *alias*, as they were all sailing under *aliases*) reveals the fact that it was at that meeting of the conspirators in Montreal, about the last of October, 1864, that the plot was matured, and arrangements made for carrying it into effect. No doubt this arrangement made between the Canada Cabinet and Booth and his fellow assassins involved a large expenditure of money — such an amount, that when the " Cabinet " came to consider the matter over they shrunk from the responsibility and called a halt until they could get the sanction of the Richmond government in such a form that they could have a voucher to show for this expenditure. Hence, their after regret that "the boys had not been allowed to act when they wanted to." This sanction was delivered to them by Surratt on the 6th of April, when Thompson, placing his hand on the despatches, exclaimed, "This makes the thing all right!" It would be a very singular coincidence, indeed, on the theory that Davis, Thompson, and the others in Canada were not in the conspiracy, that on this very day Thompson drew on his bank account for $180,000 by a deposit receipt; and that on the 8th, two days later, he drew for £446 12s., 1d., and then again on the same day for £4,000 sterling, amounting in the aggregate to over two hundred thousand dollars. Assuming this to have been the cost of the assassinations for which Booth and Surratt had made themselves responsible, and that on which they were counting to keep them well supplied with money all the balance of their lives, the question arises what became of this money? Of course their hired assassins were only to be paid when they had fulfilled their contract. The money was subject to this contingency; hence there was, no doubt, a provisional arrangement by which Thompson held control over the reward promised them, and, when we look at the final result of the thing, we can readily see that the money, in the end, reverted to Thompson.

There is another very remarkable coincidence revealed in this testimony; that is, the fact of Thompson's leaving Canada on the 14th of April, 1865, for Europe, travelling overland to Halifax, when by waiting two weeks longer he could have gone by steamer. This was such an unusual circumstance as to require explanation, and excited remarks amongst the clerks in the bank at the time. If we have been led by the evidence to the conclusion that the government fully sustained its charge and specification against Jacob Thompson, we can at once explain this coincidence of his leaving Montreal for Europe by the overland route to Halifax on the very day on which he expected the plot to be consummated. He could not afford to wait for the opening of navigation, lest his flight might be impeded by arrest, and a warrant or demand for his extradition on the charge that he was a member of the conspiracy. "The wicked flee where no man pursueth." A guilty conscience is its own accuser. This remarkable coincidence, equally with the other, is presumptive evidence of his guilt.

Booth kept his bank account in the same bank with Thompson, and there is every reason to believe that his credits were from money supplied to him by Thompson. When he drew the bill of October 27th, which was found on his person after his death, he explained that he was going to run the blockade. We have seen what he meant by that; and this gives additional evidence that the assassination plot was fully matured, as shown by the Selby letter, at that time, and that on the part of Booth, acting under the latitude of discretion contained in that letter, he was only biding his time, waiting and watching for, and seeking to make, an opportunity; and that had he not been restrained by Thompson until he could get authority from Richmond that would serve him as a voucher for the large outlay of money involved, he would have acted long before he finally did.

Now the question comes up, what became of the money deposited to Thompson's credit by the Confederate government in the banks of Canada? We have seen that he had deposited to his credit in the Ontario Bank of Montreal $649,873.28, and have learned that he had, in addition to this, large transactions in other Canada banks. The reduction of his account in the Montreal bank of over $200,000 by the drafts of the 6th and 8th of April, we have every reason to believe was dependent upon contingencies for their payment which were never fulfilled, and so this large amount reverted to Thompson. The Confederate government died suddenly and unexpectedly about this time, leaving no executor with will annexed, and no one to look after its assets, or court authorized to appoint an administrator; and so it would seem that in this case Jacob Thompson was not only a man that had achieved notoriety, but that he also had riches thrust upon him. Perhaps he and Clay, Tucker, Sanders, Cleary, and Holcombe held a court in equity, and distributed amongst them the assets thus accidentally left in their hands.

CHAPTER XV.

THE CASE OF MRS. SURRATT.

So earnest and persistent have been the efforts of rebel priests, politicians and editors to pervert public opinion in regard to the case of Mrs. Surratt that it becomes necessary to devote some special consideration to it even at the expense of some repetition. Immediately after her execution a wild howl was set up by these people for the purpose of making political capital out of the sympathy and tender feeling which we all have for her sex. Her innocence was boldly asserted, and the government was denounced for her execution. They suppressed or set at naught all the evidence against her, and made many false statements to subserve the purpose they had in view. These efforts were only made by those who had been the enemies of the government during the war — who had either asserted the right of secession, or denied the right of the government to coerce (to use their own expression) a State into submission to its authority.

Because President Lincoln felt that the obligations of his official oath required him to maintain the authority of the government and to preserve the Union they had all through the terrible struggle in which he was engaged been his bitter enemies. They were actuated by a spirit of malignant hatred of the Union cause, and stood ready to oppose and denounce every measure that the President had found necessary to the success of his purpose and work. Their hostility to the government was only rendered more intense by its success in putting down the rebellion, and so they were ready to seize on this occasion, that they might, out of it, make political capital. This effort has never been abandoned, and the case of Mrs. Surratt continues to be worked for all that it is

MRS. MARY E. SURRATT.

worth by that portion of the Northern press that inherits the old copperhead animus.

To fully understand the case of Mrs. Surratt we must make her acquaintance as early as 1863. We find her at that time living at Surrattsville, in Prince George County, Md., ten miles below Washington City. The villa called Surrattsville consisted simply of a country tavern owned and occupied by Mrs. Surratt. She was a widow with three children, two sons and a daughter. The elder son had gone to Texas and had volunteered in the rebel service. The younger son, John H. Surratt, a young man of nineteen, had left St. Charles College in the summer of 1861, not to volunteer as a soldier, but to engage in the secret service of the Confederacy. There was a United States post-office at Surrattsville; and this young man, in addition to his duties as a Confederate spy and carrier of despatches for the rebel government, handled Uncle Sam's mail and delivered it to his neighbors. From all this we can readily gather the attitude of Mrs. Surratt toward the government. On the trial of John H. Surratt, John F. Tibbetts testified that in 1863 he was carrying the mail from Washington to Charlotte Hall, and that he stopped at Surrattsville to deliver the mail at that office. On one occasion, whilst waiting for the mail there, he heard Mrs. Surratt say that she would give one thousand dollars to any one that would kill Lincoln. He also testified that when there was a Union victory he heard her son say in her presence that, "The d—d Northern army and the leader thereof ought to be sent to hell."

Here we see the deep and traitorous hostility to the government of these people who were in its service under the obligations of an official oath. In the fall of 1864 Mrs. Surratt removed to Washington, taking the house 541 on H Street. She rented her Surrattsville property to a man by the name of Lloyd. What prompted this change is not known to the writer. Her son had so won the confidence of Jefferson Davis and Judah P. Benjamin that he had for a considerable time been entrusted by them, not only with important despatches, but also with large sums of money sent to their agents in Canada.[1] Indeed, this seems to have been

---

[1] Trial John H. Surratt, p. 468, testimony of Dr. McMillen.

the only employment in which he was then engaged; and at this time the assassination plot, as we have seen, was engaging the serious attention both of Davis and his agents in Canada, and that both Surratt and Booth were in the confidence of these men, though they were as yet not personally acquainted with each other.

Booth arranged with Dr. S. A. Mudd to come to Washington to introduce him to Surratt, which he did on the 23d day of December, 1864. Their acquaintanceship ripened into the closest intimacy with a rapidity that was due to a common sympathy and a common purpose. They were from that time much together, and Booth at once became a frequent and constant visitor at the house of Mrs. Surratt.[1] From this time on the evidence begins to accumulate, showing her to be informed of the work in which they were engaged, and to have fully entered into their scheme as a helper.[2] There were a number of boarders in her house. These merely received the ordinary civilities of personal intercourse from Booth; but with John and his mother his intercourse was always of a private and confidential character.

Booth's habit was to come into that house, and after the common-place civilities to tap John on the shoulder and ask him to spare him a moment of his time, when they they would retire to an upstairs room and remain in conference sometimes for two or three hours. In John's absence (and he was frequently away) Booth would ask Mrs. Surratt to grant him a private interview, which she always did. What business could this man, who had been so recently introduced to the family, have had that required so much and such strict privacy? Whatever it was, Mrs. Surratt was trusted by him equally with her son. We have now presented the state of things in that house between these parties as shown by undisputed testimony, and will proceed to show from the further evidence in the case what the business was that they had on hand.

Shortly after John H. Surratt made the acquaintance of Booth, Atzerodt became a frequent visitor at Mrs. Surratt's.[3] The first

---

[1] Official Report of the Conspiracy Trial, p. 114, testimony of L. J. Wiechmann.

[2] See Report Conspiracy Trial, pp. 114, 115 and pp. 85–87. Testimony of L. J. Wiechmann and John M. Lloyd.

[3] Official Report Conspiracy Trial, p. 115.

time he came he inquired for "John H. Surratt or Mrs. Surratt." How did he know of Mrs. Surratt in such a way that he could make her the alternative of John? In the early part of March Payne called at the Surratt house, and inquired for John H. Surratt, but when told that he was not at home he asked to see Mrs. Surratt.[1] He was an entire stranger, but knew enough, not only about John but also about his mother, to make her the alternative in the absence of her son. He passed under the *alias* of Wood on this visit. Mrs. Surratt took him in for the night, and got her boarder, Wiechmann, to take him to his room, where she had his supper served to him. Would she thus have acted toward a stranger of whom she knew nothing? It is not to be believed. Payne carried the key to her hospitality in some secret sign that had been adopted by these conspirators. Toward the last of March Payne called again, giving the name of Payne and claiming to be a Baptist preacher. He remained in the house this time for three days, and on one of these days was surprised by Wiechmann coming into his room, where he found John H. Surratt and Payne fencing with bowie-knives, and with revolvers lying on the bed; there were also four sets of new spurs. Wiechmann spoke about what he had seen to Mrs. Surratt, saying "that he did not like the look of things," when she said, "Oh, you need not be disturbed about it; John rides a good deal in the country, and has to carry these things to protect himself."[2]

It was during this visit that Booth, Surratt, Payne, Atzerodt, Herold, and one or two others, started out on an expedition from which they returned under circumstances of disappointment and rage, as heretofore recounted, and of the import of which Mrs. Surratt was seen to have been fully informed, as she was weeping, and declined going to her dinner. Upon the failure of this expedition Booth went to New York and Payne to Baltimore. The plot, however, was not abandoned; and for its future prosecution it seemed desirable to Booth and Surratt to transfer Payne to Washington, and that in the most secret manner, and there to keep him hidden away until he was wanted. They procured a room for him at the

[1] Official Report Conspiracy Trial, p. 114.
[2] Official Report Conspiracy Trial, p. 115, and Trial of John H. Surratt, pp. 377, 378.

Herndon House, representing him to be a delicate gentleman, and stipulating that his meals should be served to him in his room.[1] It came to the knowledge of Wiechmann that Booth and Surratt had placed some one in that house, and he was naturally curious to know whom it was. Atzerodt let the secret out, and when Wiechmann spoke of its being Payne who was quartered in the Herndon House, Mrs. Surratt asked him how he knew. When he gave Atzerodt as the source of his information she manifested some displeasure. But we are not left to infer from this that she had been informed of the disposition that had been made of Payne, for a night or two after that, when returning from an evening service at St. Patrick's Church, in company with Wiechmann and three or four young ladies, she stopped when they came to the Herndon House, and asked the party to wait on her a few minutes whilst she should go in and see Payne.[2] They waited on this interview for about twenty minutes. Thus we see that she was notified of every move that was made in preparation for the assassination.

Not only were Booth, Atzerodt, and Payne visitors at Mrs. Surratt's, but also the notorious rebel spy and blockade runner, Mrs. Slater, *alias* Brown, was one of her visitors. This woman stayed all night with her toward the latter part of March, 1865, and was accompanied by Mrs. Surratt and her son John when she left on the next morning, Mrs. Surratt going as far as Surrattsville, whilst her son accompanied her to Richmond in place of a Mr. Howell whom she had expected to have for her escort, but who had been arrested, and so Surratt took his place.[3]

On one occasion Mrs. Surratt sent Mr. Wiechmann to Booth with a message that she wanted to see him on private business, to which Booth responded.

On the Tuesday before the assassination Mrs. Surratt asked Wiechmann to drive her down to Surrattsville, and upon his consenting to do so she sent him to Booth to request the use of his horse and buggy for the trip. Booth told Wiechmann that he

---

[1] Conspiracy Trial, p. 113. Trial of Surratt, pp. 377, 378.
[2] Trial of Surratt, pp. 385, 386.
[3] Trial Conspirators, pp. 113, 114, and Trial Surratt, 383, 384.

had sold his horse and buggy, but he gave him ten dollars with which to procure one.[1] As they were on their way down they met Mrs. Surratt's tenant, Lloyd, on the road, when Mrs. Surratt requested Wiechmann to stop. Lloyd, recognizing her, got out of his buggy and came to the side of Mrs. Surratt's buggy, on which she was sitting, when she leaned her head out toward him and conversed with him in so low a tone that Wiechmann did not hear what was said;[2] but Lloyd testified that she told him to "have those shooting-irons handy, as they would be called for before long." The shooting-irons to which she referred were the two Spencer carbines that had been carried to Surrattsville some time previous by J. H. Surratt, Atzerodt, and Herold, and which John H. Surratt and Lloyd had hidden away, as related heretofore. Thus we see that Mrs. Surratt was kept posted in regard to every move that was made; that she knew that these arms had been deposited there, the purpose for which they had been left there, and that they would be called for soon. We can now understand Booth's generosity in furnishing her ten dollars to pay for a conveyance — she carried his message to Lloyd. On the day of the assassination she again got Wiechmann to drive her down to Surrattsville, no doubt at Booth's request, and perhaps at his expense. She gave to Wiechmann ten dollars with which to procure a conveyance, and as he passed out of her house on this errand he met Booth at the front door, in the act, as it were, of ringing the door bell.[3] When Wiechmann returned, in passing to his room, he saw Booth in the parlor conversing with Mrs. Surratt. Booth sent by her to Lloyd, on this occasion, a field-glass and a message to have the two carbines ready, together with this glass and two bottles of whiskey, as they would be called for that night. Lloyd was absent from home when they arrived at Surrattsville, and did not return until late in the evening. Mrs. Surratt dilly-dallied until he returned, and then snatched an opportunity for a private interview with Lloyd in his back yard, where he had

---

[1] Trial Conspirators, p. 113.
[2] Trial Conspirators, pp. 118-119. Trial Conspirators, p. 85. Testimony of John M. Lloyd.
[3] Trial Conspirators, p. 113, and Trial Surratt, pp. 391, 392.

driven. She then delivered to him the field-glass and Booth's message to have the shooting-irons, etc., ready as they would be called for that night, as they were, by Booth and Herold, about midnight. Lloyd swore that this was the message which she delivered to him during that interview in the back yard.[1]

Can any one doubt now that Mrs. Surratt was fully posted in every particular of the assassination plot, that she was fully trusted by Booth and her son, and was in sympathy with their purpose and willing to do all she could in aiding its accomplishment, — that she was, in fact, a co-conspirator?

On the night of the assassination, about three o'clock in the morning, a party of detectives called at Mrs. Surratt's house for the purpose of searching it to see whom they could find there, and demanded admittance. When informed of their visit and the purpose of it by Wiechmann, she said, "For God's sake let them in. I have been expecting the house to be searched."[3] How many people in Washington were expecting detectives to come that night to search their houses? Not one who was innocent of crime. Two nights later the inmates of this house — Mrs. Surratt, her daughter, and Miss Fitzpatrick — were put under arrest by the military police; and whilst they were waiting for a conveyance at near the hour of midnight the assassin Payne rang the door bell, and was taken in and placed under arrest by the officer in charge. When Mrs. Surratt was confronted by Payne she held up her hand and solemnly said, "Before God I do not know him, and never saw him."[2] It will be remembered that he had within the last three weeks to that time stayed in her house for three days and nights, and he was a man of such marked personality that he could not have been so easily forgotten. The defense, in her case, attempted to account for this by an alleged infirmity of sight, but they were unable to establish by testimony any infirmity of sight beyond what is common to her age of about forty-five.[4] It will be remembered that Payne had been hiding and skulking for three

---

[1] Conspiracy Trial, pp. 85, etc.

[2] See supplemental affadavit of L. J. Wiechmann, and Trial of Surratt, p. 394.

[3] Trial Conspirators, pp. 121, 122.

[4] Conspiracy Trial. Testimony for the defense and testimony in rebuttal, pp. 132, 139 inclusive.

days and nights, and of all the houses in Washington her's was the only one to which he felt that he could go and entrust the secret of his presence.

He could, under the circumstances in which he was placed, only have given this confidence to a co-conspirator. Having now given a brief synopsis of the testimony on which Mrs. Surratt was found guilty by the Commission, it will be in order for my readers to form their own conclusions as to her guilt or innocence. The writer only desires to say that additional testimony going to show the justice of the finding of the Commission in her case came out incidentally on the trial of John H. Surratt, and will also be found in the affidavit of L. J. Wiechmann, made after the military trial, in which he recounts a number of circumstances that had escaped his memory when on the witness stand, and which recurred to him in his subsequent reflections on the case. The testimony of Sergeants Dye and Cooper, given on the trial of Surratt, was that in passing Mrs. Surratt's house about ten minutes after the murder, a lady which Dye (having seen Mrs. Surratt at the military trial) believed to have been her, raised a window, and thrusting her head out, asked them what was wrong down town.[1]

Here we have her sitting in her parlor at about twenty-five minutes after ten o'clock waiting anxiously to hear some news. There was as yet no excitement on the street to awaken curiosity. These two soldiers believed they were the first persons to pass that house after the assassination; the street was entirely quiet; as they passed along they met two policemen shortly after passing the house 541, where Mrs. Surratt lived, who had not yet heard the news; yet here was a woman expecting to hear some news; who hailed the first passers-by after the fatal, and evidently appointed, hour to inquire what was wrong down town. It was also proven by a servant of good character, Susan Ann Jackson, that she had on that night served supper in the dining-room, after the family and boarders had left, to a man whom Mrs. Surratt called her son, and whom this witness identified as the prisoner at the bar.[2] We can now see why she was anxiously awaiting the news.

[1] Trial of Surratt, pp. 136, 137, and pp. 186, 187, 188.
[2] Trial of Surratt, pp. 163, 164, 165.

On the trial of Surratt a good deal of the testimony introduced to show the existence of a conspiracy to assassinate the President, and that the prisoner was a member of this conspiracy, implicated his mother in it equally with himself. Most of the witnesses that had been brought before the Commission to prove the existence of such a conspiracy, and that Mary E. Surratt was an active member of it, were again produced on this trial. As the witnesses Lloyd and Wiechmann were the most important of these, their testimony being completely conclusive of the guilt both of the the prisoner and his mother, great efforts were made to discredit, especially, the testimony of Wiechmann; but this could not be done by any of the methods known to the law. He stood the test of every effort and came out unscathed from a bitter and most hostile cross-examination that occupied a day and a half. Every effort was made to make him contradict himself as to his present testimony in chief, as also to his testimony given two years before at the military trial, but without avail. No false witness could possibly have come out of such a fiery ordeal unscathed. Truth is always consistent with itself, and one truth is always consistent with every other correlated truth, and for this reason a witness that keeps the truth can never be entrapped.

He was contradicted, it is true, by negative testimony as to some points in his evidence. Persons who were in the same room with him at the time that certain declarations were made to which he testified swore that they did not hear them. But such testimony is of no value. If one person in company with many others in a room were to swear that he heard the clock strike, his testimony as to that fact could not be discredited by that of all the others swearing that they did not hear it strike. Positive testimony cannot be overthrown, or even shaken, by negative. Witnesses were also brought to prove that he had made different statements, and some to prove that he had virtually admitted that he had testified falsely as to Mrs. Surratt, and that he had been held under duress by certain officers of the government and required to state in his testimony what they dictated to him. These efforts also proved failures, as a close, scrutinizing cross-examination made it apparent that these witnessess had been suborned, and were delivering a cooked-up testimony. After every effort had been made that could be devised by the ingenuity of counsels, Wiechmann stood before the court, the jury, and the country, as an honest, conscientious, truthful man. He was also a man of superior talent, education, and intelligence. In short, he established a character that must challenge the admiration of every candid mind.

The attempt was also made to overthrow Lloyd's testimony, but without success. His testimony was assailed principally on the ground that he was drunk when he returned to his home on that evening, the 14th of April, when Mrs. Surratt snatched an opportunity to get a private interview with him, by going out to him in his back yard, as soon as he drove up, and there delivering to him the message to which he testified, and also gave him Booth's field-glass. Lloyd himself admitted that he was pretty drunk on that occasion, but he was not so drunk but that he could carry out Mrs. Surratt's instructions to the very letter. He got the carbines and all the other things and placed them where they would be handy when called for, so that they could be delivered without detaining the parties long when they should be called for.[1] He was also on hand at the time they called, and ready to get these things for them. It is evident Lloyd knew the purpose of all this. When called on by the soldiers and detectives who were in pursuit of Booth and Herold the next morning, he denied that there had been anybody there during that night. He knew nothing. But when he found a chain of ascertained facts about to fasten upon him, in great fear and trepidation he made a clean breast of it, and told all. He then gave as a reason for his course in denying all knowledge of the matter, that he knew he could not tell all that he knew without implicating Mrs. Surratt, and that he did not want to do that.

[1] Trial of Conspirators, p. 86. Trial of Surratt, pp. 282, 283.

Note and Affidavit of L. J. Wiechmann.

Col. H. L. BURNETT, *Judge Advocate*, Cincinnati, Ohio: —

COLONEL: — I stated before the Commission at Washington that I commenced to board with Mrs. Surratt in November, 1864. As a general thing I remained at home during the evenings, and consequently I heard many things which were then intended to blind me, but which now are as clear as daylight. The following facts, which have come to my recollection since the renditon of my testimony, may be of interest: —

AFFIDAVIT OF LOUIS J. WIECHMANN.

I once asked Mrs. Surratt what her son John had to do with Dr. Mudd's farm; why he made himself an agent for Booth? (She herself had told me that Booth desired to purchase Mudd's farm.) Her reply was, that Dr. Mudd and the people of Charles County had got tired of Booth, and that they had pushed him on John. Before the 4th of March she was in the habit of remarking that *something* was going to happen to "Old Abe" which would prevent him from taking his seat; that General Lee was going to execute a movement which would startle the *whole world*. What that movement was she never said. A few days after I asked her why John brought such men as Herold and Atzerodt to the house, and why he associated with them? "Oh, John wishes to make use of them for his *dirty work*," was her reply. On my desiring to know what the dirty work was, she answered that "John wanted them to clean his horses." He had two at that time. And once, when she sent me to Brooks, the stable keeper, to inquire about her son, she laughed, and remarked that "Brooks considered John H. Surratt and Booth and Herold and Atzerodt a party of young gamblers and sports, and that she wanted him to think so." Brooks has told me since the trial that such was actually the case, and that at one time he saw John H. Surratt with three one-hundred-dollar notes in his possession.

When Richmond fell and Lee's army surrendered, when Washington was illuminated, Mrs. Surratt closed her house and wept. Her house was gloomy and cheerless. To use her own expression, it was "indicative of her feelings." On Good Friday I drove her into the country, ignorant of her purpose and intentions. We started at about half-past two o'clock in the afternoon. Before leaving, she had an interview with John Wilkes Booth in the parlor. On the way down she was very lively and cheerful, taking the reins into her own hands several times and urging on the steed. We halted once, and that was about three miles from Washington, when, observing that there were pickets along the road, she hailed an old farmer and wanted to know if they would remain there all the night. On being told that they were withdrawn about eight o'clock in the evening, she said "she was glad to know it." On the return I chanced to make some remark about Booth, stating that he appeared to be without employment, and asking her when he was going to act again. "Booth is done acting," she said, "and is going to New York very soon, never to return." Then turning round, she remarked: "Yes, and Booth is crazy on one subject, and I am going to give him a good scolding the next time I see him." What that "one subject" was Mrs. Surratt never mentioned to me. She was very anxious to be at home at nine o'clock, saying that she had made an appointment with some gentleman who was to meet her at that hour. I asked her if it was Booth. She answered neither yes nor no. When about a mile from the city, and having from the top of a hill caught a view of Washington swimming in a flood of light, raising her hands, she said: "I am afraid all this rejoicing will be turned into mourning, and all this glory into sadness." I asked her what she meant. She replied that after sunshine there was always a storm, and that the people were too proud and licentious, and that God would punish them. The gentleman whom she expected at nine o'clock, on her return, called. It was, as I afterwards ascertained, Booth's last visit to Mrs. Surratt, and the third one that day. She was alone with him for a few minutes in the parlor. I was in the dining-room at the time, and as soon as I had taken tea I repaired thither. Mrs. Surratt's former cheerfulness had left her. She was now very nervous, agitated, and restless. On my asking her what was the matter, she replied that she was very nervous and did not feel well. Then looking at me, she wanted to know which way the torch-light procession was going that we had seen on the avenue. I remarked that it was a procession of the arsenal employees, who were going to serenade the President. She said that she would like to know, as she was very much interested in it. Her nervousness finally increased so much that she chased myself and the young ladies, who were making a great deal of noise and laughter, to our respective rooms. When the detectives came, at three o'clock the next morning, I rapped at her door for permission to let them in. "For God's sake, let them come in! I expected the house to be searched," she said.

When the detectives had gone, and her daughter, almost frantic, cried out: "Oh, ma! Just think of that man (John Wilkes Booth) having been here an hour before the assassination! I am afraid it will bring suspicion on us."

"Anna, come what will," she replied, "I am resigned. I think that John Wilkes Booth was only an instrument in the hands of the Almighty to punish this proud and licentious people."

(Signed)   Louis J. Wiechmann.

Sworn and subscribed before me this 11th day of August, 1865.

(Signed)   Chas. E. Pancoast,
Alderman.

CHAPTER XVI.

FATHER WALTER.

FROM the time of the trial of the conspirators by a military commission, and of the execution of Mrs. Surratt by the order of President Johnson, Father Walter, a secular priest of Washington City, has made himself conspicious by his efforts to pervert public opinion on the result of the trial of the conspirators by the Commission. Whilst rebel lawyers, editors, and politicians have boldly assailed the lawfulness of the Commission, and have denounced it as an unconstitutional tribunal, and have characterized the trial as a "Star Chamber" trial, as a contrivance for taking human life under a mockery of a judicial procedure, but with no purpose of securing the ends of justice, Father Walter and other priests whose sympathies were with the Southern Confederacy have earnestly seconded their efforts by the invention and circulation of cunningly devised falsehoods. Father Walter has every now and then bobbed up with the assertion of Mrs. Surratt's entire innocence. Knowing that not one in a thousand of our people has ever read the testimony on which she was convicted, he feels that he can boldly assert that "there was not evidence enough against her to hang a cat." He has also become bold enough to state as facts what the evidence shows to be falsehoods. As an example of this: in an article in the "Catholic Review" he asserts in regard to Mrs. Surratt's trip to Surrattsville on the afternoon of the day of the assassination that she had ordered her carriage for the trip, which was purely on private business, on the forenoon of that day, and before it was known that the President would go to the theatre. Why, if this was true, was it not proven in her defense? There was no such testimony produced. The testimony on this point against her was that shortly after two o'clock on that afternoon she went up stairs to Wiechmann's room, tapped at the door, and when it was opened she said to Mr. Wiechmann, "I have just received a letter from Mr. Calvert that makes it necessary for me to go to Surrattsville to-day and see Mr. Nothey. Would you be so good as to get a conveyance and drive me down?" Upon Wiechmann's consenting to do so, she handed him a ten dollar bill with which to procure a conveyance. Surely there is no evidence here that a carriage had been ordered already, as Wiechmann was left free to procure a conveyance where he might see fit.

Wiechmann went down stairs, and as he opened the front door he saw John Wilkes Booth, who was in the act, as it were, of pulling the front door bell. Booth entered the house.

When young Wiechmann returned, after having procured the buggy, he went up to his own room after some necessary articles of clothing, and as he again descended the stairs and passed by the parlor door he observed that Booth was in the parlor conversing with Mrs. Surratt. In a little while Booth came down to the front door steps, and waved his hand in token of adieu to Wiechmann, who was standing at the curb.

When Mrs. Surratt came and was in the act of getting into the buggy, she remembered that she had forgotten something, and said, "Wait a moment, until I go and get those things of Mr. Booth's." She returned from the parlor with a package which was done up in brown paper, the contents of which the witness did not see, but which was afterwards shown to have been the field-glass which Booth carried with him in his flight. This glass Booth sent to Lloyd by Mrs. Surratt, with a message to have it, with the two carbines and two bottles of whiskey, where they would be handy, as they would be called for that night. Lloyd swore that this was the message delivered to him by Mrs. Surratt in the private interview she sought with him in his back yard on his return home that evening, and that in accordance with these instructions he delivered them to Booth and Herold about midnight that night.[1] Now let us see about the private business on which she professed to be going, and on which she claimed on her

---

[1] See testimony of L. J. Wiechmann and John M. Lloyd on the trial of the conspirators and on the trial of J. H. Surratt. Also testimony of Trial Conspirators, p. 126.

trial that she went. The letter from Mr. Calvert was a demand for money that she owed him, and was written at Bladensburg on the 12th of April. On the afternoon of the 14th she presented herself to Wiechmann and claimed that she had just received it. It would seem very strange that it took this letter two days to reach her at a distance of only six miles. She claimed that she must go and see Mr. Nothey, who owed her, and get money from him to pay her debt to Mr. Calvert. Mr. Nothey lived five miles below Surrattsville, and as she claimed that she had just received Mr. Calvert's letter it was impossible that she could have made any arrangement with Nothey to meet her at Surrattsville that day. She did not meet him there, neither did she go to his house to see him. When she arrived at Surrattsville she took Wiechmann into the parlor at the hotel and asked him to write a letter for her to Mr. Nothey, which he did at her dictation; and this she sent to Mr. Nothey by a Mr. Bennett Gwinn, a neighbor of his, who happened to be passing down.

Now, in view of all these facts, can any one see how her private business was in any way subserved by her trip to Surrattsville on that afternoon? She could as easily have written to Mr. Nothey from Washington as from Surrattsville. A postage stamp, a sheet of paper and an envelope would have saved her six dollars, the cost of her trip, and would have served her business just as well. The truth is that this talk of going on private business of her own was all a fabrication, first to deceive Mr. Wiechmann as to the object of her trip, and then to be used, should it become necessary, in her defense. We have already seen what her real business was.

Father Walter falsifies again in the article referred to in saying that she did not see Lloyd on that afternoon, but delivered the things to his sister-in-law, Mrs. Offutt.[1] Both Lloyd and his sister-in-law testified to her interview with him in his back yard, and Lloyd testified as to what passed between them on that occassion.

It would seem that Father Walter is going on the theory that we have gotten so far past the time, and that the testimony has

---

[1] See testimony of John M. Lloyd, Trial Conspirators, pp. 85, 86, and testimony of Mrs. Emma Offutt, pp. 121–125, and Trial of Surratt, p. 281.

been so far forgotten that he can foist upon the public any statement that he may please to fabricate. We would kindly remind the reverend Father that no ultimate gain can be derived from an effort to suppress the truth. Neither can it be obliterated by our prejudices. We may misconstrue facts, but we cannot wipe them out by a mere stroke of the pen; and a fact once made can never be recalled. But I am not yet done with this Father. He prefaces his article in the "Review" with the statement that he heard Mrs. Surratt's last confession, and that whilst his priestly vows do not permit him to reveal the secrets of the confessional, yet from knowledge in his possession he is prepared to assert her entire innocence of this most atrocious crime. He means that we shall understand that were he at liberty to give her last confession to the world he could say that she then and there asserted her entire innocence.

Will Father Walter deny that under the teachings of the Roman Catholic Church he had an absolute right, with her consent, to make her confession public on this point? Nay more, could not Mrs. Surratt have compelled him to do so in vindication of her own good name, and of the honor of the church of which she was a member? And having this consent, was it not his most solemn duty to proclaim her confessed innocence in every public way, through the press, and even from the very steps of the gallows?

Why was not that confession made public? Why was it not reduced to writing and signed with her own hand? Why has it not in its entirety been given to the world? Why must the public wait twenty-seven years, and instead of having the full confession be required to content itself, in so great a case, with a mere assertion from the reverend Father, based on his alleged knowledge? Aye, just there's the rub!

That confession of Mrs. Surratt's would have proved very interesting reading, and might have let in a flood of light on some places that are now very dark; it would, indeed, have shown how far Mrs. Surratt was involved in the abduction and assassination plots, and to what degree she was the willing or unwilling tool of her son, and of John Wilkes Booth. That confession would have shown the object of Booth's visit to her on the very day and eve of the murder. It would have explained what she had in her mind when she carried Booth's field-glass into the country, and told Lloyd to have the "shooting-irons" and two bottles of whiskey ready on that fateful night of the 14th of April. And if she did not explain satisfactorily every item of testimony which bore so heavily against her, then her last confession was worth nothing.

Father Walter never had at any time Mrs. Surratt's consent to make her confession public, and he dare not do so now after twenty-seven years have elapsed since he shrove his unfortunate penitent.

Why, we repeat, did not Father Walter do this? He was interesting himself very much in her behalf in trying to get her a reprieve; why did he not use this as an argument with the President in her behalf that in her final confession she asserted her innocence? Why did he wait until the sentence had been confirmed by the President and a full cabinet without a dissenting voice, and then had been carried into execution, before he put into circulation the story of her confessed innocence? And why does he refer to his priestly vows as his excuse for this conduct, when he knows full well that having gained Mrs. Surratt's consent to make her confession public as an entirety, these vows imposed upon him no such restrictions? In vindication of the Commission, and also of the court of review,—the President and his cabinet, —we submit that the evidence shows her to have been guilty, no matter what she might have said in her final confession.

Perhaps she had been led to believe that President Lincoln was an execrable tyrant, and that his death was no more than that of the "meanest nigger in the army." Her remarks to her daughter the night her house was searched indicate the views she took of the subject. "Anna, come what will, I am resigned. I think that Booth was only an instrument in the hands of the Almighty to punish this wicked and licentious people."[1] To one who could have taken this view of the case, Booth's act could not have been regarded as a crime; and she who rendered him all the aid she could would feel no guilt. They were only co-operating with the Almighty in the execution of his vengeance. On the trial of John

[1] See supplemental affidavit of L. Wiechmann and Trial of J. H. Surratt, p. 295.

H. Surratt, Mr. Merrick brought Father Walter on to the stand and asked him if he had heard the last confession of Mrs. Surratt, to which the Father answered, "I did. I gave her communion on Friday and prepared her for death."

Mr. Merrick in his argument before the jury said: "I asked him 'Did she tell you as she was marching to the scaffold that she was an innocent woman?' I told him not to answer that question before I desired him to. He nodded his head, but did not answer that question, because he had no right, as the other side objected." Now what was the object of all this? Mr. Merrick brought the Father on to the stand and asked him a question that had not the slightest relevancy to any issue before that jury. He knew, of course, that the prosecution would object, and that the question could not be answered. It was a direct question, and could have been answered by, "She did" or "She did not." Why does not the Father answer at once? He had been cautioned not to do so until desired, and so he waits for the prosecution to object and estop him from answering the question. Mr. Merrick, however, in his argument assumes that the Father stood ready to say that, "She solemnly declared her entire innocence to me in her last confession," and throws the responsibility on the other side for not getting this answer. The argument was this: "You see that Father Walter stood ready to testify to this fact, but the prosecution objected, and so he could not do it."

Now, what has become of the Father's priestly vows behind which he has always been hiding? Or was all this a mere piece of acting, to give the counsel a point from which to denounce the government, the Commission, and all who were concerned in visiting justice upon the assassins?

We believe it to be true that the laws of his church did not forbid him to make public, with her consent or command, her last confession on this point, and that the Father in making the statements he does at this late day is simply practicing sleight-of-hand upon the public. It is a very strange circumstance, too, that whilst Payne, Arnold, O'Laughlin, Atzerodt, and even John H. Surratt admitted their connection with one or the other of the conspiracy plots, Mrs. Surratt has not left one word or line after her to explain away the incriminating evidence brought against her. The reason is plain; she could not have explained anything without involving herself and her son, and giving away the whole case.

For twenty-six years Father Walter and his rebel co-adjutors have kept a paragraph going the rounds of the papers, stating as a fact that all the members of the Commission but one are dead, and that they died miserable deaths, which marked them as the subjects of heaven's vengeance, and that some of them perished from the violence of their own hands, being crazed with remorse.

The truth is that at this writing, April, 1892, all of the members of the Commission are alive except General Hunter and General Ekin. General Hunter lived to over four score years, and General Ekin to seventy-three. The present writer is nearly seventy-nine and is still able to vindicate the truth in the interest of a true history of his period. Is it not high time that the American people should be fully informed as to this most important episode in their history, in order that they may not be misled by men who were not the friends, but the enemies, of our government in its struggle for its preservation and perpetuation?

CHAPTER XVII.

CONCLUSION.

Now come the United States and challenge an intelligent and candid world to say whether or not, in the light of all this evidence, they have vindicated their dignity and honor by showing that they had just grounds for charging Jefferson Davis, George N. Sanders, Beverly Tucker, Jacob Thompson, William C. Cleary, Clement C. Clay, George Harper, George Young, and others unknown, with combining, confederating and conspiring together with one John Wilkes Booth and John Harrison Surratt to kill and murder Abraham Lincoln, Andrew Johnson, William H. Seward, and Ulysses S. Grant, with the intent to subvert the Constitution and overthrow the government of the United States in aid of the then existing rebellion and as a means of giving it success; and that further, as specified, they, together with John H. Surratt, John Wilkes Booth, David E. Herold, George A. Atzerodt, Lewis Payne, Mary E. Surratt, Edward Spangler, Samuel Arnold, Michael O'Laughlin, and Dr. Samuel A. Mudd, did, on the night of the 14th day of April, 1865, murder Abraham Lincoln, and did attempt to murder William H. Seward, and did lie in wait to murder Andrew Johnson, in pursuance of said conspiracy, and in the purpose and intent thereof, as therein alleged. And they further say, that if, in the light of all this evidence, any persons shall feel like erecting a monument to the memory of Jefferson Davis, this is a free country; let them do so, and take the consequences that cannot fail to result to their reputation and memory in the minds of a patriotic, intelligent, and right-minded people, reared up under the influences and advantages of our free and liberal institutions of civil administration, and of their uplifting power and elevating influences on the people, who must, under these favoring conditions, ultimately reach the true ideal of human development.

CHAPTER XVIII.

FLIGHT AND CAPTURE OF JOHN H. SURRATT.

THE presence of John H. Surratt in Washington City on the day of the assassination was proven before the Military Commission by a single witness. This witness, however, was a man who was personally acquainted with him, and who swore positively to having seen him on that day. His testimony was given about a month after the event, and the circumstance was fresh in his memory. He stated the time of the day when, and the place where, he saw him; described his dress, the kind of hat he was wearing, etc., etc. He was clear in his statements, could have had no motives for swearing falsely, and it is scarcely possible that he could have been mistaken. From the description given by Sergeant Dye of the man who acted as monitor, calling the time three times in succession at short intervals, the last time calling "Ten minutes past ten," in front of the theatre, it will be remembered that the writer came to the conclusion that this was John H. Surratt. This conclusion was verified by this same witness on the trial of Surratt. Sergeant Dye had taken a seat on the platform in front of the theatre, and just before the conclusion of the second act of the play had his attention arrested by an elegantly-dressed man, who came out of the vestibule, and commenced to converse with a ruffianly-looking fellow. Then another joined them, and the three conversed together. The one who appeared to be the the leader said, "I think he will come out now," referring, as the witness supposed, to the President. The President's carriage stood near the platform on which the witness was sitting, and one of the three passed out as far as the curbstone and looked into the carriage. It would seem that they had anticipated the possibility of his departure at the close of the second act, and had intended to assassinate him at the moment of his passing out of the door. Quite a crowd of people came out at the conclusion of the act, and Booth and his companions stood near the door, awaiting the opportunity which they sought. When most of the crowd had returned into the theatre, and the would-be assassins saw that the President would remain until the close of the play, they then began to prepare for his assassination in the theatre. The writer concludes, from a careful consideration of all the circumstances, that this was a provisional arrangement, in case their plan to murder him at the door should fail.

Booth and the ruffianly-looking fellow kept their stations by the door, to make sure of not missing the opportunity of which they had planned to avail themselves, whilst the other stepped up and looked at the clock in the vestibule, and called the time. He then immediately walked rapidly up the street. He returned in a few minutes, and looking at the clock again called the time, and again walked away rapidly up the street. Very soon he returned again, and called the time louder than before, "Ten minutes past ten!" and walking rapidly away, did not return.

Booth had left the side of his companion before this long enough to go into the saloon, where he drank a glass of whiskey, and then, as soon as the time had been called the third time, went at once into the theatre, and in less than ten minutes thereafter fired the fatal shot. It is evident that it had been arranged between Booth and Payne that the assassination of Secretary Seward should be concurrent with that of President Lincoln; and that a system of signals had been arranged, of which the man who called the time was acting as monitor. The suspicions of Sergeant Dye having been aroused by the conduct of these three men, he naturally scanned them very closely, and testified that he had a good view, not only of the person, but of the face and features of the man who called the time, and had his image indelibly impressed on his memory. Upon being confronted by Surratt on his trial, he unhesitatingly and positively declared that he was the man. In addition to Reed and Dye, who testified before the Commission, there were nine others who testified on the trial of Surratt to having seen him that day in the City of Washington.

All of these persons, except four, were personally acquainted with him, and could not have been mistaken, as they were able to give the time of day when, and the place where, they saw him, as also, in the case of most of them, to describe his person, dress, hat, moustache, etc., etc., without any discrepancies in their testimony.

The other four, though not acquainted with him, identified him before the jury, more or less positively, as the man they had seen. It is worthy of remark that though they all testified with more or less of particularity in their descriptions of his person, his dress, his hat, his moustache, and as to the time of day when, and the place where, they had seen him, there was nothing incongruous or contradictory in their testimony. One witness, a colored woman, Susan Ann Jackson, who was in service at Mrs. Surratt's at the time, and had been for three or four weeks previous to the assassination, testified that under the direction of Mrs. Surratt she had made tea for the prisoner after the family and boarders had left the table on the night of the assassination, and that Mrs. Surratt had said to her on that occasion, "This is my son," and had asked her if he did not look like Annie. She said this was the first and only time she had seen him until she met him on his trial, and then she positively identified him as the man she had waited upon that night. The time was impressed on her memory by its being Good Friday, and the night of the assassination. Several of the witnesses who testified to his presence in the city on that day also testified that they saw him in company with Booth, and one, at least, with Booth and O'Laughlin. Surratt himself told his old acquaintance, St. Marie, with whom he renewed his acquaintanceship in the ranks of the Papal Zouaves at Velletri, in Italy, that he left Washington early on the morning of the 15th of April, disguised as an English tourist; and that he had a very hard time to make his escape. As the trains leaving Washington for Baltimore on the morning of the 15th were thoroughly scrutinized by the police before being permitted to leave, it is uncertain whether Surratt's disguise sufficed to get him through, or whether he went a part or all of the way to Baltimore on horseback. There was some evidence on this trial tending to the conclusion that he had escaped from the city on horseback. The next place we get track of him in his flight is at the railroad depot at Burlington, Vt., on the early morning of the 18th of April. Here he turns up with a rough-looking man, no doubt the ruffianly-looking fellow who was seen with him and Booth in front of the theatre on the night of the assassination. They had crossed Lake Champlain on a boat that ran from White Hall to Rouse's Point, on the night of the 17th, and landed at Burlington, in order to take the train to Montreal. This was the first trip the boat had made that season, and it was four hours late in reaching Burlington, arriving there about midnight. They had to wait for the morning train, which was due at four o'clock A.M. of the 18th. They requested permission to sleep at the depot, and the night watchman allowed them to sleep on the benches. He awakened them in time for the train, and after daylight, when sweeping the floor, he found a handkerchief under the bench where the taller of the two had slept, and upon examining it after it was fairly light found it marked, "J. H. Surratt 2." At Essex Junction, where they changed trains for St. Albans, these two travellers made the change, and were found by the conductor on his passing through the train standing on the platform outside. He asked them for their fare, and was told that they had no money. Surratt did all the talking. He represented that they were laboring men, had been at work in New York, and had been unfortunate and lost their money. He said they were now making their way back to Canada, and were ready to promise that if he would carry them through they would send him the fare as soon as they reached their friends. The conductor reminded them of the necessity of having money if they would travel.

Surratt disguised his speech, trying to use the dialect of a Canadian; but when he became excited from fear of being put off the train he forgot his Cannuck, and talked in good square English. The conductor also noticed that his hands were not those of a laboring man, and so concluded that the men were traveling *incognito*. This was on the early morning of the 18th of April. They arrived at St. Albans for breakfast. At the table they found everybody excited, and upon Surratt's inquiring what it meant, his next neighbor at the table, an old gentleman, informed him that the President had been assassinated, to which Surratt replied that "The news was too good to be true." The old gentleman then handed him a paper, and on looking it over he saw his own name given as one of the assassins. He dropped the paper, and found that he did not want any more breakfast. On passing out into the next room, he heard some one say that Surratt must be in town, or had passed through, as his handkerchief had been found in the street; when, upon feeling for his handkerchief, he found that he had lost it. They then left the place as quickly as possible, narrowly escaping arrest. He understood that his handkerchief had been picked up in the street of St. Albans, and no doubt, in the excitement, the news had taken that shape, but, as we have seen, he lost it at Burlington depot, and so the news must have been telegraphed to St. Albans.

It is not known how they traveled from St. Albans to Montreal, but it is most probable that they walked across the country. We find Surratt's name on the hotel register at Montreal, where he arrived at about two o'clock on the 18th of April, he having been absent from that place from the 12th. This had been to him an eventful week, full of difficulties and hazards; but he may now feel safe, as he has reached the abode of the chief conspirators, his employers, and is ready to claim his reward. He can feel that he is in the midst of sympathizing friends. But, alas! a criminal can never feel safe. An angry God is ever on the track of the guilty conscience. As it was with the first murderer, so it must be with every murderer,—a fugitive and a vagabond he is compelled to be. He had hardly recorded his name on the hotel register when he was informed that detectives were on the look-out for him, and he was at once spirited away to the house of a Mr. Porterfield. This man was a Southerner, who belonged to Thompson's cabal, but who had abjured his allegiance to his country and taken the oath of allegiance to the Queen of England, and had thus become a British subject. He knew all about the conspiracy, and the means that had been employed to carry it into effect; and was waiting and watching anxiously for the return of his co-conspirators that had been sent to Washington on their mission of assassinations. He at once

JOHN H. SURRATT.

took Surratt into his house, and kept him secreted there for several days. Finding the detectives who were in pursuit of the fugitive vigilant and determined in their search, Porterfield became fearful that he could not keep his charge concealed, and so made arrangements to get him into a place of greater security.

At this point we meet with a new element amongst the Canada conspirators, viz., the Roman Catholic priesthood. Porterfield had arranged with Father Boucher to take his charge in custody, and keep him concealed. This Father was rector of the parish of St. Liboire, a newly-settled place, about forty-five miles from Montreal — an out-of-the-way place, and so a good place in which to hide him away. The arrangements had been made in advance with this Father to take charge of Surratt, and keep him secreted at his house. He was conveyed there by one Joseph F. Du Tilley, who seems to have been priest Boucher's right hand man. The stratagem to get him away from Montreal was as follows: two carriages drove up in front of Porterfield's house late in the afternoon, when two persons, dressed as nearly as possible alike, went out together; one of these got into one of the carriages, and the other into the other, when they drove away in different directions. Father Boucher appeared at the trial of Surratt as a voluntary witness for the defense, and without any apparent sense of shame convicted himself, by his own testimony, of being an accomplice after the fact. We think that the testimony he gave warrants the conclusion, also, that another priest, Father La Pierre, placed himself in the same category. Both of these Fathers took Surratt into their houses, and kept him concealed, — the first for three, and the latter for two months, — knowing him to be charged with being a conspirator to the assassination of the President of the United States.

Father Boucher's parish being in an out-of-the-way country place, it was only necessary that he should constantly exercise a prudent vigilance in behalf of his charge. He was visited frequently by his friends whilst staying with Boucher; at one time three or four of these came together, and stayed three or four days with him. The time was spent in hunting, sporting, and revelry. It was very remarkable, however, that Father Boucher could not remember the names of any of these friends. Being a volunteer witness for the defense, he could not give their names without implicating persons whom he did not desire to compromise; hence, no doubt, his convenient Jesuitical failure of memory. Perhaps he could not have given their names without injury to the cause he desired to help. He could only say that some of their names were English names, using the word English in contra distinction from French or French-Canadian, in which sense it implied not really English, but American, — Beverly Tucker for instance, perhaps Porterfield, and likely, also, La Pierre. As two of these, Beverly Tucker and La Pierre, along with Boucher, accompanied Surratt from Montreal to Quebec, and did not leave him until they had seen him safe on board the ocean steamer, "Peruvian," when he finally was sent to Europe, it would seem highly probable that we have rightly surmised who were his visitors on the occasion referred to. Surratt was not kept in close confinement by Father Boucher, but his safety from discovery and arrest was looked after with cunning vigilance. At length the time came when it was thought safe and advisable to transfer the fugitive back to Montreal. This was affected as secretly as had been his removal from that place to the parish of St. Liboire.

Father La Pierre now took him in charge. He had provided for him a secluded upstairs room at his father's house, *right under the shadow of the bishop's window.* This Father had been a visitor of Surratt at the lonely parish of St. Liboire, and now took him under his especial protection. He kept him concealed, and never allowed him to go out until after nightfall, and then never alone, but always accompanied him. La Pierre thus kept his charge safely from the latter part of July until the 5th of September, 1865. During all of this time he was visited regularly twice a week, on Mondays and Thursdays, by Father Boucher, who always remained over night with him at each visit. How can we account for this great interest taken by these two priests in secreting the murderer of the head of the greatest nation on earth, and that with a full knowledge that he stood charged with this crime, and that a great reward was offered for his apprehension? How can we consider them less guilty, in a moral point of view, than Surratt himself?

But at length a time came when it was thought safe and advisable to send him abroad.

Early in September Father La Pierre sought an interview with Dr. Lewis J. A. McMillen, surgeon on board the ocean steamer "Peruvian," which was to sail on the 16th of that month from Quebec for Liverpool, and made arrangements to put in his care for the passage a friend of his by the name of McCarthy, who, for certain reasons, desired to embark secretly on the voyage. The doctor took a steamer at Montreal, on the 15th, to join his ship, which was to sail on the following day.

Boucher and La Pierre conveyed Surratt in a covered carriage, and went with him on board the same steamer on which the doctor had taken passage. La Pierre was in disguise, inasmuch as he was dressed in citizen's dress. They had also disguised Surratt by coloring his hair, painting his face, and putting spectacles over his eyes. On the passage from Montreal to Quebec, they kept him locked up in the state-room occupied jointly by him and Father La Pierre. When they reached Quebec and went on board the transport that was to convey them to the ocean steamer "Peruvian," in which they were to sail, the doctor was there introduced to Beverly Tucker, who had also felt enough of interest in Surratt's case to induce him to accompany him from Montreal to Quebec, and who stood in that relation to his case in the knowledge of Fathers La Pierre and Boucher that they could safely take him into their confidence in their plans for conveying Surratt out of the country. This trio saw Surratt safely on board the "Peruvian," and then bade him good-by. The interest thus manifested by Tucker in getting Surratt safely away confirms the testimony given before the Military Commission, showing him to have been justly charged by the government with being a member of the great conspiracy. Before parting from his charge Father La Pierre requested Dr. McMillen to let Surratt stay in his room until after the vessel should have sailed.

Surratt is not an innocent man carrying a good conscience, that enables him to look every man he meets squarely in the face. He is a fugitive and a vagabond, carrying the weight of a terrible crime in his memory — a weight that neither time nor distance can efface. He is haunted by his fears, having before him the vision of a detective and of capture; and so he skulks and hides from the phantom of an American detective which he cannot banish from his mind.

The vessel being now on her way, and in British waters, the fugitive ventured forth, and naturally sought the company of the surgeon of the vessel in whose care he had been placed, and whom he regarded as his friend. His social nature yearned for companionship, and all the more as a means of relief from a guilty conscience. Does he now enjoy a sense of security? To him this is impossible. He scanned closely every passenger he met, that phantom of a detective being ever present to his imagination. He sees a gentleman whom he takes to be an American. He seeks his friend McMillen, and discloses to him his fears, saying: "I think that man is an American detective." Upon being asked by the doctor what he had done that he should be afraid of a detective, he replied: "If you knew all the things I have done, it would make you stare." Murder is a crime that will out. It imposes a weight of guilt upon the conscience that will, at some unguarded moment, let the fearful secret slip through the door of the lips that are most firmly closed by a purpose of concealment. The doctor reassurred him, by reminding him that he was on board a British ship sailing on British waters, and that he had nothing to fear from an American detective. Surratt then drew a small four-barrelled revolver from his vest pocket, and remarked: "I don't care; this will settle him." The doctor now began to feel a great interest in his charge, arising from the suspicion that he was John H. Surratt. The voyage across the Atlantic occupied nine or ten days. The fugitive was so full of his terrible secret that he could not keep quiet. Every day he sought opportunities to converse with the doctor privately, and at every interview the history of his crimes kept leaking out. He was nervous, and constantly haunted by his fears; so that he could never hear any one coming up behind him without starting and looking around. Amongst his important revelations to the doctor were the following: that he had for a considerable time previously to the assassination been a bearer of despatches from

Richmond to the Confederate agents in Canada; that he had at one time carried to them from Richmond thirty thousand dollars, and at another time seventy thousand dollars; that he arrived in Montreal the last time on the 6th of April, with despatches from Davis and Benjamin, thus confirming the testimony of Conover and Merritt before the Military Commission. These despatches he claimed to have delivered to Thompson. After the military trial, and previous to the trial of Surratt, the witness, Conover, had been convicted of perjury; but this does not discredit the testimony he gave before the Commission, as it was confirmed by other witnesses who stand unimpeached, and is here also confirmed by Surratt himself in regard to one of its most important points. It will be remembered that Conover testified to having been present at a meeting of the Canada conspirators in Montreal, on the 6th of April, 1865, and that John H. Surratt, who was present, had just arrived from Richmond, bringing a cipher despatch from Jefferson Davis, and also a despatch from his Secretary of State, Benjamin, and that Thompson, laying his hand on these despatches, said: "This makes the thing all right"; and that active measures were at once entered upon for putting the assassination plot into effect. Now Surratt comes to McMillen five months later, on the face of the broad Atlantic, and confirms Conover's testimony in its major part. He also related to the doctor the particulars of his trip to Richmond late in March, 1865, when he was accompanied by a woman, who by other testimony was shown to have been Mrs. Slater, *alias* Brown, the rebel spy and blockade runner. The arrangement was made whilst he was in Canada for him to meet her in New York and accompany her to Richmond, which he did, passing through Washington. In this statement the testimony of Wiechmann is confirmed. Surratt related to the doctor the difficulty they had in crossing the Potomac. They were hailed by a gun-boat, and called upon to surrender. They said they would do so, but waited for the small boat that had been sent to bring them in to come alongside, when they suddenly arose, poured a volley into the crew of the small boat, and then, in the confusion that ensued, made their escape. There were twelve or fifteen crossing with him at the time, and all were armed with revolvers. Having gotten within the Confederate lines south of Fredericksburg, they were being pushed along by negroes on a hand-car when they met five or six forlorn, half-starved Union soldiers, who had made their escape from a rebel prison and were striking for freedom. At the suggestion of this wicked woman they shot them down, and passed on, leaving them lying on the ground.

He also related to the doctor the plot, at one time discussed, to capture the President and carry him to Richmond, but said it was found to be impracticable, and so was abandoned. He claimed that Booth and himself had spent ten thousand dollars in preparations for carrying out their plot. When we remember that neither Booth nor Surratt had any means of their own, and yet were carrying on an enterprise that called for so large an outlay of money, we may well ask who stood behind them and furnished the funds?

But if we take all of the testimony we have before us into consideration we need have no difficulty in answering this question. Jacob Thompson was the treasurer of the concern, and his government kept him amply supplied with means. It will be remembered that Clay said, "We have plenty of money to pay for anything that is worth paying for." After the assassination Surratt was in some way supplied with money to support him for a year, and carry him to Italy. In regard to the assassination, Surratt told McMillen that he received a letter from Booth at Montreal, in the beginning of the week of the assassination, which was written in New York, calling him to Washington at once, as it had become necessary to change their plans and to act quickly. He started at once, and telegraphed Booth at New York City from Elmira, but found that he had already gone to Washington. In regard to his escape from Washington after the assassination, he related all of the incidents that have already been given in regard to his experience at St. Albans, the loss of his handkerchief, his hasty departure from that place, etc., etc.

Every day during the voyage, he was filling McMillen's ears with these stories, and as they neared the end of the voyage he began to revolve in his mind whether he would land on the Irish coast or go on to Liverpool. He asked McMillen which he had better do, but McMillen, who must have known by this time who this McCarthy was, declined to give him any advice. Surratt finally said he would go on to Liverpool, but could not dismiss from his mind the fear that he might there meet a detective awaiting his arrival. Pulling out his revolver, he said, " If he did, this would settle him." Upon McMillen making the reply that " they would make short work of it with him in England if he should do such a thing as that," he said, "It is for that very reason I would do it, for I would rather be hung by an English than a Yankee hangman, and I know I would be hung should I be taken back to the United States." Upon sighting the coast of Ireland he exclaimed, " Here is a foreign country at last! I only wish that I may live two years to go back to the United States and serve Andy Johnson as we served Lincoln."

When the " Peruvian " was about to land her passengers and mail at an Irish port, Surratt sent for McMillen, and upon the latter expressing surprise at finding him dressed, and prepared to land, saying that " he thought he had concluded to go on with them to Liverpool," Surratt replied, "that he had thought the matter over carefully, and had concluded that it would be safer for him to land there, as it was then nearly midnight." McMillen then said to him, " You have been telling me a great many things, and I have come to the conclusion that the name by which you were introduced to me is not your true name. Will you be kind enough to tell me who you are?" The fugitive then whispered in his ear, " I am Surratt." He then asked the doctor to send for the barkeeper, and before leaving the ship drank so freely of brandy that the doctor found it necessary to request the chief officer at the gangway to take him by the arm and see him safely on shore. On the Wednesday following, Surratt called on the doctor at his boarding house in Birkenhead, opposite the city of Liverpool, and requested him to go over with him to the city to find a house to which he had been directed to go. The doctor had, on the previous day (which was the day after the " Peruvian " had landed in Liverpool), visited the Vice-Consul of the United States, Mr. Wildings, and made a sworn statement of the facts that Surratt had revealed to him, his purpose being to aid the United States in securing his arrest. He told the

Vice-Consul that he was only making a partial statement of Surratt's confessions during the voyage, deeming it only important that the government should be informed of Surratt's arrival in Liverpool. The doctor testified, on Surratt's trial, that Mr. Wilding told him that he had been informed by Mr. Adams, the American Minister at London, that the government was not going to prosecute Surratt; that it hadn't anything against him.

Of all this Surratt was ignorant, and the doctor went with him, as requested, across the river from Birkenhead to Liverpool, and finding a cab, gave the driver directions where to take him, and then parted from him. Surratt visited him again before the doctor started on the return voyage, and requested him to see a party in Montreal, and bring him some money. The doctor did as requested, but the person on whom he was requested to call said he had no money for him. The rebellion had collapsed; the plot had failed of its purpose, as it had also failed in part of its fulfillment; and now Surratt was to suffer the fate of Hyams — be shaken off and disowned. On the doctor's return to Liverpool Surratt called on him, but only to learn that there was no money for him. This was the last time that McMillen saw him until he saw him on his trial.

Surratt is next found in Italy, in the army of the Pope, where he had enlisted as a soldier in the ninth company of Zouaves about the middle of April, 1866. He had found friends after his escape from Washington, who had supported him, kept him secreted, watched over his safety, planned his trip from Montreal to Italy, and furnished him money for the expenses of his journey; friends who, no doubt, were accomplices before, as well as after, the fact, for we find them waiting and watching for his return to Montreal after the assassination, and ready to hurry him off into seclusion. He was to them a stranger; only known to them as a fugitive from his country, charged with the highest crime that a man could commit, — a blow at the nation's life, by murdering the nation's head, — a crime against liberty and humanity. These could not have been his friends for mere personal reasons, but from sympathy in the general purpose of this great crime, — the subversion of our free institutions.

Certainly he may now feel safe, being hid away under the *alias* of Watson, in the ranks of the Papal Zouaves, in the town of Velletri, in Italy, forty miles from Rome. But no! Here he meets Henry Benjamin St. Marie, an old acquaintance of his, and now a fellow-soldier in his company.

About the 18th or 19th of June, 1866, during an afternoon's walk, he, in his confidences with his old acquaintance, tells of the events of the 14th of April, 1865, and of the difficulty he had in making his escape from Washington on the morning of the 15th. He said he left disguised as an English traveler and succeeded in making his way out.

The American Consul was informed of his whereabouts, and upon the matter being brought to the notice of the Pope through Cardinal Antonelli, an order was issued for his arrest and delivery to the United States authorities. He was thus arrested by his comrades in the service, and kept under guard, but succeeded in making his escape from his guards (if we may believe the story), by making a bold dash down a precipice, at the risk of his life. Having thus escaped he made his way to Naples, and thence to Alexandria, in Egypt. What must have been his surprise on reaching the latter place to find an officer awaiting his arrival, and ready to make him a prisoner. He was put in chains, placed on board the United States man-of-war ship "Swatara," and brought back to Washington, where he was held to answer for his crime.

Part II.

REVIEW OF THE TRIAL OF JOHN H. SURRATT.

CHAPTER I.

INDICTMENT AND TRIAL.

ON the 4th day of February, 1867, the grand jury for the county of Washington, District of Columbia, found an indictment against John H. Surratt for the murder of Abraham Lincoln. The indictment contained four counts. The first count charged him with the murder of one Abraham Lincoln at the county of Washington, District of Columbia, on the 14th day of April, 1865. The second count charged that John H. Surratt and John Wilkes Booth did, on the 14th day of April, 1865, make an assault upon one Abraham Lincoln in the county and district aforesaid, and that John Wilkes Booth did murder the said Abraham Lincoln.

The third count charged that John H. Surratt and John Wilkes Booth, David E. Herold, George A. Atzerodt, Lewis Payne, Mary E. Surratt, and others to the jury unknown, did, on the 14th day of April, 1865, in the county and district aforesaid, make an assault upon one Abraham Lincoln, and that he was murdered by the hand of John Wilkes Booth.

The fourth count charged that John Wilkes Booth, John H. Surratt, David E. Herold, George A. Atzerodt, Lewis Payne, Mary E. Surratt, and divers other persons to the jury unknown, on the 14th day of April, 1865, at the county of Washington, District of Columbia, did unlawfully and wickedly combine, confederate, and conspire and agree together feloniously to kill and murder one Abraham Lincoln, and that the said John Wilkes Booth, John H. Surratt, David E. Herold, George A. Atzerodt, Lewis Payne, Mary E. Surratt, and other persons to the jurors unknown, did, on the 14th day of April, 1865, in pursuance of said unlawful conspiracy, make an assault, and that the said John

Wilkes Booth, in pursuance of said unlawful and wicked conspiracy, did kill and murder one Abraham Lincoln.

It will be noticed that the legal allegations designating the crime used in this indictment are the same as are used in the charge and specfications on which Surratt's co-conspirators were arraigned and tried before the Commission, except that the word "traitorously," there used, is omitted in this indictment. This indictment in its first count charged the prisoner on trial with the murder of Abraham Lincoln. This was done on the principle that when two or more persons conspire together to do an unlawful act, or to do that which is lawful by unlawful means, the act of any one of the parties thus conspiring, in pursuance of said conspiracy becomes the act of all. They are held equally guilty in law. To make this count good, it was only necessary to prove the existence of a conspiracy to do this murder—that it was done by one of the conspirators, and that the person indicted was a member of said conspiracy at the time the murder was committed, and that he aided and abetted and performed his part, whatever that might be, in accomplishing the object of the conspiracy. The second count charges that Surratt and Booth murdered Abraham Lincoln, and that the murder was actually accomplished by the hand of Booth. This implies that they acted together for the accomplishment of the crime and would be made good only by proving the presence of John H. Surratt at the time and place of its commisson, and that he was there aiding and abetting Booth in the alleged murder. The third count simply enlarges the conspiracy by designating others known to have been included in its membership, alleging also, that there were still others belonging to it, who were unknown to the jury, and that in pursuance of its object and purpose the murder was done by the hand of one of its members.

The fourth count more distinctly and emphatically alleges the combining, confederating, conspiring, and agreeing together of these persons to do this murder, and that it was so done by one of its members, viz., Booth. This would require proof to be made of such combination and agreeing together to commit this crime on the part of the persons named in the indictment; that the crime was perpetrated, and that the prisoner was a member of said conspiracy at the time of its perpetration. It will be remarked that in addition to the word "traitorously," used in the charge and specifications against the members of this conspiracy who were tried before the Commission, the political purpose of the conspiracy, as there alleged, is here omitted.

The real purpose of the conspiracy was to aid the existing rebellion in its purpose and effort to overthrow the government by assassinating the President, Vice-President, Secretary of State, and the general in command of the armies of the United States.

The parties tried before a military commission were tried under the laws of war, during a state of war, and were brought under the jurisdiction of a military tribunal because they were *secret active* enemies of the government, and were engaged in an effort to aid the rebellion. This required that the word traitorously should be used, and that the treasonable purpose of the conspiracy should be alleged. This member of the conspiracy was indicted for his participation in this crime; but he had made good his escape, and had not been brought within the jurisdiction of the authorities that could hold him to account until long after the rebellion had been suppressed, and peace had been declared; and under the political policy which had been adopted by the government in dealing with the question of treason and traitors in connection with the war, he could only be indicted for his crime, as it was a violation of civil law. Hence these omissions in framing this indictment.

The case is unique in the history of American jurisprudence. A number of his co-conspirators had been tried before a military commission under an arraignment that fully set forth, not only the crime of murder and a conspiracy to murder, but also the fact that it involved much more than the mere killing of a man — a private individual — that it was a conspiracy to murder the President of the United States, a treasonable conspiracy to subvert the government. It was a blow aimed at the nation's life. He who murders the humblest citizen sets at naught God's image impressed on man at his creation, and so commits a crime not only against a fellow man and a crime against society, but a crime against God. When Noah became the new head and progenitor of the race after the flood, God, who had just destroyed the world of mankind because they had filled the world with violence and blood, gave this law: "Whoso sheddeth man's blood by man shall his blood be shed; *for in the image of God created he him.*" God is also the author of civil government, as we read in the thirteenth of Romans: "Let every soul be subject to the higher powers, for there is no power but of God. The powers that be are ordained of God." Here we learn that civil government is the ordinance of God; and so he who assassinates a ruler, not only sets at naught God's image in man, but despises his ordinance for the welfare, protection, and peace of society.

This treasonable aspect of his crime, although it could not, for the reasons stated, be embraced in his indictment, yet, as we shall see, was a matter of which the court and jury could take judicial cognizance.

Here we have a man on trial for participation in the murder of a President; yet, in his indictment, he is only charged with the murder of one Abraham Lincoln. His fellow conspirators had been convicted of murdering Abraham Lincoln, President of the United States, and Commander-in-Chief of the armies and navy of the United States, and of attempting to kill William H. Seward, Secretary of State of the United States, and lying in wait to kill Andrew Johnson, Vice-President of the United States, and Ulysses S. Grant, commander in the field of the armies of the United States, for the purpose of overthrowing the government of the United States in aid of the existing rebellion. Under this charge they had been condemned and some of them executed. This was the result of a military trial in time of war.

This trial had been denounced by every rebel sympathizer in the land. Great lawyers and statesmen had argued with vehemence that these assassins had been tried by an unconstitutional tribunal. The dead President had been denounced as a tyrant, and usurper of authority; one who had trampled under foot the Constitution he had sworn to protect and defend by proclaiming martial law, and suspending the writ of *habeas corpus*;

and even in prosecuting a war to compel rebellious States to submit to the lawful authority of the government, and now they would tie up the hands of the government by insisting that it could only try these traitorous assassins, constitutionally, before a civil court. The country stood divided on this contention, just as it did on the issues of the war, and partisan feeling ran as high in this discussion as it did on the right of secession or the right of the government to compel submission to its authority.

The sophistry of this reasoning, when applied to a time of war, was made apparent by the results of this trial of John H. Surratt before a civil court, in time of peace. No government could protect itself under such a construction of the Constitution, because no government could ever convict a traitorous assassin before a jury made up of its enemies as well as its friends.

This trial necessarily aroused the passions and prejudices engendered by the war that gave occasion for the crime of the prisoner, and could not be conducted on a strictly judicial and legal basis. It was just as impossible now, almost two years after the close of the war, as it would have been at the time of the trial by a military commission of Surratt's fellows in crime; and a conviction by a jury in a civil court was just as impossible now as it would have been then because a jury of partisans embracing those of both sides politically can never be expected to come to an agreement in a case that appeals to their partisan feelings. This case was unique then, because it was the first case of a man on trial before a civil court for the murder of the civil head of the nation, the President of the United States, and although since that time another has been tried, convicted, and executed, for the murder of a President, the case of Surratt is still unique in this, that his crime was overshadowed by a higher crime out of which it grew — the crime of treason — of being engaged in a treasonable conspiracy to overthrow his government, and yet the circumstances surrounding the case were such that this could not be alleged in the indictment, but were of such a nature that this phase of his crime could not be excluded from view.

On the day appointed for the trial of John H. Surratt a very large number of people asssembled, and all were deeply interested in his case. The court house was crowded, and it was remarked by a most intelligent observer that the appearance and spirit of the crowd wore more of the air of a political convention than that of men assembled to participate in, and witness, the solemn scene of a fellow-being on trial for his life.

The trial was before Judge Fisher of the Criminal Court of the county of Washington, and District of Columbia, a man of great legal ability, sterling patriotism, and high moral character. The trial was a very lengthy one, and was hotly contested at every point by counsel for and against the prisoner. He was defended by lawyers who had made an enviable local reputation for ability in their profession. The District Attorney and his assistant were aided in the prosecution by that pure patriot and eminent jurist, Judge Edwards Pierrepont, of New York, who had been retained for that purpose by Attorney General Stanbury and William H. Seward, Secretary of State, and also by A. G. Riddle, Esq.

A deep partisan spirit was manifested by the defense from the first opening of their mouths to the close of the case. Every effort was made to drive the presiding judge from his fearless duty, but without avail. He stood firm as the adamantine rock. He was not only well qualified by his knowledge of law for his high position, but was also impartial, honest, and brave in his decisions on the very numerous questions of law and evidence that were raised by counsel during the trial. His carriage during that most notable trial must command the admiration of both friend and foe; and his decisions will ever command the respect of courts and lawyers.

The 10th day of June, 1867, was the day that had been set for calling up this case. The United States was represented by the District Attorney, E. C. Carrington, Esq., his assistant, Nathaniel Wilson, Esq., and associate counsel, Messrs. Edwards Pierrepont and A. G. Riddle. The prisoner was represented by Messrs. Joseph H. Bradley, R. T. Merrick, and Joseph H. Bradley, Jr. At the earnest solicitation of the Secretary of State and the Attorney General, and upon their representation that the trial would not last more than a week, Judge Pierrepont had consented to assist in the prosecution. He had just taken his seat in the convention which had met at

Albany to make a new constitution for the state of New York and in which he had been appointed on the judiciary committee, and left his place there to take a part in this trial. He was a Democrat in politics, but loyal to the government in its struggle for the perpetuation of its life. He had filled a judicial position in his own State, was a man of great legal acumen, and was noted for his patriotism and purity of character.

At ten o'clock on the 10th day of June, 1867, the Court said: "Gentlemen, this is the day assigned for the trial of John H. Surratt, indicted for the murder of Abraham Lincoln, late President of the United States. Are you ready to proceed?" To this Mr. Bradley responded, "The prisoner is ready, Sir, *and has been from the first.*" In this answer we have sounded forth the key-note to the spirit and policy of the defense. That candor and honesty of purpose which always characterize a judicial frame of mind, would have found their sufficient expression in the first clause of this reply. The addition of the declaratory clause, "And has been from the first" was not mere surplusage, but had in it the distinct and manifest intent of boldly assuming in advance, and in the face of all the adverse facts, the entire innocence of the prisoner. The purpose was at this first moment of opportunity to present the prisoner to the jury and to the country as one who was only anxious for an opportunity to exculpate himself from all guilt. The reader, if he chance to be of an imaginative turn of mind, will be able when he reads this clause of the reply of the learned counsel to see the assumed air of assurance and self-importance, and to hear the arrogant and confident tone of voice with which it was uttered. But without thus giving license to our imagination, the addition of that clause to Mr. Bradley's reply, when contrasted with the efforts of the prisoner to escape and evade a trial, creates an impression of a sinister design that is calculated to throw a taint of suspicion over all which is to follow in the line of the defense. We shall have abundant occasion, as we proceed with the review of this trial, to show that the suspicion which has been thus created is fully justified.

John H. Surratt, as was shown by the evidence on the trial, was in Washington on the 14th day of April, 1865, performing his part in the great crime. He was there aiding and abetting Booth, and co-ordinating the agencies employed in the execution of the plot, in order that all of the assassinations embraced in it might be simultaneously accomplished. Acting first as a counsellor and then as monitor, passing rapidly up and down the street to keep himself in communication with the fiends who were to do the work; calling the time loud enough to be heard at some distance; then going up the street to ascertain whether his warning could be heard by Payne, and the last time with a face deadly pale and manifesting a degree of nervous excitement, inseparable from the commission of such a crime, he called the fatal hour, "Ten minutes past ten!" and vanished from sight. He has gone, but he has left an image imprinted on the mind and memory of Sergeant Dye that can never be effaced. He now becomes a fugitive in disguise, and hies away to Canada to join the hellish clan that first conceived and then led him into his crime. Here he was at once taken in charge by sympathising friends, who kept him hidden away for five months and then, under a disguise and an *alias*, sent him across the Atlantic, and finally to Italy.

Here he is found in the Pope's army, and being charged with his crime, which he has already confessed in words as well as by flight, is arrested, escapes from his guards, flies to Naples and thence to Egypt, is met and arrested at Alexandria, and brought back to the scene of his crime, and is now put upon his trial. When asked if he is ready, he replies through his counsel, "I am ready, and have been from the first." Why, then, did he leave the city of his home, his mother and sister and all of his youthful associations, in the early morning of the 15th of April, 1865? Why did he fly to Canada disguised as an English tourist? Why did he hide in Canada for almost half a year, and then, in disguise, and under an *alias*, flee to Europe? Why did he escape from his guards in Italy at the risk (?) of his life, and flee to Egypt? Why, if innocent, did he flee to the ends of the earth, and never cease his flight until his way was hedged before him and further flight was impossible? Was it because he was innocent and desired an opportunity to prove his innocence to the world? In the presence of all these facts, what a mistake it was to say, "And has been from the first."

In how much better taste it would have been to have simply replied, "The prisoner is ready, your honor."

The District Attorney replied as follows: "If your honor please, I am happy to be able to announce that the government is ready to proceed with the trial. Before we proceed, however, sir, to impannel a jury, we desire to submit a motion to the court, which motion we have reduced to writing. With the permission of the court I will now proceed to read it to your honor. It is as follows:—

IN THE SUPREME COURT OF THE DISTRICT OF COLUMBIA.

UNITED STATES AGAINST JOHN H. SURRATT.

Indictment, Murder.

"And now, at this day, to wit, on the 10th day of June, A.D. 1867, come the United States and the said John H. Surratt, by their respective attorneys; and the jurors of the jury impanelled and summoned also come; and hereupon the said United States, by their attorney, challenge the array of the said panel, because he saith that the said jurors comprising said panel were not drawn according to law, and that the names from which said jurors were drawn were not selected according to law, wherefore he prays judgment, and that the said panel may be quashed." This motion, if your honor please, is sustained by an affidavit which I hold in my hand, and which, with the permission of your honor, I will now proceed to read. We think after this affidavit shall have been read it will be found unnecessary to introduce any oral testimony."

The motion to quash this panel, it will be observed, rests on two allegations: first, that the names were not drawn according to law; and, second, that the names from which the jury had been drawn were not selected according to law. These allegations were fully sustained by the affidavit of Samuel E. Douglas, register of Washington City, which was presented and read by the District Attorney, and more fully afterwards, upon his oral examination. The law governing the question was found in an act of Congress of June 16th, 1862, entitled, "An act providing for the selection of jurors to serve in the several courts of the District of Columbia."

Under the provisions of this act the register of the city of Washington, the clerk of the city of Georgetown, and the clerk of the levy court of the county of Washington, District of Columbia, was each required to make out a list of names of persons deemed by him to be most suitable for the duty of jurors, having respect to the exemptions and qualifications specified in the act.

The law required that such lists should be made out annually on, or before, the first day of February. The register of the city of Washington was to make out a list of names from which four hundred should be selected: the clerk of the city of Georgetown was to make out a list of names from which eighty were to be selected; and the clerk of the levy court of the county of Washington was to make out a list from which forty were to be selected, and that such lists should be preserved, and any names that had not been drawn for service during the year might be transferred to the list made up for the subsequent year.

Having thus made out their respective lists, these officers were required to meet together and jointly select from their respective lists the number specified for each one. The names thus selected were then to be written on separate and similar pieces of paper, folded, or rolled up, so that the name could not be seen; and then deposited in a box provided for the purpose. The box was required to be thoroughly shaken and sealed, and was then by these three officers to be delivered into the custody of the clerk of the court of Washington County for safe keeping. These officers were required to meet at the City Hall, in Washington City, at least ten days before the commencement of each term of the circuit court or of the criminal court, and there the clerk of the circuit court was to publicly, and in their presence, break the seal of the box and proceed to draw out the number of names required; and if it was a grand jury court, the first twenty-three names drawn were to constitute the grand jury, and the next twenty-six names drawn were to constitute the petit jury for that term. The jury or juries required, having been drawn, the box was again to be sealed and delivered to the clerk of the circuit court.

The affidavit of Samuel E. Douglas, register of the city of Washington, was offered with the motion to sustain its allegations. This affidavit was supplemented by the oral examination of Mr. Douglas, under oath. The affidavit and oral examination developed the facts that no such lists had been made out and preserved as required; also that there had been no joint action of these three officers in the selection of names, but that each one had written his respective number of names and deposited them in the box, without exhibiting them to the other two. There had been no joint selection as the law required.

Still further, the fact was developed that these offices had not sealed the box as required, but had delivered it to the clerk of the circuit court to be sealed by him. It was further shown that the names had been drawn, not by the clerk of the circuit court, but by the clerk of the city of Georgetown.

It will be seen at a glance that the affidavit and oral examination of Mr. Douglass fully sustained the allegations of the motion of the District Attorney, and that the utter disregard of all the most essential requirements of the law could have easily been made to subserve a corrupt purpose. Without charging fraud in the case, we can easily see how the clerk of the city of Georgetown, who drew this jury, and who had no right to put his hand in the box, could have carried in his own hand names of his own selection for that special purpose, and from this store to have drawn a jury without taking a single name from the box.

The substance of the affidavit and oral examination of Mr. Douglass having been incorporated with the motion of the District Attorney, the defense made the following replication: —

UNITED STATES
    vs. } *In the Criminal Court of the District of Columbia, No. ———.*
JOHN H. SURRATT.

And thereupon, the defendant saith the said motion is bad in law and in substance. The facts stated do not constitute any ground in law for a challenge of the array.

BRADLEY & MERRICK, *for defense.*

Mr. Pierrepont. — We join in the demurrer.

The question now before the court was simply one of law and of fact, and whether the facts in the case, admitted by all, constituted such a violation of the law as justified and required the setting aside of the array. It would seem that it ought to have been easily settled, and the fact the motion was hotly contested by the defense through a discussion of three days continuance, would seem to indicate that for some reason they had a special desire to have their case tried by that particular jury. The argument was opened by Mr. Merrick for the defense. His argument was first addressed to the construction of the statute, and to the contention that the facts alleged and admitted did not constitute such a violation of the law as would justify the setting aside of the array. And then as there was no statute in regard to the quashing of the panel the question was argued on the principles of the common law, and many decisions were invoked, both in England and in this country, to show that the failure of the officers to comply with the law was not such as would vitiate what they did.

The question was ably discussed on both sides, and ingeniously on the part of the defense, which did not confine itself to the legal discussion of the question, but made it the occasion for manifesting its spirit and attitude toward the government by insinuations and innuendo. Thus, Mr. Merrick said, "I hope the United States is looking for the attainment of justice in this case; I trust nothing may be developed in this case looking towards anything else. I trust the government will tread the high and honorable path which leads to the attainment of simple and, I may add, speedy justice. And entertaining this hope, I suggest to your honor, whether it is probable a jury, against whose qualification nothing is alleged, who were summoned without regard to this case, and before it was anticipated it might be tried, are not better fitted to do justice then another summoned in anticipation of the case,— a case not of an ordinary private nature, but one of great public interest, in which, while the United States as a government, I trust, will tread in the highways I have spoken of, there are individuals occupying offices in the government who may be disposed to tread lower paths which we will have to follow.

"May it please your honor, I shall say no more upon this motion than to add that after the most careful examination I have been able to give to it, the honest conclusion to which I have come is, that the ground, probably, upon which the motion rests, is to be found in the act of 1853, page 160, 10 Statutes at Large, which act provides that where a criminal case is on trial in this court and a jury has been impanelled, and another term begins during the progress of the trial, the cause shall continue; but leaves it exceedingly questionable whether unless the jury is fully impanelled before the end of the term, the cause can be tried. That other term begins Monday next, and unless a jury in this case is impanelled before Saturday night it is questionable whether this case will be tried for many days or many years."

To this sly insinuation that the government felt that it had an elephant on its hands, and that the motion was a dilatory one thus made so early in the case to influence both the jury and public opinion, Judge Pierrepont replied as follows: "They will discover before we proceed much further, that the United States are as zealous, as earnest, and as eager to try this cause as the other side, and they will discover before it is through that the public mind will be set right with regard to a great many subjects about which there have been active, numerous, and unfounded reports. Since I have been here in this city for these past few days, it has been circulated in nearly all the journals of this country that the United States dared not bring forward the diary found upon the murderer of the President, because that diary would prove things they did not want to have known. All these things will be proved to be false, and all the papers, about the suppression of which so much has been said, will be exhibited here on the trial of this case. We are anxious that it should be proceeded with at once. It has likewise been circulated through all the public journals that after the former convictions, when an effort was made to go to the President for pardon, men active here at the seat of government prevented any attempt being made, or the President even being reached for the purpose of seeing whether he would not exercise clemency; whereas, the truth, and the truth of record, which will be presented in this court, is that all this matter was brought before the President and presented to a full cabinet meeting, where it was thoroughly discussed; and after such discussion, condemnation, and execution, received not only the sanction of the President, but that of every member of his cabinet. This, and a thousand other of these false stories, will be all set at rest forever in the progress of this trial; and the gentlemen may feel assured that not only are we ready but that we are desirous of proceeding at once with the case." The insinuation of Mr. Merrick, having been thus bravely and fully met, the defense felt it necessary to shift its ground, and so Mr. Bradley, in the course of his argument, found another reason for the motion of the prosecution to quash the panel, which he artfully put forth in the form of an insinuation as follows: " I think I can see where this thing is drifting. It is not delay that is sought, but they have another motive more powerful than delay. It is to get another jury in the place of this honest jury already summoned. Why, sir, the gentleman talks about the misgivings in the public prints. I do not know that he has seen what I hold in my hand, — an article from this place denouncing this jury because sixteen of them are Catholics, as they say, but there it is — such an article has been written and published in the New York *Herald*. I know, too, that the same article, published yesterday morning, foreshadows the fact that these gentlemen were to come into court on the day they did, and make the identical motion that they have submitted here."

Mr. Merrick. "And states the ground of the motion?"

Mr. Bradley. "Yes Sir, states the ground of the motion. It looks to me as though it came from very near home."

Mr. Pierrepont. "What does it state as the ground of the motion?"

Mr. Bradley. "There it is, just the same ground precisely as was stated here that it was not a lawful panel."

Mr. Pierrepont. "Oh !" (laughingly.)

Thus we get a glimpse at the outside pressure that was brought to bear on this trial by a constant fusilade of falsehoods couched in cunningly-devised paragraphs that they might gain a general circulation through the press of the country for the purpose not only of influencing the jury in this case, but also of misleading and perverting public opinion.

The fact brought out in this paragraph is somewhat remarkable. It might have been a mere chance that sixteen out of the twenty-six drawn for the jury happened to be Catholics, but we cannot help feeling a suspicion that had the law been a little more closely followed it might have been otherwise.

To the insinuation of Mr. Bradley, the District Attorney replied as follows: "I do not rise for the purpose of arguing the motion before the court, but with the permission of your honor, and my learned friend, simply to say a word or two in regard to a certain statement in one of the newspapers of the day to which my attention has just been called. It is an item in the New York *Herald*, purporting to be telegraphed from this city.

The article is not very complimentary to myself, but as my friend is spoken of in very high terms, I am not disposed to quarrel with the writer, for, as a generous-hearted man, I am more anxious for the reputation of my friend than I am for my own. What is intimated in it, I would not think of sufficient importance to be called to the attention of the court, were it not that allusion has been made to it here by the learned counsel who last addressed your honor.

He stated that there was some reason not made known for this motion which we have submitted. I deem it due to myself to say —

Mr. Bradley. "I beg your pardon if I have said anything wrong. I thought it was a fair retort on what was said by Judge Pierrepont."

The District Attorney. "Notwithstanding the disclaimer of the gentleman to impute any wrong motive to us in submitting the motion now before your honor, I think, inasmuch as public reference has been made to it here, it is due to my position before the country to say a word. I will here say, then, that there is no one who would more earnestly and sincerely deprecate any appeal to religious prejudices than myself. Politicians may speak, think, and act as they please, but for my part I would drive from the halls of justice the demon of party spirit and religious fanaticism. I trust in God the day will never come when a judge, or a jury, will be influenced in the discharge of the most solemn duty that can possibly be devolved upon human beings by political or religious considerations."

At the assembling of the court on the morning of the 13th, Judge Fisher delivered an exhaustive opinion on the motion before him. As it is somewhat lengthy I shall only give its concluding paragraph. "Believing, therefore, that the substantial requirements of the act of Congress in this case providing for the selection of a fair and impartial jury, have not been complied with, but entirely set at naught, and that there has been grave default on the part of the officers whom that act has substituted in the place of the marshal, for the purpose of having them exercise a united judgment in the selection of all the persons whose names are to go in the jury box, I am constrained to allow the motion of challenge in this case. I do not consider the fact that the present panel were improperly drawn by the clerk of Georgetown, who had no right to put his hand into the box, because the objection which I have allowed lies even deeper than that. It is, therefore, ordered by the Court that the present panel be set aside, and that the Marshal of the District of Columbia do now proceed to summon a jury of talesmen."

Judge Fisher subsequently said: "My order is that the Marshal summon twenty-six talesmen." The process of securing a jury from talesmen occupied the next four days, and about two hundred talesmen were summoned before a panel could be secured.

Many of those summoned by the marshal were excused on showing sufficient grounds; a very large number were found disqualified on their *voire dire;* and perhaps all of the challenges, or nearly so, to which the parties were entitled, were exhausted, and it was not until the evening session of the 16th of June, that the jury was impaneled to try the case.

When a panel of twenty-six jurors had been secured, counsel for the prisoner, through Mr. Merrick, said: "If your honor please, we are now ready to proceed to empanel the jury. Before doing so, however, we think it our duty, in behalf of the prisoner, to file our challenge to the present array. Your honor has virtually decided the question, and we do not desire to take up any time in its argument. We simply wish that it may be filed so that it can be passed upon."

The challenge in word and form is as follows: —

IN THE SUPREME COURT OF THE DISTRICT OF COLUMBIA.

The United States vs. John H. Surratt.

In the Criminal Court, March Term, 1867.

And the said Marshal of the District of Columbia, in obedience to the order of the Court, made in this case on the 12th of June instant, this day makes return that he hath summoned, and now hath in court here twenty-six jurors, talesman, as a panel from which to form a jury to try the said cause, and the names of the twenty-six jurors so returned being called by the clerk of said court, and they having answered to their names as they were called, the said John H. Surratt, by his attorneys, doth challenge the array of the said panel, because he saith it doth plainly appear by the records and proceedings of the Court in this cause that no jurors have ever been summoned according to law to serve during the present term of this Court, and no names of jurors, duly and lawfully summoned, have been placed in the box provided for in the fourth section of the act of Congress, entitled, "An Act providing for the Selection of Jurors to serve in the Several Courts of the District," approved 16th of June, 1862, on or before the 1st day of February, 1867, to serve for the ensuing year, wherefore he prays judgment that the panel now returned by the said Marshal, and now in court here, be quashed.

Merrick, Bradley & Bradley,
Attorneys for Surratt.

This motion was made as a foundation for carrying the case up on a writ of error in the event of the conviction of the prisoner.

On Monday, the 18th of June, the case was opened by Mr. Nathaniel Wilson, Assistant District Attorney, as follows: " May it please your honor and gentlemen of the jury, you are doubtless aware that it is customary in criminal cases for the prosecution at the beginning of a trial to inform the jury of the nature of the offense to be inquired into, and of the proof that will be offered in support of the charges of the indictment. By making such a statement I hope to aid you in clearly ascertaining the work that is before us, and in apprehending the relevancy and significance of the testimony that will be produced as the case proceeds.

" The grand jury of the District of Columbia have indicted the prisoner at the bar, John H. Surratt, as one of the murderers of Abraham Lincoln. It has become your duty to judge whether he be guilty or innocent of that charge, — a duty than which one more solemn or momentous never was committed to human intelligence. You are to turn back the leaves of history to that red page on which is recorded in letters of blood the awful incidents of that April night on which the assassin's work was done on the body of the Chief Magistrate of the American republic,— a night on which for the first time in our existence as a nation, a blow was struck with the fell purpose not only of destroying human life, but the life of the nation, the life of liberty itself. Though more than two years have passed by since then, you scarcely need witnesses to describe to you the scene in Ford's Theatre as it was visible in the last hour of the President's conscious life. It has been present to your thoughts a thousand times since then. A vast audience were assembled, whose hearts were throbbing with a new joy, born of victory and peace, and above them the object of their gratitude and reverence,— he who had borne the nation's burdens through many and disastrous years,— sat tranquil and at rest at last, a victor indeed, but a victor in whose generous heart triumph awakened no emotions save those of kindliness, of forgiveness, and of charity. To him, in that hour of supreme tranquility, to him in the charmed circle of friendship and affection, there came the form of sudden and terrible death.

"Persons who were then present will tell you that at about twenty minutes past ten o'clock that night, the night of the 14th of April, 1865, John Wilkes Booth, armed with pistol and knife, passed rapidly from the front door of the theatre, ascended to the dress circle, and entered the President's box. By the discharge of a pistol he inflicted a death wound, then leaped upon the stage, and passing rapidly across it, disappeared into the darkness of the night.

"We shall prove to your entire satisfaction, by competent and credible witnesses, that at that time the prisoner at the bar was then present, aiding and abetting that murder; and that at ten minutes past ten o'clock that night he was in front of that theatre in company with Booth. You shall hear what he then said and did. You shall know that his cool and calculating malice was the director of the bullet that pierced the brain of the President and the knife that fell upon the venerable Secretary of State. You shall know that the prisoner at the bar was the contriver of that villainy, and that from the presence of the prisoner, Booth, drunk with theatric passion and traitorous hate, rushed directly to the execution of their mutual will. We shall further prove to you that their companionship upon that occasion was not an accidental or unexpected one, but that the butchery that ensued was the ripe result of a long premeditated plot, in which the prisoner was the chief conspirator. It will be proved to you that he is a traitor to the government that protected him; a spy in the employ of the enemies of his country in the years 1864 and 1865; passed repeatedly from Richmond to Washington, from Washington to Canada, weaving the web of his nefarious scheme, plotting the overthrow of this government, the defeat of its armies, and the slaughter of his countrymen; and as showing the venom of his intent, — as showing a mind insensible to every moral obligation and fatally bent on mischief, — we shall prove his gleeful boasts that during these journeys he had shot down in cold blood, weak and unarmed Union soldiers, fleeing from rebel prisons. It will be proved to you that he made his home in this city the rendezvous for the tools and agents in what he called his "bloody work," and that his hand deposited at Surrattsville, in a convenient place, the very weapons obtained by Booth while escaping, one of which fell or was wrenched from Booth's death grip, at the moment of his capture.

"While in Montreal, Canada, where he had gone from Richmond, on the 10th of April, on the Monday before the assassination, Surratt received a summons from his co-conspirator, Booth, requiring his immediate presence in this city. In obedience to that preconcerted signal, he at once left Canada, and arrived here on the 14th. By numerous, I had almost said a multitude, of witnesses, we shall make the proof to be as clear as the noonday sun, and as convincing as the axioms of truth, that he was here during the day of that fatal Friday, as well as present at the theatre at night, as I have before stated. We shall show him to you on Pennsylvania Avenue, booted and spurred, awaiting the arrival of the fatal moment.

"We shall show him in conference with Herold in the evening; we shall show him purchasing a contrivance for disguise an hour or two before the murder.

"When the last blow had been struck, when he had done his utmost to bring anarchy and desolation upon his native land, he turned his back upon the abomination he had wrought, he turned his back upon his home and kindred, and commenced his shuddering flight.

"We shall trace that flight, because in law flight is the criminal's inarticulate confession, and because it happened in this case as it always happens, and always must happen, that in some moment of fear or of elation, or of fancied security, he, too, to others, confessed his guilty deeds. He fled to Canada. We will prove to you the hour of his arrival there and the route he took. He there found safe concealment, and remained there several months, voluntarily absenting himself from his mother. In the following September he took his flight. Still in disguise, with painted face, and painted hair, and painted hand, he took ship to cross the Atlantic. In mid-ocean he revealed himself and related his exploits, and spoke freely of his connection with Booth in the conspiracy relating to the President. He rejoiced in the death of the President, he lifted his impious hand to heaven and expressed the wish that he might live to return to America and serve Andrew Johnson as Abraham Lincoln had been served. He was hidden for a time in England, and found there [sympathy and hospitality; but soon was made again an outcast and a wanderer by his guilty secret. From England he went to Rome, and hid himself in the ranks of the Papal army in the guise of a private soldier. Having placed almost the diameter of the globe between himself and the dead body of his victim, he might well fancy that pursuit was baffled, but by the happening of one of those events which we sometimes call accidents, but which are indeed the mysterious means by which Omnicient and Omnipotent justice reveals and punishes the doers of evil, he was discovered by an acquaintance of his boyhood. When denial would not avail he admitted his identity, and avowed his guilt in these memorable words: 'I have done the Yankees as much harm as I could. We have killed Lincoln, the nigger's friend.'

"The man to whom Surratt made this statement, did as it was his high duty to do — he made known his discovery to the American minister. There is no treaty of extradition with the Papal States; but so heinous is the crime with which Surratt is charged, such bad notoriety had his name obtained, that his Holiness the Pope and Cardinal Antonelli ordered his arrest without waiting for a formal demand from the American government. Having him arrested, he escaped from his guards by a leap down a precipice — a leap impossible to any but one to whom conscience made life valueless. He made his way to Naples, and then took passage in a steamer that carried him across the Mediterranean Sea to Alexandria, in Egypt. He was pursued, not by the 'blood hounds of the law,' that seem to haunt the imagination of the prisoner's counsel [this refers to a remark made by Mr. Merrick when discussing the motion to quash the panel], but by the very elements, by destruction itself, made a slave in the service of justice. The inexorable lightning thrilled along the wires that stretch through the waste of waters that roll between the shores of Italy and the shores of Egypt, and spake in his ear its word of terrible command; and from Alexandria, aghast and manacled, he was made to turn his face towards the land he had polluted by the curse of murder. He is here at last to be tried for his crime.

And when the facts which I have stated have been proved, as proved they assuredly will be, if anything is ever proved by hnman testimony, and when all the subterfuges of the defense have been disproved, as disproved they assuredly will be, we, having done our duty in furnishing you with that proof of the prisoner's guilt, in the name of the civilization he has dishonored, in the name of the country he has betrayed and disgraced, in the name of the law he has violated and defied, shall demand of you that retribution, though tardily, shall yet surely be done, upon the shedder of innocent and precious blood."

Before the hearing of evidence was entered upon, the prisoner presented the following petition to the Court: —

"*To the Honorable, the Justices of the Supreme Court of the District of Columbia, holding the Criminal Court in March Term, 1867.*

"The petition of John H. Surratt shows that he has been put upon his trial in a capital case in this court; that he has exhausted all his means, and such further means as have been furnished him by the liberality of his friends, in preparing for his defense, and he is now unable to procure the attendance of his witnesses. He therefore prays your honor for an order that process may issue to summon his witnesses, and to compel their attendance at the cost of the government of the United States, according to the statute in such cases made and provided."

This petition was signed, sworn to in open court, and attested by the clerk according to law, and was granted by the court.

The government introduced eighty-five witnesses in chief to sustain the various counts in the indictment, and ninety-six in rebuttal. The defense introduced ninety-eight witnesses to overthrow the testimony of the witnesses in chief on the part of the government, and twenty-three in surrebuttal, making in all three hundred and two witnesses that were examined during the trial. The examination of these witnesses occupied the period of thirty-nine days. The hearing of the evidence commenced on the 17th of June, and was concluded on the 26th of July. The arguments in the case were concluded on the 7th of August, and on that day Judge Fisher delivered his charge to the jury and gave them the case. On Saturday, the 10th day of August, just two months from the commencement of the trial, the jury reported that they stood about equally divided in favor of conviction and acquittal, and that there was no prospect of their being able to agree.

The Court inquired whether anything was to be said why the jury should not now be discharged. Mr. Bradley said: "The prisoner gave no consent to any discharge of the jury. If they were to be discharged he wants it understood that it was against his will and protest."

The District Attorney, on behalf of the government, left the whole matter with the Court.

The Court remarked that this was the third communication of a similar tenor he had received from the jury. If he thought there was any possibility of their coming to an agreement as to the guilt or innocence of the prisoner, he would have no objections to keeping them out longer, but supposing from the statement made by them, no such result could be expected, he directed the jury now to be discharged. The prisoner was then remanded to the custody of the Marshal.

A second indictment was found against him for the murder of Abraham Lincoln, and the District Attorney entered a *nolle prosequi* on this. Thus the prisoner was set at large.

The result of this trial by a civil court made it clear that no verdict could be expected from any jury that could be obtained under the law, and so the case was not further prosecuted. It does not come within the scope of the author's plan to review in detail this great mass of evidence. Neither is it necessary. It is sufficient for him to say that the charges contained in the indictment were fully proven by the testimony in chief of the witnesses for the government, and that this testimony was not impaired in any essential point by the efforts of the counsel for the defense in their cross-examination of these witnesses, nor yet by the testimony offered by the defense. It will be found upon a careful and candid scrutiny to fully sustain the statements hereinbefore given as to the conduct of Surratt in his relations to the transaction. No one can carefully read the masterly summing up of the evidence, and the fair and honest interpretation of it by Judge Pierrepont in his concluding argument, without being thoroughly convinced that Surratt was a prominent and active member of the conspiracy, and that he took an active hand through a period of more than three months in preparing for the execution of its purposes, as also in its final accomplishment. The evidence was shown to prove conclusively the fact that from the time of his introduction to Booth, on the 23d of December, 1864, to the time of the assassination, their associations were of the most intimate and confidential character; that they were much together, and co-operated in bringing together in Washington City the other members of the conspiracy, on whom they relied for important parts in the final act. It was shown that the house of Mrs. Surratt, the mother of the prisoner, was the place of rendezvous for Booth, Atzerodt, and Payne, and that her house at Surrattsville, occupied by her tenant, Lloyd, was made the place of deposit for arms to be used by Booth and Herold in their flight after the murder; that these were placed there by Surratt, and that his mother also had knowledge, not only of this fact, but of the purpose for which they had been provided, and of the time they would be called for, and was used by the conspirators to convey to her tenant, Lloyd, the notification to have them ready, as they would be called for that night.[1]

[1] As Judge Pierrepont is now dead, I deem it best to cut out a certain statement, which I had from him, with his consent to publish it.—AUTHOR.

It was here, on this civil trial, that " the scales of justice fell," and not, as alleged by the prisoner's counsel, at the trial before the Military Commission.

The District Attorney and his able assistant, Judge Pierrepont, had both expressed their confidence in the ability of the civil courts to compass the ends of justice; but the result of this trial showed that in a crime committed to further political party interests, no jury could be expected to find a verdict; and so the government refused to prosecute the case any further. The prisoner was set at large.

At the conclusion of the trial, on Aug. 10th, 1867, Surratt was remanded to prison, and on May 12th, 1868, he asked to be released on bail, but was refused. On June 22d, 1868, he was released from custody. On the 22d of September, 1868, a *nolle prosequi* was entered.

Another indictment was found against him for engaging in rebellion. Upon this he was ordered to be admitted to bail in a bond of $20,000. He first pleaded not guilty, and then asked to withdraw this plea, and to file a special plea, which was granted. The government demurred to the plea on Sept. 22d, 1869. The demurrer was overruled, and he was finally discharged.

CHAPTER II.

A CRITICISM OF THE DEFENSE.

It now remains for the writer to review the course of the defense in this trial, and to point out its policy, its spirit, its perversion of facts, and disregard of evidence in carrying out its purpose to appeal, first, to the prejudice of the jury, and then to pervert public opinion.

The prisoner was defended by counsel of known and acknowledged ability — men of reputation for their knowledge of law, and ability as advocates at the bar. But despite all this, their defense of Surratt was as unique in its character as was the case itself. Made by men learned in the law, it ignored the requirements of law, and so was managed by them more in the light of its political relations, than that of its legal requirements. In proof of this assertion I shall quote freely from the arguments of counsel, and I think I shall be able to show that I am fully justified in expressing this opinion. I shall first refer to the remarkable number of exceptions taken by the counsel for the defense to the rulings of the Court on questions of evidence, and the use made of them. I will quote first from the argument of Mr. Merrick.

"In a prosecution such as this, conducted against one of its citizens by a government, what should be the course of that government, and what is due to the jury and to the prisoner? Whatever there is that can throw light upon the alleged crime should be let into the jury box. All evidence that could go before the human mind calculated to impress it with conviction, or modify its opinions, should be allowed to come before you. What has been the case with regard to this trial? Wherever any technical rule of law could by any constraint whatever exclude a piece of testimony calculated to enlighten your judgment, it has been invoked to exclude that testimony; has been bent from its uniform application and its generally understood principle for that purpose. I shall find no fault with his honor on the bench in his rulings, for this is not my place to express an opinion about a decision of the Court.

A member of the bar should be loyal to the tribunal before which he practices, to the full extent of gentlemanly and professional courtesy, and in the court-room bow with pleasant acquiescence in whatever the judge may say. With that acquiescence I bow, and yet there is nothing — and I must say this, and say it in justice to myself — there is nothing that has fallen from his honor in the adjudiciation upon these questions of testimony that has changed my opinion that the testimony should be allowed to go to the jury. *One hundred and fifty exceptions taken by the defendant's counsel encumber this record.* It is certainly strange that there should have been so wide a difference, and I regret it. Without complaining, as I said, of the decisions of the Court, it can only be accounted for from the fact that the attorneys representing the government in this case have strained every principle of law, and invoked in their behalf every discretionary power of the court, as against the prisoner."

Notwithstanding his semblance of disclaimer, Mr. Merrick here makes an appeal to the jury, on the implied charge of partiality on the part of this Court. In giving his charge to the jury Judge Fisher very properly takes notice of this charge, and effectually rebukes the arrogance of the counsel in the following language: "Much stress has been laid by the counsel for the defense upon the fact, which they assert, that during the progress of this trial more than one hundred and fifty exceptions have been taken to the rulings of the court concerning the admissibility of evidence. If they have found themselves under the necessity of calculating the number of these exceptions, and parading them before you, with a view of having you render a verdict according to irrelevant evidence not before you, rather than according to the legal evidence which you have heard, I have no disposition to criticise their taste, but leave them to present their case in their own way. At the same time I feel it my duty to remark to you that if counsel will be so bold as to present propositions to the Court which every tyro in the profession ought to know are untenable, it does not necessarily follow that the judge must always be so weak as to sustain them. It has heretofore been supposed that exceptions to the rulings of a judge at *nisi prius* were intended to be passed in review before the appellate tribunal. I have never before known them to be neatly calculated and presented to the jury by way of argument."

A jury is sworn to decide according to the law and evidence in the case. But how are jurors to decide according to the law, not being acquainted with law? It is manifest they cannot take their instructions on the law from the counsel employed in the case, as they will naturally differ widely in their constructions of law. It is made, therefore, the duty of the court, an impartial tribunal, skilled in law, to instruct the jury on all the points of law involved in the case. In this remarkable case the counsel for the defense, feeling that the court could not sustain the interpretations of the law on several important points which they had endeavored to impress on the jury in their arguments, took the remarkable position that the jury was to be its own judge of questions of law. Mr. Merrick, in the course of his argument, took this position, and argued it at some length, as follows: " The jury is specially charged, it is true, with the fact; but they are also charged with the law. You are to instruct them by your learning, your wisdom, and by your authority. You are to advise them; but they must know and they must believe. My learned brother on the other side (Mr. Carrington) seemed to feel that it was necessary to press you, gentlemen, very hard upon your obligation to follow the instructions of the Court. I have never heard him say that before. Other cases have been tried before this, but I have never heard him talk so earnestly to the jury about being obliged to follow the instructions of the Court. Why is he so solicitous in this case? Does he think you won't dare to do right? He told you, gentlemen of the jury, that you were sworn to try this case according to the law and the fact, and that you must take the law from the court; and if you departed from the law so given you, you would be perjured. I tell you it is no such thing. If you find a verdict of guilty, and do not believe the party to be guilty in every particular, in your judgment and in your hearts, then you are perjured men, I care not what the Court's instruction is.

"Has my learned friend read the oath? I don't think he has. Mr. Clerk, will you be kind enough to read it." (The clerk then read the oath.)

Mr. Merrick resuming, said: "Where is the law? Why did you tell the jury what you did? The language is, 'And a true verdict give according to the evidence.' My learned brother has had that oath ringing in his ears for six years. Why didn't he tell you what it was? You are, gentlemen, to find a verdict according to the evidence. What sort of verdict are you to find? Guilty, or not guilty. That is all you can say. You cannot say 'Guilty,' under the Court's instruction, or 'Not guilty,' under the Court's instruction. If you say 'Guilty,' you say 'Guilty as indicted,' upon your conscience resting the weight of the guilt. If your verdict should be 'Guilty,' it will be followed by blood, for you see there is no mercy anywhere in those that represent the government. If your verdict is guilty, then, indeed, you look upon a dying man. Upon your consciences will rest the responsibility of that verdict.

"And let me say to you, gentlemen of the jury, that on that awful day when you shall stand before the last tribunal to be judged, and the All-Seeing Eye shall look into your hearts and ask you why you found this verdict of guilty, think you He will harken if you say, 'The judge's instructions made me do it.' He will say to you, 'Were you not free agents, with minds and intellects, sworn as a jury in a free country? Were you not told by the counsel for the prisoner at the bar that it was your duty to find this verdict according to your judgments, your consciences, and didn't you disregard him?'

"If Judge Fisher's instructions made you find it, bring Judge Fisher. Where is the Judge? Think you he will step forward and say, 'I will take the burden.' No, gentlemen. Let me say to you now, that by the laws of the land, and by the laws of God, the responsibility is on the judge to instruct you rightly, to guide you correctly, to give you wise and judicious counsel, not as mandatory and binding on your conscience, but as advisory to your judgment, to enlighten the pathway you are to tread in your investigations. We shall ask no instructions, and desire none. The law of murder is too plain to need any, and you, gentlemen, are too intelligent not to understand it. Indeed, if we desire some explanation, *we would prefer to give it to you in the way of argument, rather than trust it to the distinguished judge who presides.* We would trust it to argument, because, with regard to these plain questions, all men can comprehend what the law is. *We would prefer trusting it to the weight of our own character with the jury as men and lawyers.*" After this ingenious appeal to the jury, the learned advocate then proceeded to recount and expound the propositions of law on which the District Attorney had invoked the instructions of the Court.

Judge Fisher in charging the jury made the following reference to this remarkable argument by Mr. Merrick: "You have been told, gentlemen, by the counsel for the defense, in a manner not very respectful, certainly by no means complimentary to the Court, that you are the judges of the law as well as the facts in criminal cases, and that you have the right to disregard the instructions of the Court in matters of law; and they tell you that their expositions of the law, and the weight of character they possess, may be more safely relied upon than the instructions which may be given you by the Court. The weight of character of a prisoner's counsel would be a variable, and not unfrequently a very unsafe criterion by which the jury should judge as to the law of his case. Perhaps they would have you regard the court as sitting on the bench merely to discharge the duty of preserving order and decorum in the court room, which probably the crier of the court or baliff might be disposed to regard as an usurpation of his prerogative. If the jury are entirely to disregard the judge's instructions as to the law of a case, I confess I can see but little left than that for him to perform.

"It is true, gentlemen, that you have the power, and in cases where your consciences are satisfied that the instructions of the Court are dictated, not by an honest desire to enlighten the jury as to the true state of the law, but by corrupt and wicked motives, you have the right to disregard the instructions purposely intended to mislead you. But to claim that the jury are better judges of what the law may be than the Court, is about as reasonable as to assert that a plain farmer or merchant may be taken fresh from his plough or his counter, and be more capable of navigating and manœuvering a steam frigate, or to lead your armies to certain victories, than your admiral or commander-in-chief. In my opinion, you have just the same right to disregard the evidence of the witnesses who stood before you unimpeached in any matter respecting the facts involved in the cause, as you have to disregard what the Court may say to you, under an official oath, as to the law that may apply to the facts. A jury have the *power*, if they choose to exercise it, after having assumed the obligations of an oath, to say that they will neither believe the judge nor the witnesses, but decide upon the law and facts according to their own caprice, or the confidence which they may repose in the character of counsel on either side, but such is not the purpose for which juries were instituted, and they have no right so to act. When the witnesses in the cause have testified before you as to the facts, it is then the office of the judge, under his official oath, to testify to you in the spirit of truth, according to the best of his knowledge and ability, as to what is the law which may be applicable to those facts; and an honest jury will disregard neither the testimony of the witnesses nor the instructions of the judge, unless they are satisfied that corrupt motives have actuated them. They will leave the party where the law leaves him, to his legitimate redress, — a writ of error to the appellate court."

Referring to the course of counsel in this illegitimate appeal to the jury in their argument on this point, and to their appeal, based on the number of their exceptions to the rulings of the Court, the judge made this further remark in vindicating the position and dignity of the Court: "In reference to these matters I may observe that, perhaps, I owed it to the dignity of the bench to have interrupted counsel in the conduct of the case in this particular, but in a cause involving the life of the prisoner upon the one hand and the vindication of the outraged justice of a nation in mourning upon the other, I deemed it my duty to cast not an atom in the one scale or in the other which might by any possibility tend to prejudice either side of the issue."

CHAPTER III.

TREATMENT OF WITNESSES AND EVIDENCE BY THE COUNSEL FOR THE DEFENSE AND THEIR ANIMUS TOWARD THE GOVERNMENT AND APPEALS TO THE POLITICAL PREJUDICES OF JURORS.

THE conduct of this trial on the part of the defense toward the witnesses for the prosecution was most remarkable. The law prescribes the methods by which testimony is to be discredited, and the eminent lawyers who defended the prisoner were of course well acquainted with the legal methods of impeaching testimony. That they did not confine themselves to these was not only unprofessional, but was calculated to create a suspicion that they had an intuitive perception of the fact that the methods known to the law would not avail them in this case. Hence from the first they attempted to influence the jury by treating the government witnesses with supercillious contempt, and even scorn.

They did not, however, stop here, but whenever they could find or make an occasion they would throw out insinuations against the witnesses *en masse* by side remarks intended for the ears of the jury.

They spoke of the witnesses who were kept together in a room, to be called as they were needed, as being in the "penitentiary," and added to this that "they would soon be in another penitentiary."

On the examination of Dr. McMillen, the surgeon of the ocean steamer "Peruvian," in whose charge Father La Pierre had placed Surratt under the name of McCarthy, and to whom Surratt had made confessions during his voyage across the Atlantic that were conclusive of his guilt, the counsel for Surratt made themselves so offensive that the witness was provoked to a retort in self-defense.

This witness was intolerable to them because of the directness and force of his testimony. In self-defense the Doctor was provoked into making the following remark: He said he would tell the counsel (Mr Merrick), and if he was not deaf, he could hear, and repeated his answer, adding that Mr. Merrick had insulted witness the other day, and that it was the act of a coward and a sneak. The Court here cautioned the witness that such language was not becoming, but also remarked "that it was not becoming in counsel to try to worry witness into bad temper."

Witness stated "that Mr. Merrick had remarked the other day that all the witnesses in the adjoining room ought to go to the penitentiary, or something to that effect; that he was just as good as Merrick."

On the following day, at the opening of the court, Mr. Bradley said: "If your honor please, before we proceed with the trial of this case, I beg leave to call the attention of the Court to an incident which occurred just before the adjournment yesterday, and to ask that the notes of the reporter may be read. Your honor was very much occupied at the time, and I desire that the record may be read in order that you may see what passed, and what led to the attack made by the witness upon the stand upon the counsel with whom I am associated, your honor, without having heard what passed at that time, if not in precise words yet in substance, censured the counsel to whom these observations were addressed. I think, in looking at it, your honor will see that there was no provocation given; and that if there was, it is due to the dignity of this court, and to the protection of the members of the bar, to which they are entitled at the hands of the Court, that some notice should be taken of what then passed." After the reading of so much of the report as related to the matter, the Court spoke as follows: "I did not hear what was said by the witness in regard to the gunboats, for the reason that I was at the time occupied in preparing some passes for a friend. When my attention was called to the remark made use of by the witness towards the counsel, I was under the impression that he had been provoked to it by something that had been said by the counsel. I cannot, however, perceive in the record which has been read anything which ought to have called forth, or which justifies, the expression of the witness. I will say now to the witness, that although Mr. Merrick did say a few days ago, in regard to the witnesses who were in the adjoining room (which Mr. Bradley had called a penitentiary) that they (the witnesses) would soon be in another penitentiary, or words to that effect, it is not the privilege of a witness to take exception in the way he did to any remarks made in the court room. He may appeal to the Court to protect him if he is aggrieved." [Turning to witness] "You must not, hereafter, in your examination, make use of any expressions to counsel which are at all insulting in their character, however much you may feel yourself aggrieved by remarks which they may have made in reference to witnesses generally, or in reference to yourself before your examination.

"In this connection it may not be improper to observe that I have never, in all my judicial experience, seen a case in which there has been so much trouble with regard to the examination of witnesses and so much bitterness of feeling displayed.

"It may be all right, but I confess I see no reason why it should be so. I cannot, of course, enter into the feelings of counsel, and it is possible they may feel themselves aggrieved, and therefore regard themselves as justified in exhibiting this spirit. I will say, further, that I have never seen witnesses cross-examined with so much asperity as I have in the case now pending. It does not appear to me, therefore, as at all strange that witnesses should be worried into such remarks as this witness has uttered, especially when intimations are publicly thrown out by counsel as to their fitness for the penitentiary, and that, too, when some of the most respectable persons in the land, such, for instance, as General Grant and Assistant Secretary Seward, are among the number. And not even was the effect of the remark allowed to stop with the intimation, but when attention was called to it by the District Attorney, in the hope, I presume, that it would be recalled, it was repeated, and with the additional observation that the propriety of the remark could be shown. When such things occur it is not at all surprising that witnesses should come here prepared to avenge themselves by making insulting replies to the counsel. I deeply deplore it, and will endeavor, by most carefully observing all that transpires, to prevent a similar recurrence on the part of either counsel or witnesses; but however watchful the Court may be, such things will occasionally break forth at times and under circumstances when, from not expecting it, it is impossible for the Court to check them." [Again addressing himself to the witness.] "Dr. McMillen, you are highly reprehensible for having made such remarks as that to which exception has been taken. It was altogether out of place. If you felt yourself aggrieved by any remark, you should have called on the Court for protection. You will now proceed to give your evidence, and in a manner respectful to the counsel. If the counsel on either side shall treat you with what you conceive to be disrespect, you will appeal to the Court, and the Court will intervene for your protection. I would, however, suggest to gentlemen on both sides that in the examination of witnesses, if they will consult Quintilion and Allison in regard to their duty in this respect (and no doubt they have read the remarks of both these authors on the subject), they will find that those writers say nothing is to by gained by a bitterness of manner toward witnesses either on examination in chief or cross-examination, but that everything may possibly be gained by kindness and conciliatory manners; and I think it would be a decided improvement in this case if their suggestions were accepted. In the course of the five years that I was engaged in prosecuting criminal cases, I do not recollect ever to have had an unkind word with a witness on the one side or the other, and never in a civil case except on one occasion, when a witness of my own turned against me. Then I was led away by a natural quickness of temper. I advise that we should all, to the best of our ability, endeavor to control our tempers in conducting this case; and then there will be no fear of a repetition of the unpleasant occurrences that have happened during its progress."

To this Mr. Merrick replied: "I feel it incumbent upon me to say, after what has fallen from the Court, especially as your honor seems to have the impression that I intended my remarks to apply to all the witnesses, including Secretary Seward and General Grant, that while your honor misunderstood me in this regard, I do not believe I was misunderstood by some others outside, in supposing I intended to embrace all the witnesses in that remark. I will here say that I have the greatest respect for General Grant and Mr. Seward, and I apprehend that among the witnesses in the case it is perfectly well understood to whom I referred and to whom I did not refer. I apprehend that no sane man can suppose that I meant any such reference to General Grant, Mr. Seward, or Mrs. Seward, and that class of witnesses. I will only say, in conclusion, that I think, without any further explanation, or more direct pointing of the remark at present, it is perfectly well understood among the witnesses to whom the remark referred.'"

To this the Court replied: "I do not know whether it is understood or not. I cannot understand it, because I am bound not to know the witnesses, either as regards their own private character, or the character of their testimony, and I enter into the trial of this case knowing nothing, as it were, about either, scarcely ever having glanced at the testimony, and of course, therefore, I cannot enter into the feelings of counsel on the subject. I do not know to what witnesses these remarks may be directed, but this I do know, that there are certain legal methods pointed out in the text books of the law by which we are to be guided in undertaking to discredit the testimony of witnesses. One method is the discrediting of the witness by himself; by his own contradictions, and by his mode and manner of testifying. Another is by proving the witness to be utterly devoid of reputation for truth and veracity, and not to be believed on his oath. Another is by contradicting him by the conflicting testimony of other witnesses. These are the legal modes that are pointed out in the law books, and any side remarks that are made by way of prejudicing a jury, any acting in the case, the casting of sinister looks at the jury, are departures from the rules laid down.

"The examination of a witness ought to be conducted by the witness standing up and the counsel standing up, and looking each other in the face, without the counsel directing his remarks to the jury by turning towards them instead of turning towards the witness. That is the proper way to conduct either an examination in chief or a cross-examination."

The fact that the Court deemed it necessary to deliver such a lecture as this to counsel, who were men of age and experience in their profession, and who from their reading ought to have been as well informed as the Court on the proper treatment of a witness and the legal methods of discrediting testimony, indicates that he had found in their conduct such flagrant departures from the requirements of law and professional conduct a necessity for such criticism and such admonitions. The opinion of the Court as thus expressed fully justifies me in the charges I have made against the conduct of the defense and their unprofessional efforts to discredit testimony. I am still futher justified in it by the remark of Mr. Merrick that they (the counsel for the defense) " had laid at the feet of the attorneys a mass of the most corrupt battalion that was ever summoned to support a cause in a criminal court."

Here Mr. Merrick attempts to set aside all of the testimony that had been offered by the goverment proving the guilt of the prisoner, by denouncing it as corrupt throughout, and unworthy of the slightest consideration. This would certainly be as easy a method as it would be novel to throw out testimony *en masse* upon the mere *ipse dixit* of counsel, and in consequence of the legal standing and weight of character claimed by them with such manifest self complacency, but when we consider the fact that upon a candid and careful scrutiny of all the testimony in the case, it could be set aside in no other way, we could not perhaps reasonably expect them to refrain from trying to get the benefit of all the method that was left them.

The most important witnesses introduced by the government and those who most unequivocally proved the existence of a conspiracy and the connection of the prisoner with it, as also his participancy in its accomplishment, and also the fact that his mother belonged to it and performed a part in preparing for its accomplishment, had stood every test that ingenuity could devise to discredit their testimony. Some of them had been kept on the stand under cross examination for nearly two days, and could not be made to discredit their own testimony, either by contradictions or mode of answering. Neither had they been discredited by proving that they were utterly devoid of character for truth and veracity, and not to be believed on oath. The attempts at their contradiction by the conflicting testimony of other witnessess had all proven miserable failures, and so the counsel for the defense attempted to have their client declared innocent by scouting all of the evidence in the case and offering their own convictions of his entire innocence, and referring the jury to their weight of character and legal standing to enforce their opinions on the jury as grounds for a favorable verdict for their client. Never did able lawyers deal more unfairly with witnesses nor with evidence, nor more wantonly set at naught the established rules of evidence, not only in the respects referred to, but also in the efforts that they made to introduce testimony which they must have known to be inadmissible under the rules of evidence, as already shown in the number of exceptions which they not only took to the rulings of the court, but kept count of and paraded before the jury. Their animus toward the government was also shown in this matter of testimony, as also in other ways to be hereafter noticed. They charged the government with presenting testimony on this trial that it knew to be false, and withholding testimony from the military commission that would have proven the innocence of Mrs. Surratt. To sustain the first charge, they asserted in regard to the handkerchief found by Blinn at the Burlington depot, that it had been dropped by a government detective, and not lost by Surratt. Blinn, however, was positive in his testimony that he found the handkerchief on the morning of the 18th, but the handkerchief which Hallohan, the detective, claimed to have lost, was lost at Burlington on the morning of the 20th of April. He did not discover its loss, however, until he got to Essex Junction, and did not know where he had lost it. The handkerchief found by Blinn on the morning of the 18th, and put in evidence by the government, could not therefore have been the handkerchief that Hallohan claimed to have lost. There was also too heavy a cloud of uncertainty hanging over his (Hallohan's) testimony after his cross-examination, to have warranted the counsel in making so serious a charge against the government as that it knew that Hallohan, and not Surratt, lost the handkerchief.

In further proof of the charge that they disregarded and set at naught the rules of evidence, they tried to get in a statement by John Matthews of the contents of an article put into his hands by

Booth on the afternoon of the 14th of April, with a request that if he (Booth) did not see him before 10 o'clock on the following morning he should hand it to the *National Intelligencer* for publication, and which Matthews, after the assassination, had burned, thinking it would put him in danger to have such a thing found in his possession. They proposed to prove by this witness that neither the prisoner nor his mother were in the conspiracy. Of course they knew that they could not prove the contents of a paper that would have been inadmissible even if it had been presented. But if they had had the paper in their possession they could not have proven anything by it, as it was represented to be a paper prepared by Booth to justify himself in the crime he had in contemplation, and would have been no more admissible as evidence than the diary which Booth kept during his flight, every entry in it having been made in view of his probable failure to make his escape, and with the intention of palliating his crime. It was of no more value as evidence than was his assertion of the entire innocence of his companion, Herold, just a few minutes before he was shot. Yet they censured the government for not putting this diary in evidence before the Commission, asserting that its reason for withholding it was that it would have proven the innocence of Mrs. Surratt, thus by implication asserting that the government was thirsting for her blood, and was determined that she must be convicted right or wrong.

This position was boldly taken by them in their arguments, as we shall hereafter see, in the face not only of the evidence on which she was declared guilty by the Commission, but also in the face of that presented on this trial, which much more clearly and fully established her guilt. I have thus been careful to show from the record that I am justified in the strictures I am making on the course of the defense. I would be sorry to do any injustice to these men if they were here to answer for themselves, much more so now that the two senior members, Mr. Bradley and Mr. Merrick, are numbered with the dead. My charitable conclusion in their behalf is that their political opposition to the government so prejudiced their minds that they could not bring themselves into a judicial frame for the trial of this case. Their religious sympathies with Mrs. Surratt, and their ready acceptance of the assertion of Father Walter that she was "as innocent as the newborn babe," so influenced their minds that they would reject as false any testimony whatever that went to establish her guilt. Their sympathies then would naturally lead them to conduct the defense of her son in the same spirit of determination to hold him innocent in spite of all adverse testimony. The prisoner found his counsel in a state of mind to readily accept the ingenuous fabrication which he had had two years to get into form, as also no doubt the able assistance of the Reverend Fathers who so sedulously watched for his return to Canada after the murder of the President, and who at once took him under their protection on his return to Montreal, and kept him secreted for five months, until they could get him landed in the Pope's dominions; and then when he was brought back and put upon his trial, stood by him from day to day with unfaltering fidelity, until he was set at liberty.

The story which Surratt gives in his Rockville, Md., lecture, which bears throughout the marks of the "fine Italian hand" of the Jesuit, and which is contradicted in all of its most important points by the whole run of the testimony in the two trials, had no doubt been accepted by his counsel as true, and hence they would hear no testimony that conflicted with it; but were ready to accept any evidence whatever, without regard to the character of the witnesses, that corroborated it. This, in the opinion of the author, is the most charitable construction that can be put upon their conduct in the management of their case. Their eyes were blinded by their all controlling prejudices, and bitter opposition to the course of the government in sending Surratt's co-conspirators before a military commission for trial. We shall now proceed to give the evidence of their feelings toward the government in this matter. They could apparently find no words bitter enough to express their abhorrence of the trial by a commission.

As John H. Surratt and his mother were bound up in the same bundle by all the testimony in the case, and his mother had been found guilty upon this testimony by the court before which she was tried, his counsel seemed to feel the necessity of getting rid of the effect of this fact, in its bearing on their case. That I may not be accused of doing them injustice in presenting their mode of doing this, I will let them speak for themselves.

In the examination of jurors on their *voire dire*, Mr. Pierrepont asked the question: "Have you formed any opinion in regard to the guilt or innocence of the other conspirators?" The question was objected to by the counsel for the defense, and Mr. Merrick, to sustain his objection, said, among other things: "I presume there is scarcely a gentleman in the United States who has not formed and expressed the opinion that Booth shot Lincoln. I apprehend there are very few who have not formed and expressed an opinion that the mother of the prisoner at the bar suffered death without competent testimony to convict her, and so we might go through in an inquiry in relation to all the others." In replying, Mr. Pierrepont said: "The reason urged by my learned friend against it is, that he believes, I do not know but that he asserts, that there are very few in the United States who do not believe that Mrs. Surratt was illegally executed. Therefore we could not get a jury competent to try the prisoner at the bar if this question is allowed to be put."

Mr. Merrick [interrupting]. "My brother will allow me to say that he did not state my entire proposition. I said there were few intelligent persons in the United States who had not formed an opinion upon the question of Booth's participation in the killing of Lincoln; and there were also, I presumed, but few persons who had not formed an opinion that Mrs. Surratt had been executed upon insufficient evidence."

Mr. Pierrepont. "Precisely; that is the very statement, except that my friend has made it a little stronger than I did.

"I did not intend to overstate it, as there is nothing gained by overstatement, but it seems I did not come up to the mark." . . .

In his opening for the defense, Mr. Joseph H. Bradley, Jr., said: "We have at last arrived at that stage of this case when an opportunity is afforded the prisoner for saying something by way of defense, not only of his own character, his own reputation, his life and his honor, but also as it shall rise incidentally in this discussion of this evidence before you, something in the way of vindicating the pure fame of his departed mother." Again. "As to Mrs.

Surratt we hope to satisfy you that a grave error has been made in her case." Again Mr. Merrick, in his argument on the motion to strike out certain testimony, said: "The counsel had said, if it was anything favorable, the defense would insist on it; if anything unfavorable, they would not desire it. All he had to say in reply was, that he would insist on the free confession of all who had testified in the case, if he could get it. He would like to have had the privilege of putting in whatever this poor boy's butchered mother said, but had not. When he offered what she said, counsel on the other side said, 'No, you cannot prove that. We can prove what she said that will benefit the state, but you shall not throw the mantle of a mother's declarations over the child standing in the prisoner's dock.' Had we been allowed, we would have proved her declarations — proved them when tottering from the dungeon to the scaffold, with the world behind her, and nothing in the front but that God before whom she was shortly to appear, and before whom she solemnly asseverated that she was innocent of the crime for which she was being killed."

To all these charges and assumptions the District Attorney, in his argument upon the evidence, replied as follows: "Well, I do most kindly but most respectfully and emphatically repudiate the unjust imputation that Mary E. Surratt has been murdered, as was alleged by one of the counsel, and butchered as alleged by another. Where is the evidence to justify it? If they have a right to make this accusation, have we not a right to reply to it? For what purpose was it introduced before this jury? Is it to appeal to your prejudices? I make no such accusation against the gentlemen; they charge it home upon us when they say a murdered and a butchered woman. I deny it, and I undertake to prove to the contrary."

Mr. Bradley, interrupting, said "he supposed this threw the whole subject open for discussion." The District Attorney rejoined: "It had been introduced by the learned gentlemen on the other side." Mr. Bradley replied "that he was not aware what evidence there was on which this question could be discussed. But if it was understood that the whole subject was open, and that the counsel for the prisoner could not be interrupted in their discussion of it, he was satisfied."

The District Attorney. "Then why make allusion to it in the first instance? Who cast the first stone in the presence of this jury?

"I regret that it should have been necessary for an American woman to be executed by the judgment of an American tribunal. That verdict has been rendered by an American tribunal, and the consequence of it was the execution of an American woman. I know the character of the American people. I know that imagination revolts at the execution of one of the tender sex. But when the daughter of Herodias murdered John the Baptist, she deserved death. When Lucretia Borgia darkened the history of her country by her horrid crimes, she deserved death. And when Mary E. Surratt murdered Abraham Lincoln, the great moral hero of the age in which he lived, the patriot and philanthropist of the nineteenth century, she deserved death. There is no man who has a heart more capable of love for woman than myself. But when she unsexes herself, when she conceives, when she encourages, when she urges on, and is instrumental in committing the crime of murder, she places herself beyond the pale of protection. The best wife who ever lived, according to Milton, our great mother Eve, is thus represented as speaking to her husband:—

"'What thou biddest,
Unargued I obey; so God ordains:
God is thy law, thou mine.'

"I believe in submission on the part of women; submission to her God, to the laws of her country and to her husband. But when a woman opens her house to murderers and conspirators, infuses the poison of her own malice into their hearts, and urges them to the crime of murder and treason, I say boldly, as an American officer, public safety, public duty, requires that an example be made of her conduct. Murder! gentlemen of the jury. Who composed that military commission? They are no better men than you are, but you will not be offended with me if I say they are as good men as you are, or I, or any of us." Naming over the officers who constituted the tribunal by which Mrs. Surratt was tried, he continued: "I say, gentlemen of the jury, that they are good men, holding commissions under the government of the United States, and they are presumed to be honorable men. The law declares that every private citizen, and every public officer who is a servant of the American people, is presumed to be honorable until the contrary is proved.

"Your officers, your men, your representatives in the American army, in an accusation which will travel upon the telegraph wires perhaps to the four quarters of the world have been denounced, if not expressly, by implication, as murderers and butchers who took the life of an innocent woman. If so, when you come to try them, and you believe it, say it, but it is not the question submitted to you now. She may be innocent and the prisoner at the bar be guilty; the subject was introduced collaterally by the learned counsel, for what purpose I know not, except for effect. Before you brand these gentlemen with the character of murderers, see that you have relevant grounds to act upon. Take care, or you may be placed in the same situation; I have not charged it, and I do not think my friends would, upon reflection, charge men who are placed in such a solemn obligation with such a dereliction of duty. It has been said that this has been pronounced by the Supreme Court of the United States an illegal tribunal. What has that to do with the action of these officers? What has that to do with your action? What pertinency can it have to the issue now submitted to you for your decision? But, gentlemen of the jury, let us first consider the character of this crime, and then I will consider briefly the connection of Mrs. Surratt with it. I do not desire to say much about her; she has gone to her grave, and her spirit has passed before her Eternal Judge."

After recounting the character of the crime, the District Attorney thus refers to Mrs. Surratt's connection with it: "Now, gentlemen of the jury, let us view the connection of Mrs. Mary E. Surratt with this assassination. I feel the delicacy of the ground upon which I stand. I know the situation. I know that you dislike to consider this question, which has been forced upon you. I do not want to do it. My duty is to prosecute the prisoner, but one of the counsel has said she was murdered, and another that she was butchered, and it therefore becomes my

duty to trace her connection with this crime, and then leave it to
you to say whether she was guilty (though not relevant to this
case) of the crime for which she suffered. First, I call your
attention to a fact to which we have already adverted; that her
house, 541, was the rendezvous for these conspirators. Now,
gentlemen, will you pause for a moment, and let me ask you how
you can reconcile it with innocence? You remember the law,
that it is not how much a party did, but whether she had anything
to do with it. Can you, I say, reconcile it with innocence that
this woman's house should have been the rendezvous of John
Wilkes Booth, Lewis Payne, Atzerodt, Herold, and John H. Surratt? Would you not know by intuition? Would you not know
by their conversation? Would not your judgment and your hearts
tell you who they were and what they contemplated?

That is the great central truth, which I defy the learned counsel
for the defense successfully to assail. Secondly, who furnished
the arms with which the bloody deed was done? . . . The
woman who puts an arm into the hand of her lover, her son, her
brother, or her husband, who urges him on to the deed, by the
law of God and of man is equally guilty with the one who with his
own hand perpetrates the crime. According to the testimony of
John M. Lloyd this is shown. Do you believe him or disbelieve
him? My friend, Mr. Bradley, who opened this case said he was
a common drunkard; but mark you, he was an attendant and
friend of Mrs. Surratt."

Mr. Bradley. " Who says so? "

The District Attorney. " I will prove it. When I was examining that witness, and proposed to ask him certain questions in
reference to Mrs. Mary E. Surratt, he said, ' Mr. Carrington,' for
he knew me personally, ' I don't wish to speak about Mrs. Surratt, for she is not on trial.' I said ' Go on, Mr. Lloyd.' He
declined. I applied to the Court, and the Court said that it was
his duty to answer. He saw her continually. He lived in her
house; he drank her liquor. Why, this evidence shows that John
H. Surratt, Herold, and John M. Lloyd played cards and drank
together. . . . But says the friend and companion of the
prisoner at the bar, — the confiding and confidential agent of his

mother, unwilling to testify against her when put on the solemn sanction of an oath, but when required to do so he speaks out, — he says certain arms were furnished him by the prisoner at the bar; that he concealed them, the prisoner showing him where they could be safely concealed, he protesting at the time against it, protesting that it might get him into some personal difficulty. The mother knew of the transaction, for on the 11th of April we have Lloyd's own testimony; she asked him where those shooting-irons were, and said they might soon be needed, or words to that effect. But I am going too fast, for I do not desire to speak to confuse you. I say, first, that her house is the rendezvous; and that, secondly, she furnishes arms, or knows of their being furnished. On the night of the 14th of April, Booth and Herold returned, and are leaving the city of Washington in flight for their lives. At Surrattsville they called for whiskey from the agent and friend of the prisoner and his mother. She gives them a home, gives them arms, gives them whiskey, not to nerve them but to refresh them after the commission of their horrid crime.

"But Booth, in making his escape, needs something more than whiskey and arms.

"It is necessary that he should secrete himself as he traveled through the country, and that he should see persons approaching him from an immense distance, he needs a field-glass, and has it delivered to him by his friend and agent, Mrs. Surratt." With the defense no witness told the truth whose testimony went to convict their client, whilst the stories of the most infamous men, self-confessed scoundrels and accomplices after the fact, if not before, such as Father Boucher, and Reverend Cameron, must be taken as gospel truth.[1] In the face of all this testimony the counsel for the defense again bring their false accusations against the government. Mr. Merrick in the course of his argument, said: "Does the Attorney General feel that public justice demands that he should employ assistant counsel in this case, or is there somebody else behind?" . . . "Are there any other officers of the federal government that have purposes to accomplish in this case? Says

---

[1] See testimony of Father Boucher, Trial of Surratt, p. 895, and onward. Also testimony of Rev. Stephen F. Cameron, p. 793 and onward. Trial of Surratt.

the learned attorney on the other side (Mr. Pierrepont) in a speech delivered I think before you were impaneled:—

"'It has likewise been circulated through all the public journals that after the former convictions, when an effort was made to go to the President for pardon, men, active here at the seat of government, prevented any attempt being made, or the President even being reached for the purpose of seeing whether he would not exercise clemency; whereas the truth, and the truth of record, which will be presented in this court is, that all this matter was brought before the President, and presented to a full cabinet meeting, where it was thoroughly discussed, and, after such discussion, condemnation, and execution received not only the sanction of the President, but that of every member of his cabinet. This and a thousand others of these false stories will be all set at rest forever in the progress of this trail; and the gentlemen may feel assured that not only are we ready, but that we are desirous of proceeding at once with the case.' Now if this declaration of my learned brother on the other side is correct, this trial was not entered upon for the purpose alone of inquiring into the guilt or innocence of the prisoner at the bar. It was not entered upon because public justice demanded his arraignment, before you, gentlemen, but in order that a thousand false stories about men high in office might be settled at his expense.

"Then, although my learned brother is here under appointment by the Attorney General of the United States, yet it is an appointment which probably had its origin in the stimulus of some private feeling lying behind. He comes here, not to try this case alone, but he comes here to set at rest certain false stories. Has he done it?" . . . "Where is your record? Why didn't you bring it in? Did you find at the end of the record a recommendation to mercy in the case of Mrs. Surratt that the President never saw? You had the record here in court."

Mr. *Bradley.* "And offered it once and withdrew it."

Mr. *Merrick.* "Yes, sir, offered it and then withdrew it. Did you find anything at the close of it that you did not like? Why didn't you put that record in evidence, and let us have it here? We were not going to quarrel about it; we would like to know all we can about the dark secrets of those chambers whose doors are closed, but from which light enough creeps to make us anxious to look within. We only know enough to make us curious; but that is enough to make us *feel*. You were going to show, too, that nobody prevented access to the President on the part of those who waited to get a pardon. Why didn't you do it? Gentlemen of the jury, I should have been glad to have heard that proof. They have brought these charges into the case and I must meet them as part of the case. I should have been glad to have heard that proof. Who of you who was in the city of Washington, will ever forget that fatal day when the tolling of the bells reminded you of the sad fact that the hour had come when those people were to be hung? Your honor (referring to Justice Wylie, who was at the time sitting beside Judge Fisher on the bench), in your praise be it said, raised your judicial hand to prevent that murder, but it was too weak. The storm beat against your arm, and it fell powerless in the tempest. You remember that day, gentlemen. Twenty-four hours for preparation. The echoes of the announcement of impending death, scarcely dying away before the tramp of the approaching guard was heard leading to the gallows. Priest, friend, philanthrophist, and clergyman went to the Executive Mansion to get access to the President, to implore for that poor woman three days respite to prepare her soul to meet her God, but got no access. The heart-broken child — the poor daughter — went there crazed, and, stretched upon the steps that lead to the Executive chamber, she raised her hands in agony and prayed to every one that came, 'O God! let me have access, that I may ask for but one day for my poor mother — just one day.' Did she get there? No. And yet, says the counsel, there was no one to prevent access being had. Why don't you prove it? O, God! if such a thing could have been proved, how would I not have rejoiced in that fact; for when reflecting upon that sad, unfortunate, wretched hour in the history of my country — an hour when I feel she was so much degraded, I could weep until the paper be worn away with the continual dropping of my tears. Who stood between her and the seat of mercy? Has conscience lashed the chief of the Bureau of Military Justice?

[Gen. Joseph Holt.] Does memory haunt the Secretary of War? Or is it true that one who stood between her and Executive clemency now sleeps in the dark waters of the Hudson, while another died by his own violent hand in Kansas?

"The learned gentleman is right. He did come here to put these things at rest, or to endeavor to put them at rest; but he could not do it. What else is there in this case to show a feeling behind, besides public justice impelling to conviction? Gentlemen of the jury, as the counsel has stated in his speech, public rumors had gone abroad, and certain grave charges had been made. You know that political accusations had been brought against Judge Holt, Mr. Bingham, and the Secretary of War, in the House of Representatives, and that it had become a political matter." (Mr. Merrick here referred to an effort that had been made by rebel sympathizers in Congress to make political capital out of this transaction.) "There were parts of those accusations that the learned counsel was going to put at rest. Where is the proof? The proof is in this; follow me for a moment.

"I said I would show there was a conspiracy on conspiracy. What has the chief of the Bureau of Military Justice got to do with this case? Does not your honor hold an independent court? Is not the judicial tribunal of the land separate from the executive? Is it not a fundamental principle of American constitutional law that the executive and judicial departments shall be distinct and separate? The Bureau of Military Justice is a part of the executive department. What has he to do with this case? Nothing, says the counsel. Is he counsel? we ask. No, say they. Why, then, is he manipulating their witnesses in this case? Smoot, one of their witnesses, tells you that he is called up before Judge Holt, with ten others, examined, and his examination was taken down in writing. The day after giving his testimony he comes back and says that it was not Judge Holt that examined him, but was somebody else.

"I pressed him, pressed him hard, as to the place and time. He then recollected it was in the Winder Building, opposite the War Department; and when I pressed him still further, he had to say that the office he was in had written over the door 'Judge Advocate General's office.' Again I ask what had the Judge Advocate

General to do with this case? Not only was Smoot there, but Norton was there, and God only knows how many more. It is apparent, then, that he has taken a deep interest in this case. Why is he taking such an interest? It is certainly indiscreet. He has lost his prudence and he has lost his discretion; he has lost his judgment thus to expose himself and his office in a criminal prosecution.

"Mr. District Attorney, gird on your loins and answer me. Whose discretion is broken down? Whose prudence is betrayed? Is there anybody else's heart at which the vulture gnaws? Is there any high and great man who is forgetting the dignity of his office and the duties of a moral creature so far as to descend to the preparation of witnesses with which he has nothing to do to satiate his hunger with the blood of an innocent being? . . . But I am now speaking of the Bureau of Military Justice. He you know has furnished the evidence in this case."

Mr. Merrick then went on to charge the government with preparing and presenting evidence against Surratt that it knew to be false, and then proceeded as follows: "No matter whether they knew the truth in this case or not, prudence has been betrayed; discretion has been broken down; courage has been conquered. Following on Judge Pierrepont's declaration, which I have read to you, and these circumstances, comes Mr. Carrington, breaking the cerements of the tomb, and demanding your verdict against Mrs. Surratt. In God's name isn't it enough to try the living? Will you play the gnome, and bring her from the cold, cold earth and hang her corpse? Bring her in; but there is no occasion for doing so; she is here already. We have felt our blood run cold as the rustling of the garments from the grave swept by us. Her spirit moves about, and the Judge Advocate General and all these men may understand that it is the eternal law of God, though, so far as men are concerned, fresh and innocent blood may apparently vindicate innocent blood previously shed, yet the spirit will still walk beside them.

"He may shudder before her, because she is with him by day and by night; and he may say —

> "'Avaunt and quit my sight! Let the earth hide thee;
> Thy bones are marrowless; thy blood is cold.'

But the cold blood and marrowless bones are still beside him, and her whisperings are presaging that great judgment day when all men shall stand equal before the throne of God, and when Mrs. Surratt is called to testify against Joseph Holt, what will he in vindication say?

"Mr. Carrington, your honor, has gone outside of this record, and I must follow him to some extent, at least. He has gone outside of it in speaking of the military commission, defending the major generals and others. I am glad I recurred to it, for it reminds me of a statement of his that I desire to correct. He says we accused those honorable men of murder. No, sir; I refrain from any expression of opinion on that subject. It is true the most exalted judicial tribunal in the world, vindicating the liberty of American citizens and their constitutional rights against military authority, and maintaining the supremacy of the courts over military law, have pronounced that, and all other commissions similarly constituted, to be illegal; but what I denounce here is not the men who in judgment sat there, but the men conducting the trial, and who with this diary of Booth in their hands could have proved Mrs. Surratt's innocence by showing this conspiracy to have been organized on the 14th day of April, but who, though producing the toothpick and the penknife found on Booth, yet never so much as disclosed the fact that such a diary existed.

"They never made it known to those men or to the country. Do they not deserve to be denounced? Now that it has become known to the country, they come in before this jury to get them, with the diary in evidence before them, to find the same verdict that the military commission found.

"I put a question to a witness on that stand (referring to Father Walter) and asked him, 'Did you administer the consolations of religion to Mrs. Surratt?' 'I did. I gave her communion on Friday, and prepared her for death.' I asked him, 'Did she tell you as she was marching to the scaffold that she was an innocent woman?' I told him not to answer the question before I directed him to. He nodded his head, but he did not answer the question, because he had no right to, as the other side objected. If you are going to try that woman, and she being dead is unable to be here to defend herself, can you not at least have charity enough to let her last words come in in her defence? Will you try one who is not only absent from the court, but is dead? While trying one that is dead, will you deny to her the poor privilege of having the last word she uttered on earth spoken in her vindication? Were you afraid of it? Did you feel that the words would sink deep into the hearts of everybody that was here in this room, and in the United States, and cause to well up from that heart a fountain of mercy, rich and pure as the fountain that sprang from the rock at the bidding of the sacred rod? Shame on you! Prepared for the world to come, and marching to the scaffold, with her God before her and the world behind her, and a load of sin laid at the feet of Almighty God, and no hope but in that eternal mercy upon which we must all rely, I ask whether she cannot at such an hour speak for herself? No! you answer. Why not? is it likely she would lie? No, gentlemen, they will not say that. Then why is it? They did not want to hear it. Oh, they must indeed be hardened of heart, reckless of guilt, and indifferent to justice. But although they had no desire to hear it, they do hear it, and you hear it, for as that voice spoke then, it speaks now, and will continue to speak until justice is meted out. It whispers and is heard. It descends upon the head of that boy, and breaths on each of your hearts Yes, gentlemen, that woman in the nameless grave in yonder arsenal yard, the cerements of which have been broken by the government, comes here to vindicate her child. 'A nameless grave' did I say? Yes, alas! too true. Aye, sir, it would seem as if the ordinary feelings of humanity and common respect for the dead, to say nothing of regard for the honor of our country and sympathy for the sufferings of a distracted and loving daughter, would suggest to those pressing the prosecution (and who have charge of the matter) to allow this poor girl the privilege of paying a simple tribute to a mother's love by having her remains removed from a felon's grave. Yes! there that mother lies in a nameless grave, on which no flower is allowed to be strewn by that heart-broken daughter, who for the past two years has been earnestly pleading that she might have the privilege of placing those last sad, and to her, sacred relics, where filial love might weep the tear, and a filial hand plant a flower on the tomb."

Mr. Merrick then went on to meet the argument that Surratt had confessed his guilt by flight by declaring that the mad passions of the hour, and tyrannical usurpations of the government in its method of dealing with those charged with this crime, by sending them before a military commission instead of a civil court for trial, justified him in his flight.

He then went on to vindicate the Catholic Church, which he claimed had been assailed in this matter. The only reference to the Catholic Church in connection with this trial had been made in the public press. The prosecution had carefully abstained from any assault on that church, and had tried to exclude religious prejudices from the minds of the jurors.

Mr. Merrick, however, seized the occasion to pass an eulogium on that church, in which he showed as much disregard for the facts of history as he did for the proven facts in this case. Perhaps he felt this vindication to be called for from the fact that most of the conspirators were Catholics in religion, and the further fact that the friends who waited and watched for the return of his client to Montreal after the assassination, and who, on his return, spirited him away and kept him secreted for five months and then helped him off to Italy, where he was found in the ranks of the Pope's army, and who voluntarily came before the court on his trial to testify, and to procure testimony in his behalf, were priests of that church. In his eulogium on that church he forgot to mention the fact that the Pope at an early period of the war acknowledged the Southern Confederacy and wrote a sympathizing letter to Jefferson Davis, in which he called him his dear son and denounced President Lincoln as a tyrant. He could scarcely have forgotten that the Pope of Rome had sought to take advantage of the arduous struggle in which our government was engaged for the preservation of its life, to establish a Catholic Empire in Mexico, and had sent Maximillian, a Catholic prince, to reign over that, at that time, unhappy people, under the protection of the arms of France, lent to the furtherance of his unholy purpose by the last loyal son of the church that ever occupied a throne in Europe. Perhaps he did not realize that it was God who frustrated that last grasp of the drowning man at a straw that eluded his grasp, by preparing for his holiness, the Pope, and for Louis Napoleon just at that moment the Franco-Prussian war, which resulted in the final loss of his temporal power to the Pope and with it his grip on the world, and of his empire and crown to the last servile supporter of his temporal pretensions. To claim for that church, as Mr. Merrick did, friendship to civil liberty, respect for the rights of conscience and of private judgment, and love for our republican institutions, is to ignore, or set at naught, all the dogmas of that church on the above questions and all the claims of the Papacy. Mr. Merrick manifestly thought that the attitude of the Catholic clergy toward the assassination of the President could be hidden from public view by his fulsome eulogy.

The appeals made by the eminent counsel for the prisoner to the political and religious prejudices of jurors was ably seconded all through the trial by the Jesuit priesthood of Washington City and the vicinity. It will be recalled by scores of people who attended the trial that not a day passed but that some of these were in the court-room as the most interested of spectators. That they were not idle spectators may be inferred from the fact that whenever it seemed necessary to the prisoner's counsel to find witnesses to contradict any testimony that was particularly damaging to their cause they were always promptly found, and were almost uniformly Catholics in religion, as shown by their own testimony on their cross-examination. It was a remarkable fact, also, that these witnesses were scarcely ever able to come from under the fire of Judge Pierrepont's searching cross-examinations uncrippled, and also that when they took the risk of bringing two witnesses in rebuttal of the same testimony their witnesses uniformly killed each other off before they got through the ordeal that tests the truthfulness of witnesses — the cross-examination. Other outside influences were brought to bear on jurors, such as these: Father John B. Menu, from St. Charles College, spent a day in the court-room, sitting beside the prisoner all day, thus saying to the jury, "You see which side I am on." A great many of the students from the same college also visited the trial, it being vacation, and they uniformly took great pains to show their sympathy with the prisoner by shaking hands with him. The press also was prostituted almost daily by publishing cunningly devised paragraphs impugning the motives of the government in the prosecution and management of the case. Thus were the prejudices of jurors appealed to and efforts also made to pervert public opinion.

I have quoted thus at length from Mr. Merrick's argument to show, first the animus of the defense toward the government, and especially toward the Judge Advocate General, Joseph Holt, and the Secretary of War at time of the assassination, Edwin M. Stanton. These two officers of the government need no vindication at my hands before the loyal people of this country, as they were never denounced by any but rebels, whose especial venom against them would be the strongest presumptive evidence of their virtue and efficiency. A purer man, a truer patriot, a braver, more intelligent and able officer than Gen. Joseph Holt never will grace the pages of American history. He was only hated and denounced by rebels because of his faithfulness to duty and efficiency in its performance. Of Edwin M. Stanton, also, it is needless for me to say a word. His place is fixed in history, and his record cannot be blurred by the false and vile charges or insinuations of his enemies, for his enemies were only found amongst the enemies of his country, and precisely for the same reason that they were enemies of the Judge Advocate General. The charges here so boldly made that they stood between Mrs. Surratt and an appeal to the Executive for clemency, was shown to be false by Judge Pierrepont, who produced the official record of the trial of the conspirators, together with a paper signed by some members of the court recommending commutation of the sentence of Mrs. Surratt to imprisonment for life on account of her age and sex, and showed that this whole record had been laid before the President and a full cabinet, and that after mature discussion and consideration it had received their unanimous approval, with the exception of the request for the commutation of Mrs. Surratt's sentence which, though not a part of the record, was presented with it; and that the President's order for the execution of the sentence of the court had been written on the back of this very record.

These papers containing this whole record were handed to Mr. Merrick, who tossed them from him indignantly, afterwards assigning as his reason for doing so that he had learned to distrust everything that came from the Bureau of Military Justice. His real reason was that he did not desire to be estopped from reiterating the falsehoods he had so boldy proclaimed.

His denunciation of the Judge Advocate General for assisting the prosecution by furnishing them with witnesses, to prove facts found on his records, if he did indeed thus assist, is unmerited ; as it is not only the duty of every private citizen, but of every public officer as well, to assist, if it be in his power to do so, in securing the ends of justice where crimes have been committed, and the safety, peace, and welfare of society put in jeopardy. His deliberate false assumption that the prosecution had put Mrs. Surratt on trial is worthy of note, as he himself dragged her case in even before a jury was impaneled; and his colleague, Mr. Jos. H. Bradley, Jr., in his opening speech, had also brought it up in such a way that the District Attorney was forced to notice it. It was evidently a premeditated scheme of the defense, and was done for the purpose of appealing to the prejudices of jurors, and of making political capital.

Mr. Merrick's protrayal of the scenes incident to the execution of Mrs. Surratt was a fine piece of eloquent and pathetic declamation. We cannot but deplore, however, that the fine sensibilities of the counsel had not found occasion for their display in the case of the widow and orphan child of the martyred President, rather than in the person of one proven guilty of complicity in his assassination, and of being so actively engaged in that tragedy that she had traveled twenty miles on that fatal Friday afternoon to carry, at Booth's request, a field glass which he had delivered to her for the purpose, to Surrattsville, to be deposited and delivered by Lloyd, at her request, along with the carbines and the whiskey, to the assassins on that night, when fleeing from the seat of their crime, and from offended justice. It is to be deplored that he had no tears for the crazed widow and orphan child of the murdered President, when he could find such a generous fountain for his murderers. Such, however, is the deplorable effect of political and religious prejudice on frail human nature, that it perverts our moral sensibilities and warps our judgment. Mr. Merrick could see nothing but innocence in the prisoner and his mother, although the proof of their guilt was piled mountain high. It will have been noticed that he unequivocally asserts that the Supreme Court of the United States had decided that the commission that tried the assassins was an illegal tribunal. We shall have occasion hereafter to show that this is untrue.

If the counsel for the defense was not aware of this fact, it was because they had failed to grasp the meaning of the decision to which they referred, and on which they relied.

It was neither fair nor honest in them, after dragging into the trial the question of Mrs. Surratt's guilt or innocence, and that for the purpose we have above indicated, to endeavor, in the face of the facts, to shift the burden of the responsibility for this on to the prosecution. It was equally dishonest to insinuate that the prosecution of John H. Surratt was not entered upon alone for the purpose of ascertaining his guilt or innocence, but in order that the false stories that had been published in regard to the course of the government in executing Mrs. Surratt might be set at rest. The most eloquent counsel for the defence, ably assisted by his colleagues, endeavored to put the government, and not the prisoner, on trial before the jury, and before the country. They uniformly and boldly asserted his innocence, whilst they arraigned the government for having murdered, according to one, and butchered according to another, an innocent woman; and also of being in this trial engaged in an endeavor to cover up the guilt of shedding her innocent blood, by shedding the blood of her innocent son. To cap the climax of their audacity Mr. Bradley, after reiterating the charges made by Mr. Merrick and Joseph H. Bradley, Jr., asked the jury, in making up their verdict, to make a written statement at the same time of their belief that Mrs. Surratt had been unjustly condemned, and found guilty upon insufficient evidence.

They charged the government with dishonesty in withholding Booth's diary from the commission; claiming that it would have proven Mrs. Surratt's innocence. They could not have failed to know, as able lawyers, that this diary was of no account whatever as evidence. It was no more admissible than was Atzerodt's confession, as every entry that was made in it was made with the almost certainty of his capture in view, and for the purpose of concealing the greatness of the conspiracy and its personnel.

It was of no more value than was his declaration in favor of his fellow-conspirator, Herold, that he was an innocent man, made a few moments before he was shot.

In his argument on the defense of an *alibi* set up by the prisoner, Mr. Merrick makes great account of the evidence of the detectives who visited and searched Mrs. Surratt's house at two o'clock on the morning of the 15th of April, that Mrs. Surratt declared that John was not there, and that she had not seen him for two weeks.

She claimed that he was in Montreal, and that she had received a letter from him on the day previous. They well knew that her declarations had no value as testimony, and that there was evidence flatly contradicting her statements.

That she had received the letter as claimed, was true; but that that letter had been written for the very purpose of being used in the defence of an *alibi* is evident from its contents, when considered in connection with the evidence in the case. It will be remembered that Wiechmann, who was a boarder in the house, answered the door-bell, when the detectives rang it for the purpose of demanding admittance, that they might search the house. He rapped at Mrs. Surratt's door and informed her as to who was at the door and what they had come for. Her answer was, "For God's sake, let them come in; I have been expecting them."[1] When they inquired for her son she said, "He is not here; I have not seen him for two weeks." This was a sufficient answer, but her guilty conscience would not let her stop here, she had to add, "There are a great many mothers who do not know where their sons are." Let us ask ourselves at this point, how many mothers in Washington City at that hour of that eventful night were lying awake expecting their houses to be searched by detectives? Our inner consciousness will unerringly dictate the answer, "Not one who was innocent of crime." It is only necessary to say, further, in regard to this defense set up, of an *alibi*, that although there is no more common defense resorted to by criminals, because there is none more easy of establishment, there was never perhaps in all the history of jurisprudence a weaker and more unsuccessful effort made to establish it than in this defense. The effort made by the prisoner to establish an *alibi* showed plainly

[1] See p. 394, Trial of Surratt; also supplemental affidavit of L. J. Wiechmann.

that he had endeavored to prepare for it, in anticipation for his defense, and that, in this preparation he had had able help. There is good reason to conclude that he and a half dozen other of his friends in Canada had found an opportunity to visit Canandaigua in disguise, for the purpose of doctoring up a hotel register to be used in evidence. The effort after all, proved a miserable failure.

That he went from Montreal to Elmira, N.Y., leaving the former place at two o'clock on the morning of the 12th of April, was admitted. There was evidence that he was in Elmira on the morning of the 13th, and two or three credible witness were found who swore that they saw him there either on the 13th or 14th. They were willing to conclude that it might have been on the 14th; but would not positively swear that it was. On the other hand the government produced two witnesses who identified him as a man whom they saw on the road making his way towards Baltimore, on the 13th, one of whom ferried him over the Susquehanna river, and stopped mid-stream to collect his fare, and so talked with him and had a good look at him. It was then proven by nearly a dozen witnesses that they saw him in Washington City on the 14th. So that the great preponderance of evidence was against the *alibi;* and so it legally failed. The defense was lame and weak at every point in the light of the evidence, which all tended to show the prisoner's guilt. It was only strong in the bold efforts of his counsel to scout all the testimony against him, and to have the jury accept their assertions of his innocence, backed by their weight of character as lawyers, in lieu of evidence, to establish his innocence, and in contumning and rejecting that which established his guilt.

They also made great complaint that they were not allowed to prove by John Matthews, the contents of the paper which he alleged was put into his hand by Booth, a few hours before the commission of his crime, with the request that he would, on the following day, upon certain contingencies, give it to the editor of the *National Intelligencer* for publication, and which Matthews claimed to have destroyed. Of course they knew that nothing could be proven by this paper, much less by evidence as to its contents, yet, when it was not admitted by the court, they reserved an exception, and then in argument claimed that had they been allowed the benefit of this, they could have shown that the purpose of assassination was not formed until that day, and that neither the prisoner nor his mother was in it.

Matthews afterwards published what he said he desired to testify to, but was not permitted to do so by the Court. The statement that he claimed to be of Booth in this paper, gave the lie to Atzerodt's confession. These able lawyers knew full well that culprits, anticipating arrest and trial, could not be permitted to manufacture evidence in their own favor in advance. Yet they did not scruple to use, in an indirect way, in argument before the jury, this very testimony that had been excluded. Booth's diary, Booth's statement for publication, Atzerodt's confession, and the lecture of John H. Surratt, in which he makes his confession and statement of the affair, are all of a piece, and alike unworthy of credit, because they are all contradicted by sufficient and reliable testimony in every important particular. The eloquence of counsel in regard to the grave of Mrs. Surratt, who was buried in the grounds of the old arsenal, being a nameless grave, is wasted eloquence in the mind of every loyal man and woman in the country, as the heniousness of the crime of which she was convicted, made it fitting that she should sleep in a nameless grave, and that the spot of her resting-place be unknown, as an admonition to all traitors to their country, and its free institutions of government, and whose disloyalty fits them for the highest crimes that man can commit, of the infamy that awaits them in the just verdict of an outraged people. Mrs. Surratt's remains were given up to her daughter two years later, in 1869.

We will now give a few of the opening paragraphs of Judge Pierrepont's argument for the prosecution, in which he disposes of the outside and irrelevant matter that had been lugged into the defense, and out of which they had endeavored to make so much capital.

"May it please your honor, and gentlemen of the jury, I have not, in the progress of this long and tedious cause, had the opportunity as yet of addressing to you one word. My time has now arrived, 'Yea, all that a man hath will he give for his life.' When the book of Job was written, this was true, and it is just as true to-day. A man, in order to save his life, will give his property, will give his liberty, will sacrifice his good name, and will desert his father, his brother, his mother and his sister. He will lift up his hand before Almighty God and swear that he is innocent of the crime with which he is charged. He will bring perjury upon his soul, giving all that he hath in the world, and be ready to take the chances and jump the life to come; and so far as counsel place themselves in the situation of their client, and just to the degree that they absorb his feelings, his terror, and his purposes, just so far will counsel do the same.

"I am well aware, gentlemen, of the difficulties under which I labor in addressing you. The other counsel have all told you that they know you and that you know them. They know you in social life, and they know you in political affairs. They know your sympathies, your habits, your modes of thought, your prejudices even. They know how to address you, and how to awaken your sympathies, whilst I come before you a total stranger. There is not a face in those seats that I have ever beheld until this trial commenced, and yet I have a kind of feeling pervading me that we are not strangers.

"I feel as though we had a common origin, a common country, and a common religion, and that, on many grounds, we must have a common sympathy. I feel as though, if hereafter I should meet you in my native city, or in a foreign land, I should meet you, not as strangers, but as friends. It was not a pleasant thing for me to come into this case. I was called into it at a time ill-suited in every respect. I had just taken my seat in the convention called for the purpose of forming a new constitution for my State, and I was a member of the judiciary committee. The convention is now sitting, and I am now absent where I ought to be present. I feel, however, that I had no right to shirk this duty.

"The counsel asked whether I represented the Attorney General in this case. They had, perhaps, the right to ask, and so asking I give you the answer. There surely is no mystery about the matter. The District Attorney, feeling the magnitude of this case, felt that he ought to apply to the Attorney General for assistance in the prosecution of it, and he accordingly made the application. I have known the Attorney General for more than twenty years. Our relations have been most friendly, both in a social and professional point of view. The Attorney General conferred with the Secretary of State, who is, as you know, from my own State, and they determined to ask me to assist in the prosecution of this cause. On receiving a letter from the Secretary of State, I came to Washington, when I met him and the Attorney General. This is the way I happened to be here engaged in this case; and I may say that I am assured that there was no member of the cabinet but those two who ever heard or knew of my retainer until after my arrival here. I have simply tried to perform my duty as I best could, but I have, no doubt, failed to a great extent. A trial, protracted as this has been, and in such oppressive weather, is indeed a trial. It is a trial to the court, it is a trial to you, it is a trial to the counsel, it is a trial to health, it is a trial to patience, and it is a trial to temper.

"When the President of the United States was assassinated, I was one of a committee sent on by the citizens of New York to attend his funeral. When standing, as I did stand, in the east room by the side of that coffin, if some citizen sympathizing with the enemies of my country had, because my tears were falling in sorrow over the murder of the President, there insulted me, and I had at that time repelled the insult with insult, I think my fellow-citizens would have said to me that my act was deserving of condemnation; that I had no right, in that solemn hour, to let my petty passions or my personal resentments disturb the sanctity of the scene. To my mind the sancitity of this trial is far above that funeral occasion, solemn and holy as it was, and I should forever deem myself disgraced if I should ever allow any passion of mine or personal resentment of any kind to bring me here into any petty quarrel over the murder of the President of the United States. I have tried to refrain from anything like that, and God helping me, I shall so endeavor to the end.

"To me, gentlemen, this prisoner at the bar is a pure abstraction. I have no feeling toward him whatever. I never saw him until I saw him in this room, and then it was under circumstances calculated to awaken only my sympathy. I never knew one of his kindred, and never expect to know one of them. To me he is a stranger. Toward him I have no hostility, and I shall not utter any word of vituperation against him. I came to try one of the assassins of the President of the United States, as indicted before you. I laid personal considerations aside, and I hope I shall succeed in keeping them from this cause, so far as I am concerned. I believe, gentlemen, that what you wish to know in this case is the truth. I believe it is your honest desire to find out whether the accused was engaged in this plot to overthrow this government and assassinate the President of the United States. My duty is to try to aid you in coming to a just conclusion. When this evidence is reviewed, and when it is honestly and fairly presented, when passions are laid aside, and when other people who have nothing to do with the trial are kept out of the case, you will discover that in the whole history of jurisprudence no murder was ever proved with the demonstration with which this has been proven before you. The facts, the proofs, the circumstances all tend to one point, and all prove the case, not only beyond a reasonable, but beyond any doubt.

"This has been, as I have already stated, a very protracted case. The evidence is scattered. It has come in link by link, and as we could not have witnesses here in their order when you might have seen it in its logical bearings, we were obliged to take it as it came; and now it becomes my duty to put it together and show you what it is. I shall not attempt, gentlemen, to convince you by bold assertions of my own. I fancy I could make them as loudly and as confidently as the counsel on the other side, but I am not here for that purpose. The counsel are not witnesses in the cause. We have come here for the purpose of ascertaining whether under the law and on the evidence presented, this man arraigned before you is guilty as charged. I do not think it proper that I should tell you what I think about everything that may arise in the case, or that I should tell you that I know that this thing is so, and that the other is another way. My business is to prove to you from this evidence that the prisoner is guilty. If I do that I shall ask your verdict. If I do not do that, I shall neither expect nor hope for it."

"I listened, gentlemen, to the two counsel who have addressed you for several days, without one word of interruption. I listened to them respectfully and attentively. I knew their earnestness, and I know the poetry that was brought into the case, and the feeling and the passion that was attempted to be excited in your breasts, by bringing before you the ghost trailing her calico dress and making it rustle against these chairs. I have none of these powers which the gentlemen seem to possess, nor shall I attempt to invoke them. I have come to you for the purpose of proving that this party accused here was engaged in this conspiracy to overthrow this government, which conspiracy resulted in the death of Abraham Lincoln, by a shot from a pistol in the hands of John Wilkes Booth. That is all there is to be proven in this case.

"I have not come here for the purpose of proving that Mrs. Surratt was guilty or that she was innocent, and I do not understand why that subject was lugged into this case in the mode that it has been; nor do I understand why the counsel denounced the military commission who tried her, and thus indirectly censured, in the severest manner, the President of the United States. The counsel certainly knew when they were talking about that tribunal, and when they were thus denouncing it, that President Johnson, President of the United States, ordered it with his own hand; that President Johnson, President of the United States, signed the warrant that directed the execution; that President Johnson, President of the United States, when that record was presented to him, laid it before his cabinet, and that every single member voted to confirm the sentence, and that the President with his own hand, wrote his confirmation of it, and with his own hand signed the warrant. I hold in my hand the original record, and no other man, as it appears from that paper, ordered it. No other one touched this paper; and when it was suggested by some of the members of the commission that in consequence of the age and the sex of Mrs. Surratt it might possibly be well to change her sentence to imprisonment for life, he signed the warrant for her death with the paper right before his eyes — and there it is (handing the paper to Mr. Merrick). My friend can read it for himself.

"My friends on the other side have undertaken to arraign the government of the United States against the prisoner. They have talked very loudly and eloquently about this great government of twenty-five or thirty millions of people being engaged in trying to bring to conviction one poor young man, and have treated it as though it was a hostile act, as though two parties were litigants before you, the one trying to beat the other. Is it possible that it has come to this, that, in the city of Washington, where the President has been murdered, that when under the form of law, and before a court and jury of twelve men, an investigation is made to ascertain whether the prisoner is guilty of this great crime, that the government are to be charged as seeking his blood, and its officers as lapping their tongues in the blood of the innocent? I quote the language exactly. It is a shocking thing to hear. What is the purpose of a government? What is the business of a government? According to the gentlemen's notion, when a murder is committed the government should not do anything towards ascertaining who perpetrated that murder; and if the government did undertake to investigate the matter and endeavor to find out whether the man charged with the crime is guilty or not guilty the government and all connected with it must be expected to be assailed as 'blood hounds of the law,' and as seeking 'to lap their tongues in the blood of the innocent.' Is that the business of government, and is it the business of counsel under any circumstances thus to charge the government? What is government for? It is instituted for your protection, for my protection, for the protection of us all. What could we do without it? Tell me, my learned and eloquent counsel on the other side, what would you do without a government? What would you do in this city? Suppose, for instance, a set of young men, who choose to lead an idle life, say to themselves that it is not right that some rich man living here should be enjoying his hoarded wealth, and they break into his house at night and steal therefrom. My learned friend would say, when you came to prosecute them for that robbery, 'What! would you have this great and generous government of twenty-five or thirty millions of people pursue these poor young men, who merely tried to break into the house of one of your citizens and steal his money? Should not this government be generous and let them go? Oh, yes! Let them off. Well, they are let off, and a few days afterward they break into the house of my friend, Mr. Merrick, for the purpose of stealing his money, when he, a brave man, undertakes to resist them, and in doing so they strike him down in death. Oh, generous government! with twenty-five or thirty millions of people, let the young men off. Why should a great and generous government with all its powers be pursuing the young men who thus murdered Mr. Merrick while attempting to prevent a robbery at his house?

"Why should the officers of the government be 'lapping their tongues in the blood of the innocent?' Suppose this view as to the duty of a government were universally entertained, what would be the result? How long would your government last? How long would you hold a dollar of property? How long would the safety of your daughters be secure? How long would the life of your sons, who stand in resistance to lust and rapine, be safe? I have never heard such shocking sentiments uttered in relation to the duty of government from any human lips, or from any writer on the face of the earth. We have been told here that our government has nothing of divinity that hedges it about; that it is only the government of man's making. The Bible tells us that all government is of God; that the powers that be are ordained of God; and I can tell you, gentlemen, if such are the sentiments of this country that there is no divinity and no power of God that hedges about this government, its days are numbered, its condemnation is already written, and it will lie in the dust before many years have rolled by. No government that is not of God will last. It will soon come to naught. No other government ever did long exist. No other government can exist. Every government which is a government of the people is of God, and the powers that be are ordained of God. When you come together to the polls, and you elect as the ruler of this great nation a President, he is made so by the sanction of your votes, and in that act the voice of the people becomes the voice of God. I repeat, a government which is thus instituted is ordained of God, and it is as much hedged about as that of any king that ever reigned on England's throne. Is it possible that our countrymen will say that the government which we thus have made, which our fathers established, and which we are thus cherishing, has nothing of divinity hedging it about?

"Does it rest alone on human whim, without having anything sacred about it, and without any protection of the Almighty over it? If so, let me again repeat, its days are numbered; it will soon pass away. Once there was an empire in Rome. It was an empire which was in its day the greatest which the human mind had ever reared; but it did not believe, or rather ceased to believe, that there was a God who ruled; that government was of God; and they ceased to punish great crimes, such as treason, rapine, and murder, and it happened a very short time after they ceased to inflict punishment for such crimes — ceased to exercise the powers which belong to government — that the Roman empire tumbled into ruins.

"It was trampled down by the barbarians, and now not a son of the Cæsars lives on the face of the earth, and not a descendant of a Roman matron exists anywhere in this wide universe. The empire perished, and crumbled into dust; nothing but its ashes remain. And thus will it ever be whenever a people cease to obey God, and cease to think that government is of God. Let us see what the Bible says on this subject; what views were entertained in the Old Testament, and what in the New." Mr. Pierrepont then read from 1st Samuel, chapter xv, as follows: —

"'Samuel also said unto Saul, the Lord sent me to anoint thee to be king over his people, over Israel; now therefore hearken thou unto the voice of the words of the Lord.

"'Thus saith the Lord of hosts, I remember that which Amalek did to Israel, how he laid wait for him in the way, when he came up from Egypt.

"'Now go and smite Amalek, and utterly destroy all that they have, and spare them not; but slay both man and woman, infant and suckling, ox and sheep, camel and ass.

"'And Saul gathered the people together, and numbered them in Telaim, two hundred thousand foot-men, and ten thousand men of Judah.

"'And Saul came to a city of Amalek, and laid wait in the valley.

"'And Saul said unto the Kenites, go, depart, get you down from among the Amalekites, lest I destroy you with them; for ye showed kindness to all the children of Israel, when they came up out of Egypt. So the Kenites departed from among the Amalekites.

"'And Saul smote the Amalekites, from Havilah *until* thou comest to Shur, that is over against Egypt.

"'And he took Agag, the king of the Amalekites, alive, and utterly destroyed all the people with the edge of the sword.

"'But Saul and the people spared Agag, and the best of the sheep, and of the oxen, and of the fatlings, and of the lambs, and all *that was* good, and would not utterly destroy them; but every thing *that was* vile and refuse, that they destroyed utterly.

"'Then came the word of the Lord unto Samuel, saying, It repenteth me that I have set up Saul *to be* king; for he is turned back from following me, and hath not performed my commandments. And it grieved Samuel, and he cried unto the Lord all night.

"'And when Samuel rose early to meet Saul in the morning, it was told Samuel, saying, Saul came to Carmel, and behold, he set him up a place, and is gone about, and passed on, and gone down to Gilgal.

"'And Samuel came to Saul, and Saul said unto him, blessed be thou of the Lord; I have performed the commandment of the Lord.

"'And Samuel said, what meaneth then this bleating of sheep in mine ears, and the lowing of the oxen which I hear?

"'And Saul said, they have brought them from the Amalekites; for the people spared the best of the sheep, and of the oxen, to sacrifice unto the Lord thy God, and the rest we have utterly destroyed.

"'Then Samuel said unto Saul, stay, and I will tell thee what the Lord hath said to me this night. And he said unto him say on.

"'And Samuel said, when thou *wast* little in thine own sight, *wast* thou not *made* the head of the tribes of Israel, and the Lord anointed thee king over Israel?

"'And the Lord sent thee on a journey, and said, go and utterly destroy the sinners of the Amalekites, and fight against them until they be consumed.

"'Wherefore then didst thou not obey the voice of the Lord, but didst fly upon the spoil, and didst evil in the sight of the Lord.

"'And Saul said unto Samuel, yea, I have obeyed the voice of the Lord, and have gone the way which the Lord sent me, and have brought Agag, the king of Amalek, and have utterly destroyed the Amalekites.

"'But the people took of the spoil, sheep and oxen, the chief of the things, which should have been utterly destroyed to sacrifice to the Lord thy God in Gilgal.

"'And Samuel said, hath the Lord as great delight in burnt offerings and sacrifices as in obeying the voice of the Lord? Behold to obey is better than sacrifice, and to hearken than the fat of rams.

"'For rebellion *is as* the sin of witchcraft, and stubbornness *is as* iniquity and idolatry; because thou hast rejected the word of the Lord, he hath also rejected thee from being king.

"'And Saul said unto Samuel, I have sinned, for I have transgressed the commandment of the Lord, and thy words; because I feared the people, and obeyed their voice.

"'Now, therefore, I prayed thee, pardon my sin, and turn again with me that I may worship the Lord.

"'And Samuel said unto Saul, I will not return with thee; for thou hast rejected the word of the Lord, and the Lord hath rejected thee from being king over Israel.

"'And as Samuel turned about to go away, he laid hold upon the skirt of his mantle, and it rent.

"'And Samuel said unto him, the Lord hath rent the kingdom of Israel from thee this day, and hath given it to a neighbor of thine, *that is* better than thou.

"'And also the strength of Israel will not lie nor repent; for he *is* not a man that he should repent.

"'Then he said, I have sinned; *yet* honor me now, I pray thee, before the elders of my people, and before Israel, and turn again with me, that I may worship the Lord thy God.

"'So Samuel turned again after Saul, and Saul worshiped the Lord.

"' Then said Samuel, bring ye hither to me Agag, the king of the Amalekites. And Agag came unto him delicately. And Agag said, surely the bitterness of death is past.

"' And Samuel said, as thy sword has made women childless, so shall thy mother be childless among women. And Samuel hewed Agag in pieces before the Lord in Gilgal.

"' Then Samuel went to Ramah; and Saul went up to his house to Gibeah of Saul.

"' And Samuel came no more to see Saul until the day of his death; nevertheless, Samuel mourned for Saul; and the Lord repented that he had made Saul king over Israel.'"

Mr. Pierrepont then read from the eighteenth chapter of St. Matthew as follows:—

"'Woe unto the world because of offences, for it must needs be that offences come; but woe unto that man by whom the offence cometh. . . . It were better for him that a millstone were hanged about his neck, and that he were drowned in the depth of the sea.'

"Such was the order in the times of this Book. All government is of God. The powers that be are ordained of God. Now, from whom come those words? Not from the Old Testament, but they come from the meek and lowly Jesus, the Saviour of the world, who died for you, for me, for all. It is true as the counsel have said, that God is a God of mercy; but he says: 'Though I am a God of mercy, I will by no means clear the guilty.' Now the counsel who has addressed you, you will remember, said in his speech, with great earnestness: 'We have had blood enough; let us have peace.' The question before you, gentlemen, is not about blood. The question is not about peace. The question before you is whether you have not had murder enough, and assassination enough, and crime enough, to enable us to have at least once before a civil tribunal in this land a trial and a verdict. Not a single one of all those engaged in the conspiracy has been tried before a civil tribunal; and the question now is, have you not had enough of this murder, enough of this assassination, to have at least one jury of the country say so, and to say that we will stop it? You and I have nothing to do with the consequences. All we have to do is to do our duty, and ascertain whether the man is guilty. You do not punish the man; I do not punish the man. I have not a feeling toward him of punishment, and you have no such feeling. The duty does not lie with you, nor with me; we have nothing to do with that. The question for us is to see whether this man is guilty of this violation of the law of the land as charged; and if so, to so declare; and then, if for any cause, the Executive sees fit to show leniency, he will show it. If he does not, he will not. It is not for you or for me to have to say what the leniency should be. It is not for you or for me to have anything to say upon that question. Our business is, I repeat, to ascertain whether he is guilty of this violation of the law, and if he is guilty, so to say, and then afterward to say whatever we thought fit to be said with regard to any leniency. Our duty is, and the duty of the court is, to find out that one fact, and to have you pronounce your verdict, under your oath, according to the facts as you find them.

"There are one or two other things that I must notice before I come to the main question. One of these is in regard to the attacks which were made by counsel yesterday upon the learned District Attorney and myself. Have you seen anything in the conduct of the District Attorney in this case that was improper? Have you seen anything but an earnest desire to discharge his duty? If I understood the counsel aright yesterday, he said that if he should stand in the place and should have done as the District Attorney had, he would expect the women, as they passed him, to gather their skirts and pull them aside, lest they be contaminated by the touch. I did not at that time know why there was so much bitterness of feeling thus expressed, but I have been shown since last night this record called the 'Rebellion Record,' and I find in it that on the 5th of January, 1861, Edward C. Carrington, now District Attorney, issued to the public a stirring letter calling out the militia of this District for the purpose of aiding in the protection of the government of the United States; calling upon them to rally; and they did rally at his call. The fact of this native born citizen of Virginia, one of your own number and living in your midst, having thus early and practically taken the side in favor of the government, when even his own State had deserted him, of course would be likely to call down the greatest bitterness and hatred against this loyal and noble citizen on the part of a certain class. We have been told, gentlemen, by the counsel upon the other side, that the Judge Advocate General had done a great many wrong things in his life. We have been told that the military commission which Mr. Johnson had established, and he alone, had done wrong things in their prosecution; and we have been told, likewise, that the Supreme Court of the United States had decided that this commission was illegal. Now you would hardly expect an eminent lawyer to make such a statement unless he believed it. But he is wholly mistaken. No court in the United States has declared this commission to have been illegal. There is no such decision on record — not any.

"Some of these very persons are now in confinement, and if the Supreme Court of the United States had declared the commission that tried them illegal, why should they now, in a time of profound peace, be kept in prison? If such were the case would not an application have been immediately made by my learned brother for a writ of *habeas corpus* to release them? But nothing of the kind is done. And why? Because no such decision has ever been pronounced. No court has, and in my judgment no court will, pronounce this commission, thus formed by the President of the United States, to have been illegal."

As this is a question of the gravest importance we all ought to know whether, as claimed twice in the arguments of defendant's counsel, the military commission which tried the conspirators and assassins has been decided by the Supreme Court of the United States to have been an illegal tribunal. Judge Pierrepont, as we have seen, asserts boldly that in his judgment no such decision had ever been given by that tribunal, or ever would be. That the counsel for the defense did not really so understand it he clearly shows by the fact that they had never asked for a writ of *habeas corpus* in behalf of those who were working out the sentence of the commission. To his opinion I will now add that of Judge Fisher as given in his charge to the jury. It is as follows: —

"You have been told, gentlemen, in the argument of this case, that those who were tried before that military commission, and hung upon its findings, were themselves the victims of a base and disgraceful conspiracy to murder. Brave, gallant, and honest soldiers of their country have been held up before you as inhuman butchers of innocent men. It has been said in support of this denunciation, that the Supreme Court of the United State have, in the case of Milligan, declared that the military court which tried Herold and others for the murder of Abraham Lincoln was an illegal tribunal, organized without law, without right, and without warrant in the Constitution — a mere convocation of military men, having no right to try the cause committed to them by President Johnson; and it has been said that it was convoked not to try but to condemn.

"In my humble judgment the Supreme Court has made no such decision. If so, why have not the prisoners now confined upon the Dry Tortugas for complicity in the greatest crime of the age been released from their confinement? They have sympathizing friends enough to have applied any such decision in the direction of their deliverance, and they would not have remained there a week after the decision had been made to the effect that they were unlawfully restrained of their liberty. If I understand the decision in Milligan's case aright, it went upon the ground that the commission which tried Milligan was not organized in obedience to the act of Congress providing for the punishment of such crimes as he was charged with committing, and the opinion of the majority of the court went upon the additional ground that no hostile foot had ever pressed the soil of Indiana at the time when he was arraigned before a military tribunal there, and that, therefore, that tribunal which condemned him for acts of treason committed in that State had no authority to try him, notwithstanding the whole nation was involved in the most terrible struggle for its life. The majority opinion being thus predicated upon a misapprehension of historic truth, we could not, perhaps, have looked for a more rightful deduction.

"Unprepared, however, as all loyal hearts were for such an anouncement, the American people would be even yet more astounded to have it declared by any court in this country that the commander-in-chief of the army and navy, the President of the United States, has not the power in time of war to institute a military commission for the purpose of trying a gang of spies and traitors who have found their way within the intrenched encampments of the nation's capital to take the life of the chief of the army and navy, to assassinate all the heads of the executive departments, in the interest of the pretended government with which the federal government was engaged in war. They who maintain such a doctrine profess to defend it upon the ground that no such power is delegated by the constitution, as *they* did who could find no warrant there to coerce seceding States into submission to the federal authority; but the day has passed by when honest statesmen will longer, if they ever did, regard the sovereignty of the federal Union as possessing no powers save those expressly enumerated in the Constitution.

"The government of the United States was doubtless created by the adoption of the Constitution. But when it had once been spoken into being it stood upon the same level with other nations, and was clothed with all the powers incident to an independent sovereignty under the laws of nature and of nations, and among these was the power, in time of war or great public emergency, to arrest and inflict upon spies and traitors the most summary punishment, whenever and wherever the strong hand of military justice can be laid upon them. It is a power incident to the right and duty of self preservation, and ought to be exercised, just as the individual owes it to himself to strike down the assassin who is feeling for his heartstrings, without waiting to lose his own life, in order that the courts of justice may, at their leisure, proceed to try the felon according to the formularies of the law and the Constitution. The right of self-defense needs not to be inscribed upon parchment, either for individuals or for sovereign states. The Almighty impressed this right and duty upon the hearts and minds of men long before he wrote the decalogue upon the tables of stone. To say that this government has not the power in time of war to exercise this great duty of self-preservation, for want of warrant in the Constitution, is to condemn the action of the government in acquiring from France and Spain and Mexico and Russia territory lying far beyond the limits of the original thirteen States, because such power of acquisition and growth is not provided for by the Constitution. Both these powers are but the incidents of sovereignty, requiring no warrant in written governmental charter; they are derived from the common law of nations, and are co-existent with sovereignty.

"But with this military commission, gentlemen, you have no concern at this time; whether it was a legel or illegal tribunal, is not the matter on which you are now called to decide. The oath that you have taken requires that you shall 'well and truly try, and true deliverance make between the United States of America and John H. Surratt, the prisoner at the bar, whom you have in charge, and a true verdict give according to your evidence.' The prisoner stands before you indicted for the murder of Abraham Lincoln on the 14th day of April, 1865, in this city. About the time and place and manner of the death of your late President no controversy has been made in the case. If there had been your recollection of a nation in tears, and of a whole civilized world in mourning would have revived your memory of the sad and terrible fact. The only question, therefore, for you to determine is, whether the prisoner at the bar participated with John Wilkes Booth and the others named in the indictment, or either or any of them, in the diabolical crime. If, from all the evidence in the case, your minds shall be convinced beyond a reasonable doubt growing out of that evidence that the prisoner did co-operate with them; if that shall have produced a moral conviction in your minds that the prisoner did participate in the conspiracy to murder, or in a plot to do some unlawful act which resulted in this foul murder, no consideration as to the legality or illegality of the tribunal which tried the prisoner's mother; no feelings of sympathy for other members of the family; no consideration of his youth, or that other lives have already been forfeited for the crime, should for a single moment, tempt you to step aside from the plain pathway of duty."

The last paragraph quoted is directed to some of the many artful appeals made to the political prejudices or to the feelings of the jury to swerve them from the duty devolved upon them by their oath. The former paragraphs may well be said to set at rest forever the question of the right of a government to defend its life when the occasion requires it by sending offenders against its life before a military commission for trial. This question may be taken as settled, as is the question of the right of the federal government to coerce into submission a refractory State. The opportunity thus sought by the prisoner's counsel to foist upon the public mind the assertion that the Supreme Court of the United States had made a decision denying to the government this right, thus gave occasion not only for denying that such opinion had ever been delivered, but also for showing that it never could be.

It will be remembered that for reasons heretofore given the crime charged in the indictment was simply that of murder — the murder of Abraham Lincoln.

The fact of his being, at the time of his murder, the President of the United States was not mentioned. The treasonable purpose of that murder was also omitted no reference being made to the political reasons that moved the conspirators to the commission of the crime. The counsel for the defense contended most earnestly that because of these omissions the fact of the official position of Abraham Lincoln and of the political motives that inspired the crime could not be taken into consideration in the trial of the prisoner. They argued that it must be regarded in law simply as the murder of a man, and as a crime no more henious in character than the murder of the humblest citizen. Had the crime of treason been alleged in the indictment the defense would have been entitled to have a list of the witnesses by whom the government expected to prove the crime in advance of the trial; and it would have taken two witnesses to have established an overt act. The defense contended that because they were not entitled to these advantages under this indictment the prosecution could derive no advantages from the consideration of these facts; and that the case must be treated simply as a case of murder. The spirit of their argument would rather indicate that they really regarded it in the same light that Miss Anna Surratt did, as "nothing more than the death of the meanest nigger in the Union army."[1] The following is Mr. Pierrepont's reply to their argument on this point: —

"Our learned friends on the other side have told us, in the progress of their argument, that they could not subscribe in the least

[1] Testimony of L. J. Wiechmann, p. 454, Report of the trial of John H. Surratt.

degree to the doctrine that it was a higher crime to conspire against the government of the United States, and through that conspiracy commit a murder upon the Chief Magistrate, than it was to murder the humblest vagabond in the streets, or words to that effect. Now that is not the doctrine of a statesman; it is not the doctrine of the Bible; it is not the doctrine of the law. It is a far more heinous crime to conspire against the government of the United States and to murder its President for the purpose of bringing anarchy and confusion on the land, than to murder a single individual. It is because its consequences are so much more terrible. It is because it is involving the lives of hundreds and of thousands. It is because it is involving considerations affecting the stability, the protection, the life, and the liberty, it may be, of a nation. The law of England, which I have cited, but which it would seem, my friends have not read, lays it down, and without a statute, but as the common law, that it is a crime of such heniousness as to admit of no accessories.

"They, however, undertake to say that the crime of the murder of the President of the United States in time of war or great civil commotion, is not as henious a crime as it would be in England to murder the Chief of their country; and that there is no divinity about our government. What is its origin? All government is either of God or the devil, and they will have to take their choice. I say that the government is of God, and that no other government will stand. What says the civilized world upon this subject? I wrote a note to the Secretary of State two days ago, asking him to send me the letters that were transmitted from the different governments of the civilized world upon the subject of this murder, and what do you think he sent me? He sent me the note I hold in my hand and with it this large printed volume. It takes every line and word of that book, a book of 717 pages, closely printed, to contain the letters of condolence that were written to this government from the foreign governments of the world. Entire Christendom wrote, entire Christendom looked upon it as one of the most horrible of crimes — one that required every nation, even to the Turk, to write for the purpose of expressing their abhorrence of the crime. And, gentlemen, I hold in my hand the original paper sent by some 13,000 rebel prisoners, and our prisoners, at Point Lookout. Here is the paper in which these rebel prisoners, met together, passed their resolutions of condemnation, and their curse upon this crime. I would try this case before any twelve of those rebel prisoners, and feel certain of a verdict, and yet the gentlemen tell us this murder is like that of the commonest vagabond that ever walked the streets, and the crime no higher. Not so thought the rebels; not so thought any honorable man in arms against us; not so thinks any right-minded man upon the face of the earth."

The judge in giving his charge to the jury, addressing himself to this point, spoke as follows:—

"Historians and text writers on the law may treat of the heinousness of the crime of imagining the death of a weak or a wicked king or of a wise or benignant monarch, but you know, gentlemen, as well as you know that you exist, that to murder the duly elected President of the most powerful people on earth, is not less atrocious in its character than to compass the death of a king, or an emperor, albeit he may have sprang from the loins of the people, who have made him their representative head, and may have no royal blood coursing through his veins. You may be told that it is a crime surpassingly heinous to take or compass the life of him who has occupied a throne simply because he may be the king of an enslaved people, but that to take the life of the President of a free republic is an offense of no greater magnitude than to murder the 'veriest vagabond that walks your streets'; but an American jury will only believe this doctrine when the people have become so demoralized and corrupt, so devoid of the love of liberty and patriotic feeling, as to prefer to have a king and ruler foisted upon them by the accident of birth or fortunate adventure, rather than have the making of their own selection of him who is to execute their laws, and, for the time being, to stand as the representative head of their collective sovereignty.

"It is a mistake to suppose that a free people in any country will ever consider it a more henious crime to kill a king, or even to desire his death, than it is to assassinate a President. It is of no avail to tell you that to surround the life of a President of a republic with safeguards as sacred and powerful as those which, in monarchies, are thrown about a king, as you have been told in the argument, is a modern idea, 'entertained only by those whose eyes have been dazzled by visions of stars and garters, and who are desirous of changing our free institutions for a monarchical form of government.'

"On the contrary, they can only be opposed to guarding with sacred vigilance the life of the President of a free people who are themselves prepared to submit to the rule of a despot. Why should the people be less proud or less regardful of the life of a ruler selected by themselves, from among themselves, than they would be of the life of him who claimed to rule over them of his own right? When this question can be sensibly answered, I shall be willing to admit that the life of a President is less worth preserving than that of a king, and that to destroy the life of a President is a crime of less atrocity than to merely desire the death of a prince; but not till then; nor do I believe you will."

The practical legal bearing of this question on the trial was as to whether the prisoner, being proven to have been a member of the conspiracy which resulted in the death of President Lincoln by the hands of a fellow-conspirator, should be held as a principal in the crime, or only an accessory before the fact. In other words whether the court and jury could take cognizance of the official position of Abraham Lincoln without its being alleged in the indictment. If he could be regarded as a principal and not as an accessory he could be held equally guilty with Booth although he might not have been present and assisting in the assassination.

Practically, however, this was not a matter of any consequence in this trial, because it was proven beyond a doubt that the prisoner was actually present, acting a conspicious part in the execution of the plot. It was also proven by the testimony of one witness whose testimony was in no way impeached that it was he, and not Spangler, who prepared and fitted the bar to the door to prevent Booth being followed into the box at the theatre. The summing up of the evidence by Judge Pierrepont in his concluding speech is one of the most admirable and masterly efforts that can be anywhere found. In the first place it is a model of judicial fairness and honesty. To him the prisoner was evidently a pure abstraction toward whom he had no feelings. His only effort was to weigh impartially the evidence in the case, and to give to it a fair and common sense interpretation. He brushed away all side issues and every effort of the prisoner's counsel to bring the trial under the influence of political and of religious perjudices, and held them strictly to the question of the guilt or innocence of the prisoner, as shown by the evidence. Again it was a model effort in its logical ability in bringing the evidence before the jury. He had so completely analyzed the testimony that he was able to present it in its logical connection as to time, purpose, and circumstances; tracing the plot through the evidence before him, from its incipiency to its completion, step by step, showing the bearing and relation that one thing sustained to another in a most conclusive and unanswerable way.

He had systematically and logically arranged the testimony, which had necessarily been presented in a most desultory and unsatisfactory way, from the fact that the evidence had to be taken just as witnesses were found to be present. By great care and labor the judge had arranged the evidence just in the order in which he would have chosen to introduce it had the witnesses all been at his command at the moment he would have chosen to use them. Having thus arranged the testimony, he simply read it to the jury, stopping when necessary to comment on it and interpret it. His fair, natural, common sense interpretation of the facts proven could not fail to bring conviction to every intelligent, and candid mind. That the proof before him had brought to the mind of this eminent and experienced advocate and jurist the most complete conviction of the prisoner's guilt, is shown throughout his argument. He did not, however, leave the matter of his own convictions to be the subject merely of inference, but left himself on record on this point as follows: —

" In this case I feel justified in saying, that the prisoner is proved to be guilty, and in as overwhelming a manner as any man was ever proven guilty in the history of jurisprudence. I appeal to any judge, any lawyer, any man who has had experience, if there was ever a case where the guilt of the party, was more clearly demonstrated. He is proven guilty not only beyond a reasonable doubt, but beyond the possibility of any doubt. There is not a man of you who can doubt it. It has been a strange case. It was a strange providence that brought the man back here to be tried. And now that he is here, you, the twelve men who in the providence of God have been selected to try the case, are to say whether what he has done is right or not right; whether he is guilty or not guilty.

"That is for you to say, not for me. I know he is proved guilty. About that there can be no doubt. I do not believe that any of you have any doubt whatever on that subject."

That the purpose of this conspiracy was to assassinate the heads of the government from its very first inception, is made clear by the whole run of the evidence brought out on the two trials. Atzerodt, in his confession, which he had gotten up to be used in his defence, claims that he was a member of a conspiracy to kidnap the President, and carry him to Richmond. John H. Surratt, in his Rockville lecture, claims the same thing. They both claim that when Booth laid aside this plan as impracticable, and proposed to change it to a conspiracy to assassinate, that they withdrew, and would have nothing further to do with it. It is evident that the statements of both are false, both as regards the original purpose of the conspiracy, and also their abandonment of it. Surratt in his confessions to McMillen stated that he received a letter from Booth in Montreal on the 10th of April. This letter was written from New York, and summoned him to Washington at once, as it had become necessary for them to change their plans and to act quickly.

He left Montreal in obedience to this summons on the 12th of April, and was in Elmira on the morning of the 13th. In his defense of an *alibi*, he tried to prove that he remained at Elmira until after the 15th, and then returned to Montreal, where he arrived on the 18th.

His counsel argued that the plan up to that time had been to capture, and that it was then for the first time that Booth had determined to assassinate; that this was the change of plan referred to in his letter, and that, as Surratt, according to their plea, never saw him after this change of plan had been determined upon, he knew nothing about it, and was never a member of a conspiracy to assassinate. He admitted that he left Montreal in response to Booth's letter, but claimed that he did not go any further than Elmira, in his defense.

This, also, is his story in his Rockville lecture, in which he admits that he was a member of the conspiracy to capture the President, but asserts that he was never a member of the conspiracy to assassinate him. Why did he obey Booth's summons which required him to come at once to Washington? Why did he come by way of Elmira? He says in his lecture that he went to Elmira in the interest of a plan to liberate the rebel prisoners that were held at that place. He had just been to Richmond, carrying dispatches from Davis and Benjamin to their agents in Canada. Active measures were at once resorted to to accomplish the assassinations that had been planned without delay, and had the scheme been fully realized it was no doubt a part of this plan to bring into active service at once all the secret treasonable military organizations throughout the North, liberate all the rebel prisoners held in Northern prisons, and inaugurate a new rebellion in the North, in aid of the existing rebellion in the South. Surratt admits that he went to Elmira on this business. He went there no doubt to arrange with other conspirators there for carrying out this purpose when notified of the success of the assassination plot. No doubt similar arrangements had been made at Chicago to liberate the prisoners at Camp Douglass; and perhaps at other places. The partial failure of the assassination plot, and the signal triumph of our arms, admonished these Northern traitors that they had better not enter the arena of actual war, and frustrated all the plans of Jefferson Davis and his Canada Cabinet. Surratt's admissions are right in the line of our theory, and tend to prove its correctness; but his claim that he was only a member of a conspiracy to capture is manifestly untrue. Let us hear the conclusion of that eminent jurist, Judge Pierrepont, founded on a careful consideration of all the evidence on this point. "Now you see gentlemen, what is meant by a change of plan. In the spring of 1864 the plan was to murder Mr. Lincoln. They laid various plans for its accomplishment.

They thought to do it as he went to the Soldiers' Home, by the telescopic rifle, and they did not intend, in the event of concluding to carry out that plan, to let his wife or his child stand in their way. They then thought to do it by having Payne call upon Mr. Lincoln, get into conversation with him, listen to his stories, seem to be interested in them, and then, at that moment, to strike the knife home, deep into his heart. They at another time thought to poison him, and for this purpose tried the cup; but it seemed that that failed them once, and, as Booth said, might fail them again. They finally concluded they would try to kill him in the theatre, instead of on his way to the Soldiers' Home, and have Payne kill Secretary Seward at his house. That plan they carried out. But, gentlemen, notwithstanding this change of plan, never was there for more than a year any other purpose than to murder. They had long since abandoned the idea of kidnapping, for that required too much machinery, too many men, and subjected them to too much danger; and the changes in plan that had taken place recently were simply as to the mode of killing, and the men who should strike the fatal blow." Here we have the mature opinion of an eminent jurist, founded on a thorough and careful examination of all the evidence, and we feel confident that no candid, intelligent man who studies all the evidence with care can come to any other.

Having had occasion to follow the history of this sad affair from its incipiency to its conclusion, as revealed by the evidence produced before the commission, and that brought out on the civil trial, my purpose in writing this book has been fulfilled. It was, first, to correct many grave errors in public opinion that have grown out of a wilful and ingenious suppression of the truth and an unblushing publication of falsehoods, in order to cover up from view the fact that the assassination of President Lincoln was the result of a deep-laid political scheme to subvert the government of the United States in aid of the rebellion; that it was not merely the rash act of Booth and his co-conspirators, to whom the work was intrusted; but that behind these stood Jefferson Davis and his Canada cabinet; that it was the work of a great conspiracy.

The second object of the author was to vindicate the government in its method of dealing with the assassins, and to show that the decisions of the commission were founded on adequate testimony. And, lastly, to so gather up and present the truth, as shown by the evidence, that his work might be of some service to the future historian. He feels that he has kept faithful to his purpose to present nothing but the truth. He feels that by this he has not only vindicated the government, but that also in doing this he has vindicated the commission. He has shown that a military commission was the only tribunal before which the conspirators and assassins could properly be tried; that the right of the government to try offenses of this character is a power inherent in sovereignty as is the right of personal self-defence a right that inheres to the individual; that the laws of war recognize this right and justify its exercise. The wisdom of the government in dealing thus summarily with these offenders was seen in its effect on the Canada conspirators, who at first were swearing that "they were not done yet," but who were driven to their holes by the prompt and wise action of the government in dealing thus summarily with their hired assassins as fast as they were caught. The government thus compelled its enemies to respect its authority.

And, finally, the result of the trial of one of the conspirators before a civil court, more than anything else, vindicates its wisdom in sending these prisoners before a military tribunal for trial.

Side Lights on the Conspiracy.

John Matthews gives us the substance of a paper put into his hands by Booth on the afternoon of the assassination, which closed as follows: "Men who love their country better than their lives — Booth, Payne, Atzerodt, and Herold."[1] It will be observed that Booth here identifies Atzerodt with the conspiracy and the evidence shows that he relied on Atzerodt at that time to perform the part he assigned to him: to assassinate Vice-President Johnson. He had transferred Atzerodt from the Pennsylvania House, where he had been boarding, to the Kirkwood House on the morning of that day, having engaged his room but for one day, and paying for

[1] In a communication to a Philadelphia paper.

it in advance. This change was made because the Vice-President was stopping at the Kirkwood.

That Booth had visited Atzerodt at his room during the day was shown by the fact that his coat, containing his bank book and handkerchiefs marked in his name, was found in Atzerodt's room where he had hung it up and then forgotten to take it again when he left. That the purpose was a murderous purpose was shown by the fact that a pistol, loaded and capped, together with a large dagger, were found hid away in the bed. Booth had been there schooling Atzerodt in his part, and had had such assurances from Atzerodt that he felt safe in coupling his name with his own and those of Payne and Herold in the paper referred to. Matthews stated that whilst he was in conversation with Booth, General Grant passed rapidly down the Avenue in an open carriage, having his baggage along with him; that he called Booth's attention to this fact, when Booth left him abruptly and galloped down the avenue after General Grant. Why did he do this? What did this mean? When Atzerodt had made his way into the country, and was eating his dinner on Sabbath, the 16th, at the house of Hezekiah Metz, he was asked if it was true, as had been reported, that General Grant had been killed, answered, "If the man who was to follow him had done so, it was likely to be true." This explains Booth's purpose in galloping after General Grant when he saw that he was about to leave the city. He hurried to inform O'Laughlin of the fact and to have him follow the General and assassinate him on the road or at the end of his journey, and had told Atzerodt of this arrangement. We can in this way account for the fact that Atzerodt knew that a man had had orders to follow him. The fact that Booth, in the paper referred to, coupled Atzerodt's name with his own and those of Payne and Herold as "men who loved their country better than their lives" shows that he fully expected Atzerodt to perform the part he had assigned him in the tragedy. O'Laughlin was no doubt the man who had orders to follow the General, but upon reflection, wisely declined to do so.

Dr. Mudd voluntarily confessed to Captain Dutton, who had charge of the convicts who were sent to the Dry Tortugas, whilst on their voyage thither, that he knew Booth when he came to his house on the morning of the 15th of April; and said that he denied it because he was afraid of endangering his own life, and the lives of his family. He also admitted that he went to Washington by appointment to introduce Booth to Surratt, and that Wiechmann's testimony on this point was true. Why, if innocent, should he have been afraid to let it be known that Booth and Herold called at his house on that morning, and what he had done for them? This fear could only have come from a consciousness of guilt, and shows that he not only knew what they had done, but, also, that he was implicated in their guilt by his previous knowledge of what they were going to do. John H. Surratt, after he had been set at liberty, delivered a lecture at Rockville, Maryland, in which he denied that he ever knew of the plot to assassinate, but admitted that he was a member of a conspiracy to capture President Lincoln and carry him a prisoner to Richmond. He asserts that this was Booth's purpose whilst he was co-operating with him, and that they had spent a great deal of money ($10,000) in preparations to effect their object. He claims that neither the Richmond government, nor its agents in Canada, knew anything about their scheme, and that they alone were responsible for it. Where then did they get their $10,000 to spend on it? They were both without means of their own, and without employment. The Rockville lecture is simply a plausible tissue of falsehoods, well put together, but altogether inconsistant with the whole tenure of the evidence in the case. It is contradicted at almost every point by the testimony we have had under review. Yet its admissions are important, as they establish the theory of the conspiracy which we have maintained. He admits that he was engaged in the secret service of the Confederate government almost constantly from the time he left college in the summer of 1861, and that he enjoyed that service greatly, and was very active in it. He claims that he was entrusted with dispatches for the agents of that government in Canada, and that he passed from the one place to the other frequently. He admits that he reached Montreal on the 6th of April with dispatches from Davis and Benjamin to Thompson. Of course he does not say that he also carried Bills of Exchange on Liverpool at the same time for $70,000, or that he carried funds at any time; but we have had the proof of this fact. He admits that he went from Montreal on the 12th of April, to Elmira, New York, and claims that he remained there until after the assassination.

This we have seen was proven to be a falsehood, yet his purpose in going to Elmira, as claimed by himself, confirms our theory that the plan of the conspirators was in connection with the assassinations which they had planned to get up a Northern rebellion in aid of that of the South, through the agency of the secret disloyal organizations with whom they were in correspondence throughout the Northwestern and Middle States, and to liberate all the rebel prisoners held in Northern prisons to augment their forces, and in the state of anarchy and confusion, consequent upon the deprivation of the government of a civil head, and the army of a lawful commander, they thus intended inaugurating a reign of terror throughout the North that would make a further prosecution of the war impossible, and by this means establish the Southern Confederacy. Surratt says in his lecture that he went to Elmira for the purpose of preparing for the release of the more than five thousand rebel prisoners that were held at that place. The author, after a very careful scrutiny of all the evidence relating to the question of Surratt's presence in Washington on the night of the assassination, and of his participation in it, has not hesitated to express the opinion that this was proven. By all legal rules the plea of an *alibi* failed as the vast preponderance of evidence went to prove his presence as charged. But even if we admit that he was at Elmira, as claimed, on the night of the assassination, and that he remained there until the 16th of April, he is not by this admission disconnected with the conspiracy, but was by his own admission acting there in the interest of its purposes by setting at large the five thousand rebel prisoners held there by the government. The effort to aid the rebellion by this step was contingent upon the accomplishment of all of the assassinations that had been planned. The failure to do this rendered his mission there useless. If he was there, he was there in the interest of the conspiracy. That he had all of its guilt upon his conscience is shown by the facts of his flight and concealment.

Thompson and his gang claimed, in the fall of 1864, it will be remembered, that they had eight hundred men hid away in Chicago for the purpose of liberating the rebel prisoners held in Camp Douglass. They were only waiting for a safe opportunity, for which they were planning to secure an opportune moment. Why did Vallandigham break his parole in the summer of 1864 and return to Ohio to become a candidate for the governorship of that state? It was no doubt in the interest of this new rebellion that had been planned, and that he might be in a position to carry out the details of these nefarious schemes. It will be remembered that he had been elected Supreme Commander of the order of American Knights at their annual meeting in February, 1863. During Vallandigham's enforced absence, Robert Holloway acted as Lieutenant-General, or Deputy Supreme Commander, and Doctor Massey of Ohio was Secretary of State. The organization was a military one, of which Vallandigham was recognized as General, and had a complete army organization, and was, in 1864, arming, drilling, and preparing for a Northern rebellion, and the accomplishment of the assassinations that were planned and arranged for was no doubt to have been the signal for a general uprising. It may be asked, why, if this theory be correct, was not this purpose carried out? We answer simply because that God who planted, and has hitherto watched over our nation, frustrated the scheme. He so ordered the events of his providence that the carrying out of this wicked scheme became manifestly impossible. The plan to deprive the government of a civil head and the army of a lawful commander failed. The collapse of the rebellion was precipitated so rapidly that it was manifestly useless to attempt to give it aid. The valor, prowess, skill, and loyalty of our victorious legions was a menace to copperheadism. This secret army concluded that discretion was the better part of valor, and sought safely in seclusion, but not quite in silence. They still continued to hiss.

To God's over-ruling and protecting care we owe our thanks for the preservation of our government, and for the peace and prosperity with which we have been blessed, and it is in Him alone that we can found our hopes for the future. Let us reverently study and learn the lessons of our great civil war, that we may learn to avert future judgments by putting away all our idols, and all the abominations of our national life, remembering that it is righteousness alone that exalteth a nation, and gives to it peace and prosperity, and that sin is not only a reproach to any people, but that national sins, if persisted in, justified and incorporated into national policy, will inevitably call down the judgments of a holy, righteous, and just God.

APPENDIX.

PREFACE TO APPENDIX.

In presenting the great argument of the Hon. John A. Bingham, Assistant Judge Advocate, on the trial of the assassins, the author feels that he does not need to offer an apology to his readers, notwithstanding its length.

In addition to what he has already said by way of commending it to the careful perusal of his readers, he will add by way of preface, the following extracts from Barnes's 40th Congress, Vol. I, showing the light in which that great effort was viewed by competent judges at the time; and also giving extracts from his great argument before the United States Senate on the articles of impeachment found against Andrew Johnson, President of the United States, for high crimes and misdemeanors, in vindication of the high encomiums bestowed by him on this distinguished statesman and advocate.

EXTRACTS FROM "THE FORTIETH CONGRESS OF THE UNITED STATES."

BY WILLIAM H. BARNES:—1ST VOL., 40TH CONGRESS.

Mr. Bingham served as Special Judge Advocate in the great trial of the conspirators, who were tried for the assassination of Abraham Lincoln, etc. Immense labor devolved upon him during this difficult and protracted trial, and for eight weeks his arduous duties allowed him but brief intervals of rest. He occupied nine hours in the delivery of the closing arguments, in which he ably elucidated the law and the testimony in the case, and conclusively proved the guilt of the conspirators. Mr. Bingham's success in this great trial attracted general attention, and awakened a wide-spread curiosity to know his history. Soon after the close of the trial, a correspondent of the *Philadelphia Press*, having expressed the deep interest he had felt in arriving at a well founded conclusion as to "the guilt of the conspirators and the constitutionality of the court," wrote as follows:—

"Grant me space in your columns to give expression to my most unqualified admiration of the great arguments, on these two main points, presented to the court by the Special Judge Advocate, Gen. John A. Bingham. In the entire range of my reading, I have known of no productions that have so literally led me captive. For careful analysis, logical argumentation, profound and most extensive research; for overwhelming unravelment of complications that would have involved an ordinary mind only with inextricable bewilderment, and for a literal rending to tatters of all the metaphysical subleties of the array of legal talent engaged on the other side, I know of no two productions in the English language superior to these. They are literally as the spear of Ithuriel, dissolving the hardest substances at their touch; as the thread of Dædalus, leading out of the labyrinths of error, no matter how thick and mazy. Not Locke or Bacon were more profound; not Daniel Webster was clearer and more penetrating; not Chillingworth was more logical. I feel sure that the author of these two unrivalled papers must possess a legal mind unrivalled in America, and must be, too, one of our rising statesmen. But who is John A. Bingham, who by his industry and learning displayed on this wonderful trial, has placed the country under such a heavy debt of obligation? He may be well known to others moving in a public sphere, like yourself, but to me, so absorbed in a different line of duty, he has appeared so suddenly, and yet with such vividness, that I long to know some, at least, of his antecedents."

Upon which the editor remarked:—

"The question of our esteemed correspondent is natural to one who has not, probably, watched the individual actors on the great stage of public affairs with the interest of the historical and political student. We are not surprised that the arguments of Mr. Bingham before the military commission should have filled him with delight. It was worthy of the great subject confided to that accomplished statesman by the Government, and of his own fame. When the assassins of Mr. Lincoln were sent for trial before the military court by President Johnson, the Government wisely left the whole management to Judge Holt and his eloquent associate, Mr. Bingham, and to the latter was committed the stupendous labor of sifting the mass of evidence, of replying to the corps of lawyers for the defence, of setting forth the guilt of the accused and of vindicating the policy and the duty of the executive in an exigency so novel and so full of tragic solemnity. The crime was so enormous, and the trial of those who committed it so important in all its issues, immediate, contingent and remote, as to awaken an excitement that embraced all nations. The murder itself was almost forgotten by those who wished to screen the murderers, and the most wicked theories were broached and sown broadcast by men, who, under cloak of reverence for what they called the law, toiled with herculean energy to weaken the arm of the Government, extended in time of war to save the servants of the people from being slaughtered by assassins in public places, and tracked even to their firesides by the agents and friends of slavery. These poisons of plausibility, blunting the sharpest horrors of any age, and sanctifying the most hellish offenses, required an antidote as swift to cure. Mr. Bingham's two great arguments, alluded to by our correspondent, have supplied the remedy. They are monuments of reflection, research, and argumentation; and they are presented in the language of a scholar and with the fervor of an orator. In the great volume of proof and counter-proof, rhetoric, and controversy that forever preserves the record of this great trial, the efforts of Mr. Bingham will ever remain to be first studied with an eager and admiring interest. That they came, after all that has and can be said against the Government, is rather an inducement to their more satisfactory and critical consideration. For from that study the American student and citizen must, more than ever, realize how irresistible is Truth when in conflict with Falsehood, and how poor and puerile are all the professional tricks of the lawyer when opposed to the moral power of the patriot."

In Congress Mr. Bingham has had a distinguished career, marked by important services to the country. In the XXXVIIth Congress he was earnest and successful in advocating many important measures to promote the vigorous prosecution of the war, which had just begun. Returning to Congress in 1865, after an absence of two years, he at once took a prominent position. Upon the formation of the joint committee on Reconstruction, December 14th, 1865, he was appointed one of the nine members on the part of the House. He was active in advocating the great measures of Reconstruction, which were proposed and passed in the XXXIXth and XLth Congresses. The House of Representatives having resolved that Andrew Johnson should be impeached for "high crimes and misdemeanors," Mr. Bingham was appointed on the committee to which was intrusted the important duty of drawing up the Articles of Impeachment. This work having been done to the satisfaction of the House, Mr. Bingham was elected chairman of the managers to conduct the impeachment of the President before the Senate.

On him devolved the duty of making the closing argument. His speech on this occasion ranks among the greatest forensic efforts of any age. He began the delivery of his argument on Monday, May 4th, and occupied the attention of the Senate, and a vast auditory on the floor and in the galleries, during three successive days. At the close of his argument, the immense audience in the galleries, wrought up to the highest pitch of enthusiasm, gave vent to such an unanimous and continued outburst of applause as has never before been heard in the Capitol. Ladies and gentlemen, who could not have been induced deliberately to trespass on the decorum of the Senate, by whose courtesy they were admitted to the galleries, overcome by their feelings, joined in the utterance of applause, knowing that for so doing the Sergeant-at-arms would be required to expel them from the galleries. The history of the country records no similar tribute to the oratorial efforts of the ablest advocates or statesmen. From so long and so well-sustained an argument, it is impossible to select particular passages which would give an adequate idea of the whole. The following historical argument for the supremacy of the law will always be read with interest, whether as an extract, or in its original setting: —

"Is it not in vain, I ask you, Senators, that the people have thus vindicated by battle the supremacy of their own Constitution and laws, if, after all, their President is permitted to suspend their laws and dispense with the execution thereof at pleasure, and defy the power of the people to bring him to trial and judgment before the only tribunal authorized by the Constitution to try him? That is the issue that is presented before the Senate for decision by these articles of impeachment. By such acts of usurpation on the part of the ruler of a people, I need not say to the Senate, the peace of nations is broken, as it is only by obedience to law that the peace of nations is maintained, and their existence perpetuated. Law is the voice of God and the harmony of the world: —

"'It doth preserve the stars from wrong,
Through it the eternal heavens are fresh and strong.'

"All history is but philosophy, teaching by example. God is in history, and through it teaches to men and nations the profoundest lessons which they learn. It does not surprise me, Senators, that the learned counsel for the accused asked the Senate, in the consideration of this question, to close that volume of instruction, not to look into the past, and not to listen to its voices. Senators, from that day when the inscription was written upon the graves of the heroes of Thermopylæ, 'Stranger, go tell the Lacedemonians that we lie here in obedience to their laws,' to this hour, no profounder lesson than this has come down to us: that through obedience to law comes the strength of nations and the safety of men.

"No more fatal provision ever found its way into the Constitutions of States than that contended for in this defense which recognizes the right of a single despot or of the many to discriminate in the administration of justice between the ruler and the citizen, between the strong and the weak. It was by this unjust discrimination that Aristides was banished because he was just. It was by this unjust discrimination that Socrates, the wonder of the Pagan world, was doomed to drink the hemlock because of his transcendant virtues. It was in honorable protest against this unjust discriminatton that the great Roman Senator, father of his country, declared that the force of the law consists in its being made for the whole community. Senators, it is the pride and boast of that great people from whom we are descended, as it is the pride and boast of every American, that the law is the supreme power of the State, that it is for the protection of each, by the combined power of all. By the Constitution of England the hereditary monarch is no more above the law than the humblest subject; and by the Constitution of the United States, the President is no more above the law than the poorest and most friendless beggar in your streets. The usurpations of Charles I. inflicted untold injuries upon the people of England, and finally cost the usurper his life. The subsequent usurpations of James II., and I only refer to it because there is between his official conduct and that of this accused President, the most remarkable parallel that I have ever read in history, filled the heart and brain of England with conviction that new securities must be taken to restrain the prerogatives asserted by the crown, if they would maintain their ancient Constitution and perpetuate their liberties. It is well said by Hallam that the usurpations of James swept away the solemn ordinances of the legislature. Out of those usurpations came the great revolution of 1688, which resulted in the dethronement and banishment of James, in the elevation of William and Mary, and in the immortal Declaration of Rights.

" I ask the Senate to notice that these charges against James are substantially the charges presented against this accused President, and confessed here of record, that he has suspended the laws, and dispensed with the execution of laws, and in order to do this has usurped authority as the executive of the nation, declaring himself entitled under the Constitution to suspend the laws and dispense with their execution. He has further, like James, attempted to control the appropriated money of the people contrary to law. And he has further, like James, although it is not alleged against him in the Articles of Impeachment, it is confessed in his answer, and attempted to cause the question of his responsibility to the people to be tried, not in the King's Bench, but in the Supreme Court, when that question is alone cognizable in the Senate of the United States. Surely, Senators, if these usurpations, if these endeavors on the part of James thus to subvert the liberties of the people of England, cost him his crown and kingdom, the like offenses committed by Andrew Johnson ought to cost him his office, and to subject him to that perpetual disability pronounced by the people through the Constitution upon him for his high crimes and misdemeanors.

" I ask you, Senators, how long men would deliberate upon the question whether a private citizen arraigned at the bar of one of your tribunals of justice for a criminal violation of the law, should be permitted to interpose a plea in justification of his criminal act, that his only purpose was to interpret the Constitution and laws for himself, that he violated the law in the exercise of his prerogative to test its validity hereafter at such a day as might suit his own convenience in the courts of justice. Surely it is as competent for the private citizen to interpose such justification in answer to crime in one of your tribunals of justice, as it is for the President to interpose it, and for the simple reason that the Constitution is no respecter of persons, and rests neither in the private citizen judicial power.

" Can it be that by your decree you are at last to make this discrimination between the ruler of the people and the private citizen, and to allow him to interpose his assumed right to interpret judicially your Constitution and laws? Are you to solemnly proclaim by your decree : —

" ' Plate sin with gold,
And the strong lance of justice heartless breaks;
Arm it in rags and a pigmy's straw doth pierce it? '

" I put away the possibility that the Senate of the United States, equal in dignity to any tribunal in the world, is capable of recording any such decision even upon the petition and prayer of the accused and guilty President. Can it be that by reason of his great office the President is to be protected in his high crimes and misdemeanors, violative alike of his oath, of the Constitution and of the express letter of your written law, enacted by the legislative department of the government?

"I ask you, Senators, to consider that I speak before you this day in behalf of the violated law of a free people, who commission me. I ask you to remember this, that I speak this day under the obligations of this my oath. I ask you to consider that I am not insensible to the significance of the words of which mention was made by the learned counsel from New York; justice, duty, law, oath. I ask you to remember that the great principles of constitutional liberty for which I speak this day, have been taught to men and nations by all the trials and triumphs, by all the agonies and martyrdoms of the past; that they are the wisdom of the centuries uttered by the elect of the human race.

"I ask you to consider that we stand this day pleading for the violated majesty of the law, by the graves of half a million of martyred hero-patriots who sacrificed themselves for their country, the Constitution, and the laws, and who by their sublime examples have taught us that all must obey the law; that none are above the law; that no man lives for himself alone, but each for all, that some must die that the State may live; that the citizen is but for to-day, that the commonwealth is for all time, and that position, however high, patronage however powerful, cannot be permitted to shelter crime to the peril of the Republic."

ARGUMENT OF JOHN A. BINGHAM,

SPECIAL JUDGE ADVOCATE,

IN REPLY TO THE SEVERAL ARGUMENTS IN DEFENCE OF MARY E. SURRATT AND OTHERS, CHARGED WITH CONSPIRACY AND THE MURDER OF ABRAHAM LINCOLN, LATE PRESIDENT OF THE UNITED STATES, ETC.

MAY IT PLEASE THE COURT: The conspiracy here charged and specified, and the acts alleged to have been committed in pursuance thereof, and with the intent laid, constitute a crime the atrocity of which has sent a shudder through the civilized world. All that was agreed upon and attempted by the alleged inciters and instigators of this crime constitutes a combination of atrocities with scarcely a parallel in the annals of the human race. Whether the prisoners at your bar are guilty of the conspiracy and the acts alleged to have been done in pursuance thereof, as set forth in the charge and specification, is a question the determination of which rests solely with this honorable court, and in passing upon which this court are the sole judges of the law and the fact.

In presenting my views upon the questions of law raised by the several counsel for the defence, and also on the testimony adduced for and against the accused, I desire to be just to them, just to you, just to my country, and just to my own convictions. The issue joined involves the highest interests of the accused, and, in my judgment, the highest interests of the whole people of the United States.

It is a matter of great moment to all the people of this country that the prisoners at your bar be lawfully tried and lawfully convicted or acquitted. A wrongful and illegal conviction or a wrongful and illegal acquittal upon this dread issue would impair somewhat the security of every man's life, and shake the stability of the republic.

The crime charged and specified upon your record is not simply the crime of murdering a human being, but it is the crime of killing and murdering on the 14th day of April, A. D. 1865, within the military department of Washington and the intrenched lines thereof, Abraham Lincoln, then President of the United States, and Commander-in-Chief of the army and navy thereof; and then and there assaulting, with intent to kill and murder, William H. Seward, then Secretary of State of the United States; and then and there lying in wait to kill and murder Andrew Johnson, then Vice-President of the United States, and Ulysses S. Grant, then lieutenant-general and in command of the armies of the United States, in pursuance of a treasonable conspiracy entered into by the accused with one John Wilkes Booth, and John H. Surratt, upon the instigation of Jefferson Davis, Jacob Thompson, and George N. Sanders and others, with intent thereby to aid the existing rebellion and subvert the Constitution and laws of the United States.

The rebellion, in aid of which this conspiracy was formed and this great public crime committed, was prosecuted for the vindication of no right, for the redress of no wrong, but was itself simply a criminal conspiracy and gigantic assassination. In resisting and crushing this rebellion the American people take no step backward and cast no reproach upon their past history. That people now, as ever, proclaim the self-evident truth that whenever government becomes subversive of the ends of its creation, it is the right and duty of the people to alter or abolish it; but during these four years of conflict they have as clearly proclaimed, as was their right and duty, both by law and by arms, that the government of their own choice, humanely and wisely administered, oppressive of none and just to all, shall not be overthrown by privy conspiracy or armed rebellion.

What wrong had this government or any of its duly constituted agents done to any of the guilty actors in this atrocious rebellion? They themselves being witnesses, the government which they assailed had done no act, and attempted no act, injurious to them, or in any sense violative of their rights as citizens and men; and yet for four years, without cause of complaint or colorable excuse, the inciters and instigators of the conspiracy charged upon your record have, by armed rebellion, resisted the lawful authority of the government, and attempted by force of arms to blot the republic from the map of nations. Now that their battalions of treason are broken and flying before the victorious legions of the republic, the chief traitors in this great crime against your government secretly conspire with their hired confederates to achieve by assassination, if possible, what they have in vain attempted by wager of battle — the overthrow of the government of the United States and the subversion of its Constitution and laws. It is for this secret conspiracy in the interest of the rebellion, formed at the instigation of the chiefs in that rebellion, and in pursuance of which the acts charged and specified are alleged to have been done and with the intent laid, that the accused are upon trial.

The government, in preferring this charge, does not indict the whole people of any State or section, but only the alleged parties to this unnatural and atrocious conspiracy and crime. The President of the United States, in the discharge of his duty as Commander-in-Chief of the army, and by virtue of the power vested in him by the Constitution and laws of the United States, has constituted you a military court, to hear and determine the issue joined against the accused, and has constituted you a court for no other purpose whatever. To this charge and specification the defendants have pleaded, first, that this court has no jurisdiction in the premises; and, second, not guilty. As the court has already overruled the plea to the jurisdiction, it would be passed over in silence by me but for the fact that a grave and elaborate argument has been made by counsel for the accused not only to show the want of jurisdiction, but to arraign the President of the United States before the country and the world as a usurper of power over the lives and the liberties of the prisoners. Denying the authority of the President to constitute this commission is an averment that this tribunal is not a court of justice, has no legal existence, and therefore no power to hear and determine the issue joined. The learned counsel for the accused, when they make this averment by way of argument, owe it to themselves and to their country to show how the President could otherwise lawfully and efficiently discharge the duty enjoined upon him by his oath to protect, preserve, and defend the Constitution of the United States, and to take care that the laws be faithfully executed.

An existing rebellion is alleged and not denied. It is charged that in aid of this existing rebellion a conspiracy was entered into by the accused, incited and instigated thereto by the chiefs of this rebellion, to kill and murder the executive officers of the government and the commander of the armies of the United States, and that this conspiracy was partly executed by the murder of Abraham Lincoln, and by a murderous assault upon the Secretary of State; and counsel reply, by elaborate argument, that although the facts be as charged, though the conspirators be numerous and at large, able and eager to complete the horrid work of assassination already begun within your military encampment, yet the successor of your murdered President is a usurper if he attempts by military force and martial law, as Commander-in-Chief, to prevent the consummation of this traitorous conspiracy in aid of this treasonable rebellion. The civil courts, say the counsel, are open in the District. I answer, they are closed throughout half the republic, and were only open in this District on the day of this confederation and conspiracy, on the day of the traitorous assassination of your President, and are only open at this hour by force of the bayonet. Does any man suppose that if the military forces which garrison the intrenchments of your capital, fifty thousand strong, were all withdrawn, the rebel bands who this day infest the mountain passes in your vicinity would allow this court, or any court, to remain open in this District for the trial of these their confederates, or would permit your executive officers to discharge the trust committed to them, for twenty-four hours?

At the time this conspiracy was entered into, and when this court was convened and entered upon this trial, the country was in a state of civil war. An army of insurrectionists have, since this trial begun, shed the blood of Union soldiers in battle. The conspirator, by whose hand his co-conspirators, whether present or absent, jointly murdered the President on the 14th of last April, could not be and was not arrested upon civil process, but was pursued by the military power of the government, captured, and slain. Was this an act of usurpation? — a violation of the right guaranteed to that fleeing assassin by the very Constitution against which and for the subversion of which he had conspired and murdered the President? Who in all this land is bold enough or base enough to assert it?

I would be glad to know by what law the President, by a military force, acting only upon his military orders, is justified in pursuing, arresting, and killing one of these conspirators, and is condemned for arresting in like manner, and by his order subjecting to trial, according to the laws of war, any or all of the other parties to this same damnable conspiracy and crime, by a military tribunal of justice — a tribunal, I may be pardoned for saying, whose integrity and impartiality are above suspicion, and pass unchallenged even by the accused themselves.

The argument against the jurisdiction of this court rests upon the assumption that even in time of insurrection and civil war no crimes are cognizable and punishable by military commission or court-martial, save crimes committed in the military or naval service of the United States, or in the militia of the several states when called into the actual service of the United States. But that is not all the argument: it affirms that under this plea to the jurisdiction the accused have the right to demand that this court shall decide that it is not a judicial tribunal and has no legal existence.

This is a most extraordinary proposition — that the President, under the Constitution and laws of the United States, was not only not authorized, but absolutely forbidden, to constitute this court for the trial of the accused, and, therefore, the act of the President is void, and the gentlemen who compose the tribunal without judicial authority or power, and are not in fact or in law a court.

That I do not misstate what is claimed and attempted to be established on behalf of the accused, I ask the attention of the court to the following as the gentleman's (Mr. Johnson's) propositions: —

That Congress has not authorized, and, under the Constitution, cannot authorize the appointment of this commission.

That this commission has, "as a court, no legal existence or authority," because the President, who alone appointed the commission, has no such power.

That his act "is a mere nullity — the usurpation of a power not vested in the Executive, and conferring no authority upon you."

We have had no common exhibition of law learning in this defence, prepared by a Senator of the United States; but with all his experience, and all his learning and acknowledged ability, he has failed, utterly failed, to show how a tribunal constituted and sworn, as this has been, to duly try and determine the charge and specification against the accused, and by its commission not authorized to hear or determine any other issues whatever, can rightfully entertain, or can by any possibility pass upon, the proposition presented by this argument of the gentleman for its consideration.

The members of this court are officers in the army of the United States, and by order of the President, as Commander-in-Chief, are required to discharge this duty, and are authorized in this capacity to discharge no other duty, to exercise no other judicial power. Of course, if the commission of the President constitutes this a court for the trial of this case only, as such court it is competent to decide all questions of law and fact arising in the trial of the case. But this court has no power, as a court, to declare the authority by which it was constituted null and void, and the act of the President a mere nullity, a usurpation. Has it been shown by the learned gentleman, who demands that this court shall so decide, that officers of the army may lawfully and constitutionally question in this manner the orders of their Commander-in-Chief, disobey, set them aside, and declare them a nullity and a usurpation? Even if it be conceded that the officers thus detailed by order of the Commander-in-Chief may question and utterly disregard his order and set aside his authority, is it possible, in the nature of things, that any body of men, constituted and qualified as a tribunal of justice, can sit in judgment upon the proposition that they are not a court for any purpose, and finally decide judicially, as a court, that the government which appointed them was without authority? Why not crown the absurdity of this proposition by asking the several members of this court to determine that they are not men — living, intelligent, responsible men? This would be no more irrational than the question upon which they are asked to pass. How can any sensible man entertain it? Before he begins to reason upon the proposition he must take for granted, and therefore decide in advance, the very question in dispute, to wit, his actual existence.

So with the question presented in this remarkable argument for the defence: before this court can enter upon the inquiry of the want of authority in the President to constitute them a court, they must take for granted and decide the very point in issue, that the President had the authority, and that they are in law and in fact a judicial tribunal; and having assumed this, they are gravely asked, as such judicial tribunal, to finally and solemnly decide and declare that they are not in fact or in law a judicial tribunal, but a mere nullity and nonentity. A most lame and impotent conclusion!

As the learned counsel seems to have great reverence for judicial authority, and requires precedent for every opinion, I may be pardoned for saying that the objection which I urge against the possibility of any judicial tribunal, after being officially qualified as such, entertaining, much less judicially deciding, the proposition that it has no legal existence as a court, and that the appointment was a usurpation and without authority of law, has been solemnly ruled by the Supreme Court of the United States.

That court say: "The acceptance of the judicial office is a recognition of the *authority* from which it is derived. If a court should enter upon the inquiry (whether the *authority* of the government which established it existed), and should come to the conclusion that the government under which it acted had been put aside, it would cease to be a court and be *incapable* of pronouncing a judicial decision upon the question it undertook to try. If it decides at all as a court, it necessarily affirms the existence and *authority* of the government under which it is exercising judicial power."—(Luther *vs.* Borden, 7 Howard, 40.)

That is the very question raised by the learned gentleman in his argument — that there was no *authority* in the President, by whose act alone this tribunal was constituted, to vest it with judicial power to try this issue; and by the order upon your record, as has already been shown, if you have no power to try this issue for want of authority in the Commander-in-Chief to constitute you a court, you are no court, and have no power to try any issue, because his order limits you to this issue, and this alone.

It requires no very profound legal attainments to apply the ruling of the highest judicial tribunal of this country, just cited, to the point raised, not by the pleadings, but by the argument. This court exists as a judicial tribunal by authority only of the President of the United States; the acceptance of the office is an acknowledgment of the validity of the authority conferring it, and if the President had no authority to order, direct, and constitute this court to try the accused, and, as is claimed, did, in so constituting it, perform an unconstitutional and illegal act, it necessarily results that the order of the President is void and of no effect; that the order did not and could not constitute this a tribunal of justice, and therefore its members are incapable of pronouncing a judicial decision upon the question presented.

There is a marked distinction between the question here presented and that raised by a plea to the jurisdiction of a tribunal whose existence as a court is neither questioned nor denied. Here it is argued, through many pages, by a learned Senator, and a distinguished lawyer, that the order of the President, by whose authority alone this court is constituted a tribunal of military justice, is unlawful; if unlawful it is void and of no effect, and has created no court; therefore this body, not being a court, can have no more power as a court to decide any question whatever than have its individual members power to decide that they as men do not in fact exist.

It is a maxim of the common law — the perfection of human reason — that what is impossible the law requires of no man.

How can it be possible that a judicial tribunal can decide the question that it does not exist, any more than that a rational man can decide that he does not exist?

The absurdity of the proposition so elaborately urged upon the consideration of this court cannot be saved from the ridicule and contempt of sensible men by the pretence that the court is not asked judicially to decide that it is not a court, but only that it has no jurisdiction; for it is a fact not to be denied that the whole argument for the defence on this point is that the President had not the lawful authority to issue the order by which alone this court is constituted, and that the order for its creation is null and void.

Gentlemen might as well ask the Supreme Court of the United States upon a plea to the jurisdiction to decide, as a court, that the President had no lawful authority to nominate the judges thereof severally to the Senate, and that the Senate had no lawful authority to advise and consent to their appointment, as to ask this court to decide, as a court, that the order of the President of the United States, constituting it a tribunal for the sole purpose of this trial, was not only without authority of law, but against and in violation of law. If this court is not a lawful tribunal, it has no existence, and can no more speak as a court than the dead, much less pronounce the judgment required at his hands — that it is not a court, and that the President of the United States, in constituting it such to try the question upon the charge and specification preferred, has transcended his authority, and violated his oath of office.

Before passing from the consideration of the proposition of the learned senator, that this is not a court, it is fit that I should notice that another of the counsel for the accused (Mr. Ewing) has also advanced the same opinion, certainly with more directness and candor, and without any qualification. His statement is, "You," gentlemen, "are no court under the Constitution." This remark of the gentleman cannot fail to excite surprise, when it is remembered that the gentleman, not many months since, was a general in the service of the country, and as such in his department in the West proclaimed and enforced martial law by the constitution of military tribunals for the trial of citizens not in the land or naval forces, but who were guilty of military offences, for which he deemed them justly punishable before military courts, and accordingly he punished them. Is the gentleman quite sure, when that account comes to be rendered for these alleged unconstitutional assumptions of power, that he will not have to answer for more of these alleged violations of the rights of citizens by illegal arrests, convictions, and executions, than any of the members of this court? In support of his opinion that this is no court, the gentleman cites the 3d article of the Constitution, which provides "that the judicial power of the United States shall be vested in one supreme court, and such inferior courts as Congress may establish," the judges whereof "shall hold their offices during good behavior."

It is a sufficient answer to say to the gentleman, that the power of this government to try and punish military offences by military tribunals is no part of the "judicial power of the United States," under the 3d article of the Constitution, but a power conferred by the 8th section of the 1st article, and so it has been ruled by the Supreme Court in Dyres *vs.* Hoover, 20 Howard, 78. If this power is so conferred by the 8th section, a military court authorized by Congress, and constituted as this has been, to try all persons for military crimes in time of war, though not exercising "the judicial power" provided for in the 3d article, is nevertheless a court as constitutional as the Supreme Court itself. The gentleman admits this to the extent of the trial by courts-martial of persons in the military or naval service, and by admitting it he gives up the point. There is no *express* grant for any such tribunal, and the power to establish such a court, therefore, is *implied* from the provisions of the 8th section, 1st article, that "Congress shall have power to provide and maintain a navy," and also "to make rules for the government of the land and naval forces." From these grants the Supreme Court infer the power to establish courts-martial, and from the grants in the same 8th section, as I shall notice hereafter, that "Congress shall have power to declare war," and "to pass all laws necessary and proper to carry this and all other powers into effect," it is necessarily implied that in time of war Congress may authorize military commissions, to try all crimes committed in aid of the public enemy, as such tribunals are *necessary* to give effect to the power to make war and suppress insurrection.

Inasmuch as the gentleman (General Ewing), for whom, personally, I have a high regard as the military commander of a Western department, made a liberal exercise, under the order of the Commander-in-Chief of the army, of this power to arrest and try military offenders not in the land or naval forces of the United States, and inflicted upon them, as I am informed, the extreme penalty of the law, by virtue of his military jurisdiction, I wish to know whether he proposes, by his proclamation of the personal responsibility awaiting all such usurpations of judicial authority, that he himself shall be subjected to the same stern judgment which he invokes against others — that, in short, he shall be drawn and quartered for inflicting the extreme penalties of the law upon citizens of the United States in violation of the Constitution and laws of his country? I trust that his error of judgment in pronouncing this military jurisdiction a usurpation and violation of the Constitution may not rise up in judgment to condemn him, and that he may never be subjected to pains and penalties for having done his duty heretofore in exercising this rightful authority, and in bringing to judgment those who conspired against the lives and liberties of the people.

Here I might leave this question, committing it to the charitable speeches of men, but for the fact that the learned counsel has been more careful in his extraordinary argument to denounce the President as a usurper than to show how the court could possibly decide that it has no judicial existence, and yet that it has judicial existence.

A representative of the people and of the rights of the people before this court, by the appointment of the President, and which appointment was neither sought by me nor desired, I cannot allow all that has been here said by way of denunciation of the murdered President and his successor to pass unnoticed. This has been made the occasion by the learned counsel, Mr. Johnson, to volunteer, not to defend the accused, Mary E. Surratt, not to make a judicial argument in her behalf, but to make a political harangue, a partisan speech against his government and country, and thereby swell the cry of the armed legions of sedition and rebellion that but yesterday shook the heavens with their infernal enginery of treason, and filled the habitations of the people with death. As the law forbids a senator of the United States to receive compensation or fee for defending, in cases before civil or military commissions, the gentleman volunteers to make a speech before this court, in which he denounces the action of the Executive Department in proclaiming and executing martial law against rebels in arms, their aiders and abettors, as a usurpation and a tyranny. I deem it my duty to reply to this denunciation, not for the purpose of presenting thereby any question for the decision of this court, for I have shown that the argument of the gentleman presents no question for its decision as a court, but to repel, as far as I may be able, the unjust aspersion attempted to be cast upon the memory of our dead President, and upon the official conduct of his successor.

I propose now to answer fully all that the gentleman (Mr. Johnson) has said of the want of jurisdiction in this court, and of the alleged usurpation and tyranny of the Executive, that the enlightened public opinion to which he appeals may decide whether all this denunciation is just — whether indeed conspiring against the whole people, and confederation and agreement, in aid of insurrection to murder all the executive officers of the government, cannot be checked or arrested by the Executive power. Let the people decide this question; and in doing so, let them pass upon the action of the senator as well as upon the action of those whom he so arrogantly arraigns. His plea in behalf of an expiring and shattered rebellion is a fit subject for public consideration and for public condemnation.

Let that people also note that, while the learned gentleman (Mr. Johnson), as a volunteer, without pay, thus condemns as a usurpation the means employed so effectually to suppress this gigantic insurrection, the New York *News*, whose proprietor, Benjamin Wood, is shown by the testimony upon your record to have received from the agents of the rebellion twenty-five thousand dollars, rushes into the lists to champion the cause of the rebellion, its aiders and abettors, by following to the letter his colleague (Mr. Johnson), and with greater plainness of speech, and a fervor intensified, doubtless, by the twenty-five thousand dollars received, and the hope of more, denounces the court as a usurpation and threatens the members with the consequences!

The argument of the gentleman, to which the court has listened so patiently and so long, is but an attempt to show that it is unconstitutional for the government of the United States to arrest upon military order and try before military tribunals and punish upon conviction, in accordance with the laws of war and the usages of nations, all criminal offenders acting in aid of the existing rebellion. It does seem to me that the speech in its tone and temper is the same as that which the country has heard for the last four years uttered by the armed rebels themselves and by their apologists, averring that it was unconstitutional for the government of the United States to defend by arms its own rightful authority and the supremacy of its laws.

It is as clearly the right of the republic to live and to defend its life until it forfeits that right by crime, as it is the right of the individual to live so long as God gives him life, unless he forfeits that right by crime. I make no argument to support this proposition. Who is there here or elsewhere to cast the reproach upon my country that for her crimes she must die? Youngest born of the nations! is she not immortal by all the dread memories of the past — by that sublime and voluntary sacrifice of the present, in which the bravest and noblest of her sons have laid down their lives that she might live, giving their serene brows to the dust of the grave, and lifting their hands for the last time amidst the consuming fires of battle? I assume, for the purposes of this argument, that self-defence is as clearly the right of nations as it is the acknowledged right of men, and that the American people may do in the defence and maintenance of their own rightful authority against organized armed rebels, their aiders and abettors, whatever free and independent nations anywhere upon this globe, in time of war, may of right do.

All this is substantially denied by the gentleman in the remarkable argument which he has here made. There is nothing further from my purpose than to do injustice to the learned gentleman or to his elaborate and ingenious argument. To justify what I have already said, I may be permitted here to remind the court that nothing is said by the counsel touching the conduct of the accused, Mary E. Surratt, as shown by the testimony; that he makes confession at the end of his arraignment of the government and country, that he has not made such argument, and that he leaves it to be made by her other counsel. He does take care, however, to arraign the country and the government for conducting a trial with closed doors and before a secret tribunal, and compares the proceedings of this court to the Spanish Inquisition, using the strongest words at his command to intensify the horror which he supposes his announcement will excite throughout the civilized world.

Was this dealing fairly by this government? Was there anything in the conduct of the proceedings here that justified any such remark? Has this been a secret trial? Has it not been conducted in open day in the presence of the accused, and in the presence of seven gentlemen learned in the law, who appeared from day to day as their counsel? Were they not informed of the accusation against them? Were they deprived of the right of challenge? Was it not secured to them by law, and were they not asked to exercise it? Has any part of the evidence been suppressed? Have not all the proceedings been published to the world? What, then, was done, or intended to be done, by the government, which justifies this clamor about a Spanish Inquisition?

That a people assailed by organized treason over an extent of territory half as large as the continent of Europe, and assailed in their very capital by secret assassins banded together and hired to do the work of murder by the instigation of these conspirators, may not be permitted to make inquiry, even with closed doors, touching the nature and extent of the organization, ought not to be asserted by any gentleman who makes the least pretensions to any knowledge of the law, either common, civil, or military. Who does not know that at the common law all inquisition touching crimes and misdemeanors, preparatory to indictment by the grand inquest of the state, is made with closed doors?

In this trial no parties accused, nor their counsel, nor the reporters of this court, were at any time excluded from its deliberations when any testimony was being taken; nor has there been any testimony taken in the case with closed doors, save that of a few witnesses, who testified, not in regard to the accused or either of them, but in respect to the traitors and conspirators not on trial, who were alleged to have incited this crime. Who is there to say that the American people, in time of armed rebellion and civil war, have not the right to make such an examination as secretly as they may deem necessary, either in a military or civil court?

I have said this, not by way of apology for anything the government has done or attempted to do in the progress of this trial, but to expose the animus of the argument, and to repel the accusation against my country sent out to the world by the counsel. From anything that he has said, I have yet to learn that the American people have not the right to make their inquiries secretly, touching a general conspiracy in aid of an existing rebellion, which involves their nationality and the peace and security of all.

The gentleman then enters into a learned argument for the purpose of showing that, by the Constitution, the people of the United States cannot, in war or in peace, subject any person to trial before a military tribunal, whatever may be his crime or offence, unless such person be in the military or naval service of the United States. The conduct of this argument is as remarkable as its assaults upon the government are unwarranted, and its insinuations about the revival of the Inquisition and secret trials are inexcusable. The court will notice that the argument, from the beginning almost to its conclusion, insists that no person is liable to be tried by military or martial law before a military tribunal, save those in the land and naval service of the United States. I repeat, the conduct of this argument of the gentleman is remarkable. As an instance, I ask the attention not only of this court, but of that public whom he has ventured to address in this tone and temper, to the authority of the distinguished Chancellor Kent, whose great name the counsel has endeavored to press into his service in support of his general proposition, that no person save those in the military or naval service of the United States is liable to be tried for any crime whatever, either in peace or in war, before a military tribunal.

The language of the gentleman, after citing the provision of the Constitution, "that no person shall be held to answer for a capital or otherwise infamous crime unless on a presentment or indictment of a grand jury, except in cases arising in the land or naval forces or in the militia, when in actual service in time of war or public danger," is, "that this exception is designed to leave in force, not to enlarge, the power vested in Congress by the original Constitution to make rules for the government and regulation of the land and naval forces; that the land or naval forces are the terms used in both, have the same meaning, and until lately have been supposed by every commentator and judge to exclude from military jurisdiction offences committed by citizens not belonging to such forces." The learned gentleman then adds: "Kent, in a note to his 1st Commentaries, 341, states, and with accuracy, that 'military and naval crimes and offences committed while the party is attached to and under the immediate authority of the army and navy of the United States and in actual service, are not cognizable under the common-law jurisdiction of the courts of the United States.'" I ask this court to bear in mind that this is the only passage which he quotes from this note of Kent in his argument, and that no man possessed of common sense, however destitute he may be of the exact and varied learning in the law to which the gentleman may rightfully lay claim, can for a moment entertain the opinion that the distinguished chancellor of New York, in the passage just cited, intimates any such thing as the counsel asserts, that the Constitution excludes from military jurisdiction offences committed by citizens not belonging to the land or naval forces.

Who can fail to see that Chancellor Kent, by the passage cited, only decides that military and naval crimes and offences committed by a party attached to and under the immediate authority of the army and navy of the United States, and in actual service, are not cognizable under the common-law jurisdiction of the courts of the United States? He only says they are not cognizable under its common-law jurisdiction; but by that he does not say or intimate what is attempted to be said by the counsel for him, that "all crimes committed by citizens are by the Constitution excluded from military jurisdiction," and that the perpetrators of them can under no circumstances be tried before military tribunals. Yet the counsel ventures to proceed, standing upon this passage quoted from Kent, to say that, "according to *this* great authority, every other class of persons and every other species of offences are within the jurisdiction of the civil courts, and entitled to the protection of the proceeding by presentment or indictment and the public trial in such a court."

Whatever that great authority may have said elsewhere, it is very doubtful whether any candid man in America will be able to come to the very learned and astute conclusion that Chancellor Kent has so stated in the note or any part of the note which the gentleman has just cited. If he has said it elsewhere, it is for the gentleman, if he relies upon Kent for authority, to produce the passage. But was it fair treatment of this "great authority": was it not taking an unwarrantable privilege with the distinguished chancellor and his great work, the enduring monument of his learning and genius, to so mutilate the note referred to as might leave the gentleman at liberty to make his deductions and assertions under cover of the great name of the New York chancellor, to suit the emergency of his case by omitting the following passage, which occurs in the same note, and absolutely excludes the conclusion so defiantly put forth by the counsel to support his argument? In that note Chancellor Kent says: —

"*Military* law is a system of regulations for the government of the armies in the service of the United States, authorized by the act of Congress of April 10, 1806, known as the Articles of War, and *naval* law is a similar system for the government of the navy, under the act of Congress of April 23, 1800. But *martial* law is quite a distinct thing, and is founded upon paramount necessity and proclaimed by a *military chief*."

However unsuccessful, after this exposure, the gentleman appears in maintaining his monstrous proposition, that the American people are by their own Constitution forbidden to try the aiders and abettors of armed traitors and rebellion before military tribunals, and subject them, according to the laws of war and the usages of nations, to just punishment for their great crimes, it has been made clear from what I have already stated that he has been eminently successful in mutilating this beautiful production of that great mind; which act of mutilation every one knows is violative alike of the laws of peace and war. Even in war the divine creations of art and the immortal productions of genius and learning are spared.

In the same spirit, and it seems to me with the same unfairness as that just noted, the learned gentleman has very adroitly pressed into his service by an extract from the autobiography of the war-worn veteran and hero, General Scott, the names of the late secretary of war, Mr. Marcy, and the learned ex-attorney general, Mr. Cushing. This adroit performance is achieved in this way: after stating the fact that General Scott in Mexico proclaimed martial law for the trial and punishment by military tribunals of persons guilty of "assassination, murder, and poisoning," the gentleman proceeds to quote from the autobiography, "that this order when handed to the then secretary of war (Mr. Marcy) for his approval, 'a startle at the title (martial law order) was the only comment he then or ever made on the subject,' and that it was 'soon silently returned as too explosive for safe handling.' 'A little later (he adds) the attorney general (Mr. Cushing) called and asked for a copy, and the law officer of the government, whose business it is to speak on all such matters, was stricken with *legal dumbness.*'" Thereupon the learned gentleman proceeds to say: "How much more startled and more paralyzed would these great men have been had they been consulted on such a commission as this! A commission, not to sit in another country, and to try offences not provided for in any law of the United States, civil or military, then in force, but in their own country, and in a part of it where there are laws providing for their trial and punishment, and civil courts clothed with ample powers for both, and in the daily and undisturbed exercise of their jurisdiction."

I think I may safely say, without stopping to make any special references, that the official career of the late secretary of war (Mr. Marcy) gave no indication that he ever doubted or denied the constitutional power of the American people, acting through their duly constituted agents, to do any act justified by the laws of war for the suppression of a rebellion or to repel invasion. Certainly there is nothing in this extract from the autobiography which justifies any such conclusion. He was startled we are told. It may have been as much the admiration he had for the boldness and wisdom of the conqueror of Mexico as any abhorrence he had for the trial and punishment of "assassins, poisoners, and murderers," according to the laws and usages of war.

But the official utterances of the ex-attorney general, Cushing, with which the gentleman doubtless was familiar when he prepared this argument, by no means justify the attempt here made to quote him as authority against the proclamation and enforcement of martial law in time of rebellion and civil war. That distinguished man, not second in legal attainments to any who have held that position, has left an official opinion of record touching this subject. Referring to what is said by Sir Mathew Hale, in his "History of the Common Law," concerning martial law, wherein he limits it, as the gentleman has seemed by the whole drift of his argument desirous of doing, and says that it is "not in truth and in reality law, but something indulged rather than allowed as a law — the necessity of government, order, and discipline in an army," Mr. Cushing makes this just criticism: "This proposition is a mere composite blunder, a total misapprehension of the matter. It confounds *martial law* and *law military;* it ascribes to the former the uses of the latter; it erroneouly assumes that the government of a body of troops is a necessity more than of a body of civilians or citizens. It confounds and confuses all the relations of the subject, and is an apt illustration of the incompleteness of the notions of the common-law jurists of England in regard to matters not comprehended in that limited branch of legal science . . . Military law, it is now perfectly understood in England, is a branch of the law of the land, applicable only to certain acts of a particular class of persons and administered by special tribunals;

but neither in that nor in any other respect essentially differing as to foundation in constitutional reason from admiralty, ecclesiastical, or indeed chancery and common law. . . . It is the system of rules for the government of the army and navy established by successive acts of Parliament. . . . Martial law, as exercised in any country by the commander of a foreign army, is an element of the *jus belli*.

"It is incidental to the state of solemn war, and appertains to the law of nations. . . . Thus, while the armies of the United States occupied different provinces of the Mexican republic, the respective commanders were not limited in authority by any local law. They allowed, or rather required, the magistrates of the country, municipal or judicial, to continue to administer the laws of the country among their countrymen; but in subjection always to the military power, which acted summarily and according to discretion, when the belligerent interests of the conqueror required it, and which exercised jurisdiction, either summarily or by means of military commissions for the protection or the punishment of citizens of the United States in Mexico."— *Opinions of Attorneys General*, vol. viii., 366-69.

Mr. Cushing says, "That, it would seem, was one of the forms of martial law"; but he adds that such an example of martial law administered by a foreign army in the enemy's country "does not enlighten us in regard to the question of martial law in one's own country, and as administered by its military commanders. That is a case which the law of nations does not reach. Its regulation is of the domestic resort of the organic laws of the country itself, and regarding which, as it happens, there is no definite or explicit legislation in the United States, as there is none in England.

"Accordingly, in England, as we have seen, Earl Grey assumes that when martial law exists it has no legal origin, but is a mere fact of necessity to be legalized afterwards by a bill of indemnity if there be occasion. I am not prepared to say that, under existing laws, such may not also be the case in the United States."— *Ibid.*, 370.

After such a statement, wherein ex-Attorney General Cushing very clearly recognizes the right of this government, as also of England, to employ martial law as a means of defence in a time of war, whether domestic or foreign, he will be as much surprised when he reads the argument of the learned gentleman, wherein he is described as being struck with *legal dumbness* at the mere mention of proclaiming martial law and its enforcement by the commander of our army in Mexico, as the late secretary of war was startled with even the mention of its title.

Even some of the reasons given, and certainly the power exercised by the veteran hero himself, would seem to be in direct conflict with the propositions of the learned gentleman.

The lieutenant-general says he "excludes from his order cases already cognizable by court-martial, and limits it to cases not provided for in the act of Congress establishing rules and articles for the government of the armies of the United States." Has not the gentleman who attempts to press General Scott into his service argued and insisted upon it that the commander of the army cannot subject the soldiers under his command to any control or punishment whatever, save that which is provided for in the articles?

It will not do, in order to sustain the gentleman's hypothesis, to say that these provisions of the Constitution, by which he attempts to fetter the power of the people to punish such offences in time of war within the territory of the United States, may be disregarded by an officer of the United States in command of its armies, in the trial and punishment of its soldiers in a foreign war. The law of the United States for the government of its own armies follows the flag upon every sea and in every land.

The truth is, that the right of the people to proclaim and execute martial law is a necessary incident of war, and this was the right exercised, and rightfully exercised, by Lieutenant-General Scott in Mexico. It was what Earl Grey has justly said was a " fact of necessity," and I may add, an act as clearly authorized as was the act of fighting the enemy when they appeared before him.

In making this exception, the lieutenant-general followed the rule recognized by the American authorities on military law, in which it is declared that "many crimes committed even by military officers, enlisted men, or camp-retainers, cannot be tried under the rules and articles of war. Military commissions must be resorted to for such cases, and these commissions should be ordered by the same authority, be constituted in a similar manner, and their proceedings be conducted according to the same general rules as general courts-martial."—*Benet*, 15.

There remain for me to notice, at present, two other points in this extraordinary speech: first, that martial law does not warrant a military commission for the trial of military offences — that is, offences committed in time of war in the interests of the public enemy and by concert and agreement with the enemy; and second, that martial law does not prevail in the United States, and has never been declared by any competent authority.

It is not necessary, as the gentleman himself has declined to argue the first point, — whether martial law authorizes the organization of military commissions by order of the commander-in-chief to try such offences, — that I should say more than that the authority just cited by me shows that such commissions are authorized under martial law, and are created by the commander for the trial of all such offences when their punishment by court-martial is not provided for by the express statute law of the country.

The second point, — that martial law has not been declared by any competent authority, — is an arraignment of the late murdered President of the United States for his proclamation of September 24, 1862, declaring martial law throughout the United States, and of which, in Lawrence's edition of Wheaton on International Law, p. 522, it is said, "Whatever may be the inference to be deduced either from constitutional or international law, or from the usages of European governments, as to the legitimate depository of the power of suspending the writ of *habeas corpus*, the virtual abrogation of the judiciary in cases affecting individual liberty, and the establishment as *matter of fact* in the United States, by the Executive alone, of martial law, not merely in the insurrectionary districts or in cases of military occupancy, but throughout the entire Union, and not temporarily, but as an institution as permanent as the insurrection on which it professes to be based, and capable on the same principle of being revived in all cases of foreign as well as civil war, are placed beyond question by the President's proclamation of September 24, 1862." That proclamation is as follows: —

"BY THE PRESIDENT OF THE UNITED STATES OF AMERICA.

"A PROCLAMATION.

"Whereas it has become necessary to call into service not only volunteers, but also portions of the militia of the states, by a draft, in order to suppress the insurrection existing in the United States, and disloyal persons are not adequately restrained by the ordinary processes of law from hindering this measure and from giving aid and comfort in various ways to the insurrection: Now, therefore, be it ordered that, during the existing insurrection, and as a necessary means for suppressing the same, all rebels and insurgents, their aiders and abettors, within the United States, and all persons discouraging volunteer enlistments, resisting militia drafts, or guilty of any disloyal practice affording aid and comfort to rebels, against the authority of the United States, shall be subject to martial law and liable to trial and punishment by courts-martial or military commission.

"Second. That the writ of *habeas corpus* is suspended in respect to all persons arrested, or who are now, or hereafter during the rebellion shall be, imprisoned in any fort, camp, arsenal, military prison, or other place of confinement, by any military authority or by the sentence of any court-martial or military commission.

"In witness whereof, I have hereunto set my hand and caused the seal of the United States to be affixed.

"Done at the city of Washington, this 24th day of September, A.D. 1862, and of the independence of the United States the eighty-seventh.

"ABRAHAM LINCOLN.

"By the President:
 "WILLIAM H. SEWARD,
  "*Secretary of State.*"

This proclamation is duly certified from the War Department to be in full force and not revoked, and is evidence of record in this case; and but a few days since a proclamation of the President, of which this court will take notice, declares that the same remains in full force.

It has been said by another of the counsel for the accused (Mr. Stone) in his argument, that, admitting its validity, the proclamation ceases to have effect with the insurrection, and is terminated by it. It is true the proclamation of martial law only continues during the insurrection; but inasmuch as the question of the existence of an insurrection is a political question, the decision of which belongs exclusively to the political department of the government, that department alone can declare its existence, and that department alone can declare its termination, and by the action of the political department of the government every judicial tribunal in the land is concluded and bound. That question has been settled for fifty years in this country by the Supreme Court of the United States: First, in the case of Brown *vs.* The United States (8 Cranch); also in the prize cases (2 Black, 641). Nothing more, therefore, need be said upon this question of an *existing* insurrection than this: The political department of the government has heretofore proclaimed an insurrection; that department has not yet declared the insurrection ended, and the event on the 14th of April, which robbed the people of their chosen Executive, and clothed this land in mourning, bore sad but overwhelming witness to the fact that the rebellion is not ended. The fact of the insurrection is not an open question to be tried or settled by parol, either in a military tribunal or in a civil court.

The declaration of the learned gentleman who opened the defence (Mr. Johnson), that martial law has never been declared by any competent authority, as I have already said, arraigns Mr. Lincoln for a usurpation of power. Does the gentleman mean to say that, until Congress authorizes it, the President cannot proclaim and enforce martial law in the suppression of armed and organized rebellion? Or does he only affirm that this act of the late President is a usurpation?

The proclamation of martial law in 1862 a usurpation! though it armed the people in that dark hour of trial with the means of defence against traitorous and secret enemies in every state and district of the country; though by its use some of the guilty were brought to swift and just judgment, and others deterred from crime or driven to flight; though by this means the innocent and defenceless were protected; though by this means the city of the gentleman's residence was saved from the violence and pillage of the mob and the torch of the incendiary. But, says the gentleman, it was a usurpation, forbidden by the laws of the land!

The same was said of the proclamations of blockade issued April 19 and 27, 1861, which declared a blockade of the ports of the insurgent states, and that all vessels violating the same were subjects of capture, and, together with the cargo, to be condemned as prize. Inasmuch as Congress had not then recognized the fact of civil war, these proclamations were denounced as void. The Supreme Court decided otherwise, and affirmed the power of the Executive thus to subject property on the seas to seizure and condemnation. I read from that decision: —

"The Constitution confers upon the President the whole executive power, he is bound to take care that the laws be faithfully executed; he is Commander-in-Chief of the army and navy of the United States, and of the militia of the several states when called into the actual service of the United States. . . . Whether the President, in fulfilling his duties as Commander-in-Chief in suppressing an insurrection, has met with such armed hostile resistance and a civil war of such alarming proportions as will compel him to accord to them the character of belligerents, is a question to be decided *by him*, and this court must be governed by the decisions and acts of the political department of the government to which this power was intrusted. He must determine what degree of force the crisis demands.

"The proclamation of blockade is itself official and conclusive evidence to the court that a state of war existed which demanded and authorized a recourse to such a measure under the circumstances peculiar to the case." (2 Black, 670.)

It has been solemnly ruled by the same tribunal, in an earlier case, "that the power is confided to the Executive of the Union to determine when it is necessary to call out the militia of the states to repel invasion," as follows: "That he is necessarily constituted the judge of the existence of the exigency in the first instance, and is bound to act according to his belief of the facts. If he does so act, and decides to call forth the militia, his orders for this purpose are in strict conformity with the provisions of the law; and it would seem to follow as a necessary consequence, that every act done by a subordinate officer in obedience to such orders, is equally justifiable. The law contemplates that, under such circumstances, orders shall be given to carry the power into effect; and it cannot therefore be a correct inference that any other person has a just right to disobey them. The law does not provide for any appeal from the judgment of the President, or for any right in subordinate officers to review his decision, and in effect defeat it. Whenever a statute gives a discretionary power to any person, to be exercised by him upon his own opinion of certain facts, it is a sound rule of construction that the statute constitutes him the sole and exclusive judge of the existence of those facts." (12 Wheaton, 31.)

In the light of these decisions, it must be clear to every mind that the question of the existence of an insurrection, and the necessity of calling into requisition for its suppression both the militia of the states and the army and navy of the United States, and of proclaiming martial law, which is an essential condition of war, whether foreign or domestic, must rest with the officer of the government who is charged by the express terms of the Constitution with the performance of this great duty for the common defence and the execution of the laws of the Union.

But it is further insisted by the gentleman in this argument, that Congress has not authorized the establishment of military commissions, which are essential to the judicial administration of martial law and the punishment of crimes committed during the existence of a civil war, and especially that such commissions are not so authorized to try persons other than those in the military or naval service of the United States, or in the militia of the several States, when in the actual service of the United States. The gentleman's argument assuredly destroys itself, for he insists that the Congress, as the legislative department of the government, can pass no law which, either in peace or war, can constitutionally subject any citizen not in the land or naval forces to trial for crime before a military tribunal, or otherwise than by a jury in the civil courts.

Why does the learned gentleman now tell us that Congress has not authorized this to be done, after declaring just as stoutly that by the fifth and sixth amendments to the Constitution no such military tribunals can be established for the trial of any person not in the military or naval service of the United States, or in the militia when in actual service, for the commission of any crime whatever in time of war or insurrection? It ought to have occurred to the gentleman when commenting upon the exception in the fifth article of the Constitution, that there was a reason for it very different from that which he saw fit to assign, and that reason manifestly upon the face of the Constitution itself, was, that by the eighth section of the first article, it is expressly provided that Congress shall have power to make rules for the government of the land and naval forces, and to provide for organizing, arming, and disciplining the militia, and for *governing* such part of them as may be employed in the service of the United States, and that, inasmuch as military discipline and order are as essential in an army in time of peace as in time of war, if the Constitution would leave this power to Congress in peace, it must make the exception, so that rules and regulations for the government of the army and navy should be operative in time of peace as well as in time of war; because the provisions of the Constitution give the right of trial by jury IN TIME OF PEACE, in all criminal prosecutions by indictment, in terms embracing every human being that may be held to answer for crime in the United States; and therefore if the eighth section of the first article was to remain in full force IN TIME OF PEACE, the exception must be made; and, accordingly, the exception was made. But by the argument we have listened to, this court is told, and the country is told, that IN TIME OF WAR — a war which involves in its dread issue the lives and interests of us all — the guarantees of the Constitution are in full force for the benefit of those who conspire with the enemy, creep into your camps, murder in cold blood, in the interest of the invader or insurgent, the Commander-in-Chief of your army, and secure to him the slow and weak provisions of the civil law, while the soldier, who may, when overcome by the demands of exhausted nature which cannot be resisted, have slept at his post, is subject to be tried upon the spot by a military tribunal and shot. The argument amounts to this: that as military courts and military trials of civilians in time of war are a usurpation and tyranny, and as soldiers are liable to such arrests and trial, Sergeant Corbett, who shot Booth, should be tried and executed by sentence of a military court; while Booth's co-conspirators and aiders should be saved from any such indignity as a military trial! I confess that I am too dull to comprehend the logic, the reason, or the sense of such a conclusion! If there is any one *entitled* to this privilege of a civil trial at a remote period, and by a jury of the district, IN TIME OF CIVIL WAR, when the foundations of the republic are rocking beneath the earthquake tread of armed rebellion, that man is the defender of the republic. It will never do to say, as has been said in this argument, that the soldier is not liable to be tried in time of war by a military tribunal for any other offence than those prescribed in the rules and articles of war. To my mind, nothing can be clearer than that citizen and soldier alike, in time of civil or foreign war, after a proclamation of martial law, are triable by military tribunals for all offences of which they may be guilty, in the interests of, or in concert with the enemy.

These provisions, therefore, of your Constitution for indictment and trial by jury in civil courts of *all crimes* are, as I shall hereafter show, silent and inoperative in time of war when the public safety requires it.

The argument to which I have thus been replying, as the court will not fail to perceive, nor that public to which the argument is addressed, is a labored attempt to establish the proposition, that, by the Constitution of the United States, the American people cannot, even in a civil war the greatest the world has ever seen, employ martial law and military tribunals as a means of successfully asserting their authority, preserving their nationality, and securing protection to the lives and property of all, and especially to the persons of those to whom they have committed, officially, the great trust of maintaining the national authority. The gentleman says, with an air of perfect confidence, that he denies the jurisdiction of military tribunals for the trial of civilians in time of war, because neither the Constitution nor laws justify, but on the contrary repudiate them, and that all the experience of the past is against it. I might content myself with saying that the practice of all nations is against the gentleman's conclusion. The struggle for our national independence was aided and prosecuted by military tribunals and martial law, as well as by arms. The contest for American nationality began with the establishment, very soon after the firing of the first gun at Lexington on the 19th day of April, 1775, of military tribunals and martial law. On the 30th of June, 1775, the Continental Congress provided that "whosoever, *belonging to the continental army*, shall be convicted of holding correspondence with, or giving intelligence to the enemy, either indirectly or directly, shall suffer such punishment as by a court-martial shall be ordered." This was found not sufficient, inasmuch as it did not reach those *civilians* who, like certain civilians of our day, claim the protection of the civil law in time of war against military arrests and military trials for military crimes. Therefore the same Congress, on the 7th of November, 1775, amended this provision by striking out the words "belonging to the continental army," and adopting the article as follows: —

"*All persons* convicted of holding a treacherous correspondence with, or giving intelligence to the enemy, shall suffer death or such other punishment as a general court-martial shall think proper."

And on the 17th of June, 1776, the Congress added an additional rule —

"That all persons not members of, nor owing allegiance to, any of the United States of America, who should be found lurking as spies in or about the fortifications or encampments of the armies of the United States, or any of them, shall suffer death, according to the law and usage of nations, by the sentence of a court-martial or such other punishment as a court-martial shall direct."

Comprehensive as was this legislation, embracing as it did soldiers, citizens, and aliens, subjecting all alike to trial for their military tribunals of justice, according to the law and the usage of nations, it was found to be insufficient to meet that most dangerous of all crimes committed in the interests of the enemy by citizens in time of war — the crime of conspiring together to assassinate or seize and carry away the soldiers and citizens who were loyal to the cause of the country. Therefore, on the 27th of February, 1778, the Congress adopted the following resolution: —

"*Resolved*, That whatever inhabitant of these states shall kill, or seize, or take any loyal citizen or citizens thereof and convey him, her, or them to any place within the power of the enemy, or shall ENTER INTO ANY COMBINATION for such purpose, or attempt to carry the same into execution, or hath assisted or shall assist therein; or shall, by giving intelligence, acting as a guide, or in any manner whatever, aid the enemy in the perpetration thereof, he shall suffer death by the judgment of a court-martial as a traitor, assassin, or spy, if the offence be committed within seventy miles of the headquarters of the grand or other armies of these states where a general officer commands." — *Journals of Congress*, vol. ii, pp. 459, 460.

So stood the law until the adoption of the Constitution of the United States. Every well-informed man knows that at the time of the passage of these acts the courts of justice, having cognizance of all crimes against persons, were open in many of the states, and that by their several constitutions and charters, which were then the supreme law for the punishment of crimes committed within their respective territorial limits, no man was liable to conviction but by the verdict of a jury. Take, for example, the provisions of the constitution of North Carolina, adopted on the 10th of November, 1776, and in full force at the time of the passage of the last resolution by Congress above cited, which provisions are as follows: —

"That no freeman shall be put to answer any criminal charge but by indictment, presentment or impeachment."

"That no freeman shall be convicted of any crime but by the unanimous verdict of a jury of good and lawful men in open court, as heretofore used."

This was the law in 1778 in all the states, and the provision for a trial by jury every one knows meant a jury of twelve men, impanelled and qualified to try the issue in a civil court. The conclusion is not to be avoided, that these enactments of the Congress under the Confederation set aside the trial by jury within the several states, and expressly provided for the trial by court-martial of "any of the inhabitants" who, during the revolution, might, contrary to the provisions of said law, and in aid of the public enemy, give them intelligence, or kill any loyal citizens of the United States, or enter into any combination to kill or carry them away. How comes it, if the argument of the counsel be true, that this enactment was passed by the Congress of 1778, when the constitutions of the several states at that day as fully guaranteed trial by jury to every person held to answer for a crime as does the Constitution of the United States at this hour? Notwithstanding this fact, I have yet to learn that any loyal man ever challenged, during all the period of our conflict for independence and nationality, the validity of that law for the trial, for military offences, by military tribunals, of all offenders, as the law, not of peace, but of war, and absolutely essential to the prosecution of war. I may be pardoned for saying that it is the accepted common law of nations, that martial law is, at all times and everywhere, essential to the successful prosecution of war, whether it be a civil or a foreign war. The validity of these acts of the Continental and Confederate Congress I know was challenged, but only by men charged with the guilt of their country's blood.

Washington, the peerless, the stainless, and the just, with whom God walked through the night of that great trial, enforced this just and wise enactment upon all occasions. On the 30th of September, 1780, Joshua H. Smith, by the order of General Washington, was put upon his trial before a court-martial, convened in the State of New York, on the charge of there aiding and assisting Benedict Arnold, in a combination with the enemy, to *take, kill*, and *seize* such loyal citizens or soldiers of the United States as were in garrison at West Point. Smith objected to the jurisdiction, averring that he was a private citizen, not in the military or naval service, and therefore was only amenable to the civil authority of the State, whose constitution had guaranteed the right of trial by jury to all persons held to answer for crime. ("Chandler's Criminal

Trials," vol. 2, p. 187.) The constitution of New York then in force had so provided; but, notwithstanding that, the court overruled the plea, held him to answer, and tried him. I repeat, that when Smith was thus tried by court-martial the constitution of New York as fully guaranteed trial by jury in the civil courts to all civilians charged and held to answer for crimes within the limits of that State as does the Constitution of the United States guarantee such trial within the limits of the District of Columbia. By the second of the Articles of Confederation each State retained "its sovereignty," and every power, jurisdiction, and right not *expressly* delegated to the United States in Congress assembled. By those articles there was no express delegation of judicial power; therefore the States retained it fully.

If the military courts, constituted by the commander of the army of the United States under the Confederation, who was appointed only by a resolution of the Congress, without any *express* grant of power to authorize it — his office not being created by the act of the people in their fundamental law — had jurisdiction in every State to try and put to death "any inhabitant" thereof who should *kill* any loyal citizen or enter into "any combination" for any such purpose therein in time of war, notwithstanding the provisions of the constitution and laws of such States, how can any man conceive that under the Constitution of the United States, which is the supreme law over every State, anything in the constitution and laws of such State to the contrary notwithstanding, and the supreme law over every territory of the republic as well, the Commander-in-Chief of the army of the United States, who is made such by the Constitution, and by its supreme authority clothed with the power and charged with the duty of directing and controlling the whole military power of the United States in time of rebellion or invasion, has not that authority?

I need not remind the court that one of the marked differences between the Articles of Confederation and the Constitution of the United States was, that under the Confederation the Congress was the sole depository of all federal power. The Congress of the Confederation, said Madison, held "the command of the army." (Fed., No. 38.) Has the Constitution, which was ordained by the people the better "to insure domestic tranquillity and to provide for the common defence," so fettered the great power of self-defence against armed insurrection or invasion that martial law, so essential in war, is forbidden by that great instrument? I will yield to no man in reverence for or obedience to the Constitution of my country, esteeming it, as I do, a new evangel to the nations, embodying the democracy of the New Testament — the absolute equality of all men before the law, in respect of those rights of human nature which are the gift of God, and therefore as universal as the material structure of man. Can it be that this Constitution of ours, so divine in its spirit of justice, so beneficent in its results, so full of wisdom and goodness and truth, under which we became one people, a great and powerful nationality, has in terms or by implication denied to this people the power to crush armed rebellion by war, and to arrest and punish, during the existence of such rebellion, according to the laws of war and the usages of nations, secret conspirators who aid and abet the public enemy?

Here is a conspiracy, organized and prosecuted by armed traitors and hired assassins, receiving the moral support of thousands in every State and district, who pronounced the war for the Union a failure, and your now murdered but immortal Commander-in-Chief a tyrant; the object of which conspiracy, as the testimony shows, was to aid the tottering rebellion which struck at the nation's life. It is in evidence that Davis, Thompson, and others, chiefs in this rebellion, in aid of the same, agreed and conspired with others to poison the fountains of water which supply your commercial metropolis, and thereby murder its inhabitants; to secretly deposit in the habitations of the people and in the ships in your harbors inflammable materials, and thereby destroy them by fire; to murder by the slow and consuming torture of famine your soldiers, captive in their hands; to import pestilence in infected clothes to be distributed in your capital and camps, and thereby murder the surviving heroes and defenders of the republic, who, standing by the holy graves of your unreturning brave, proudly and defiantly challenge to honorable combat and open battle all public enemies, that their country may live; and finally, to crown this horrid catalogue of crime, this sum of all human atrocities, conspired, as charged upon your record, with the accused and John Wilkes Booth and John H. Surratt, to kill and murder in your capital the executive officers of your government and the commander of your armies. When this conspiracy, entered into by these traitors, is revealed by its attempted execution, and the foul and brutal murder of your President in the capital, you are told that it is unconstitutional, in order to arrest the further execution of the conspiracy, to interpose the military power of this government for the arrest, without civil process, of any of the parties thereto, and for their trial by a military tribunal of justice. If any such rule had obtained during our struggle for independence we never would have been a nation. If any such rule had been adopted and acted upon now, during the fierce struggle of the past four years no man can say that our nationality would have thus long survived.

The whole people of the United States by their Constitution have created the office of President of the United States and Commander-in-Chief of the army and navy, and have vested, by the terms of that Constitution, in the person of the President and Commander-in-Chief, the power to enforce the execution of the laws, and preserve, protect, and defend the Constitution.

The question may well be asked: If, as Commander-in-Chief, the President may not, in time of insurrection or war, proclaim and execute martial law, according to the usages of nations, how he can successfully perform the duties of his office — execute the laws, preserve the Constitution, suppress insurrection, and repel invasion?

Martial law and military tribunals are as essential to the successful prosecution of war as are men and arms and munitions. The Constitution of the United States has vested the power to declare war and raise armies and navies exclusively in the Congress, and the power to prosecute the war and command the army and navy exclusively in the President of the United States. As, under the Confederation, the commander of the army, appointed only by the Congress, was by the resolution of that Congress empowered to act as he might think proper for the good and welfare of the service, subject only to such restraints or orders as the Congress might give, so, under the Constitution, the President is, by the people who ordained that Constitution and declared him Commander-in-Chief of the army and navy, vested with full power to direct and control the army and navy of the United States, and employ all the forces necessary to preserve, protect, and defend the Constitution and execute the laws, as enjoined by his oath and the very letter of the Constitution, subject to no restriction or direction save such as Congress may from time to time prescribe.

That these powers for the common defence, intrusted by the Constitution exclusively to the Congress and the President, are, in time of civil war or foreign invasion, to be exercised without limitation or restraint, to the extent of the public necessity, and without any intervention of the federal judiciary or of State constitutions or State laws, are facts in our history not open to question.

The position is not to be answered by saying you make the American Congress thereby omnipotent, and clothe the American Executive with the asserted attribute of hereditary monarchy — the king can do no wrong. Let the position be fairly stated — that the Congress and President, in war as in peace, are but the agents of the whole people, and that this unlimited power for the common defence against armed rebellion or foreign invasion is but the power of the people intrusted exclusively to the legislative and executive departments as their agents, for any and every abuse of which these agents are directly responsible to the people — and the demagogue cry of an omnipotent Congress, and an Executive invested with royal prerogatives, vanishes like the baseless fabric of a vision. If the Congress, corruptly or oppressively, or wantonly abuse this great trust, the people, by the irresistible power of the ballot, hurl them from place. If the President so abuse the trust, the people by their Congress withhold supplies, or by impeachment transfer the trust to better hands, strip him of the franchises of citizenship and of office, and declare him forever disqualified to hold any position of honor, trust, or power, under the government of his country.

I can understand very well why men should tremble at the exercise of this great power by a monarch whose person, by the constitution of his realm, is inviolable, but I cannot conceive how any American citizen, who has faith in the capacity of the whole people to govern themselves, should give himself any concern on the subject. Mr. Hallam, the distinguished author of the Constitutional History of England, has said: —

"Kings love to display the divinity with which their flatterers invest them in nothing so much as in the instantaneous execution of their will, and to stand revealed, as it were, in the storm and thunderbolt when their power breaks through the operation of secondary causes and awes a prostate nation without the intervention of law."

How just are such words when applied to an irresponsible monarch! how absurd when applied to a whole people, acting through their duly appointed agents, whose will, thus declared, is the supreme law, to awe into submission and peace and obedience, not a prostrate nation, but a prostrate rebellion! The same great author utters the fact which all history attests, when he says: —

"It has been usual for all governments during actual rebellion to proclaim martial law for the suspension of civil jurisdiction; and this anomaly, I must admit," he adds, "is very far from being less indispensable at such unhappy seasons where the ordinary mode of trial is by jury than where the right of decision resides in the court." — *Const. Hist.*, vol. i, ch. 5, p. 326.

That the power to proclaim martial law and fully or partially suspend the civil jurisdiction, federal and state, in time of rebellion or civil war, and punish by military tribunals all offences committed in aid of the public enemy, is conferred upon Congress and the Executive, necessarily results from the unlimited grants of power for the common defence to which I have already briefly referred. I may be pardoned for saying that this position is not assumed by me for the purposes of this occasion, but that early in the first year of this great struggle for our national life I proclaimed it as a representative of the people, under the obligation of my oath, and, as I then believed and still believe, upon the authority of the great men who formed and fashioned the wise and majestic fabric of American government.

Some of the citations which I deemed it my duty at that time to make, and some of which I now reproduce, have, I am pleased to say, found a wider circulation in books that have since been published by others.

When the Constitution was on trial for its deliverance before the people of the several States, its ratification was opposed on the ground that it conferred upon Congress and the Executive unlimited power for the common defence. To all such objectors — and they were numerous in every State — that great man, Alexander Hamilton, whose words will live as long as our language lives, speaking to the listening people of all the States and urging them not to reject that matchless instrument which bore the name of Washington, said: —

"The authorities essential to the care of the common defence are these: To raise armies; to build and equip fleets; to prescribe rules for the government of both; to direct their operations; to provide for their support. These powers ought to exist WITHOUT LIMITATION; because it is impossible to foresee or define the extent and variety of national exigencies, and the correspondent extent and variety of the means which may be necessary to satisfy them.

"The circumstances that endanger the safety of nations are infinite; and for this reason no constitutional shackles can wisely be imposed on the power to which the care of it is committed. . . . This power ought to be under the direction of the same councils which are appointed to preside over the common defence. . . . It must be admitted, as a necessary consequence, that there can be no limitation of that authority which is to provide for the defence and protection of the community in any manner essential to its efficacy; that is, in any matter essential to the formation, direction, or support of the national forces."

He adds the further remark: "This is one of those truths which, to a correct and unprejudiced mind, carries its own evidence along with it; and may be obscured, but cannot be made plainer by argument or reasoning. It rests upon axioms as simple as they are universal — the *means* ought to be proportioned to the *end;* the persons from whose agency the attainment of any *end* is expected ought to possess the means by which it is to be attained." — *Federalist*, No. 23.

In the same great contest for the adoption of the Constitution, Madison, sometimes called the "Father of the Constitution," said: —

"Is the power of declaring war necessary? No man will answer this question in the negative. . . . Is the power of raising armies and equipping fleets necessary? . . . It is involved in the power of self-defence. . . . With what color of propriety could the force necessary for defence be limited by those who cannot limit the force of offence? . . . The means of security can only be regulated by the means and the danger of attack. . . . It is in vain to oppose constitutional barriers to the impulse of self-preservation. It is worse than in vain, because it plants in the Constitution itself necessary usurpations of power." — *Federalist*, No. 41.

With this construction, proclaimed both by the advocates and opponents of its ratification, the Constitution of the United States was accepted and adopted, and that construction has been followed and acted upon by every department of the government to this day.

It was as well understood then in theory as it has since been illustrated in practice, that the judicial power, both federal and State, had no voice and could exercise no authority in the conduct and prosecution of a war, except in subordination to the political department of the government. The Constitution contains the significant provision, "The privilege of the writ of *habeas corpus* shall not be suspended, unless when in cases of rebellion or invasion the public safety may require it."

What was this but a declaration, that in time of rebellion or invasion the public safety is the highest law? — that so far as necessary the civil courts (of which the Commander-in-Chief, under the direction of Congress, shall be the sole judge) must be silent, and the rights of each citizen, as secured in time of peace, must yield to the wants, interests, and necessities of the nation? Yet we have been gravely told by the gentleman in his argument, that the maxim, *salus populi suprema est lex*, is but fit for a tyrant's use. Those grand men, whom God taught to build the fabric of empire, thought otherwise when they put that maxim into the Constitution of their country. It is very clear that the Constitution recognizes the great principle which underlies the structure of society and of all civil government; that no man lives for himself alone, but each for all; that, if need be, some must die that the State may live, because at best the individual is but for to-day, while the commonwealth is for all time. I agree with the gentleman in the maxim which he borrows from Aristotle, "Let the public weal be under the protection of the law "; but I claim that in war, as in peace, by the very terms of the Constitution of the country, the public safety is under the protection of the law; that the Constitution itself has provided for the declaration of war for the common defense, to suppress rebellion, to repel invasion, and, by express terms, has declared that whatever is necessary to make the prosecution of the war successful, may be done, and ought to be done, and is therefore constitutionally lawful.

Who will dare to say that in time of civil war "no person shall be deprived of life, liberty, and property without due process of law"? This is a provision of your Constitution than which there is none more just or sacred in it; it is, however, only the law of peace, not of war. In peace, that wise provision of the Constitution must be, and is, enforced by the civil courts; in war it must be, and is, to a great extent, inoperative and disregarded. The thousands slain by your armies in battle were deprived of life "without due process of law." All spies arrested, convicted, and executed by your military tribunals in time of war are deprived of liberty and life " without due process of law "; all enemies captured and held as prisoners of war are deprived of liberty " without due process of law "; all owners whose property is forcibly seized and appropriated in war are deprived of their property " without due process of law." The Constitution recognizes the principle of common law, that every man's house is his castle; that his home, the shelter of his wife and children, is his most sacred possession; and has therefore specially provided, "that no soldier shall *in time of peace* be quartered in any house without the consent of its owner, nor in time of war, but in a manner to be prescribed by law [III Amend.]; thereby declaring that, in time of war, Congress may by law authorize, as it has done, that without the consent and against the consent of the owner, the soldier may be quartered in any man's house and upon any man's hearth. What I have said illustrates the proposition, that in time of war the civil tribunals of justice are wholly or partially silent, as the public safety may require; that the limitations and provisions of the Constitution in favor of life, liberty, and property are therefore wholly or partially suspended. In this I am sustained by an authority second to none with intelligent American citizens. Mr. John Quincy Adams, than whom a purer man or a wiser statesman never ascended the chair of the chief magistracy in America, said in his place in the House of Representatives, in 1836, that: —

"In the authority given to Congress by the Constitution of the United States to declare war, all the powers incident to war are by necessary implication conferred upon the government of the United States. Now the powers incident to war are derived, not from their internal municipal source, but from the laws and usages of nations. There are, then, in the authority of Congress and the Executive, two classes of powers altogether different in their nature and often incompatible with each other — the war power and the peace power. The peace power is limited by regulations and restricted by provisions prescribed within the Constitution itself. The war power is limited only by the laws and usage of nations. This power is tremendous; it is strictly constitutional, but it breaks down every barrier so anxiously erected for the protection of liberty, of property, and of life."

If this be so, how can there be trial by jury for military offenses in time of civil war? If you cannot, and do not, try the armed enemy before you shoot him, or the captured enemy before you imprison him, why should you be held to open the civil courts and try the spy, the conspirator, and the assassin, in the secret service of the public enemy, by jury, before you convict and punish him? Why not clamor against holding imprisoned the captured armed rebels, deprived of their liberty without due process of law? Are they not citizens? Why not clamor against slaying for their crime of treason, which is cognizable in the civil courts, by your rifled ordnance and the leaden hail of your musketry in battle, these public enemies, without trial by jury? Are they not citizens? Why is the clamor confined exclusively to the trial by military tribunals of justice of traitorous spies, traitorous conspirators, and assassins hired to do secretly what the armed rebel attempts to do openly — murder your nationality by assassinating its defenders and its executive officers? Nothing can be clearer than that the rebel captured prisoner, being a citizen of the republic, is as much entitled to trial by jury before he is committed to prison, as the spy, or the aider and abetter of the treason by conspiracy and assassination, being a citizen, is entitled to such trial by jury, before he is subjected to the just punishment of the law for his great crime. I think that in time of war the remark of Montesquieu, touching the civil judiciary is true: that "it is next to nothing." Hamilton well said, "The Executive holds the sword of the community; the judiciary has no direction of the strength of society; it has neither force nor will; it has judgment alone, and is dependent for the execution of that upon the arm of the Executive." The people of these States so understood the Constitution and adopted it, and intended thereby, without limitation or restraint, to empower their Congress and Executive to authorize by law, and execute by force, whatever the public safety might require to suppress rebellion or repel invasion.

Notwithstanding all that has been said by the counsel for the accused to the contrary, the Constitution has received this construction from the day of its adoption to this hour. The Supreme Court of the United States has solemnly decided that the Constitution has conferred upon the government authority to employ all the means necessary to the faithful execution of all the powers which that Constitution enjoins upon the government of the United States, and upon every department and every officer thereof. Speaking of that provision of the Constitution which provides that "Congress shall have power to make all laws that may be necessary and proper to carry into effect all powers granted to the government of the United States, or to any department or officer thereof," Chief Justice Marshall, in his great decision in the case of McCulloch *vs.* State of Maryland, says: —

"The powers given to the government imply the ordinary means of execution, and the government, in all sound reason and fair interpretation, must have the choice of the means which it deems the most convenient and appropriate to the execution of the power. . . . The powers of the government were given for the welfare of the nation; they were intended to endure for ages to come, and to be adapted to the various crises in human affairs. To prescribe the specific means by which government should, in all future time, execute its power, and to confine the choice of means to such narrow limits as should not leave it in the power of Congress to adopt any which might be appropriate and conducive to the end, would be most unwise and pernicious." — 4 Wheaton, 420.

Words fitly spoken! which illustrated at the time of their utterance the wisdom of the Constitution in providing this general grant of power to meet every possible exigency which the fortunes of war might cast upon the country, and the wisdom of which words, in turn, has been illustrated to-day by the gigantic and triumphant struggle of the people during the last four years for the supremacy of the Constitution, and in exact accordance with its provisions. In the light of these wonderful events, the words of Pinckney, uttered when the illustrious Chief Justice had concluded this opinion, "The Constitution of my country is immortal!" seem to have become words of prophecy. Has not this great tribunal, through the chief of all its judges, by this luminous and profound reasoning, declared that the government may by law authorize the Executive to employ, in the prosecution of war, the ordinary means, and all the means necessary and adapted to the end? And in the other decision before referred to, in the 8th of Cranch, arising during the late war with Great Britain, Mr. Justice Story said : —

"When the legislative authority, to whom the right to declare war is confided, has declared war in its most unlimited manner, the executive authority, to whom the execution of the war is confided, is bound to carry it into effect. He has a discretion vested in him as to the manner and extent, but he cannot lawfully transcend the rules of warfare established among civilized nations. He cannot lawfully exercise powers or authorize proceedings which the civilized world repudiates and disclaims. The sovereignty, as to declaring war and limiting its effects, rests with the legislature. The sovereignty as to its execution rests with the President. — Brown *vs.* United States, 8 Cranch, 153.

Has the Congress, to whom is committed the sovereignty of the whole people to declare war, by legislation restricted the President, or attempted to restrict him, in the prosecution of this war for the Union, from exercising all the "powers" and adopting all the "proceedings" usually approved and employed by the civilized world? He would, in my judgment, be a bold man who asserted that Congress has so legislated; and the Congress which should by law fetter the executive arm when raised for the common defense would, in my opinion, be false to their oath. That Congress may prescribe rules for the government of the army and navy and the militia when in actual service, by articles of war, is an express grant of power in the Constitution which Congress has rightfully exercised, and which the Executive must and does obey. That Congress may aid the Executive by legislation in the prosecution of a war, civil or foreign, is admitted. That Congress may restrain the Executive, and arraign, try, and condemn him for wantonly abusing the great trust, is expressly declared in the Constitution. That Congress shall pass all laws NECESSARY to enable the Executive to execute the laws of the Union, suppress insurrection, and repel invasion, is one of the express requirements of the Constitution, for the performance of which the Congress is bound by an oath.

What was the legislation of Congress when treason fired its first gun on Sumter? By the act of 1795 it is provided that whenever the laws of the United States shall be opposed, or the execution thereof obstructed, in any State, by combinations too powerful to be suppressed by the ordinary course of judicial proceeding or by the powers vested in the marshals, it shall be lawful by this act for the President to call forth the militia of such State, or of any other State or States, as may be necessary to suppress such combinations and to cause the laws to be executed (1st Statutes at Large, 424). By the act of 1807 it is provided that in case of insurrection or obstruction to the laws, either of the United States or of any individual State or territory, where it is lawful for the President of the United States to call forth the militia for the purpose of suppressing such insurrection or of causing the laws to be duly executed, it shall be lawful for him to employ for such purpose such part of the land or naval forces of the United States as shall be judged necessary (2d Statutes at Large, 443).

Can any one doubt that by these acts the President is clothed with full power to determine whether armed insurrection exists in any State or territory of the Union; and if so, to make war upon it with all the force he may deem necessary or be able to command? By the simple exercise of this great power it necessarily results that he may, in the prosecution of the war for the suppression of such insurrection, suspend as far as may be necessary the civil administration of justice by substituting in its stead martial law, which is simply the common law of war. If in such a moment the President may make no arrests without civil warrant, and may inflict no violence or penalties on persons (as is claimed here for the accused), without first obtaining the verdict of juries and the judgment of civil courts, then is this legislation a mockery, and the Constitution, which not only authorized but enjoined its enactment, but a glittering generality and a splendid bauble. Happily, the Supreme Court has settled all controversy on this question. In speaking of the Rhode Island insurrection, the court say: —

"The Constitution of the United States, as far as it has provided for an emergency of this kind and authorized the general government to interfere in the domestic concerns of a State, has treated the subject as political in its nature and placed the power in the hands of that department." . . . "By the act of 1795 the power of deciding whether the exigency has arisen upon which the government of the United States is bound to interfere is given to the President."

The court add: —

"When the President has acted and called out the militia, is a circuit court of the United States authorized to inquire whether his decision was right? If it could, then it would become the duty of the court, provided it came to the conclusion that the President had decided incorrectly, to discharge those who were arrested or detained by the troops in the service of the United States." . . . "If the judicial power extends so far, the guarantee contained in the Constitution of the United States is a guarantee of anarchy and not of order." . . . "Yet if this right does not reside in the courts when the conflict is raging, if the judicial power is at that time bound to follow the decision of the political, it must be equally bound when the contest is over. It cannot, when peace is restored, punish as offenses and crimes the acts which it before recognized and was bound to recognize as lawful." — Luther *vs.* Borden, 7 Howard, 42, 43.

If this be law, what becomes of the volunteer advice of the volunteer counsel, by him given without money and without price, to this court, of their responsibility — their *personal* responsibility, for obeying the orders of the President of the United States in trying persons accused of the murder of the Chief Magistrate and Commander-in-Chief of the army and navy of the United States in time of rebellion, and in pursuance of a conspiracy entered into with the public enemy? I may be pardoned for asking the attention of the court to a further citation from this important decision, in which the court say, the employment of military power to put down an armed insurrection "is essential to the existence of every government, and is as necessary to the States of this Union as to any other government; and if the government of the State deem the armed opposition so formidable as to require the use of military force and the declaration of MARTIAL LAW, we see no ground upon which this court can question its authority" (*Ibid*). This decision in terms declared that under the act of 1795 the President had power to decide and did decide the question so as to exclude further inquiry whether the State government which thus employed force and proclaimed martial law was the government of the State, and therefore was permitted to act. If a State may do this to put down armed insurrection, may not the federal government as well? The reason of the man who doubts it may justly be questioned. I but quote the language of that tribunal, in another case before cited, when I say the Constitution confers upon the President the whole executive power.

We have seen that the proclamation of blockade made by the President was affirmed by the Supreme Court as a lawful and valid act, although its direct effect was to dispose of the property of whoever violated it, whether citizen or stranger. It is difficult to perceive what course of reasoning can be adopted, in the light of that decision, which will justify any man in saying that the President had not the like power to proclaim martial law in time of insurrection against the United States, and to establish, according to the customs of war among civilized nations, military tribunals of justice for its enforcement and for the punishment of all crimes committed in the interests of the public enemy.

These acts of the President have, however, all been legalized by the subsequent legislation of Congress, although the Supreme Court decided, in relation to the proclamation of blockade, that no such legislation was necessary. By the act of August 6, 1861, ch. 63, sec. 3, it is enacted that —

"All the acts, proclamations, and orders of the President of the United States, after the 4th of March, 1861, respecting the army and navy of the United States, and calling out, or relating to, the militia or volunteers from the States, are hereby approved in all respects, legalized, and made valid to the same extent and with the same effect as if they had been issued and done under the previous express authority and direction of the Congress of the United States." — 12 Statutes at Large, 326.

This act legalized, if any such legalization was necessary, all that the President had done from the day of his inauguration to that hour, in the prosecution of the war for the Union. He had suspended the privilege of the writ of *habeas corpus*, and resisted its execution when issued by the Chief Justice of the United States; he had called out and accepted the services of a large body of volunteers for a period not previously authorized by law; he had declared a blockade of the Southern ports; he had declared the Southern States in insurrection; he had ordered the armies to invade them and suppress it; thus exercising, in accordance with the laws of war, power over the life, the liberty, and the property of the citizens. Congress ratified it and affirmed it.

In like manner and by subsequent legislation did the Congress ratify and affirm the proclamation of martial law of September 25, 1862. That proclamation, as the court will have observed, declares that during the existing insurrection all rebels and insurgents, their aiders and abettors within the United States, and all persons guilty of any disloyal practice affording aid and comfort to the rebels against the authority of the United States, shall be subject to martial law and liable to trial and punishment by courts-martial or *military commission;* and second, that the writ of *habeas corpus* is suspended in respect to all persons arrested, or who are now, or hereafter during the rebellion shall be, imprisoned in any fort, etc., by any military authority, or by the sentence of any court-martial or *military commission*.

One would suppose that it needed no argument to satisfy an intelligent and patriotic citizen of the United States that, by the ruling of the Supreme Court cited, so much of this proclamation as declares that all rebels and insurgents, their aiders and abettors, shall be subject to martial law and be liable to trial and punishment by court-martial or military commission, needed no ratification by Congress. Every step that the President took against rebels and insurgents was taken in pursuance of the rules of war and was an exercise of martial law. Who says that he should not deprive them, by the authority of this law, of life and liberty? Are the aiders and abettors of these insurgents entitled to any higher consideration than the armed insurgents themselves? It is against these that the President proclaimed martial law, and against all others who were guilty of any disloyal practice affording aid and comfort to rebels against the authority of the United States. Against these he suspended the privilege of the writ of *habeas corpus;* and these, and only such as these, were by that proclamation subjected to trial and punishment by court-martial or military commission.

That the Proclamation covers the offense charged here, no man will, or dare, for a moment deny. Was it not a disloyal practice? Was it not aiding and abetting the insurgents and rebels to enter into a conspiracy with them to kill and murder, within your capital and your intrenched camp, the Commander-in-Chief of our army, your Lieutenant General, and the Vice-President, and the Secretary of State, with intent thereby to aid the rebellion, and subvert the Constitution and laws of the United States? But it is said that the President could not establish a court for their trial, and therefore Congress must ratify and affirm this Proclamation. I have said before that such an argument comes with ill grace from the lips of him who declared as solemnly that neither by the Congress nor by the President could either the rebel himself or his aider or abettor be lawfully and constitutionally subjected to trial by any military tribunal, whether court-martial or military commission. But the Congress did ratify, in the exercise of the power vested in them, every part of this Proclamation. I have said, upon the authority of the fathers of the Constitution, and of its judicial interpreters, that Congress has power by legislation to aid the Executive in the suppression of rebellion, in executing the laws of the Union when resisted by armed insurrection, and in repelling invasion.

By the act of March 3, 1863, the Congress of the United States, by the first section thereof, declared that during the present rebellion the President of the United States, whenever in his judgment the public safety may require it, is authorized to suspend the writ of *habeas corpus* in any case throughout the United States or any part thereof. By the fourth section of the same act it is declared that any order of the President, or under his authority, made at any time during the existence of the present rebellion, shall be a defense in all courts to any action or prosecution, civil or criminal, pending or to be commenced, for any search, seizure, arrest, or imprisonment, made, done, or committed, or acts omitted to be done, under and by virtue of such order. By the fifth section it is provided that, if any suit or prosecution, civil or criminal, has been or shall be commenced in any State court against any officer, civil or military, or against any other person, for any arrest or imprisonment made, or other trespasses or wrongs done or committed, or any act omitted to be done at any time during the present rebellion, by virtue of or under color of any authority derived from or exercised by or under the President of the United States, if the defendant shall, upon appearance in such court, file a petition stating the facts upon affidavit, etc., as aforesaid, for the removal of the cause for trial to the circuit court of the United States, it shall be the duty of the State court, upon his giving security, to proceed no further in the cause or prosecution; thus declaring that all orders of the President, made at any time during the existence of the present rebellion, and all acts done in pursuance thereof, shall be held valid in the courts of justice. Without further inquiry, these provisions of this statute embrace Order 141, which is the proclamation of martial law, and necessarily legalize every act done under it, either before the passage of the act of 1863 or since.

Inasmuch as that Proclamation ordered that all rebels, insurgents, their aiders and abettors, and persons guilty of any disloyal practice affording aid and comfort to rebels against the authority of the United States, at any time during the existing insurrection, should be subject to martial law, and liable to trial and punishment by a *military commission*, the sections of the law just cited declaring lawful all acts done in pursuance of such order, including, of course, the trial and punishment by military commission of all such offenders, as directly legalized this order of the President as it is possible for Congress to legalize or authorize any executive act whatever. — 12 Statutes at Large, 755, 756.

But after assuming and declaring with great earnestness in his argument that no person could be tried and convicted for such crimes by any military tribunal, whether a court-martial or a military commission, save those in the land or naval service in time of war, the gentleman makes the extraordinary statement that the creation of a military commission must be authorized by the legislative department, and demands, if there be any such legislation, "let the statute be produced." The statute has been produced. The power so to try, says the gentleman, must be authorized by Congress, when the demand is made for such authority. Does not the gentleman thereby give up his argument, and admit, that if the Congress has so authorized the trial of all aiders and abettors of rebels or insurgents for whatever they do in aid of such rebels and insurgents during the insurrection, the statute and proceedings under it are lawful and valid? I have already shown that the Congress have so legislated by expressly legalizing Order No. 141, which directed the trial of all rebels, their aiders and abettors, by military commission. Did not Congress expressly legalize this order by declaring that the order shall be a defense in all courts to any action or prosecution, civil or criminal, for acts done in pursuance of it? No amount of argument could make this point clearer than the language of the statute itself. But, says the gentleman, if there be a statute authorizing trials by military commission, "let it be produced."

By the act of March 3, 1863, it is provided in section thirty that in time of war, insurrection, or rebellion, murder and assault with intent to kill, etc., when committed by persons in the military service, shall be punishable by the sentence of a court-martial or *military commission*, and the punishment of such offenses shall never be less than those inflicted by the laws of the State or district in which they may have been committed. By the thirty-eighth section of the same act it is provided that all persons who, in time of war or rebellion against the United States, shall be found lurking or acting as spies in or about the camps, etc., of the United States, or elsewhere, shall be triable by a *military commission*, and shall, upon conviction, suffer death. Here is a statute which expressly declares that all persons, whether citizens or strangers, who in time of rebellion shall be found acting as spies, shall suffer death upon conviction by a military commission. Why did not the gentleman give us some argument upon this law? We have seen that it was the existing law of the United States under the Confederation. Then, and since, men not in the land or naval forces of the United States have suffered death for this offense upon conviction by courts-martial. If it was competent for Congress to authorize their trial by courts-martial, it was equally competent for Congress to authorize their trial by military commission, and accordingly they have done so. By the same authority the Congress may extend the jurisdiction of military commissions over all military offenses or crimes committed in time of rebellion or war in aid of the public enemy; and it certainly stands with right reason, that if it were just to subject to death, by the sentence of a military commission, all persons who should be guilty merely of lurking as spies in the interests of the public enemy in time of rebellion, though they obtained no information, though they inflicted no personal injury, but were simply overtaken and detected in the endeavor to obtain intelligence for the enemy, those who enter into conspiracy with the enemy, not only to lurk as spies in your camp, but to lurk there as murderers and assassins, and who, in pursuance of that conspiracy, commit assassination and murder upon the Commander-in-Chief of your army within your camp and in aid of rebellion, should be subject in like manner to trial by military commission. — Statutes at Large 12, 736, 737, ch. 8.

Accordingly, the President having so declared, the Congress, as we have stated, have affirmed that his order was valid, and that all persons acting by authority, and consequently as a court pronouncing such sentence upon the offender as the usage of war requires, are justified by the law of the land. With all respect, permit me to say that the learned gentleman has manifested more acumen and ability in his elaborate argument by what he has omitted to say than by anything which he has said. By the act of July 2, 1864, cap. 215, it is provided that the commanding general in the field, or the commander of the department, as the case may be, shall have power to carry into execution all sentences against guerilla marauders for robbery, arson, burglary, etc., and for violation of the laws and customs of war, as well as sentences against spies, mutineers, deserters, and murderers.

From the legislation I have cited, it is apparent that military commissions are expressly recognized by the law-making power; that they are authorized to try capital offenses against citizens not in the service of the United States, and to pronounce the sentence of death upon them; and that the commander of a department, or the commanding general in the field, may carry such sentence into execution. But, says the gentleman, grant all this to be so; Congress has not declared in what manner the court shall be constituted. The answer to that objection has already been anticipated in the citation from Benét, wherein it appeared to be the rule of the law martial that in the punishment of all military offenses not provided for by the written law of the land, military commissions are constituted for that purpose by the authority of the commanding officer or the Commander-in-Chief, as the case may be, who selects the officers of a court-martial; that they are similarly constituted, and their proceedings conducted according to the same general rules. That is a part of the very law martial which the President proclaimed, and which the Congress has legalized. The Proclamation has declared that all such offenders shall be tried by military commissions. The Congress has legalized the same by the act which I have cited; and by every intendment it must be taken that, as martial law is by the Proclamation declared to be the rule by which they shall be tried, the Congress, in affirming the act of the President, simply declared that they should be tried according to the customs of martial law; that the commission should be constituted by the Commander-in-Chief according to the rule of procedure known as martial law; and that the penalties inflicted should be in accordance with the laws of war and the usages of nations. Legislation no more definite than this has been upon your statute-book since the beginning of the century, and has been held by the Supreme Court of the United States valid for the punishment of offenders.

By the thirty-second article of the act of 23d April, 1800, it is provided that "all crimes committed by persons belonging to the navy which are not specified in the foregoing articles shall be punished according to the laws and customs in such cases at sea." Of this article the Supreme Court of the United States say, that when offences and crimes are not given in terms or by definition, the want of it may be supplied by a comprehensive enactment such as the thirty-second article of the rules for the government of the navy; which means that courts-martial have jurisdiction of such crimes as are not specified, but which have been recognized to be crimes and offenses by the usages in the navies of all nations, and that they shall be punished according to the laws and customs of the sea.— Dynes *vs.* Hoover, 20 Howard, 82.

But it is a fact that must not be omitted in the reply which I make to the gentleman's argument, that an effort was made by himself and others in the Senate of the United States, on the 3d of March last, to condemn the arrests, imprisonments, etc., made by order of the President of the United States in pursuance of his Proclamation, and to reverse, by the judgment of that body, the law which had been before passed affirming his action, which effort most signally failed.

Thus we see that the body which by the Constitution, if the President had been guilty of the misdemeanors alleged against him in this argument of the gentleman, would, upon presentation of such charge in legal form against the President, constitute the high court of impeachment for his trial and condemnation, has decided the question in advance, and declared upon the occasion referred to, as they had before declared by solemn enactment, that this order of the President declaring martial law and the punishment of all rebels and insurgents, their aiders and abettors, by military commission, should be enforced during the insurrection, as the law of the land, and that the offenders should be tried, as directed, by military commission. It may be said that this subsequent legislation of Congress, ratifying and affirming what had been done by the President, can have no validity. Of course it cannot if neither the Congress nor the Executive can authorize the proclamation and enforcement of martial law in the suppression of rebellion for the punishment of all persons committing military offenses in aid of that rebellion. Assuming, however, as the gentleman seemed to assume, by asking for the legislation of Congress, that there is such power in Congress, the Supreme Court of the United States has solemnly affirmed that such ratification is valid. — 2 Black, 671.

The gentleman's argument is full of citations of English precedent. There is a late English precedent bearing upon this point — the power of the legislature, by subsequent enactment, to legalize executive orders, arrests, and imprisonment of citizens — that I beg leave to commend to his consideration. I refer to the statute of 11 and 12 Victoria, ch. 35, entitled "An act to empower the lord lieutenant, or other chief governor or governors of Ireland, to apprehend and detain until the first day of March, 1849, such persons as he or they shall *suspect* of conspiring against her Majesty's person and government," passed July 25, 1848, which statute in terms declares that all and every person and persons who is, are, or shall be, within that period, within that part of the United Kingdom of England and Ireland called Ireland at or on the day the act shall receive her Majesty's royal assent, or after, by warrant for high treason or treasonable practices, or *suspicion* of high treason or treasonable practices, signed by the lord lieutenant, or other chief governor or governors of Ireland for the time being, or his or their chief secretary, for such causes as aforesaid, may be detained in safe custody without bail or main prize, until the first day of March, 1849; and that no judge or justice shall bail or try any such person or persons so committed, without order from her Majesty's privy council, until the said first day of March, 1849, any law or statute to the contrary notwithstanding. The second section of this act provides that, in cases where any persons have been, *before* the passing of the act, arrested, committed, or detained for such cause by warrant or warrants signed by the officers aforesaid, or either of them, it may be lawful for the person or persons to whom such warrants have been or shall be directed, to detain such person or persons in his or their custody in any place whatever in Ireland; and that such person or persons to whom such warrants have been or shall be directed shall be deemed and taken, to all intents and purposes, lawfully authorized to take into safe custody and be the lawful jailers and keepers of such persons so arrested, committed, or detained.

Here the power of arrest is given by the act of Parliament to the governor or his secretary; the process of the civil courts was wholly suspended; bail was denied and the parties imprisoned, and this not by process of the courts, but by warrant of a chief governor or his secretary; not for crimes charged to have been committed, but for being *suspected* of treasonable practices. Magna Charta, it seems, opposes no restraint, notwithstanding the parade that is made about it in this argument, upon the power of the Parliament of England to legalize arrests and imprisonments made before the passage of the act upon an executive order, and without colorable authority of statute law, and to authorize like arrests and imprisonments of so many of six million of people as such executive officers might *suspect* of treasonable practices.

But, says the gentleman, whatever may be the precedents, English or American, whatever may be the provisions of the Constitution, whatever may be the legislation of Congress, whatever may be the proclamations and orders of the President as Commander-in-Chief, it is a usurpation and a tyranny in time of rebellion and civil war to subject any citizen to trial for any crime before military tribunals, save such citizens as are in the land or naval forces, and against this usurpation, which he asks this court to rebuke by solemn decision, he appeals to public opinion. I trust that I set as high value upon enlightened public opinion as any man. I recognize it as the reserved power of the people which creates and dissolves armies, which creates and dissolves legislative assemblies, which enacts and repeals fundamental laws, the better to provide for personal security by the due administration of justice. To that public opinion upon this very question of the usurpation of authority, of unlawful arrests, and unlawful imprisonments, and unlawful trials, condemnations, and executions by the late President of the United States, an appeal has already been taken. On this very issue the President was tried before the tribunal of the people, that great nation of freemen who cover this continent, looking out upon Europe from their eastern and upon Asia from their western homes. That people came to the consideration of this issue not unmindful of the fact that the first struggle for the establishment of our nationality could not have been, and was not, successfully prosecuted without the proclamation and enforcement of martial law, declaring, as we have seen, that any inhabitant who, during that war, should kill any loyal citizen, or enter into any combination for that purpose, should, upon trial and conviction before a military tribunal, be sentenced as an assassin, traitor, or spy, and should suffer death, and that in this last struggle for the maintenance of American nationality the President but followed the example of the illustrious Father of his Country. Upon that issue the people passed judgment on the 8th day of last November, and declared that the charge of usurpation was false.

From this decision of the people there lies no appeal on this earth. Who can rightfully challenge the authority of the American people to decide such questions for themselves? The voice of the people, thus solemnly proclaimed, by the omnipotence of the ballot in favor of the righteous order of their murdered President, issued by him for the common defense, for the preservation of the Constitution, and for the enforcement of the laws of the Union, ought to be accepted, and will be accepted, I trust, by all just men, as the voice of God.

May it please the Court: I have said thus much touching the right of the people, under their Constitution, in time of civil war and rebellion, to proclaim through their Executive, with the sanction and approval of their Congress, martial law, and enforce the same according to the usage of nations.

I submit that it has been shown that, by the letter and spirit of the Constitution, as well as by its contemporaneous construction, followed and approved by every department of the government, this right is in the people; that it is inseparable from the condition of war, whether civil or foreign, and absolutely essential to its vigorous and successful prosecution; that according to the highest authority upon constitutional law, the proclamation and enforcement of martial law are "usual under all governments in time of rebellion"; that our own highest judicial tribunal has declared this, and solemnly ruled that the question of the necessity for its exercise rests exclusively with Congress and the President; and that the decision of the political departments of the government, that there is an armed rebellion and a necessity for the employment of military force and martial law in its suppression concludes the judiciary.

In submitting what I have said in support of the jurisdiction of this honorable court, and of its constitutional power to hear and determine this issue, I have uttered my own convictions; and for their utterance in defense of my country, and its right to employ all the means necessary for the common defense against armed rebellion and secret treasonable conspiracy in aid of such rebellion, I shall neither ask pardon nor offer apology. I find no words with which more fitly to conclude all I have to say upon the question of the jurisdiction and constitutional authority of this court than those employed by the illustrious Lord Brougham to the House of Peers in the support of the bill before referred to, which empowered the lord lieutenant of Ireland, and his deputies, to apprehend and detain, for the period of seven months or more, all such persons within that island as they should *suspect* of conspiracy against her Majesty's person and government. Said that illustrious man: "A friend of liberty I have lived, and such will I die; nor care I how soon the latter event may happen, if I cannot be a friend of liberty without being a friend of traitors at the same time — a protector of criminals of the deepest dye — an accomplice of foul rebellion and of its concomitant, civil war, with all its atrocities and all its fearful consequences." — Hansard's Debates, 3d series, vol. 100, p. 635.

May it please the Court: It only remains for me to sum up the evidence and present my views of the law arising upon the facts in the case on trial. The questions of fact involved in the issue are: —

First, did the accused, or any two of them, confederate and conspire together as charged? and —

Second, did the accused, or any of them, in pursuance of such conspiracy, and with the intent alleged, commit either or all of the several acts specified?

If the conspiracy be established, as laid, it results that whatever was said or done by either of the parties thereto, in the furtherance or execution of the common design, is the declaration or act of all the other parties to the conspiracy; and this, whether the other parties, at the time such words were uttered or such acts done by their confederates, were present or absent — here, within the intrenched lines of your capital, or crouching behind the intrenched lines of Richmond, or awaiting the results of their murderous plot against their country, its Constitution and laws, across the border, under the shelter of the British flag.

The declared and accepted rule of law in cases of conspiracy is that —

"In prosecutions for conspiracy it is an established rule that where several persons are proved to have combined together for the same illegal purpose, any act done by one of the party, in pursuance of the original concerted plan, and in reference to the common object, is, in the contemplation of law as well as in sound reason, the act of the whole party; and, therefore, the proof of the act will be evidence against any of the others who were engaged in the same general conspiracy, without regard to the question whether the prisoner is proved to have been concerned in the particular transaction." — Phillips on Evidence, p. 210.

The same rule obtains in cases of treason: "If several persons agree to levy war, some in one place and some in another, and one party do actually appear in arms, this is a levying of war by all, as well those who were not in arms as those who were, if it were done in pursuance of the original concert, for those who made the attempt were emboldened by the confidence inspired by the general concert, and therefore these particular acts are in justice imputable to all the rest." — 1 East., Pleas of the Crown, p. 97; Roscoe, 84.

In *Ex parte Bollman and Swartwout*, 4 Cranch, 126, Marshall, Chief Justice, rules: "If war be actually levied, — that is, if a body of men be actually assembled, for the purpose of effecting, by force, a treasonable purpose, — all those who perform any part, *however minute, or however remote from the scene of action*, and who are actually leagued in the general conspiracy, are to be considered as traitors."

In United States *vs*. Cole *et al*, 5 McLean, 601, Mr. Justice McLean says: "A conspiracy is rarely, if ever, proved by positive testimony. When a crime of high magnitude is about to be perpetrated by a combination of individuals, they do not act openly but covertly and secretly. The purpose formed is known only to those who enter into it. Unless one of the original conspirators betray his companions and give evidence against them, their guilt can be proved only by circumstantial evidence. . . . It is said by some writers on evidence that such circumstances are stronger than positive proof. A witness swearing positively, it is said, may misapprehend the facts or swear falsely, but that circumstances cannot lie.

"The common design is the essence of the charge; and this may be made to appear when the defendants steadily pursue the same object, whether acting separately or together, by common or different means, all leading to the same unlawful result. And where *prima facie* evidence has been given of a combination, the acts or confessions of one are evidence against all. . . . It is reasonable that where a body of men assume the attribute of individuality, whether for commercial business or for the commission of a crime, that the association should be bound by the acts of one of its members in carrying out the design."

It is a rule of the law, not to be overlooked in this connection, that the conspiracy or agreement of the parties, or some of them, to act in concert to accomplish the unlawful act charged, may be established either by direct evidence of a meeting or consultation for the illegal purpose charged, or more usually, from the very nature of the case, by circumstantial evidence. — 2 Starkie, 232.

Lord Mansfield ruled that it was not necessary to prove the actual fact of a conspiracy, but that it might be collected from collateral circumstances. — Parson's Case, 1 W. Blackstone, 392.

"If," says a great authority on the law of evidence, "on a charge of conspiracy, it appear that two persons by their acts are pursuing the same object, and often by the same means, or one performing part of the act and the other completing it, for the

APPENDIX. 359

attainment of the same object, the jury may draw the conclusion there is a conspiracy. If a conspiracy be formed, and a person join in it afterwards, he is equally guilty with the original conspirators." — Roscoe, 415.

"The rule of the admissibility of the acts and declarations of any one of the conspirators, said or done in furtherance of the common design, applies in cases as well where only part of the conspirators are indicted or upon trial as where all are indicted and upon trial. Thus, upon an indictment for murder, if it appear that others, together with the prisoner, conspired to commit the crime, the act of one, done in pursuance of that intention, will be evidence against the rest." — 2d Starkie, 237.

They are all alike guilty as principals. — Commonwealth *vs.* Knapp, 9 Pickering, 496; 10 Pickering, 477; 6 Term Reports, 528; 11 East., 584.

What is the evidence, direct and circumstantial, that the accused, or either of them, together with John H. Surratt, John Wilkes Booth, Jefferson Davis, George N. Sanders, Beverly Tucker, Jacob Thompson, William C. Cleary, Clement C. Clay, George Harper, and George Young, did combine, confederate, and conspire, in aid of the existing rebellion, as charged, to kill and murder, within the military department of Washington, and within the fortified and intrenched lines thereof, Abraham Lincoln, late, and at the time of the said combining, confederating, and conspiring, President of the United States of America and Commander-in-Chief of the army and navy thereof; Andrew Johnson, Vice-President of the United States; William H. Seward, Secretary of State of the United States; and Ulysses S. Grant, Lieutenant General of the armies thereof, and then in command, under the direction of the President?

The time, as laid in the charge and specification, when this conspiracy was entered into, is immaterial, so that it appear by the evidence that the criminal combination and agreement were formed before the commission of the acts alleged. That Jefferson Davis, one of the conspirators named, was the acknowledged chief and leader of the existing rebellion against the government of the United States, and that Jacob Thompson, George N. Sanders, Clement C. Clay, Beverly Tucker, and others named in the specification, were his duly accredited and authorized agents to act in the interests of said rebellion, are facts established by the testimony in this case beyond all question. That Davis, as the leader of said rebellion, gave to those agents, then in Canada, commissions in blank, bearing the official signature of his war minister, James A. Seddon, to be by them filled up and delivered to such agents as they might employ to act in the interests of the rebellion within the United States, and intended to be a cover and protection for any crimes they might therein commit in the service of the rebellion, is also a fact established here, and which no man can gainsay. Who doubts that Kennedy, whose confession made in view of immediate death, as proved here, was commissioned by those accredited agents of Davis to burn the city of New York? — that he was to have attempted it on the night of the presidential election, and that he did, in combination with his confederates, set fire to four hotels in the city of New York on the night of the 25th of November last? Who doubts that, in like manner, in the interests of the rebellion and by the authority of Davis, these his agents also commissioned Bennett H. Young to commit arson, robbery, and the murder of unarmed citizens, in St. Albans, Vt.? Who doubts, upon the testimony shown, that Davis, by his agents, deliberately adopted the system of starvation for the murder of our captive soldiers in his hands; or that, as shown by the testimony, he sanctioned the burning of hospitals and steamboats, the property of private persons, and paid therefor from his stolen treasure the sum of thirty-five thousand dollars in gold? By the evidence of Joseph Godfrey

Hyams it is proved that Thompson, the agent of Jefferson Davis, paid him money for the service he rendered in the infamous and fiendish project of importing pestilence into our camps and cities to destroy the lives of citizens and soldiers alike, and into the house of the President for the purpose of destroying his life. It may be said, and doubtless will be said, by the pensioned advocates of this rebellion, that Hyams, being infamous, is not to be believed. It is admitted that he is infamous, as it must be conceded that any man is infamous who either participates in such a crime or attempts in any wise to extenuate it. But it will be observed that Hyams is supported by the testimony of Mr. Sanford Conover, who heard Blackburn and the other rebel agents in Canada speak of this infernal project, and by the testimony of Mr. Wall, the well-known auctioneer of this city, whose character in unquestioned, that he received this importation of pestilence (of course without any knowledge of the purpose), and that Hyams consigned the goods to him in the name of J. W. Harris, a fact in itself an acknowledgment of guilt; and that he received afterwards a letter from Harris, dated Toronto, Canada West, December 1, 1864, wherein Harris stated that he had not been able to come to the States since his return to Canada, and asked for an account of the sale. He identifies the Godfrey Joseph Hyams who testified in court as the J. W. Harris who imported the pestilence. The very transaction shows that Hyams's statement is truthful. He gives the names of the parties connected with this infamy (Clement C. Clay, Dr. Blackburn, Rev. Dr. Stuart Robinson, J. C. Holcombe — all refugees from the Confederacy in Canada), and states that he gave Thompson a receipt for the fifty dollars paid to him, and that he was by occupation a shoemaker; in none of which facts is there an attempt to discredit him. It is not probable that a man in his position in life would be able to buy five trunks of clothing, ship them all the way from Halifax to Washington, and then order them to be sold at auction, without regard to price, solely upon his own account. It is a matter of notoriety that a part of his statement is verified by the results at New Berne, N.C., to which point he says a portion of the infected goods were shipped, through a sutler; the result of which was, that nearly two thousand citizens and soldiers died there about that time with yellow fever.

That the rebel chief, Jefferson Davis, sanctioned these crimes, committed and attempted through the instrumentality of his accredited agents in Canada — Thompson, Clay, Tucker, Sanders, Cleary, etc., — upon the persons and property of the people of the North, their is positive proof on your record. The letter brought from Richmond, and taken from the archives of his late pretended government there, dated February 11, 1865, and addressed to him by the late rebel senator from Texas, W. S. Oldham, contains the following significant words: "When Senator Johnson, of Missouri, and myself waited on you a few days since, in relation to the project of annoying and harassing the enemy by means of burning their shipping, towns, etc., etc., there were several remarks made by you upon the subject which I was not fully prepared to answer, but which, upon subsequent conference with parties proposing the enterprise, I find cannot apply as objections to the scheme. First, the 'combustible materials' consist of several preparations, and not one alone, and can be used without exposing the party using them to the least danger of detection whatever. . . . Second, there is no necessity for sending persons in the military service into the enemy's country, but the work may be done by agents. . . . I have seen enough of the effects that can be produced to satisfy me that in most cases, without any danger to the parties engaged, and in others but very slight, we can, first, burn every vessel that leaves a foreign port for the United States; second, we can burn every transport that leaves the harbor of New York, or other Northern port, with supplies for the armies of the enemy in the South; third, burn every transport and gunboat on the Mississippi River, as well as devastate the country of the enemy and fill his people with terror and consternation. . . . For the purpose of satisfying your mind upon the subject, I respectfully, but earnestly, request that you will give an interview with General Harris, formerly a member of Congress from Missouri, who, I think, is able, from conclusive proofs, to convince you that what I have suggested is perfectly feasible and practicable."

No one can doubt, from the tenure of this letter, that the rebel Davis only wanted to be satisfied that this system of arson and murder could be carried on by his agents in the North successfully and without detection. With him it was not a crime to do these acts, but only a crime to be detected in them. But Davis, by his indorsement on this letter, dated the 20th of February, 1865, bears witness to his own complicity and his own infamy in this proposed work of destruction and crime for the future, as well as to his complicity in what had before been attempted without complete success. Kennedy, with his confederates, had failed to burn the city of New York. "The combustibles" which Kennedy had employed were, it seems, defective. This was "a difficulty to be overcome." Neither had he been able to consummate the dreadful work without subjecting himself *to detection*. This was another "*difficulty* to be overcome." Davis, on the 20th of February, 1865, indorsed upon this letter these words: "Secretary of State, at his convenience, see General Harris and learn what plan he has for *overcoming the difficulties heretofore experienced. J. D.*"

This indorsement is unquestionably proved to be the handwriting of Jefferson Davis, and it bears witness on its face that the monstrous proposition met his approval, and that he desired his rebel Secretary of State, Benjamin, to see General Harris and learn how to overcome *the difficulty heretofore experienced*, to wit: the inefficiency of "the combustible materials" that had been employed, and the liability of his agents to detection. After this, who will doubt that he had endeavored, by the hand of incendiaries, to destroy by fire the property and lives of the people of the North, and thereby "fill them with terror and consternation"; that he knew his agents had been unsuccessful; that he knew his agents had been detected in their villainy and punished for their crime; that he desired through a more perfect "chemical preparation," by the science and skill of Professor McCulloch, to accomplish successfully what had before been unsuccessfully attempted?

The intercepted letter of his agent, Clement C. Clay, dated St. Catherine's, Canada West, November 1, 1864, is an acknowledgment and confession of what they had attempted, and a suggestion made through J. P. Benjamin, rebel Secretary of State, of what remained to be done in order to make the "chemical preparations" efficient. Speaking of this Bennett H. Young, he says: "You have doubtless learned through the press of the United States of the raid on St. Albans by about twenty-five Confederate soldiers, led by Lieut. Bennett H. Young; of their attempt and failure to burn the town; of their robbery of three banks there of the aggregate amount of about two hundred thousand dollars; of their arrest in Canada by United States forces; of their commitment and the pending preliminary trial." He makes application, in aid of Young and his associates, for additional documents, showing that they acted upon the authority of the Confederate States government, taking care to say, however, that he held such authority at the time, but that it ought to be more explicit so far as regards the particular acts complained of. He states that he met Young at Halifax in May, 1864, who developed his plans for retaliation on the enemy; that he, Clay, recommended him to the rebel

Secretary of War; that after this "Young was sent back by the Secretary of War with a commission as second lieutenant to execute his plans and purposes, but to report to Hon. —— and myself." Young afterwards "proposed passing through New England, burning some towns and robbing them of whatever he could convert to the use of the Confederate government. This I approved as justifiable retaliation. He attempted to burn the town of St. Albans, Vt., and would have succeeded but for the failure of the *chemical preparation* with which he was armed. He then robbed the banks of funds amounting to over two hundred thousand dollars. That he was not prompted by selfish or mercenary motives I am as well satisfied as I am that he is an honest man. He assured me before going that his effort would be to destroy towns and farm-houses, but not to plunder or rob; but he said if, after firing a town, he saw he could take *funds* from a bank or any house, and thereby might inflict injury upon the enemy and benefit his own government, he would do so. He added most emphatically, that *whatever* he took should be turned over to the government or *its representatives in foreign lands*. My instructions to him were to destroy whatever was valuable; not to stop to rob, but if, after firing a town, he could seize and carry off money or treasury or bank notes, he might do so upon condition that they were delivered to the proper authorities of the Confederate States " — that is, to Clay himself.

When he wrote this letter it seems that this accredited agent of Jefferson Davis was as strongly impressed with the *usurpation and despotism* of Mr. Lincoln's administration as some of *the advocates* of his aiders and abettors seem to be at this day; and he indulges in the following statement: "All that a large portion of the Northern people, especially in the northwest, want to resist the *oppressions* of the *despotism* at Washington is a *leader*. They are ripe for resistance, *and it may come soon after the presidential election*. At all events, it must come if our armies are not overcome, or destroyed, or dispersed. No people of the Anglo-Saxon blood can long endure *the usurpations and tyrannies of Lincoln*." Clay does not sign the despatch, but indorses the bearer of it as a person who can identify him and give his name. The bearer of that letter was the witness Richard Montgomery, who saw Clay write a portion of the letter, and received it from his hands, and subsequently delivered it to the Assistant Secretary of War of the United States, Mr. Dana. That the letter is in Clay's handwriting is clearly proved by those familiar with it. Mr. Montgomery testifies that he was instructed by Clay to deliver this letter to Benjamin, the rebel Secretary of State, if he could get through to Richmond, and to tell him what names to put in the blanks.

This letter leaves no doubt, if any before existed in the mind of any one who had read the letter of Oldham and Davis's indorsement thereon, that "the chemical preparations" and "combustible materials" had been tried and had failed, and it had become a matter of great moment and concern that they should be so prepared as, in the words of Davis, "to overcome the difficulties heretofore experienced"; that is to say, complete the work of destruction, and secure the perpetrators against personal injury or detection in the performance of it.

It only remains to be seen whether Davis, the procurer of arson and of the indiscriminate murder of the innocent and unoffending necessarily resultant therefrom, was capable also of endeavoring to procure, and in fact did procure, the murder, by direct assassination, of the President of the United States and others charged with the duty of maintaining the government of the United States, and of suppressing the rebellion in which this arch-traitor and conspirator was engaged.

The official papers of Davis, captured under the guns of our victorious army in his rebel capital, identified beyond question or shadow of doubt, and placed upon your record, together with the declaration and acts of his co-conspirators and agents, proclaim to all the world that he was capable of attempting to accomplish his treasonable procuration of the murder of the late President, and other chief officers of the United States, by the hands of hired assassins.

In the fall of 1864 Lieutenant W. Alston addresses to "his excellency" a letter now before the court, which contains the following words: —

"I now offer you my services, and if you will favor *me in my designs* I will proceed, as soon as my health will permit, to rid *my* country of some of her deadliest enemies, by striking at the very *hearts' blood* of those who seek to enchain her in slavery. I consider nothing *dishonorable* having such a tendency. All I ask of you is, to favor me by granting me the necessary papers, etc., to travel on. . . . *I am perfectly familiar with the North*, and feel confident that I can *execute* anything I undertake. I was in the raid last June in Kentucky, under General John H. Morgan; . . . was taken prisoner; . . . escaped from them by dressing myself in the garb of a citizen. . . . I went through to the Canadas, from whence, by the assistance of *Colonel J. P. Holcomb*, I succeeded in working my way around and through the blockade. . . . I should like to have a *personal* interview with you in order to perfect the arrangements before starting."

Is there any room to doubt that this was a proposition to *assassinate*, by the hand of this man and his associates, such persons in the North as he deemed the "deadliest enemies" of the rebellion? The weakness of the man who for a moment can doubt that such was the proposition of the writer of this letter is certainly an object of commiseration. What had Jefferson Davis to say to this proposed assassination of the "deadliest enemies" in the North of his great treason? Did the atrocious suggestion kindle in him indignation against the villain who offered, with his own hand, to strike the blow? Not at all. On the contrary, he ordered his private secretary, on the 29th of November, 1864, to endorse upon the letter these words: "Lieutenant W. Alston; accompanied raid into Kentucky, and was captured, but escaped into *Canada*, from whence he found his way back. Now offers his services to rid the country of some of its *deadliest enemies;* asks for papers, etc. Respectfully referred, by direction of the President, to the honorable Secretary of War." It is also indorsed, for attention, "by order. (Signed) J. A. Campbell, Assistant Secretary of War."

Note the fact in this connection, that Jefferson Davis himself, as well as his subordinates, had, before the date of this indorsement, concluded that Abraham Lincoln was "the deadliest enemy" of the rebellion. You hear it in the rebel camp in Virginia, in 1863, declared by Booth, then and there present, and assented to by rebel officers, that "Abraham Lincoln must be killed." You hear it in that slaughter-pen in Georgia — Andersonville — proclaimed among rebel officers, who, by the slow torture of starvation, inflicted cruel and untimely death on ten thousand of your defenders, captives in their hands — whispering, like demons, their horrid purpose, "Abraham Lincoln must be killed." And in Canada, the accredited agents of Jefferson Davis, as early as October, 1864, and afterwards, declared that "Abraham Lincoln must be killed" if his re-election could not be prevented. These agents in Canada, on the 13th of October, 1864, delivered, in cipher, to be transmitted to Richmond by Richard Montgomery, the witness, whose reputation is unchallenged, the following communication: —

"OCTOBER 13, 1864.

"We again urge the immense necessity of our gaining immediate advantages. Strain every nerve for victory. We now look upon the re-election of *Lincoln* in

November as almost certain, and we need to whip his hirelings to prevent it. Besides, with *Lincoln* re-elected, and his armies victorious, we need not hope even for recognition, much less the help mentioned in our last. Holcomb will explain this. Those figures of the Yankee armies are correct to a unit. *Our friends shall be immediately set to work as you direct.*"

To which an official reply, in cipher, was delivered to Montgomery by an agent of the state department in Richmond, dated October 19, 1864, as follows: —

"Your letter of the 13th instant is at hand. There is yet time enough to colonize many *voters* before November. A blow will shortly be stricken here. It is not quite time. General Longstreet is to attack Sheridan without delay, and then move north as far as practicable toward unprotected points. This will be made instead of movement before mentioned. He will endeavor to assist the *republicans in collecting their ballots*. Be watchful and assist him."

On the very day of the date of this Richmond despatch, Sheridan was attacked, with what success history will declare. The court will not fail to notice that the *re-election of Mr. Lincoln* is to be prevented, if possible, by any and every means. Nor will they fail to notice that *Holcombe* is to "explain this" — the same person who, in Canada, was the friend and advisor of *Alston*, who proposed to Davis the assassination of the "deadliest enemies" of the rebellion.

In the despatch of the 13th of October, which was borne by Montgomery, and transmitted to Richmond in October last, you will find these words: "Our friends shall be immediately set to work as you direct." Mr. Lincoln is the subject of that despatch. Davis is therein notified that his agents in Canada look upon the re-election of Mr. Lincoln in November as almost certain. In this connection he is assured by those agents that the *friends* of their cause are to be set to work as Davis *had directed*. The conversations, which are proved by witnesses whose character stands unimpeached, disclose what "work" the "friends" were to do under the *direction* of Davis himself. Who were these "friends," and what was "the work" which his agents, Thompson, Clay, Tucker, and Sanders, had been directed to set them at? Let Thompson answer for himself. In a conversation with Richard Montgomery in the summer of 1864, Thompson said that he "*had his friends*, confederates, all over the Northern States, who were ready and willing to go any lengths for the good of the cause of the South, and he could at any time have the *tyrant Lincoln* or *any other of his advisers* that he chose *put out of his way ;* that they would not consider it *a crime* when done for the cause of the Confederacy." This conversation was repeated by the witness in the summer of 1864, to Clement C. Clay, who immediately stated: "That is so ; we are all devoted to our cause and ready to go any length — to do anything under the sun."

At and about the time that these declarations of Clay and Thompson were made, *Alston*, who made the proposition, as we have seen, to Davis to be furnished with papers *to go north* and rid the Confederacy of some of its "deadliest enemies," was in Canada. He was doubtless one of the "friends" referred to. As appears by the testimony of Montgomery, Payne, the prisoner at your bar, was about that time in Canada, and was seen standing by Thompson's door, engaged in a conversation with Clay, between whom and the witness some words were interchanged, when Clay stated he (Payne) was one of *their friends* — "we trust him." It is proved beyond a shadow of doubt that in October last John Wilkes Booth, the assassin of the President, was also in Canada, and upon intimate terms with Thompson, Clay, Sanders, and other rebel agents. Who can doubt, in the light of the events which have since transpired, that he was one of the "friends" to be "set to work," as Davis had already directed — not, perhaps, as yet to assassinate the President, but to do that other work which is suggested in the letter of Oldham, indorsed by Davis in his own hand, and spread upon your record — the work of a secret incendiary, which was to "fill the people of the North with terror and consternation." The other "work" spoken of by Thompson — putting the *tyrant Lincoln* and *any of his advisers out of the way* — was work doubtless to be commenced only after the re-election of Mr. Lincoln, which they had already declared in their despatch to their employer, Davis, was with them a foregone conclusion. At all events, it was not until after the presidental election in November that Alston proposed to Davis to go north on the work of assassination ; nor was it until after that election that Booth was found in possession of the letter which is in evidence, and which dicloses the purpose to assassinate the President. Being assured, however, when Booth was with them in Canada, as they had already declared in their despatch, that the re-election of Mr. Lincoln was certain, in which event there would be no hope for the Confederacy, they doubtless entered into the arrangement with Booth as one of their "friends," that as soon as that fact was determined he should go to "work," and as soon as might be "rid the Confederacy of the tyrant Lincoln and of his advisers."

That these persons named upon your record, — Thompson, Sanders, Clay, Cleary, and Tucker, — were the agents of Jefferson Davis, is another fact established in this case beyond a doubt. They made affidavit of it themselves, of record here, upon the examination of their "friends" charged with the raid upon St. Albans, before Judge Smith, in Canada. It is in evidence also by the letter of Clay, before referred to.

The testimony to which I have thus briefly referred shows, by the letter of his agents of the 13th of October, that Davis had before directed those agents to set his *friends to work*. By the letter of Clay it seems that his direction had been obeyed, and his friends had been set to work in the burning and robbery and murder at St. Albans, in the attempt to burn the city of New York, and in the attempt to introduce pestilence into this capital and into the house of the President. It having appeared, by the letter of Alston, and the indorsement thereon, that Davis had in November entertained the proposition of sending agents, that is to say "friends," to the North to not only "spread terror and consternation among the people" by means of his "chemical preparations," but also, in the words of that letter, to "strike," by the hands of assassins, "at the heart's blood" of the deadliest enemies in the North to the Confederacy of traitors ; it has also appeared by the testimony of many respectable witnesses, among others the attorneys who represented the people of the United States and the State of Vermont, in the preliminary trial of the raiders in Canada, that Clay, Thompson, Tucker, Sanders, and Cleary declared themselves the agents of the Confederacy. It also clearly appears by the correspondence referred to, and the letter of Clay, that they were holding, and at any time able to command, blank commissions from Jefferson Davis to authorize *their friends* to do whatever work they appointed them to do in the interests of the rebellion, by the destruction of life and property in the North.

If a *prima facie* case justifies, as we have seen by the law of evidence it does, the introduction of all declarations and acts of any of the parties to a conspiracy, uttered or done in the prosecution of the common design, as evidence against all the rest, it results that whatever was said or done in furtherance of the common design, after this month of October, 1864, by either of these agents in Canada, is evidence not only against themselves, but against Davis as well, of his complicity with them in the conspiracy.

Mr. Montgomery testifies that he met Jacob Thompson in January at Montreal, when he said that "a proposition had been made to him to rid the world of the tyrant Lincoln, Stanton, Grant, and some others; that he knew the men who had made the proposition were bold, daring men, able to execute what they undertook; that he himself was in favor of the proposition, but had determined to defer his answer until he had consulted his government at Richmond; that he was then only awaiting their approval." This was about the middle of January, and consequently more than a month after Alston had made his proposition direct to Davis, in writing, to go north and rid their Confederacy of some of its "deadliest enemies." It was at the time of this conversation that Payne, the prisoner, was seen by the witness standing at Thompson's door in conversation with Clay. This witness also shows the intimacy between Thompson, Clay, Cleary, Tucker, and Sanders.

A few days after the assassination of the President, Beverly Tucker said to this witness "that President Lincoln deserved his death long ago; that it was a pity he didn't have it long ago, and it was too bad that the boys had not been allowed to act when they wanted to."

This remark undoubtedly had reference to the propositions made in the fall to Thompson, and also to Davis, to rid the South of its deadliest enemies by their assassination. Cleary, who was accredited by Thompson as his confidential agent, also stated to this witness that Booth was one of the party to whom Thompson had referred in the conversation in January, in which he said he knew the men who were ready to rid the world of the tyrant Lincoln, and of Stanton and Grant. Cleary also said, speaking of the assassination, "that it was a pity that the whole work had not been done," and added, "they had better look out — we are not done yet"; manifestly referring to the statement made by his employer, Thompson, before in the summer, that not only the tyrant Lincoln, but Stanton and Grant, and others of his advisers, should be put out of the way. Cleary also stated to this witness that Booth had visited Thompson twice in the winter, the last time in December, and had also been there in the summer.

Sanford Conover testified that he had been for some time a clerk in the war department at Richmond; that in Canada he knew Thompson, Sanders, Cleary, Tucker, Clay, and other rebel agents; that he knew John H. Surratt and John Wilkes Booth; that he saw Booth there upon one occasion, and Surratt upon several successive days; that he saw Surratt (whom he describes) in April last in Thompson's room, and also in company with Sanders; that about the 6th or 7th of April, Surratt delivered to Jacob Thompson a despatch brought by him from Benjamin at Richmond, enclosing one in cipher from Davis. Thompson had before this proposed to Conover to engage in a plot to assassinate President Lincoln and his cabinet, and on this occasion he laid his hand upon these despatches and said, "This makes the thing all right," referring to the assent of the rebel authorities, and stated that the rebel authorities had consented to the plot to assassinate Lincoln, Johnson, the Secretary of War, Secretary of State, Judge Chase, and General Grant. Thompson remarked further that the assassination of these parties would leave the government of the United States entirely without a head; that there was no provision in the Constitution of the United States by which they could elect another President if these men were put out of the way.

In speaking of this assassination of the President and others, Thompson said that it was only removing them from office, that the killing of a tyrant was no murder. It seems that he had learned precisely the same lesson that Alston had learned in November, when he communicated with Davis, and said, speaking of the President's assassination, "he did not think anything dishonorable that would serve their cause."

Thompson stated at the same time that he had conferred a commission on Booth, and that everybody engaged in the enterprise would be commissioned, and if it succeeded, or failed, and they escaped into Canada, they could not be reclaimed under the extradition treaty. The fact that Thompson and other rebel agents held blank commissions, as I have said, has been proved, and a copy of one of them is of record here.

This witness also testifies to a conversation with William C. Cleary, shortly after the surrender of Lee's army, and on the day before the President's assassination, at the St. Lawrence Hotel, Montreal, when speaking of the rejoicing in the States over the capture of Richmond, Cleary said, "they would put the laugh on the other side of their mouth *in a day or two*." These parties knew that Conover was in the secret of the assassination, and talked with him about it as freely as they would speak of the weather. Before the assassination he had a conversation also with Sanders, who asked him if he knew Booth well, and expressed some apprehension that Booth would "make a failure of it; that he was desperate and reckless, and he was afraid the whole thing would prove a failure."

Dr. James D. Merritt testifies that George Young, one of the parties named in the record, declared in his presence, in Canada, last fall, that Lincoln should never be inaugurated; that they had friends in Washington who, I suppose, were some of the same friends referred to in the despatch of October 13, and which Davis had directed them "to set to work." George N. Sanders also said to him "that Lincoln would keep himself mighty close if he did serve another term"; while Steele and other Confederates declared that the tyrant never should serve another term. He heard the assassination discussed at a meeting of these rebel agents in Montreal in February last. "Sanders said they had *plenty of money* to accomplish the assassination, and named over a number of persons who were ready and willing to engage in undertaking to remove the President, Vice-President, the cabinet, and some of the leading generals. At this meeting he read a letter which he had received from Davis, which justified him in making any arrangements that he could to accomplish the object." This letter the witness heard read, and it, in substance, declared that if the people in Canada and the Southerners in the States were willing to submit to be governed by such a tyrant as Lincoln, he didn't wish to recognize them as friends. The letter was read openly; it was also handed to Colonel Steele, George Young, Hill, and Scott, to be read. This was about the middle of February last. At this meeting Sanders named over the persons who were willing to accomplish the assassination, and among the persons thus named was Booth, whom the witness had seen in Canada in October; also George Harper, one of the conspirators named on the record, Caldwell, Randall, Harrison, and Surratt.

The witness understood, from the reading of the letter, that if the President, Vice-President, and cabinet could be disposed of it would satisfy the people of the North that the Southerners had *friends* in the North; that a peace could be obtained on better terms; that the rebels had endeavored to bring about a war between the United States and England, and that Mr. Seward, through his energy and sagacity, had thwarted all their efforts; that was given as a reason for removing him. On the 5th or 6th of last April this witness met George Harper, Caldwell, Randall, and others, who are spoken of in this meeting at Montreal as engaged to assassinate the President and cabinet, when Harper said they were going to the States to make a row such as had never been heard of, and added that "if I (the witness) did not hear of the death of Old Abe, of the Vice-President, and of General Dix in less than ten days I might put him down as a fool. That was on the 6th of April. He mentioned that Booth was in Washington at that time. He said they had plenty of friends in Washington, and that some fifteen or twenty were going."

This witness ascertained, on the 8th of April, that Harper and others had left for the States. The proof is that these parties could come through to Washington from Montreal or Toronto in thirty-six hours. They did come, and within the ten days named by Harper the President was murdered! Some attempts have been made to discredit this witness (Dr. Merritt), not by the examination of witnesses in court, not by any apparent want of truth in the testimony, but by the *ex parte* statements of these rebel agents in Canada and their hired advocates in the United States. There is a statement upon the record verified by an official communication from the War Department, which shows the truthfulness of this witness, and that is, that before the assassination, learning that Harper and his associates had started for the States, informed as he was of their purpose to assassinate the President, cabinet, and leading generals, Merritt deemed it his duty to call, and did call, on the 10th of April, upon a justice of the peace in Canada, named Davidson, and gave him the information that he might take steps to stop these proceedings. The correspondence on this subject with Davidson has been brought into court. Dr. Merritt testifies further that after this meeting in Montreal he had a conversation with Clement C. Clay, in Toronto, about the letter from Jefferson Davis which Sanders had exhibited, in which conversation Clay gave the witness to understand that he knew the nature of the letter perfectly, and remarked that he thought "the end would justify the means." The witness also testifies to the presence of Booth with Sanders in Montreal last fall, and of Surratt in Toronto in February last.

The court must be satisfied by the manner of this and other witnesses to the transactions in Canada, as well as by the fact that they are wholly uncontradicted in any material matter that they state, that they speak the truth, and that the several parties named on your record — Davis, Thompson, Cleary, Tucker, Clay, Young, Harper, Booth, and John H. Surratt — did combine and conspire together in Canada to kill and murder Abraham Lincoln, Andrew Johnson, William H. Seward, and Ulysses S. Grant. That this agreement was substantially entered into by Booth and the agents of Davis in Canada as early as October there cannot be any doubt. The language of Thompson at that time and before was, that he was in favor of the assassination. His further language was that he knew the men who were ready to do it; and Booth it was shown was there at that time, and, as Thompson's secretary says, was one of the men referred to by Thompson.

The fact that others, besides the parties named on the record, were, by the terms of the conspiracy to be assassinated in no wise affects the case now on trial. If it is true that these parties did conspire to murder other parties, as well as those named upon the record, the substance of the charge is proved.

It is also true that if, in pursuance of that conspiracy, Booth, confederated with Surratt and the accused, killed and murdered Abraham Lincoln, the charge and specification is proved literally as stated on your record, although their conspiracy embraced other persons. In law the case stands, though it may appear that the conspiracy was to kill and murder the parties named in the record and others not named in the record. If the proof is that the accused, with Booth, Surratt, Davis, etc., conspired to kill and murder one or more of the persons named, the charge of the conspiracy is proved.

The declaration of Sanders, as proved, that there was plenty of money to carry out this assassination, is very strongly corroborated by the testimony of Mr. Campbell, cashier of the Ontario Bank, who states that Thompson, during the current year preceding the assassination, had upon deposit in the Montreal branch of the Ontario Bank six hundred and forty-nine thousand dollars, beside large sums to his credit in other banks in the province.

There is a further corroboration of the testimony of Conover as to the meeting of Thompson and Surratt in Montreal, and the delivery of the despatches from Richmond, on the 6th or 7th of April, first, in the fact which is shown by the testimony of Chester, that in the winter or spring Booth said he himself or some other party must go to Richmond, and second, by the letter of Arnold, dated 27th of March last, that he preferred Booth's first query, that he would first go to Richmond and see how they would take it, manifestly alluding to the proposed assassination of the President. It does not follow because Davis had written a letter in February which, in substance, approved the general object, that the parties were fully satisfied with it; because it is clear there was to be some arrangement made about the funds; and it is also clear that Davis had not before as distinctly approved and sanctioned this act as his agents either in Canada or here desired. Booth said to Chester, "We must have money; there is money in this business, and if you will enter into it I will place three thousand dollars at the disposal of your family; but I have no money myself, and must go to Richmond," or one of the parties must go, "to get money to carry out the enterprise." This was one of the arrangements that was to be "made right in Canada." The funds at Thompson's disposal, as the banker testifies, were exclusively raised by drafts of the secretary of the treasury of the Confederate States upon London, deposited in their bank to the credit of Thompson.

Accordingly, about the 27th of March, Surratt did go to Richmond. On the 3rd of April he returned to Washington, and the same day left for Canada. Before leaving, he stated to Wiechmann that when in Richmond he had had a conversation with Davis and with Benjamin. The fact in this connection is not to be overlooked, that on or about the day Surratt arrived in Montreal, April 6, Jacob Thompson, as the cashier of the Ontario bank states, drew of these Confederate funds the sum of one hundred and eighty thousand dollars in the form of certificates, which, as the bank officer testifies, "might be used anywhere."

What more is wanting? Surely no word further need be spoken to show that John Wilkes Booth was in this conspiracy; that John H. Surratt was in this conspiracy; and that Jefferson Davis and his several agents named, in Canada, were in this conspiracy. If any additional evidence is wanting to show the complicity of Davis in it, let the paper found in the possession of his hired assassin, Booth, come to bear witness against him. That paper contained the secret cipher which Davis used in his state department at Richmond which he employed in communicating with his agents in Canada, and which they employed in the letter of October 13, notifying him that "their friends would be set to work as *he had directed*." The letter in cipher found in Booth's possession is translated here by the use of the cipher machine now in court, which, as the testimony of Mr. Dana shows, he brought from the rooms of Davis's state department in Richmond. Who gave Booth this secret cipher? Of what use was it to him if he was not in confederation with Davis?

But there is one other item of testimony that ought, among honest and intelligent people at all conversant with this evidence, to end all further inquiry as to whether Jefferson Davis was one of the parties, with Booth, as charged upon this record, in the conspiracy to assassinate the President and others. That is that on the fifth day after the assassination, in the city of Charlotte, N. C., a telegraphic despatch was received by him, at the house of Mr. Bates, from John C. Breckinridge, his rebel Secretary of War, which despatch is produced here, identified by the telegraph agent, and placed upon your record in the words following: —

"GREENSBORO', April 19, 1865.

"*His Excellency President Davis:* —

"President Lincoln was assassinated in the theatre in Washington on the night of the 14th inst. Seward's house was entered on the same night and he was repeatedly stabbed, and is probably mortally wounded.

"JOHN C. BRECKINRIDGE."

At the time this despatch was handed to him, Davis was addressing a meeting from the steps of Mr. Bates's house, and after reading the despatch to the people, he said: "If it were to be done, it were *better* it were well done." Shortly afterwards, in the house of the witness, in the same city, Breckinridge, having come to see Davis, stated his regret that the occurrence had happened, because he deemed it unfortunate for the people of the South at that time. Davis replied, referring to the assassination, "Well, general, I don't know; if it were to be done at all, it were *better* that it were well done; and if the same had been done to Andy Johnson, the beast, and to Secretary Stanton, the job would then be *complete*."

Accomplished as this man was in all the arts of a conspirator, he was not equal to the task — as happily, in the good providence of God, no mortal man is — of concealing, by any form of words, any great crime which he may have meditated or perpetrated either against his government or his fellow-men. It was doubtless furthest from Jefferson Davis's purpose to make confession, and yet he did make a confession. His guilt demanded utterance; that demand he could not resist; therefore his words proclaimed his guilt, in spite of his purpose to conceal it. He said, "if it were to be done, it were *better* it were *well done*." Would any man ignorant of the conspiracy be able to devise and fashion such a form of speech as that? Had not the President been murdered? Had he not reason to believe that the Secretary of State had been mortally wounded? Yet he was not satisfied, but was compelled to say, "it were *better* it were *well done*" — that is to say, all that had been agreed to be done had not been done. Two days afterwards, in his conversation with Breckinridge, he not only repeats the same form of expression, "if it were to be done it were *better* it were *well done*," but adds these words: "And if the same had been done to Andy Johnson, the beast, and to Secretary Stanton, the *job* would *then be complete*." He would accept the assassination of the President, the Vice-President, of the Secretary of State, and the Secretary of War, as a complete execution of the "job," which he had given out upon contract, and which he had "made all right," so far as the pay was concerned, by the despatches he had sent to Thompson by Surratt, one of his hired assassins. Whatever may be the conviction of others, my own conviction is that Jefferson Davis is as clearly proven guilty of this conspiracy as is John Wilkes Booth, by whose hand Jefferson Davis inflicted the mortal wound upon Abraham Lincoln. His words of intense hate and rage and disappointment are not to be overlooked — that the assassins had not done their work *well;* that they had not succeeded in robbing the people altogether of their constitutional Executive and his advisers; and hence he exclaims, "If they had killed Andy Johnson, the beast!" Neither can he conceal his chagrin and disappointment that the war minister of the republic, whose energy, incorruptible integrity, sleepless vigilance, and executive ability had organized day by day, month by month, and year by year, victory for our arms, had escaped the knife of the hired assassins. The job, says this procurer of assassination, was not well done; it had been *better* if it had been well done! Because Abraham Lincoln had been clear in his great office, and had saved the nation's life by enforcing the nation's laws, this traitor declares he must be murdered; because Mr. Seward, as the foreign secretary of the country, had thwarted the purposes of treason to plunge his country into a war with England, he must be murdered; because, upon the murder of Mr. Lincoln, Andrew Johnson would succeed to the presidency, and because he had been true to the Constitution and government, faithful found among the faithless of his own State, clinging to the falling pillars of the republic when others had fled, he must be murdered; and because the Secretary of War had taken care, by the faithful discharge of his duties, that the republic should live and not die, he must be murdered. Inasmuch as these two faithful officers were not also assassinated, assuming that the Secretary of State was mortally wounded, Davis could not conceal his disappointment and chagrin that the work was not "well done," that "the job was not complete!"

Thus it appears by the testimony that the proposition made to Davis was to kill and murder the deadliest enemies of the Confederacy — not to kidnap them, as is now pretended here; that by the declaration of Sanders, Tucker, Thompson, Clay, Cleary, Harper, and Young, the conspirators in Canada, the agreement and combination among them was to kill and murder Abraham Lincoln, William H. Seward, Andrew Johnson, Ulysses S. Grant, Edwin M. Stanton, and others of his advisors, and not to kidnap them; it appears from every utterance of John Wilkes Booth, as well as from the Charles Selby letter, of which mention will presently be made, that, as early as November, the proposition with him was to kill and murder, not to kidnap.

Since the first examination of Conover, who testified, as the court will remember, to many important facts against these conspirators and agents of Davis in Canada — among others, the terrible and fiendish plot disclosed by Thompson, Pallen, and others, that they had ascertained the volume of water in the reservoir supplying New York City, estimated the quantity of poison required to render it deadly, and intended thus to poison a whole city — Conover returned to Canada, by direction of this court, for the purpose of obtaining certain documentary evidence. There, about the 9th of June, he met Beverley Tucker, Sanders, and other conspirators, and conversed with them. Tucker declared that Secretary Stanton, whom he denounced as "a scoundrel," and Judge Holt, whom he called "a bloodthirsty villain," "could protect themselves as long as they remained in office by a guard, but that would not always be the case, and, by the Eternal, he had a large account to settle with them." After this, the evidence of Conover here having been published, these parties called upon him and asked him whether he had been to Washington and had testified before this court. Conover denied it; they insisted, and took him to a room where, with drawn pistols, they compelled him to consent to make an affidavit that he had been falsely personated here by another, and that he would make that affidavit before a Mr. Kerr, who would witness it. They then called in Mr. Kerr to certify to the public that Conover had made such a denial. They also compelled this witness to furnish for publication an advertisement offering a reward of five hundred dollars for the arrest of the "infamous and perjured scoundrel" who had recently personated James W. Wallace under the name of Sanford Conover, and testified to a tissue of falsehoods before the military commission at Washington, which advertisement was published in the papers.

To these facts Mr. Conover now testifies, and also discloses the fact that these same men published, in the report of the proceedings before Judge Smith, an affidavit purporting to be his, but which he never made. The affidavit which he in fact made, and which was published in a newspaper at that time, produced here, is set out substantially upon your record, and agrees with the testimony upon the same point given by him in this court.

To suppose that Conover ever made such an affidavit voluntarily as the one wrung from him as stated is impossible. Would he advertise for his own arrest and charge himself with falsely personating himself? But the fact cannot evade observation, that when these guilty conspirators saw Conover's testimony before this court in the public prints, revealing to the world the atrocious plots of these felon conspirators, conscious of the truthfulness of his statements, they cast about at once for some defense before the public, and devised the foolish and stupid invention of compelling him to make an affidavit that he was not Sanford Conover, was not in this court, never gave this testimony, but was a practicing lawyer in Montreal! This infamous proceeding, coupled with the evidence before detailed, stamps these ruffian plotters with the guilt of this conspiracy.

John Wilkes Booth having entered into this conspiracy in Canada, as has been shown, as early as October, he is next found in the city of New York on the 11th day, as I claim, of November, in disguise, in conversation with another, the conversation disclosing to the witness, Mrs. Hudspeth, that they had some matter of personal interest between them; that upon one of them the lot had fallen to go to Washington — upon the other to go to New Berne. This witness, upon being shown the photograph of Booth, swears "that the face is the same" as that of one of those men, who, she says, was a young man of education and culture, as appeared by his conversation, and who had a scar like a bite near the jaw-bone. It is a fact proved here by the Surgeon General that Booth had such a scar on the side of his neck. Mrs. Hudspeth heard him say he would leave for Washington the day after to-morrow. His companion appeared angry because it had not fallen on him to go to Washington. This took place after the presidential election in November. She cannot fix the precise date, but says she was told that General Butler left New York on that day. The testimony discloses that General Butler's army was on the 11th of November leaving New York. The register of the National Hotel shows that Booth left Washington on the early morning train, November 11, and that he returned to this city on the 14th. Chester testifies positively to Booth's presence in New York early in November. This testimony shows most conclusively that Booth was in New York on the 11th of November. The early morning train on which he left Washington would reach New York early in the afternoon of that day. Chester saw him there early in November, and Mrs. Hudspeth not only identifies his picture, but describes his person. The scar upon his neck near his jaw was peculiar and is well described by the witness as like a bite. On that day Booth had a letter in his possession which he accidentally dropped in a street car in the presence of Mrs. Hudspeth, the witness, who delivered it to Major General Dix the same day, and by whom, as his letter on file before this court shows, the same was transmitted to the War Department, November 17, 1864. That letter contains these words: —

"DEAR LOUIS: — The time has at last come that we have all so wished for, and upon you everything depends. As it was decided, before you left, we were to cast lots, we accordingly did so, and you are to be the Charlotte Corday of the nineteenth century. When you remember the fearful, solemn vow that was taken by us, you will feel there is no drawback. *Abe* must *die*, and *now*. You can choose your weapons —

the cup, the knife, the bullet. The cup failed us once, and might again. Johnson, who will give *this*, has been like an enraged demon since the meeting, because it has not fallen upon him to rid the world of the monster. . . . You know where *to find your friends.* Your *disguises* are so perfect and complete that without *one* knew your *face* no police telegraphic despatch would catch you. The English gentleman, *Harcourt*, must not act hastily. Remember, he has ten days. *Strike for your home, strike for your country; bide your time, but strike sure.* Get introduced; congratulate him; listen to his stories (not many more will the brute tell to earthly friends); do anything but fail, and meet us at the appointed place within the fortnight. You will probably hear from me in Washington. Sanders is doing us no good in Canada.

"CHAS. SELBY."

The learned gentleman (Mr. Cox), in his very able and carefully considered argument in defense of O'Laughlin and Arnold, attached importance to this letter, and doubtless very clearly saw its bearing upon the case, and therefore undertook to show that the witness, Mrs. Hudspeth, must be mistaken as to the person of Booth. The gentleman assumes that the letter of General Dix, of the 17th of November last, transmitting this letter to the War Department, reads that the party who dropped the letter was heard to say that he would start to Washington on Friday night next, although the word "next" is not in the letter, neither is it in the quotation which the gentleman makes, for he quotes it fairly; yet he concludes that this would be the 18th of November.

Now the fact is, the 11th of November last was Friday, and the register of the National Hotel bears witness that Mrs. Hudspeth is not mistaken; because her language is, that Booth said he would leave for Washington day after to-morrow, which would be Sunday, the 13th, and if in the evening, would bring him to Washington on Monday, the 14th of November, the day on which, the register shows, he did return to the National Hotel. As to the improbability which the gentleman raises, on the conversation happening in a street car, crowded with people, there was nothing that transpired, although the conversation was earnest, which enabled the witness, or could have enabled any one, in the absence of this letter or of the subsequent conduct of Booth, to form the least idea of the subject-matter of their conversation. The gentleman does not deal altogether fairly in his remarks touching the letter of General Dix, because, upon a careful examination of the letter, it will be found that he did not form any such judgment as that it was a hoax for the *Sunday Mercury;* but he took care to forward it to the Department, and asked attention to it, when, as appears by the testimony of the Assistant Secretary of War, Mr. Dana, the letter was delivered to Mr. Lincoln, who considered it important enough to indorse it with the word "Assassination," and file it in his office, where it was found after the commission of this crime, and brought into this court to bear witness against his assassins.

Although this letter would imply that the assassination spoken of was to take place speedily, yet the party was *to bide his time.* Though he had entered into the preliminary arrangements in Canada, although conspirators had doubtless agreed to co-operate with him in the commission of the crime, and lots had been cast for the chief part in the bloody drama, yet it remained for him, as the leader and principal of the hired assassins, by whose hand their employers were to strike the murderous blow, to collect about him and bring to Washington such persons as would be willing to lend themselves for a price to the horrid crime, and likely to give the necessary aid and support in its consummation. The letter declares that Abraham Lincoln must die, and *now*, meaning as soon as the agents can be employed and the work done. To that end you will *bide your time.* But, says the gentleman, it could not have been the same conspiracy charged here to which this letter refers. Why not? It is charged here that Booth, with the accused and others, conspired to kill and murder Abraham Lincoln; that is precisely the conspiracy disclosed in the letter. Granted that the parties on trial had not then entered into the combination; if they at any time afterward entered into it they became parties to it, and the conspiracy was still the same. But, says the gentleman, the words of the letter imply that the conspiracy was to be executed within the fortnight. Booth is directed, by the name of Louis, to meet the writer within the fortnight. It by no means follows that he was to strike within the fortnight, because he was to meet his co-conspirator within that time, and any such conclusion is excluded by the words, "Bide your time." Even if the conspiracy was to be executed within the fortnight, and was not so executed, and the same party, Booth, afterwards by concert and agreement with the accused and others, did execute it by "striking sure" and killing the President, that act, whenever done, would be but the execution of the same conspiracy. The letter is conclusive evidence of so much of this conspiracy as relates to the murder of President Lincoln. As Booth was to do anything but fail, he immediately thereafter sought out the agents to enable him to strike sure and execute all that he had agreed with Davis and his co-confederates in Canada to do — to murder the President, the Secretary of State, the Vice-President, General Grant, and Secretary Stanton.

Even Booth's co-conspirator, Payne, now on his trial, by his defense admits all this, and says Booth had just been to Canada, "was filled with a mighty scheme, and was lying in wait for agents." Booth asked the co-operation of the prisoner, Payne, and said: "I will give you as much money as you want; but first you must swear to stick by me. It is in the oil business." This you are told by the accused was early in March last. Thus guilt bears witness against itself.

We find Booth in New York in November, December, and January, urging Chester to enter into this combination, assuring him that there was *money* in it; that they had "friends on the other side"; that if he would only participate in it he would never want for money while he lived, and all that was asked of him was to stand at and open *the back door of Ford's Theatre*. Booth, in his interviews with Chester, confesses that *he is without money himself*, and allows Chester to reimburse him the fifty dollars which he (Booth) had transmitted to him in a letter for the purpose of paying his expenses to Washington as one of the parties to this conspiracy. Booth told him, although he himself was penniless, "*there is money in this* — we have friends on the other side"; and if you will but engage, I will have three thousand dollars deposited at once for the use of your family.

Failing to secure the services of Chester, because his soul recoiled with abhorrence from the foul work of assassination and murder, he found more willing instruments in others whom he gathered about him. Men to commit the assassinations, horses to secure speedy and certain escape, were to be provided, and to this end Booth, with an energy worthy of a better cause, applies himself. For this latter purpose he told Chester he had already expended five thousand dollars. In the latter part of November, 1864, he visits Charles County, Md., and is in company with one of the prisoners, Dr. Samuel A. Mudd, with whom he lodged over night, and through whom he procures of Gardner one of the several horses which were at his disposal and used by him and his co-conspirators in Washington on the night of the assassination.

Some time in January last, it is in testimony that the prisoner Mudd introduced Booth to John H. Surratt and the witness Wiechmann; that Booth invited them to the

National Hotel; that when there, in the room to which Booth took them, Mudd went out into the passage, called Booth out and had a private conversation with him, leaving the witness and Surratt in the room. Upon their return to the room, Booth went out with Surratt, and upon their coming in, all three — Booth, Surratt, and Samuel A. Mudd — went out together and had a conversation in the passage, leaving the witness alone. Up to the time of this interview it seems that neither the witness nor Surratt had any knowledge of Booth, as they were then introduced to him by Dr. Mudd. Whether Surratt had in fact previously known Booth it is not important to inquire. Mudd deemed it necessary, perhaps a wise precaution, to introduce Surratt to Booth; he also deemed it necessary to have a private conversation with Booth shortly afterwards, and directly upon that to have a conversation together with Booth and Surratt alone. Had this conversation, no part of which was heard by the witness, been perfectly innocent, it is not to be presumed that Dr. Mudd, who was an entire stranger to Wiechmann, would have deemed it necessary to hold the conversation secretly, nor to have volunteered to tell the witness, or rather pretend to tell him, what the conversation was; yet he did say to the witness, upon their return to the room, by way of apology, I suppose, for the privacy of the conversation, that Booth had some private business with him and wished to purchase his farm. This silly device, as is often the case in attempts at deception, failed in the execution; for it remains to be shown how the fact that Mudd had private business with Booth, and that Booth wished to purchase his farm, made it at all necessary, or even proper, that they should both volunteer to call out Surratt, who, up to that moment, was a stranger to Booth. What had Surratt to do with Booth's purchase of Mudd's farm? And if it was necessary to withdraw and talk by themselves secretly about the sale of the farm, why should they disclose the fact to the very man from whom they had concealed it?

Upon the return of these three parties to the room, they seated themselves at a table, and upon the back of an envelope Booth traced lines with a pencil, indicating, as the witness states, the direction of roads. Why was this done? As Booth had been previously in that section of country, as the prisoner in his defense has taken great pains to show, it was certainly not necessary to anything connected with the purchase of Mudd's farm that at that time he should be indicating the direction of roads to or from it; nor is it made to appear, by anything in this testimony, how it comes that Surratt, as the witness testifies, seemed to be as much interested in the marking out of these roads as Mudd or Booth. It does not appear that Surratt was in any wise connected with or interested in the sale of Mudd's farm. From all that has transpired since this meeting at the hotel, it would seem that this plotting the roads was intended, not so much to show the road to Mudd's farm, as to point out the shortest and safest route for flight from the capital, by the houses of all the parties to this conspiracy, to their "friends on the other side."

But, says the learned gentleman (Mr. Ewing), in his very able argument in defense of this prisoner, why should Booth determine that his flight should be through Charles County? The answer must be obvious, upon a moment's reflection, to every man, and could not possibly have escaped the notice of the counsel himself, but for the reason that his zeal for his client constrained him to overlook it. It was absolutely essential that this murderer should have his co-conspirators at convenient points along his route, and it does not appear in evidence that by the route to his friends, who had then fled from Richmond, which the gentleman (Mr. Ewing) indicates as the more direct, but of which there is not the slightest evidence whatever, Booth had co-conspirators at an equal distance from Washington. The testimony discloses, further, that on the route selected by him for his flight there is a large population that would be most likely to favor and aid him in the execution of his wicked purpose and in making his escape. But it is a sufficient answer to the gentleman's question that Booth's co-conspirator, Mudd, lived in Charles County.

To return to the meeting at the hotel. In the light of other facts in this case, it must become clear to the court that this secret meeting between Booth, Surratt, and Mudd was a conference looking to the execution of this conspiracy. It so impressed the prisoner — it so impressed his counsel, that they deemed it necessary and absolutely essential to their defense to attempt to destroy the credibility of the witness Wiechmann.

I may say here, in passing, that they have not attempted to impeach his general reputation for truth by the testimony of a single witness, nor have they impeached his testimony by calling a single witness to discredit one material fact to which he has testified in this issue. Failing to find a breath of suspicion against Wiechmann's character, or to contradict a single fact to which he testified, the accused had to fly to the last resort, an *alibi*, and very earnestly did the learned counsel devote himself to the task.

It is not material whether this meeting in the hotel took place on the 23d of December or in January. But, says the counsel, it was after the commencement or close of the Congressional holiday. That is not material; but the concurrent resolution of Congress shows that the holiday commenced on the 22d of December, the day before the accused spent the evening in Washington. The witness is not certain about the date of this meeting. The material fact is, did this meeting take place — either on the 23d of December or in January last? Were the private interviews there held, and was the apology made, as detailed, by Mudd and Booth, after the secret conference, to the witness? That the meeting did take place, and that Mudd did explain that these secret interviews, with Booth first, and with Booth and Surratt directly afterward, had relation to the sale of his farm, is confessedly admitted by the endeavor of the prisoner, through his counsel, to show that negotiations had been going on between Booth and Mudd for the sale of Mudd's farm. If no such meeting was held, if no such explanation was made by Mudd to Wiechmann, can any man for a moment believe that a witness would have been called here to give any testimony about Booth having negotiated for Mudd's farm? What conceivable connection has it with this case, except to show that Mudd's explanation to Wiechmann for his extraordinary conduct was in exact accordance with the fact? Or was this testimony about the negotiations for Mudd's farm intended to show so close an intimacy and intercourse with Booth that Mudd could not fail to recognize him when he came flying for aid to his house from the work of assassination? It would be injustice to the able counsel to suppose that.

I have said that it was wholly immaterial whether this conversation took place on the 23d of December or in January; it is in evidence that in both these months Booth was at the National Hotel; that he occupied a room there; that he arrived there on the 22d and was there on the 23d of December last, and also on the 12th day of January. The testimony of the witness is, that Booth said he had just come in. Suppose this conversation took place in December, on the evening of the 23d, the time when it is proved by J. T. Mudd, the witness for the accused, that he, in company with Samuel A. Mudd, spent the night in Washington City. Is there anything in the testimony of that or any other witness to show that the accused did not have and could not have had an interview with Booth on that evening? J. T. Mudd testifies that he separated from the prisoner, Samuel A. Mudd, at the National Hotel early in the evening of that day, and did not meet him again until the accused came in for the night at the Pennsylvania House, where he stopped. Where was Dr. Samuel A. Mudd during this interval? What does his witness know about him during that time? How can he say that Dr. Mudd did not go up on Seventh Street in company with Booth, then at the National; that he did not on Seventh Street meet Surratt and Wiechmann; that he did not return to the National Hotel; that he did not have this interview, and afterwards meet him, the witness, as he testifies, at the Pennsylvania House? Who knows that the Congressional holiday had not in fact commenced on that day? What witness has been called to prove that Booth did not on either of those occasions occupy the room that had formerly been occupied by a member of Congress, who had temporarily vacated it, leaving his books there? Wiechmann, I repeat, is not positive as to the date, he is only positive as to the fact; and he disclosed voluntarily to this court that the date could probably be fixed by a reference to the register of the Pennsylvania House; that register cannot, of course, be conclusive of whether Mudd was there in January or not, for the very good reason that the proprietor admits that he did not know Samuel A. Mudd, therefore Mudd might have registed by any other name. Wiechmann does not pretend to know that Mudd had registered at all. If Mudd was here in January, as a party to this conspiracy, it is not at all unlikely that, if he did register at that time in the presence of a man to whom he was wholly unknown, his kinsman not then being with him, he would register by a false name. But if the interview took place in December, the testimony of Wiechmann bears as strongly against the accused as if it had happened in January. Wiechmann says he does not know what time was occupied in this interview at the National Hotel; that it probably lasted twenty minutes; that, after the private interviews between Mudd and Surratt and Booth, which were not of very long duration, had terminated, the parties went to the Pennsylvania House, where Dr. Mudd had rooms, and after sitting together in the common sitting-room of the hotel, they left Dr. Mudd there about ten o'clock P.M., who remained during the night. Wiechmann's testimony leaves no doubt that this meeting on Seventh Street and interview at the National took place after dark, and terminated before or about ten o'clock P.M. His own witness, J. T. Mudd, after stating that he separated from the accused at the National Hotel, says after he had got through a conversation with a gentleman of his acquaintance, he walked down the Avenue, went to several clothing stores, and "after a while" walked round to the Pennsylvania House, and "very soon after" he got there Dr. Mudd came in, and they went to bed shortly afterwards. What time he spent in his "walk alone" on the Avenue, looking at clothing; what period he embraces in the terms "after a while," when he returned to the Pennsylvania House, and "soon after" which Dr. Mudd got there, the witness does not disclose. Neither does he intimate, much less testify, that he saw Dr. Mudd when he first entered the Pennsylvania House on that night after their separation. How does he know that Booth and Surratt and Wiechmann did not accompany Samuel A. Mudd to that house that evening? How does he know that the prisoner and those persons did not converse together some time in the sitting-room of the Pennsylvania Hotel? Jeremiah Mudd has not testified that he met Dr. Mudd in that room, or that he was in it himself. He has, however, sworn to the fact, which is disproved by no one, that the prisoner was separated from him long enough that evening to have had the meeting with Booth, Surratt, and Wiechmann, and the interviews in the National Hotel, and at the Pennsylvania House, to which Wiechmann has testified? Who is there to disprove it? Of what importance is it whether it was on the 23d day of December or in January? How does that affect the credibility of Wiechmann? He is a man, as I have before said, against whose reputation for truth and good conduct they have not been able to bring one witness. If this meeting did by possibility take place that night, is there anything to render it improbable that Booth and Mudd and Surratt did have the conversation at the National Hotel to which Wiechmann testifies? Of what avail, therefore, is the attempt to prove that Mudd was not here during January, if it was clear that he was here on the 23d of December, 1864, and had this conversation with Booth? That this attempt to prove an *alibi* during January has failed, is quite as clear as is the proof of the fact that the prisoner was here on the evening of the 23d of December, and present in the National Hotel, where Booth stopped. The fact that the prisoner, Samuel A. Mudd, went with J. T. Mudd on that evening to the National Hotel, and there separated from him, is proved by his own witness, J. T. Mudd; and that he did not rejoin him until they retired to bed in the Pennsylvania House is proved by the same witness and contradicted by nobody. Does any one suppose there would have been such assiduous care to prove that the prisoner was with his kinsman all the time on the 23d of December, in Washington, if they had not known that Booth was then at the National Hotel, and that a meeting of the prisoner with Booth, Surratt, and Wiechmann on that day would corroborate and confirm Wiechmann's testimony in every material statement he made concerning that meeting?

The accused having signally failed to account for his absence after he separated from his witness, J. T. Mudd, early in the evening of the 23d of December, at the National Hotel, until they had again met at the Pennsylvania House, when they retired to rest, he now attempts to prove an *alibi* as to the month of January. In this he has failed, as he failed in the attempt to show that he could not have met Booth, Surratt, and Wiechmann on the 23d of December.

For this purpose the accused calls Betty Washington. She had been at Mudd's house every night since the Monday after Christmas last, except when here at court, and says that the prisoner, Mudd, has only been away from home three nights during that time. This witness forgets that Mudd has not been at home any night or day since this court assembled. Neither does she account for the three nights in which she swears to his absence from home. First, she says he went to Gardner's party; second, he went to Giesboro, then to Washington. She does not know in what month he was away, the second time, all night. She only knows where he went from what he and his wife said, which is not evidence; but she does testify that when he left home and was absent over night the second time, it was about two or three weeks after she came to his house, which would, if it were three weeks, make it just about the 15th of January, 1865; because she swears she came to his house on the first Monday after Christmas last, which was the 26th day of December; so that the 15th of January would be three weeks, less one day, from that time; and it might have been a week earlier according to her testimony, as, also, it might have been a week earlier, or more, by Wiechmann's testimony, for he is not positive as to the time. What I have said of the register of the Pennsylvania House, the headquarters of Mudd and Atzerodt, I need not here repeat. That record proves nothing, save that Dr. Mudd was there on the 23d of December, which, as we have seen, is a fact, along with others, to show that the meeting at the National then took place. I have also called the attention of the court to the fact that if Mudd was at that house again in January, and did not register his name, that fact proves nothing; or, if he did, the register only proves that he registered falsely; either of which facts might have happened without the knowledge of the witness called by the accused from that house, who does not know Samuel A. Mudd personally.

The testimony of Henry L. Mudd, his brother, in support of this *alibi*, is, that the prisoner was in Washington on the 23d of March, and on the 10th of April, four days before the murder! But he does not account for the absent night in January, about which Betty Washington testifies. Thomas Davis was called for the same purpose, but stated that he was himself absent one night in January, after the 9th of that month, and he could not say whether Mudd was there on that night or not. He does testify to Mudd's absence over night three times, and fixes one occasion on the night of the 26th of January. In consequence of his own absence one night in January, this witness cannot account for the absence of Mudd on the night referred to by Betty Washington.

This matter is entitled to no further attention. It can satisfy no one, and the burden of proof is upon the prisoner to prove that he was not in Washington in January last. How can such testimony convince any rational man that Mudd was not here in January, against the evidence of an unimpeached witness, who swears that Samuel A. Mudd was in Washington in the month of January? Who that has been examined here as a witness knows that he was not?

The Rev. Mr. Evans swears that he saw him in Washington last winter, and that at the same time he saw Jarboe, the one coming out of, and the other going into, a house on H Street, which he was informed on inquiry was the house of Mrs. Surratt. Jarboe is the only witness called to contradict Mr. Evans, and he leaves it in extreme doubt whether he does not corroborate him, as he swears that he was here himself last winter or fall, but cannot state exactly the time. Jarboe's silence on questions touching his own credibility leaves no room for any one to say that his testimony could impeach Mr. Evans, whatever he might swear.

Miss Anna H. Surratt is also called for the purpose of impeaching Mr. Evans. It is sufficient to say of her testimony on that point that she swears negatively only — that she does not see either of the persons named at her mother's house. This testimony neither disproves, nor does it even tend to disprove, the fact put in issue by Mr. Evans. No one will pretend, whatever the form of her expression in giving her testimony, that she could say more than that she did not know the fact, as it was impossible that she could know who was, or who was not, at her mother's house, casually, at a period so remote. It is not my purpose, neither is it needful here, to question in any way the integrity of this young woman.

It is further in testimony that Samuel A. Mudd was here on the 3d day of March last, the day preceding the inauguration, when Booth was to strike the traitorous blow; and it was, doubtless, only by the interposition of that God who stands within the shadow and keeps watch above his own, that the victim of this conspiracy was spared that day from the assassin's hand that he might complete his work and see the salvation of his country in the fall of Richmond and the surrender of its great army. Dr. Mudd was here on that day (the 3d of March) to abet, to encourage, to nerve his co-conspirator for the commission of this great crime. He was carried away by the awful purpose which possessed him, and rushed into the room of Mr. Norton, at the National Hotel, in search of Booth, exclaiming excitedly: "I'm mistaken; I thought this was Mr. Booth's room." He is told Mr. Booth is above, on the next floor. He is followed by Mr. Norton, because of his rude and excited behavior, and being followed, conscious of his guilty errand, he turns away, afraid of himself and afraid to be found in concert with his fellow confederate. Mr. Norton identifies the prisoner, and has no doubt that Samuel A. Mudd is the man.

The Rev. Mr. Evans also swears that, after the 1st and before the 4th day of March last, he is certain that within that time, and on the 2d or 3d of March, he saw Dr. Mudd drive into Washington City. The endeavor is made by the accused in order to break down this witness, by proving another *alibi*. The sister of the accused, Miss Fanny Mudd, is called. She testifies that she saw the prisoner at breakfast in her father's house, on the 2d of March, about five o'clock in the morning, and not again until the 3d of March at noon. Mrs. Emily Mudd swears substantially to the same statement. Betty Washington, called for the accused, swears that he was at home all day at work with her on the 2d of March, and took breakfast at home. Frank Washington swears that Mudd was at home all day; that he saw him when he first came out in the morning about sunrise from his own house, and knows that he was there all day with them. Which is correct, the testimony of his sisters or the testimony of his servants? The sisters say that he was at their father's house for breakfast on the morning of the 2d of March; the servants say he was at home for breakfast with them on that day. If this testimony is followed, it proves one *alibi* too much. It is impossible, in the nature of things, that the testimony of all these four witnesses can be true.

Seeing this weakness in the testimony brought to prove this second *alibi*, the endeavor is next made to discredit Mr. Norton for truth; and two witnesses, not more, are called, who testify that his reputation for truth has suffered by contested litigation between one of the impeaching witnesses and others. Four witnesses are called, who testify that Mr. Norton's reputation for truth is very good; that he is a man of high character for truth, and entitled to be believed whether he speaks under the obligation of an oath or not. The late Postmaster General, Hon. Horatio King, not only sustains Mr. Norton as a man of good reputation for truth, but expressly corroborates his testimony, by stating that in March last, about the 4th of March, Mr. Norton told him the same fact to which he swears here: that a man came into his room under excitement, alarmed his sister, was followed out by himself, and went down stairs instead of going up; and that Mr. Norton told him this before the assassination, and about the time of the inauguration. What motive had Mr. Norton at that time to fabricate this statement? It detracts nothing from his testimony that he did not at that time mention the name of this man to his friend, Mr. King; because it appears from his testimony — and there is none to question the truthfulness of his statement — that at that time he did not know his name. Neither does it take from the force of this testimony, that Mr. Norton did not, in communicating this matter to Mr. King, make mention of Booth's name; because there was nothing in the transaction, at the time, he being ignorant of the name of Mudd, and equally ignorant of the conspiracy between Mudd and Booth, to give the least occasion for any mention of Booth or of the transaction further than as he detailed it. With such corroboration, who can doubt the fact that Mudd did enter the room of Mr. Norton, and was followed by him, on the 3d of March last? Can he be mistaken in the man? Whoever looks at the prisoner carefully once will be sure to recognize him again.

For the present I pass from the consideration of the testimony showing Dr. Mudd's connection with Booth in this conspiracy, with the remark that it is in evidence, and I think established, both by the testimony adduced by the prosecution and that by the prisoner, that since the commencement of this rebellion, John H. Surratt visited the prisoner's house; that he concealed Surratt and other rebels and traitors in the woods near his house, where for several days he furnished them with food and bedding; that the shelter of the woods by night and by day was the only shelter that the prisoner dare furnish *these friends* of his; that in November, Booth visited him and remained over night; that he accompanied Booth at that time to Gardner's, from whom he purchased one of the horses used on the night of the assassination to aid the escape of one of his confederates; that the prisoner had secret interviews with Booth and Surratt, as sworn to by the witness Wiechmann, in the National Hotel, whether on the 23d of December or in January is a matter of entire indifference; that he rushed into Mr. Norton's room on the 3d of March in search of Booth; and that he was here again on the 10th of April, four days before the murder of the President. Of his conduct after the assassination of the President, which is confirmatory of all this — his conspiring with Booth and his sheltering, concealing, and aiding the flight of his co-conspirator, this felon assassin — I shall speak hereafter, leaving him for the present with the remark that the attempt to prove his character has resulted in showing him in sympathy with the rebellion, so cruel that he shot one of his slaves and declared his purpose to send several of them to work on the rebel batteries in Richmond.

What others, besides Samuel A. Mudd and John H. Surratt and Lewis Payne, did Booth, after his return from Canada, induce to join him in this conspiracy to murder the President, the Vice-President, the Secretary of State, and the Lieutenant General, with the intent thereby to aid the rebellion and overthrow the government and laws of the United States?

On the 10th of February the prisoners Arnold and O'Laughlin came to Washington and took rooms in the house of Mrs. Vantyne; were armed; were then visited frequently by John Wilkes Booth, and alone; were occasionally absent when Booth called, who seemed anxious for their return — would sometimes leave notes for them, and sometimes a request that when they came in they should be told to come to the stable. On the 18th of March last, when Booth played in "The Apostate," the witness, Mrs. Vantyne, received from O'Laughlin complimentary tickets. These persons remained there until the 20th of March. They were visited, so far as the witness knows, during their stay at her house only by Booth, save that on a single occasion an unknown man came to see them, and remained with them over night. They told the witness they were in the "oil business." With Mudd, the guilty purpose was sought to be concealed by declaring that he was in the "land business"; with O'Laughlin and Arnold it was attempted to be concealed by the pretence that they were in the "oil business." Booth, it is proved, had closed up all connection with oil business last September. There is not a word of testimony to show that the accused, O'Laughlin and Arnold, ever invested or sought to invest, in any way or to any amount, in the oil business; their silly words betray them; they forgot when they uttered that false statement that truth is strong, next to the Almighty, and that their crime must find them out was the irrevocable and irresistible law of nature and of nature's God.

One of their co-conspirators, known as yet only to the guilty parties to this damnable plot and to the Infinite, who will unmask and avenge all blood-guiltiness, comes to bear witness, unwittingly, against them. This unknown conspirator, who dates his letter at South Branch Bridge, April 6, 1865, mailed and postmarked Cumberland, Md., and addressed to John Wilkes Booth, by his initials, "J. W. B., National Hotel, Washington, D.C.," was also in the "oil speculation." In that letter he says:—

"FRIEND WILKES:— I received yours of March 12th, and reply as soon as practicable. I saw French, Brady, and others about the oil speculation. The subscription to the stock amounts to eight thousand dollars, and I add one thousand myself, which is about all I can stand. Now, when you sink your well, go *deep enough; don't fail;* everything depends upon you and your *helpers*. If you cannot get through on *your trip* after you strike oil, strike through Thornton gap and across by Capon, Romney, and down the Branch. I can keep you *safe* from all hardships for a year. I am clear of all surveillance now that infernal Purdy is beat. . . .

"I send this by Tom, and if he don't get drunk you will get it the 9th. At all events, it cannot be *understood* if lost. . . .

"No more, only *Jake* will be at Green's *with the funds*. (Signed) "Lon."

That this letter is not a fabrication is made apparent by the testimony of Purdy, whose name occurs in the letter. He testified that he had been a detective in the government service, and that he had been falsely accused, as the letter recites, and put under arrest; that there was a noted rebel, by the name of Green, living at Thornton gap; that there was a servant, who drank, known as "Tom," in the neighborhood of South Branch Bridge; that there is an obscure route through the gap, and as described in the letter; and that a man commonly called "Lon" lives at South Branch Bridge. If the court are satisfied — and it is for them to judge — that this letter was written before the assassination, as it purports to have been, and on the day of its date, there can be no question with any one who reads it that the writer was in the conspiracy, and knew that the time of its execution drew nigh. If a conspirator, every word of its contents is evidence against every other party to this conspiracy.

Who can fail to understand this letter? His words, "go deep enough," "don't fail," "everything depends on you and your helpers," "if you can't get through on your *trip* after you *strike oil*, strike through Thornton gap," etc., and "I can keep you safe from all hardships for a year," necessarily imply that when he "*strikes oil*" there will be an occasion for *a flight;* that *a trip*, or route, has already been determined upon; that he may not be able to go through by that route; in which event he is to strike for Thornton gap, and across by Capon and Romney, and down the branch, for the shelter which his co-conspirator offers him. "I am clear of all serveillance now" — does any one doubt that the man who wrote those words wished to assure Booth that he was no longer watched, and that Booth could safely hide with him from his pursuers? Does any one doubt, from the further expression in this letter, "Jake will be at Green's with the funds," that this was a part of the price of blood, or that the eight thousand dollars subscribed by others, and the one thousand additional, subscribed by the writer, were also a part of the price to be paid?

"The oil business," which was the declared business of O'Laughlin and Arnold, was the declared business of the infamous writer of this letter; was the declared business of John H. Surratt; was the declared business of Booth himself, as explained to Chester and Payne; was *" the business"* referred to in his telegrams to O'Laughlin, and meant the murder of the President, of his cabinet, and of General Grant. The first of these telegrams is dated Washington, 13th March, and is addressed to M. O'Laughlin, No. 57 North Exeter Street, Baltimore, Md., and is as follows: "Don't you fear to neglect your business; you had better come on at once. J. Booth." The telegraphic operator, Hoffman, who sent this despatch from Washington, swears that John Wilkes Booth delivered it to him in person on the day of its date; and the handwriting of the original telegram is established beyond question to be that of Booth. The other telegram is dated Washington, March 27, addressed, "M. O'Laughlin, Esq., 57 North Exeter Street, Baltimore, Md.," and is as follows: "Get word to Sam. Come on with or without him on Wednesday morning. We sell that day sure; don't fail. J. Wilkes Booth." The original of this telegram is also proved to be in the handwriting of

APPENDIX.

Booth. The sale referred to in this last telegram was doubtless the murder of the President and others — the "oil speculation," in which the writer of the letter from South Branch Bridge, dated April 6, had taken a thousand dollars, and in which Booth said there was money, and Sanders said there was money, and Atzerodt said there was money. The words of this telegram, "get word to Sam," mean Samuel Arnold, his co-conspirator, who had been with him during all his stay in Washington, at Mrs. Vantyne's. These parties to this conspiracy, after they had gone to Baltimore, had additional correspondence with Booth, which the court must infer had relation to carrying out the purposes of their confederation and agreement. The colored witness, Williams, testifies that John Wilkes Booth handed him a letter for Michael O'Laughlin, and another for Samuel Arnold, in Baltimore, some time in March last; one of which he delivered to O'Laughlin at the theatre in Baltimore, and the other to a lady at the door where Arnold boarded in Baltimore.

Their agreement and co-operation in the common object having been thus established, the letter written to Booth by the prisoner Arnold, dated March 27, 1865, the handwriting of which is proved before the court, and which was found in Booth's possession after the assassination, becomes testimony against O'Laughlin, as well as against the writer Arnold, because it is an act done in furtherance of their combination. That letter is as follows: —

"DEAR JOHN: — Was business so important that you could not remain in Baltimore till I saw you? I came in as soon as I could, but found you had gone to Washington. I called also to see *Mike*, but learned from his mother he had gone out with you and had not returned. I concluded, therefore, he had gone with you. How inconsiderate you have been! When I left you, you stated that *we would not meet* in a month or so, and therefore I made application for employment, an answer to which I shall receive during the week. I told my parents I had ceased with you. Can I, then, under existing circumstances, act as you request? You know full well that the government suspicions something is going on there, therefore the *undertaking* is becoming more complicated. Why not, *for the present,* desist? — for various reasons, which, if you look into, you can readily see without my making any mention thereof. You, nor any one, can censure me for my present course. You have been its cause, for how can I now come after telling them I had left you? Suspicion rests upon me now from my whole family, and even parties in the country. I will be compelled to leave home any how, and how soon I care not. None, no, not one, were more in favor of the enterprise than myself, and to-day would be there had you not done as you have. By this I mean manner of proceeding. I am, as you well know, in *need*. I am, you may say, in rags, whereas, to-day, I ought to be *well clothed*. I do not feel right stalking about with *means*, and more from appearances a beggar. I feel my dependence. But even all this would have been, and was, forgotten, for I *was one with you*. Time more *propitious* will arrive yet. Do not act rashly or in haste. I would prefer your first query, 'Go and see how it will be taken in Richmond,' and *ere long* I shall be better prepared *to again be with you*. I dislike writing. Would sooner verbally make known my views. Yet your now waiting causes me thus to proceed. Do not in anger peruse this. Weigh all I have said, and, as a rational man and a *friend*, you cannot censure or upbraid my conduct. I sincerely trust this, nor aught else that shall or may occur, will ever be an obstacle to obliterate our former friendship and attachment. Write me to Baltimore, as I expect to be in about Wednesday or Thursday; or, if you can possibly come on, I will Tuesday meet you at Baltimore at B.

"Ever I subscribe myself, your friend,   "SAM."

Here is the confession of the prisoner Arnold, that he was one with Booth in this conspiracy; the further confession that they are suspected by the government of their country, and the acknowledgment that *since they parted* Booth had communicated, among other things, a suggestion which leads to the remark in this letter, "I would prefer your first query, 'Go and see how it will be taken at Richmond,' and *ere long* I shall be better prepared *to again be with you.*" This is a declaration that affects Arnold, Booth, and O'Laughlin alike, if the court are satisfied, and it is difficult to see how they can have doubt on the subject, that the matter to be referred to Richmond is the matter of the assassination of the President and others, to effect which these parties had previously agreed and conspired together. It is a matter in testimony, by the declaration of John H. Surratt, who is as clearly proved to have been in this conspiracy and murder as Booth himself, that about the very date of this letter, the 27th of March, upon the suggestion of Booth, and with his knowledge and consent, he went to Richmond, not only to see "how it would be taken there," but to get funds with which to carry out the enterprise, as Booth had already declared to Chester in one of his last interviews, when he said that he or "some one of the party" would be constrained to go to Richmond for funds to carry out the conspiracy. Surratt returned from Richmond, bringing with him some part of the money for which he went, and was then going to Canada, and, as the testimony discloses, bringing with him the despatches from Jefferson Davis to his chief agents in Canada, which, as Thompson declared to Conover, made the proposed assassination "all right." Surratt, after seeing the parties here, left immediately for Canada and delivered his despatches to Jacob Thompson, the agent of Jefferson Davis. This was done by Surratt upon the suggestion, or in exact accordance with the suggestion, of Arnold, made on the 27th of March in his letter to Booth just read, and yet you are gravely told that four weeks before the 27th of March Arnold had abandoned the conspiracy.

Surratt reached Canada with these despatches, as we have seen, about the 6th or 7th of April last, when the witness Conover saw them delivered to Jacob Thompson and heard their contents stated by Thompson, and the declaration from him that these despatches made it "all right." That Surratt was at that time in Canada is not only established by the testimony of Conover, but it is also in evidence that he told Wiechmann on the 3d of April that he was going to Canada, and on that day left for Canada, and afterwards, two letters addressed by Surratt over the *fictitious* signature of John Harrison, to his mother and to Miss Ward, dated at Montreal, were received by them on the 14th of April, as testified by Wiechmann and by Miss Ward, a witness called for the defense. Thus it appears that the condition named by Arnold in his letter had been complied with. Booth had "gone to Richmond," in the person of Surratt, "to see how it would be taken." The rebel authorities at Richmond had approved it, the agent had returned; and Arnold was, in his own words, thereby the better prepared to rejoin Booth in the prosecution of this conspiracy.

To this end Arnold went to Fortress Monroe. As his letter expressly declares, Booth said when they parted, "we would not meet in a month or so, and *therefore* I made application for employment — an answer to which I shall receive during the week." He did receive the answer that week from Fortress Monroe, and went there to await the "more propitious time," bearing with him the weapon of death which Booth had provided, and ready to obey his call, as the act had been approved at Richmond and been made "all right." Acting upon the same fact that the conspiracy had been approved in Richmond and the *funds* provided, O'Laughlin came to Washington to identify General Grant, the person who was to become the victim of his violence in the final consummation of this crime — General Grant, whom, as is averred in the specification, it had become the part of O'Laughlin by his agreement in this conspiracy to kill and murder. On the evening preceding the assassination — the 13th of April — by the testimony of three reputable witnesses, against whose truthfulness not one word is uttered here or elsewhere, O'Laughlin went into the house of the Secretary of War, where General Grant then was, and placed himself in position in the hall where he could see him, having declared before he reached that point, to one of these witnesses, that he wished to see General Grant. The house was brilliantly illuminated at the time; two, at least, of the witnesses conversed with the accused and the other stood very near to him, took special notice of his conduct, called attention to it, and suggested that he be put out of the house, and he was accordingly put out by one of the witnesses. These witnesses are confident, and have no doubt, and so swear upon their oaths, that Michael O'Laughlin is the man who was present on that occasion. There is no denial on the part of the accused that he was in Washington during the day and during the night of April 13, and also during the day and during the night of the 14th; and yet, to get rid of this testimony, recourse is had to that common device — an *alibi;* a device never, I may say, more frequently resorted to than in this trial. But what an *alibi!* Nobody is called to prove it, save some men who, by their own testimony, were engaged in a drunken debauch through the evening. A reasonable man who reads their evidence can hardly be expected to allow it to outweigh the united testimony of three unimpeached and unimpeachable witnesses who were clear in their statements, who entertain no doubt of the truth of what they say, whose opportunities to know were full and complete, and who were constrained to take special notice of the prisoner by means of his extraordinary conduct.

These witnesses describe accurately the appearance, stature, and complexion of the accused, but because they describe his clothing as dark or black, it is urged that as part of his clothing, although dark, was not black, the witnesses are mistaken. O'Laughlin and his drunken companions (one of whom swears that he drank ten times that evening) were strolling in the streets and in the direction of the house of the Secretary of War, up the Avenue; but you are asked to believe that these witnesses could not be mistaken in saying they were not off the Avenue above Seventh Street, or on K Street. I venture to say that no man who reads their testimony can determine satisfactorily all the places that were visited by O'Laughlin and his drunken associates that evening from seven to eleven o'clock P.M. All this time, from seven to eleven o'clock P.M., must be accounted for satisfactorily before the *alibi* can be established. Laughlan does not account for all the time, for he left O'Laughlin after seven o'clock, and rejoined him, as he says, "I suppose about eight o'clock." Grillet did not meet him until *half-past ten,* and then only casually saw him in passing the hotel. May not Grillet have been mistaken as to the fact, although he did meet O'Laughlin after eleven o'clock the same evening, as he swears?

Purdy swears to seeing him in the bar with Grillet about half-past ten, but, as we have seen by Grillet's testimony, it must have been after eleven o'clock. Murphy contradicts *as to time* both Grillet and Purdy, for he says it was half-past eleven or twelve o'clock when he and O'Laughlin returned to Rullman's from Platz's, and Early swears the accused went from Rullman's to Second Street to a dance about a quarter-past eleven o'clock, when O'Laughlin took the lead in the dance and stayed about one hour. I follow these witnesses no further. They contradict each other, and do not account for O'Laughlin all the time from seven to eleven o'clock. I repeat that no man can read their testimony without finding contradictions most material *as to time,* and coming to the conviction that they utterly fail to account for O'Laughlin's whereabouts on that evening. To establish an *alibi* the witnesses *must know the fact* and *testify* to it. Laughlan, Grillet, Purdy, Murphy, and Early utterly fail to prove it, and only succeed in showing that they did not know where O'Laughlin was all this time, and that some of them were grossly mistaken in what they testified, both as to *time and place.* The testimony of James B. Henderson is equally unsatisfactory. He is contradicted by other testimony of the accused as *to place.* He says O'Laughlin went up the Avenue above Seventh Street, but that he did not go to Ninth Street. The other witnesses swear he went to Ninth Street. He swears he went to Canterbury about nine o'clock, after going back from Seventh Street to Rullman's. Laughlan swears that O'Laughlin was with him at the corner of the Avenue and Ninth Street at nine o'clock, and went from there to Canterbury, while Early swears that O'Laughlin went up as far as Eleventh Street and returned with him and took supper at Welcker's about eight o'clock. If these witnesses prove an *alibi,* it is really against each other. It is folly to pretend that they prove facts which make it impossible that O'Laughlin could have been at the house of Secretary Stanton, as three witnesses swear he was, on the evening of the 13th of April, looking for General Grant.

Has it not, by the testimony thus reviewed, been established *prima facie* that in the months of February, March, and April, O'Laughlin had combined, confederated, and agreed with John Wilkes Booth and Samuel Arnold to kill and murder Abraham Lincoln, William H. Seward, Andrew Johnson, and Ulysses S. Grant? It is not established, beyond a shadow of doubt, that Booth had so conspired with the rebel agents in Canada as early as October last; that he was in search of agents to do the work *on pay,* in the interests of the rebellion, and that in this speculation Arnold and O'Laughlin had joined as early as February; that then, and after, with Booth and Surratt, they were in the "oil business," which was the business of assassination by contract as a speculation? If this conspiracy on the part of O'Laughlin with Arnold is established even *prima facie,* the declarations and acts of Arnold and Booth, the other conspirators, in furtherance of the common design, is evidence against O'Laughlin as well as against Arnold himself or the other parties. The rule of law is, that the act or declaration of one conspirator, done in pursuance or furtherance of the common design, is the act or declaration of all the conspirators.— *1 Wharton, 706.*

The letter, therefore, of his co-conspirator, Arnold, is evidence against O'Laughlin, because it is an act in the prosecution of the common conspiracy, suggesting what should be done in order to make it effective, and which suggestion, as has been stated, was followed out. The defense has attempted to avoid the force of this letter by reciting the statement of Arnold, made to Horner at the time he was arrested, in which he declared, among other things, that the purpose was to abduct President Lincoln and take him South; that it was to be done at the theatre by throwing the President out of the box upon the floor of the stage, when the accused was to catch him. The very announcement of this testimony excited derision that such a tragedy meant only to take the President and carry him gently away! This pigmy to catch the giant as the assassins hurled him to the floor from an elevation of twelve feet! The court has viewed the theatre, and must be satisfied that Booth, in leaping from the President's box, broke his limb. The court cannot fail to conclude that this statement of Arnold was but another silly device, like that of the "oil business," which, for the time being, he employed to hide from the knowledge of his captor the fact that the purpose was to murder the President. No man can, for a moment, believe that any one of these conspirators hoped or desired, by such a proceeding as that stated by this prisoner, to take the President alive in the presence of thousands assembled in the theatre after he had been thus thrown upon the floor of the stage, much less to carry him through the city, through the lines of your army, and deliver him into the hands of the rebels. No such purpose was expressed or hinted by the conspirators in Canada, who commissioned Booth to let these assassinations on contract. I shall waste not a moment more in combatting such an absurdity.

Arnold does confess that he was a conspirator with Booth in this purposed murder; that Booth had a letter of introduction to Dr. Mudd; that Booth, O'Laughlin, Atzerodt, Surratt, a man with an *alias* "Mosby," and another whom he does not know, and himself, were parties to this conspiracy, and that Booth had furnished them all with arms. He concludes this remarkable statement to Horner with the declaration that at that time, to wit, the first week of March, or four weeks before he went to Fortress Monroe, he left the conspiracy, and that Booth told him to sell his arms if he chose. This is sufficiently answered by the fact that, four weeks *afterwards*, he wrote his letter to Booth, which was found in Booth's possession after the assassination, suggesting to him what to do in order to make the conspiracy a success, and by the further fact that at the very moment he uttered these declarations part of his arms were found upon his person, and the rest not disposed of, but at his father's house.

A party to a treasonable and murderous conspiracy against the government of his country cannot be held to have abandoned it because he makes such a declaration as this, when he is in the hands of the officer of the law, arrested for his crime, and especially when his declaration is in conflict with and expressly contradicted by his written acts, and unsupported by any conduct of his which becomes a citizen and a man.

If he abondoned the conspiracy, why did he not make known the fact to Abraham Lincoln and his constitutional advisers that these men, armed with the weapons of assassination, were daily lying in wait for their lives? To pretend that a man who thus conducts himself for weeks after the pretended abandonment, volunteering advice for the successful prosecution of the conspiracy, the evidence of which is in writing, and about which there can be no mistake, has, in fact, abandoned it, is to insult the common understanding of men. O'Laughlin having conspired with Arnold to do this murder, is, therefore, as much concluded by the letter of Arnold of the 27th of March as is Arnold himself. The further testimony touching O'Laughlin, that of Streett, establishes the fact that about the 1st of April he saw him in confidential conversation with J. Wilkes Booth, in this city, on the Avenue. Another man, whom the witness does not know, was in conversation. O'Laughlin called Streett to one side, and told him Booth was busily engaged with his friend — was *talking privately* to his friend. This remark of O'Laughlin is attempted to be accounted for, but the attempt failed; his counsel taking the pains to ask what induced O'Laughlin to make the remark, received the fit reply: "I did not see the interior of Mr. O'Laughlin's mind; I cannot tell." It is the province of this court to infer why that remark was made and what it signified.

That John H. Surratt, George A. Atzerodt, Mary E. Surratt, David E. Herold, and Louis Payne entered into this conspiracy with Booth, is so very clear upon the testimony that little time need be occupied in bringing again before the court the evidence which establishes it. By the testimony of Wiechmann, we find Atzerodt in February at the house of the prisoner, Mrs. Surratt. He inquired for her or for John when he came and remained over night. After this and before the assassination he visited there frequently, and at that house bore the name of "Port Tobacco," the name by which he was known in Canada among the conspirators there. The same witness testifies that he met him on the street, when he said he was going to visit Payne at the Herndon House, and also accompanied him, along with Herold and John H. Surratt, to the theatre in March to hear Booth play in "The Apostate." At the Pennsylvania House, one or two weeks previous to the assassination, Atzerodt made the statement to Lieutenant Keim, when asking for his knife which he had left in his room, a knife corresponding in size with the one exhibited in court, " I want that; if one fails I want the other," wearing at the same time his revolver at his belt. He also stated to Greenawalt, of the Pennsylvania House, in March, that he was nearly broke, but had friends enough to give him as much money as *would see him through*, adding, " I am going away some of these days, but will return with as much gold as will keep me all my lifetime." Mr. Greenawalt also says that Booth had frequent interviews with Atzerodt, sometimes in the room, and at other times Booth would walk in and immediately go out, Atzerodt following.

John M. Lloyd testifies that some six weeks before the assassination, Herold, Atzerodt, and John H. Surratt came to his house at Surrattsville, bringing with them two Spencer carbines with ammunition, also a rope and wrench. Surratt asked the witness to take care of them and to conceal the carbines. Surratt took him into a room in the house, it being his mother's house, and showed the witness where to put the carbines, between the joists on the second floor. The carbines were put there, according to his directions, and concealed. Marcus P. Norton saw Atzerodt in conversation with Booth at the National Hotel about the 2d or 3d of March; the conversation was confidential, and the witness accidentally heard them talking in regard to President Johnson, and say that "the class of witnesses would be of that character that there could be little proven by them." This conversation may throw some light on the fact that Atzerodt was found in possession of Booth's bank book!

Colonel Nevens testifies that on the 12th of April last he saw Atzerodt at the Kirkwood House; that Atzerodt there asked him, a stranger, if he knew where Vice-President Johnson was, and where Mr. Johnson's *room was*. Colonel Nevens showed him where the room of the Vice-President was, and told him that the Vice-President was then at dinner. Atzerodt then looked into the dining-room where Vice-President Johnson was dining alone. Robert R. Jones, the clerk at the Kirkwood House, states that on the 14th, the day of the murder, two days after this, Atzerodt registered his name at the hotel, G. A. Atzerodt, and took No. 126, retaining the room that day, and carrying away the key. In this room, after the assassination, were found the knife and revolver with which he intended to murder the Vice-President.

The testimony of all these witnesses leaves no doubt that the prisoner, George A. Atzerodt, entered into this conspiracy with Booth; that he expected to receive a large compensation for the service that he would render in its execution; that he had undertaken the assassination of the Vice-President for a price; that he, with Surratt and Herold, rendered the important service of depositing the arms and ammunition to be used by Booth and his confederates as a protection in their flight after the conspiracy had been executed; and that he was careful to have his intended victim pointed out to him, and the room he occupied in the hotel, so that when he came to perform his horrid work he would know precisely where to go and whom to strike.

I take no further notice now of the preparation which this prisoner made for the successful execution of this part of the traitorous and murderous design. The question is, did he enter into this conspiracy? His language overheard by Mr. Norton excludes every other conclusion. Vice-President Johnson's name was mentioned in that secret conversation with Booth, and the very suggestive expression was made between them that "little could be proved by the witnesses." His confession in his defense is conclusive of his guilt.

That Payne was in this conspiracy is confessed in the defense made by his counsel, and is also evident, from the facts proved, that when the conspiracy was being organized in Canada by Thompson, Sanders, Tucker, Cleary, and Clay, this man Payne stood at the door of Thompson, was recommended and indorsed by Clay with the words, "We trust him"; that after coming hither he first reported himself at the house of Mrs. Mary E. Surratt, inquired for her and for John H. Surratt, remained there for four days, having conversation with both of them; having provided himself with means of disguise, was also supplied with pistols and a knife, such as he afterwards used, and spurs, preparatory to his flight; was seen with John H. Surratt, practicing with knives such as those employed in this deed of assassination and now before the court; was afterwards provided with lodging at the Herndon House, at the instance of Surratt; was visited there by Atzerodt, and attended Booth and Surratt to Ford's Theatre, occupying with those parties the box, as I believe and which we may readily infer, in which the President was afterwards murdered.

If further testimony be wanting that he had entered into the conspiracy, it may be found in the fact sworn to by Wiechmann, whose testimnoy no candid man will discredit, that about the 20th of March, Mrs. Surratt, in great excitement and weeping, said that her son John had gone away not to return, when, about three hours subsequently, in the afternoon of the same day, John H. Surratt reappeared, came rushing in a state of frenzy into the room, in his mother's house, armed, declaring he would shoot whoever came into the room, and proclaiming that his prospects were blasted and his hopes gone; that soon Payne came into the same room, also armed and under great excitement, and was immediately followed by Booth, with his riding-whip in his hand, who walked rapidly across the floor from side to side, so much excited that for some time he did not notice the presence of the witness. Observing Wiechmann, the parties then withdrew, upon a suggestion from Booth, to an upper room, and there had a private interview. From all that transpired on that occasion, it is apparent that when these parties left the house that day it was with the full purpose of completing some act essential to the final execution of the work of assassination, in conformity with their previous confederation and agreement. They returned foiled — from what cause is unknown — dejected, angry, and covered with confusion.

It is almost imposing upon the patience of the court to consume time in demonstrating the fact which none conversant with the testimony of this case can for a moment doubt, that John H. Surratt and Mary E. Surratt were as surely in the conspiracy to murder the President as was John Wilkes Booth himself. You have the frequent interviews between John H. Surratt and Booth, his intimate relations with Payne, his visits from Atzerodt and Herold, his deposit of the arms to cover their flight after the conspiracy should have been executed; his own declared visit to Richmond to do what Booth himself said to Chester must be done, to wit, that he or some of the party must go to Richmond in order to get funds to carry out the conspiracy; that he brought back with him gold, the price of blood, confessing himself that he was there; that he immediately went to Canada, delivered despatches in cipher to Jacob Thompson from Jefferson Davis, which were interpreted and read by Thompson in the presence of the witness Conover, and in which the conspiracy was approved, and, in the language of Thompson, the proposed assassination was "made all right."

One other fact, if any other fact be needed, and I have done with the evidence which proves that John H. Surratt entered into this combination; that is, that it appears by the testimony of the witness, the cashier of the Ontario Bank, Montreal, that Jacob Thompson, about the day that these despatches were delivered, and while Surratt was then present in Canada, drew from that bank of the rebel funds there on deposit the sum of one hundred and eighty thousand dollars. This being done, Surratt, finding it safer, doubtless, to go to Canada for the great bulk of funds which were to be distributed amongst these hired assassins than to attempt to carry it through our lines direct from Richmond, immediately returned to Washington and was present in this city, as is proven by the testimony of Mr. Reid, *on the afternoon of the 14th of April*, the day of the assassination, booted and spurred, ready for the flight whenever the fatal blow should have been struck. If he was not a conspirator and a party to this great crime, how comes it that from that hour to this no man has seen him in the capital, nor has he been reported anywhere outside of Canada, having arrived at Montreal, as the testimony shows, on the 18th of April, four days after the murder? Nothing but his conscious coward guilt could possibly induce him to absent himself from his mother, as he does, upon her trial. Being one of these conspirators, as charged, every act of his in the prosecution of this crime is evidence against the other parties to the conspiracy.

That Mary E. Surratt is as guilty as her son of having thus conspired, combined, and confederated to do this murder, in aid of this rebellion, is clear. First, her house was the headquarters of Booth, John H. Surratt, Atzerodt, Payne, and Herold. She is inquired for by Atzerodt; she is inquired for by Payne; and she is visited by Booth, and holds private conversations with him. His picture, together with that of the chief conspirator, Jefferson Davis, is found in her house. She sends to Booth for a carriage to take her, on the 11th of April, to Surrattsville for the purpose of perfecting the arrangement deemed necessary to the successful execution of the conspiracy, and especially to facilitate and protect the conspirators in their escape from justice. On that occasion Booth, having disposed of his carriage, gives to the agent she employed ten dollars with which to hire a conveyance for that purpose. And yet the pretence is made that Mrs. Surratt went on the 11th to Surrattsville exclusively upon her own private and lawful business. Can any one tell, if that be so, how it comes that she should apply *to Booth* for a conveyance, and how it comes that he of his own accord, having no conveyance to furnish her, should send her ten dollars with which to procure it? There is not the slightest indication that Booth was under any obligation to her, or that she had any claim upon him, either for a conveyance or for the means with which to procure one, except that he was bound to contribute, being the agent of the conspirators in Canada and Richmond, whatever money might be necessary to the consummation of this infernal plot. On that day, the 11th of April, John H. Surratt had not returned from Canada with the funds furnished by Thompson!

Upon that journey of the 11th the accused, Mary E. Surratt, met the witness John M. Lloyd at Uniontown. She called him; he got out of his carriage and came to her, and she whispered to him in so low a tone that her attendant could not hear her words, though Lloyd, to whom they were spoken, did distinctly hear them, and testifies that she told him he should have those "shooting-irons" ready, meaning the carbines which her son and Herold and Atzerodt had deposited with him, and added the reason, "for they would soon be called for." On the day of the assassination she again sent for Booth, had an interview with him in her own house, and immediately went again to Surrattsville, and then, at about six o'clock in the afternoon, she delivered to Lloyd a field-glass, and told him " to have two bottles of whiskey and the carbines ready, as they would be called for that night." Having thus perfected the arrangement she returned to Washington to her own house, at about half-past eight o'clock in the evening, to await the final result. How could this woman anticipate on Friday afternoon, at six o'clock, that these arms would be called for and would be needed that night unless she was in the conspiracy and knew the blow was to be struck, and the flight of the assassins attempted and by that route? Was not the private conversation which Booth held with her in her parlor on the afternoon of the 14th of April, just before she left on this business, in relation to the orders she should give to have the arms ready?

An endeavor is made to impeach Lloyd. But the court will observe that no witness has been called who contradicts Lloyd's statement in any material matter; neither has his general character for truth been assailed. How, then, is he impeached? Is it claimed that his testimony shows that he was a party to the conspiracy? Then it is conceded by those who set up any such pretence that there was a conspiracy. A conspiracy between whom? There can be no conspiracy without the co-operation or agreement of two or more persons. Who were the other parties to it? Was it Mary E. Surratt? Was it John H. Surratt, George A. Atzerodt, David E. Herold? Those are the only persons, so far as his own testimony or the testimony of any other witness discloses, with whom he had any communication whatever on any subject immediately or remotely touching this conspiracy before the assassination. His receipt and concealment of the arms are, unexplained, evidence that he was in the conspiracy.

The explanation is that he was dependent upon Mary E. Surratt; was her tenant; and his declaration, given in evidence by the accused herself, is that "she had ruined him and brought this trouble upon him." But because he was weak enough, or wicked enough, to become the guilty depositary of these arms, and to deliver them on the order of Mary E. Surratt to the assassins, it does not follow that he is not to be believed on oath. It is said that he concealed the facts that the arms had been left and called for. He so testifies himself, but he gives the reason that he did it only from apprehension of danger to his life. If he were in the conspiracy, his general credit being unchallenged, his testimony being uncontradicted in any material matter, he is to be believed, and cannot be disbelieved if his testimony is substantially corroborated by other reliable witnesses. Is he not corroborated touching the deposit of arms by the fact that the arms are produced in court, one of which was found upon the person of Booth at the time he was overtaken and slain, and which is identified as the same which had been left with Lloyd by Herold, Surratt, and Atzerodt? Is he not corroborated in the fact of the first interview with Mrs. Surratt by the joint testimony of Mrs. Offut and Lewis J. Wiechmann, each of whom testified (and they are contradicted by no one), that on Tuesday, the 11th day of April, at Uniontown, Mrs. Surratt called Mr. Lloyd to come to her, which he did, and she held a *secret* conversation with him? Is he not corroborated as to the last conversation on the 14th of April by the testimony of Mrs. Offut, who swears that upon the evening of the 14th of April she saw the prisoner, Mary E. Surratt, at Lloyd's house, approach and hold conversation with him? Is he not corroborated in the fact, to which he swears, that Mrs. Surratt delivered to him at that time the field-glass wrapped in paper, by the sworn statement of Wiechmann that Mrs. Surratt took with her on that occasion two packages, both of which were wrapped in paper, and one of which he describes as a small package about six inches in diameter? The attempt was made by calling Mrs. Offut to prove that no such package was delivered, but it failed; she merely states that Mrs. Surratt delivered a package wrapped in paper to her after her arrival there, and before Lloyd came in, which was laid down in the room. But whether it was *the* package about which Lloyd testifies, or the other package of the *two* about which Wiechmann testifies, as having been carried there that day by Mrs. Surratt, does not appear. Neither does this witness pretend to say that Mrs. Surratt, after she had delivered it to her, and the witness had laid it down in the room, did not again take it up, if it were the same, and put it in the hands of Lloyd. She only knows that she did not see that done; but she did see Lloyd with a package like the one she received in the room before Mrs. Surratt left. How it came into his possession she is not able to state; nor what the package was that Mrs. Surratt first handed her; nor which of the packages it was she afterwards saw in the hands of Lloyd.

But there is one other fact in this case that puts forever at rest the question of the guilty participation of the prisoner, Mrs. Surratt, in this conspiracy and murder; and that is that Payne, who had lodged four days in her house — who during all that time had sat at her table, and who had often conversed with her — when the guilt of his great crime was upon him, and he knew not where else he could so safely go to find a co-conspirator, and he could trust none that was not like himself, guilty, with even the knowledge of his presence — under cover of darkness, after wandering for three days and nights, skulking before the pursuing officers of justice, at the hour of midnight found his way to the door of Mrs. Surratt, rang the bell, was admitted, and upon being asked, "Whom do you want to see?" replied, "Mrs. Surratt." He was then asked by the officer, Morgan, what he came at that time of night for, to which he replied, "to dig a gutter in the morning; Mrs. Surratt had sent for him." Afterwards he said "Mrs. Surratt knew he was a poor man and *came to him.*" Being asked where he last worked, he replied, "sometimes on 'I' street"; and where he boarded, he replied, "he had no boarding-house, and was a poor man who got his living with the pick," which he bore upon his shoulder, having stolen it from the intrenchments of the capital. Upon being pressed again why he came there at that time of night to go to work, he answered that he simply called to see what time he should go to work in the morning. Upon being told by the officer, who fortunately had preceded him to this house, that he would have to go to the provost marshal's office, he moved and did not answer, whereupon Mrs. Surratt was asked to step into the hall and state whether she knew this man. Raising her right hand, she exclaimed, "Before God, sir, I have not seen that man before; I have not hired him; I do not know anything about him." The hall was brilliantly lighted.

If not one word had been said, the mere act of Payne in flying to her house for shelter would have borne witness against her, strong as proofs from Holy Writ. But when she denies, after hearing his declarations, that she had sent for him, or that she had gone to him and hired him, and calls her God to witness that she had never seen him, and knew nothing of him, when, in point of fact, she had seen him for four successive days in her own house, in the same clothing which he then wore, who can resist for a moment the conclusion that these parties were alike guilty?

The testimony of Spangler's complicity is conclusive and brief. It was impossible to hope for escape after assassinating the President, and such others as might attend him in Ford's Theatre, without arrangements being first made to aid the flight of the assassin and to some extent prevent immediate pursuit.

A stable was to be provided close to Ford's Theatre, in which the horses could be concealed and kept ready for the assassin's use whenever the murderous blow was struck. Accordingly, Booth secretly, through Maddox, hired a stable in rear of the theatre and connecting with it by an alley, as early as the 1st of January last; showing that at that time he had concluded, notwithstanding all that has been said to the contrary, to murder the President in Ford's Theatre and provide the means for immediate and successful flight. Conscious of his guilt, he paid the rent for this stable through Maddox, month by month, giving him the money. He employed Spangler, doubtless for the reason that he could trust him with the secret, as a carpenter to fit up this shed, so that it would furnish room for two horses, and provide the door with lock and key. Spangler did this work for him. Then, it was necessary that a carpenter having access to the theatre should be employed by the assassin to provide a bar for the outer door of the passage leading to the President's box, so that when he entered upon his work of assassination he would be secure from interruption from the rear. By the evidence, it is shown that Spangler was in the box in which the President was murdered on the afternoon of the 14th of April, and when there damned the President and General Grant, and said the President ought to be cursed, he had got so many good men killed; showing not only his hostility to the President, but the cause of it — that he had been faithful to his oath and had resisted that great rebellion in the interest of which his life was about to be sacrificed by this man and his co-conspirators. In performing the work which had doubtless been intrusted to him by Booth, a mortise was cut in the wall. A wooden bar was prepared, one end of which could be readily inserted in the mortise and the other pressed against the edge of the door on the inside so as to prevent its being opened. Spangler had the skill and the opportunity to do that work and all the additional work which was done.

It is in evidence that the screws in "the keepers" to the locks on each of the inner doors of the box occupied by the President were drawn. The attempt has been made, on behalf of the prisoner, to show that this was done some time before, accidentally, and with no bad design, and had not been repaired by reason of inadvertence; but that attempt has utterly failed, because the testimony adduced for that purpose relates exclusively to but one of the two inner doors, while the fact is, that the screws were drawn in *both*, and the additional precaution taken to cut a small hole through one of these doors through which the party approaching and while in the private passage would be enabled to look into the box and examine the exact posture of the President before entering. It was also deemed essential, in the execution of this plot, that some one should watch at the outer door, in the rear of the theatre, by which alone the assassin could hope for escape. It was for this work Booth sought to employ Chester in January, offering three thousand dollars down of the money of his employers, and the assurance that he should never want. What Chester refused to do Spangler undertook and promised to do. When Booth brought his horse to the rear door of the theatre, on the evening of the murder, he called for Spangler, who went to him, when Booth was heard to say to him, "Ned, you'll help me all you can, won't you?" To which Splangler replied, "Oh, yes."

When Booth made his escape, it is testified by Colonel Stewart, who pursued him across the stage and out through the same door, that as he approached it some one slammed it shut. Ritterspaugh, who was standing behind the scenes when Booth fired the pistol and fled, saw Booth run down the passage toward the back door, and pursued him; but Booth drew his knife upon him and passed out, slamming the door after him. Ritterspaugh opened it and went through, leaving *it open* behind him, leaving Spangler inside, and in a position from which he readily could have reached the door. Ritterspaugh also states that very quickly after he had passed through this door he was followed by a large man, the first who followed him, and who was, doubtless, Colonel Stewart. Stewart is very positive that he saw this door slammed; that he himself was constrained to open it, and had some difficulty in opening it. He also testifies that as he approached the door a man stood near enough to have thrown it to with his hand, and this man, the witness believes, was the prisoner Spangler. Ritterspaugh has sworn that he left the door open behind him when he went out, and that he was first followed by the large man, Colonel Stewart. Who slammed that door behind Ritterspaugh? It was not Ritterspaugh; it could not have been Booth, for Ritterspaugh swears that Booth was mounting his horse at the time; and Stewart swears that Booth was upon his horse when he came out. That it was Spangler who slammed the door after Ritterspaugh may not only be inferred from Stewart's testimony, but it is made very clear by his own conduct afterwards upon the return of Ritterspaugh to the stage. The door being then open, and Ritterspaugh being asked which way Booth went, had answered. Ritterspaugh says: "Then I came back on the stage, where I had left Edward Spangler; he hit me on the face with his hand and said, 'Don't say which way he went.' I asked him what he meant by slapping me in the mouth? He said, 'For God's sake, shut up.'"

The testimony of Withers is adroitly handled to throw doubt upon these facts. It cannot avail, for Withers says he was knocked in the scene by Booth, and when he "come to" he got a side view of him. A man knocked down and senseless, on "coming to" might mistake anybody by a side view for Booth.

An attempt has been made by the defense to discredit this testimony of Ritterspaugh, by showing his contradictory statements to Gifford, Garlan, and Lamb, neither of whom do in fact contradict him, but substantially sustain him. None but a guilty man would have met the witness with a blow for stating which way the assassin had gone. A like confession of guilt was made by Spangler when the witness Miles, the same evening, and directly after the assassination, came to the back door, where Spangler was standing with others, and asked Spangler who it was that held the horse, to which Spangler replied: "Hush; don't say anything about it." He confessed his guilt again when he denied to Mary Anderson the fact, proved here beyond all question, that Booth had called him when he came to that door with his horse, using the emphatic words, "No, he did not; he did not call me." The rope comes to bear witness against him, as did the rope which Atzerodt and Herold and John H. Surratt had carried to Surrattsville and deposed there with the carbines.

It is only surprising that the ingenious counsel did not attempt to explain the deposit of the rope at Surrattsville by the same method that he adopted in explanation of the deposit of this rope, some sixty feet long, found in the carpet-sack of Spangler, unaccounted for save by some evidence which tends to show that he may have carried it away from the theatre.

It is not needful to take time in the recapitulation of the evidence, which shows conclusively that David E. Herold was one of these conspirators. His continued association with Booth, with Atzerodt, his visits to Mrs. Surratt's, his attendance at the theatre with Payne, Surratt, and Atzerodt, his connection with Atzerodt on the evening of the murder, riding with him on the street in the direction of and near to the theatre at the hour appointed for the work of assassination, and his final flight and arrest, show that he, in common with all the other parties on trial, and all the parties named upon your record not upon trial, and combined and confederated to kill and murder in the interests of the rebellion, as charged and specified against them.

That this conspiracy was entered into by all these parties, both present and absent, is thus proved by the acts, meetings, declarations, and correspondence of all the parties, beyond any doubt whatever. True it is circumstantial evidence, but the court will remember the rule before recited, that circumstances cannot lie; that they are held sufficient in every court where justice is judicially administered to establish the fact of a conspiracy. I shall take no further notice of the remark made by the learned counsel who opens for the defense, and which has been followed by several of his associates, that under the Constitution it requires two witnesses to prove the overt act of high treason, than to say, this is not a charge of high treason, but of a treasonable conspiracy, in aid of a rebellion, with intent to kill and murder the executive officer of the United States, and commander of its armies, and of the murder of the President in pursuance of that conspiracy, and with the intent laid, etc. Neither by the Constitution, nor by the rules of the common law, is any fact connected with this allegation required to be established by the testimony of more than one witness. I might say, however, that every substantive averment against each of the parties named upon this record has been established by the testimony of more than one witness.

That the several accused did enter into this conspiracy with John Wilkes Booth and John H. Surratt to murder the officers of this government named upon the record, in pursuance of the wishes of their employers and instigators in Richmond and Canada, and with intent thereby to aid the existing rebellion and subvert the Constitution and laws of the United States, as alleged, is no longer an open question.

The intent as laid was expressly declared by Sanders in the meeting of the conspirators at Montreal in February last, by Booth in Virginia and New York, and by Thompson to Conover and Montgomery; but if there were no testimony directly upon this point, the law would presume the intent, for the reason that such was the natural and necessary tendency and manifest design of the act itself.

The learned gentleman (Mr. Johnson) says the government has survived the assassination of the President, and thereby would have you infer that this conspiracy was not entered into and attempted to be executed with the intent laid. With as much show of reason it might be said that because the government of the United States has survived this unmatched rebellion, it therefore results that the rebel conspirators waged war upon the government with no purpose or intent thereby to subvert it. By the law we have seen that, without any direct evidence of previous combination and agreement between these parties, the conspiracy might be established by evidence of the acts of the prisoners, or of any others with whom they co-operated, concurring in the execution of the common design. — *Roscoe, 416.*

Was there co-operation between the several accused in the execution of this conspiracy? That there was is as clearly established by the testimony as is the fact that Abraham Lincoln was killed and murdered by John Wilkes Booth. The evidence shows that all of the accused, save Mudd and Arnold, were in Washington on the 14th of April, the day of the assassination, together with John Wilkes Booth and John H. Surratt; that on that day Booth had a secret interview with the prisoner, Mary E. Surratt; that immediately thereafter she went to Surrattsville to perform her part of the preparation necessary to the successful execution of the conspiracy, and did make that preparation; that John H. Surratt had arrived here from Canada, notifying the parties that the price to be paid for this great crime had been provided for, at least in part, by the deposit receipts of April 6th for $180,000, procured by Thompson of the Ontario Bank, Montreal, Canada; that he was also prepared to keep watch, or strike a blow, and ready for the contemplated flight; that Atzerodt, on the afternoon of that day, was seeking to obtain a horse, the better to secure his own safety by flight, after he should have performed the task which he had voluntarily undertaken by contract in the conspiracy — the murder of Andrew Johnson, then Vice-President of the United States; that he did procure a horse for that purpose at Naylor's, and was seen about nine o'clock in the evening to ride to the Kirkwood House, where the Vice-President then was, dismount and enter. At a previous hour Booth was in the Kirkwood House, and left his card, now in evidence, doubtless intended to be sent to the room of the Vice-President, and which was in these words: "Don't wish to disturb you. Are you at home? J. Wilkes Booth." Atzerodt, when he made application at Brooks's in the afternoon for the horse, said to Wiechmann, who was there, he was going to ride in the country, and that "he was going to get a horse and send for Payne." He did get a horse for Payne, as well as for himself; for it is proven that on the 12th he was seen in Washington riding the horse which had been procured by Booth, in company with Mudd, last November, from Gardner. A similar horse was tied before the door of Mr. Seward on the night of the murder, was captured after the flight of Payne, who was seen to ride away, and which horse is now identified as the Gardner horse. Booth also procured a horse on the same day, took it to his stable in the rear of the theatre, where he had an interview with Spangler, and where he concealed it. Herold, too, obtained a horse in the afternoon, and was seen between nine and ten o'clock riding with Atzerodt down the Avenue from the Treasury, then up Fourteenth and down F Street, passing close by Ford's Theatre.

O'Laughlin had come to Washington the day before, had sought out his victim (General Grant) at the house of the Secretary of War, that he might be able with certainty to identify him, and at the very hour when these preparations were going on was lying in wait at Rullman's on the Avenue, keeping watch, and declaring, as he did, at about ten o'clock P.M., when told that the fatal blow had been struck by Booth, "I don't believe Booth did it." During the day, and the night before, he had been visiting Booth, and doubtless encouraging him, and at that very hour was in position, at a convenient distance, to aid and protect him in his flight, as well as to execute his own part of the conspiracy by inflicting death upon General Grant, who, happily, was not at the theatre nor in the city, having left the city that day. Who doubts that Booth, having ascertained in the course of the day that General Grant would not be present at the theatre, O'Laughlin, who was to murder General Grant, instead of entering the box with Booth, was detailed to lie in wait, and watch and support him.

His declarations of his reasons for changing his lodgings here and in Baltimore, after the murder, so ably and so ingeniously presented in the argument of his learned counsel (Mr. Cox), avail nothing before the blasting fact that he did change his lodgings, and declared "he knew nothing of the affair whatever." O'Laughlin, who lurked here, conspiring daily with Booth and Arnold for six weeks to do this murder, declares "he knew nothing of the affair." O'Laughlin, who said he was "in the oil business," which Booth and Surratt and Payne and Arnold have all declared meant this conspiracy, says he "knew nothing of the affair." O'Laughlin, to whom Booth sent the despatches of the 13th and 27th of March — O'Laughlin, who is named in Arnold's letter as one of the conspirators, and who searched for General Grant on Thursday night, laid in wait for him on Friday, was defeated by that Providence "which shapes our ends," and laid in wait to aid Booth and Payne, declares "he knows nothing of the matter." Such a denial is as false and inexcusable as Peter's denial of our Lord.

Mrs. Surratt had arrived at home, from the completion of her part in the plot, about half past eight o'clock in the evening. A few moments afterwards she was called to the parlor and there had a private interview with some one unseen, but whose retreating footsteps were heard by the witness Wiechmann. This was doubtless the secret and last visit of John H. Surratt to his mother, who had instigated and encouraged him to strike this traitorous and murderous blow against his country.

While all these preparations were going on, Mudd was awaiting the execution of the plot, ready to faithfully perform his part in securing the safe escape of the murderers. Arnold was at his post at Fortress Monroe, awaiting the meeting referred to in his letter of March 27th, wherein he says they were not "to meet for a month or so," which month had more than expired on the day of the murder, for his letter and the testimony disclose that this month of suspension began to run from about the first week in March. He stood ready with the arms which Booth had furnished him to aid the escape of the murderers by *that route*, and secure their communication with their employers. He had given the assurance in that letter to Booth, that although the government "suspicioned them," and the undertaking was "becoming complicated," yet "a time more propitious would arrive" for the consummation of this conspiracy in which he "was one" with Booth, and when he would "be better prepared to again be with him."

Such were the preparations. The horses were in readiness for the flight; the ropes were procured, doubtless for the purpose of tying the horses at whatever point they might be constrained to delay and to secure their boats to their moorings in making their way across the Potomac. The five murderous camp knives, the two carbines, the eight revolvers, the derringer, in court and identified, all were ready for the work of death. The part that each had played has already been in part stated in this argument, and needs no repetition.

Booth proceeded to the theatre about nine o'clock in the evening, at the same time that Atzerodt and Payne and Herold were riding the streets, while Surratt, having parted with his mother at the brief interview in her parlor, from which his retreating steps were heard, was walking the Avenue, booted and spurred, and doubtless consulting with O'Laughlin. When Booth reached the rear of the theatre, he called Spangler to him (whose denial of that fact, when charged with it, as proven by three witnesses is very significant) and received from Spangler his pledge to help him all he could, when with Booth he entered the theatre by the stage-door, doubtless to see that the way was clear from the box to the rear door of the theatre, and look upon their victim, whose exact position they could study from the stage. After this view, Booth passes to the street in front of the theatre, where, on the pavement with other conspirators yet unknown, among them one described as a low-browed villain, he awaits the appointed moment. Booth himself, impatient, enters the vestibule of the theatre from the front and asks the time. He is referred to the clock, and returns. Presently, as the hour of ten o'clock approached, one of his guilty associates called the time; they wait; again, as the moments elapsed, this conspirator upon watch called the time; again, as the appointed hour draws nigh, he calls the time; and finally, when the fatal moment arrives, he repeats in a louder tone, "Ten minutes past ten o'clock!" Ten minutes past ten o'clock! The hour has come when the red right hand of these murderous conspirators should strike, and the dreadful deed of assassination be done.

Booth, at the appointed moment, entered the theatre, ascended to the dress-circle, passed to the right, paused a moment, looking down, doubtless to see if Spangler was at his post, and approached the outer door of the close passage leading to the box occupied by the President, pressed it open, passed in, and closed the passage door behind him. Spangler's bar was in its place, and was readily adjusted by Booth in the mortise, and pressed against the inner side of the door, so that he was secure from interruption from without. He passes on to the next door, immediately behind the President, and there stopping, looks through the aperture in the door into the President's box, and deliberately observes the precise position of his victim, seated in the chair which had been prepared by the conspirators as the altar for the sacrifice, looking calmly and quietly down upon the glad and grateful people whom by his fidelity he had saved from the peril which had threatened the destruction of their government, and all they held dear this side of the grave, and whom he had come upon invitation to greet with his presence, with the words still lingering upon his lips which he had uttered with uncovered head and uplifted hand before God and his country, when on the 4th of last March he took again the oath to preserve, protect, and defend the Constitution, declaring that he entered upon the duties of his great office "with malice toward none — with charity for all." In a moment more, strengthened by the knowledge that his co-conspirators were all at their posts, seven at least of them present in the city, two of them, Mudd and Arnold, at their appointed places, watching for his coming, this hired assassin moves stealthily through the door, the fastenings of which had been removed to facilitate his entrance, fires upon his victim, and the martyr spirit of Abraham Lincoln ascends to God.

> "Treason has done his worst; nor steel, nor poison,
> Malice domestic, foreign levy, nothing
> Can touch him further."

At the same hour, when these accused and their co-conspirators in Richmond and Canada, by the hand of John Wilkes Booth, inflicted this mortal wound which deprived the republic of its defender, and filled this land from ocean to ocean with a strange, great sorrow, Payne, a very demon in human form, with the words of falsehood upon his lips, that he was the bearer of a message from the physician of the venerable Secretary of State, sweeps by his servant, encounters his son, who protests that the assassin shall not disturb his father, prostrate on a bed of sickness, and receives for answer the assassin's blow from the revolver in his hand, repeated again and again, rushes into the room, is encountered by Major Seward, inflicts wound after wound upon him with his murderous knife, is encountered by Hansell and Robinson, each of whom he also wounds, springs upon the defenseless and feeble Secretary of State, stabs first on one side of his throat, then on the other, again in the face, and is only prevented from literally hacking out his life by the persistence and courage of the attendant Robinson. He turns to flee, and, his giant arm and murderous hand for a moment paralyzed by the consciousness of guilt, he drops his weapons of death, one in the house, the other at the door, where they were taken up, and are here now to bear witness against him. He attempts escape on the horse which Booth and Mudd had procured of Gardner, with what success has already been stated.

Atzerodt, near midnight, returns to the stable of Naylor the horse which he had procured for this work of murder, having been interrupted in the execution of the part assigned him at the Kirkwood House by the timely coming of citizens to the defense of the Vice-President, and creeps into the Pennsylvania House at two o'clock in the morning with another of the conspirators, yet unknown. There he remained until about five o'clock, when he left, found his way to Georgetown, pawned one of his revolvers, now in court, and fled northward into Maryland.

He is traced to Montgomery County, to the house of Mr. Metz, on the Sunday succeeding the murder, where, as is proved by the testimony of three witnesses, he said that if the man that was to follow General Grant *had* followed him, it was likely that Grant was shot. To one of these witnesses (Mr. Layman) he said he did not think Grant had been killed; or if he had been killed he was killed by a man who got on the cars at the same time that Grant did; thus disclosing most clearly that one of his co-conspirators was assigned the task of killing and murdering General Grant, and that Atzerodt knew that General Grant had left the city of Washington, a fact which is not disputed, on the Friday evening of the murder, by the evening train. Thus this intended victim of the conspiracy escaped, for that night, the knives and revolvers of Atzerodt and O'Laughlin and Payne and Herold and Booth and John H. Surratt and, perchance, Harper and Caldwell, and twenty others, who were then here lying in wait for his life.

In the mean time Booth and Herold, taking the route before agreed upon, make directly after the assassination for the Anacostia bridge. Booth crosses first, gives his name, passes the guard, and is speedily followed by Herold. They make their way directly to Surrattsville, where Herold calls to Lloyd, "Bring out those things," showing that there had been communication between them and Mrs. Surratt after her return. Both the carbines being in readiness, according to Mary E. Surratt's directions, both were brought out. They took but one. Booth declined to carry the other, saying that his limb was broken. They then declared that they had murdered the President and the Secretary of State. They then make their way directly to the house of the prisoner Mudd, assured of safety and security. They arrived early in the morning before day, and no man knows at what hour they left. Herold rode towards Bryantown with Mudd about three o'clock that afternoon, in the vicinity of which place he parted with him, remaining in the swamp, and was afterwards seen returning the same afternoon in the direction of Mudd's house, about which time, a little before sundown, Mudd returned from Bryantown towards his home. This village at the time Mudd was in it was thronged with soldiers in pursuit of the murderers of the President, and although great care has been taken by the defense to deny that any one said in the presence of Dr. Mudd, either there or elsewhere on that day, who had committed this crime, yet it is in evidence by two witnesses, whose truthfulness no man questions, that upon Mudd's return to his own house that afternoon, he stated that Booth was the murderer of the President, and Boyle the murderer of Secretary Seward, but took care to make the further remark that Booth had brothers, and he did not know which of them had done the act. When did Dr. Mudd learn that Booth had brothers? And what is still more pertinent to this inquiry, from whom did he learn that either John Wilkes Booth or any of his brothers had murdered the President? It is clear that Booth remained in his house until some time in the afternoon of Saturday; that Herold left the house alone, as one of the witnesses states, being seen to pass the window; that he alone of these two assassins was in the company of Dr. Mudd on his way to Bryantown. It does not appear when Herold returned to Mudd's house. It is a confession of Dr. Mudd himself, proven by one of the witnesses, that Booth left his house on crutches and went in the direction of the swamp. How long he remained there, and what became of the horses which Booth and Herold rode to his house and which were put into his stable, are facts nowhere disclosed by the evidence. The owners testify that they have never seen the horses since. The accused give no explanation of the matter, and when Herold and Booth were captured they had not these horses in their possession. How comes it that, on Mudd's return from Bryantown, on the evening of Saturday, in his conversation with Mr. Hardy and Mr. Farrell, the witnesses before referred to, he gave the name of Booth as the murderer of the President, and that of Boyle as the murderer of Secretary Seward and his son, and carefully avoided intimating to either that Booth had come to his house early that day and had remained there until the afternoon; that he left him in his house and had furnished him a razor with which Booth attempted to disguise himself by shaving off his moustache? How comes it, also, that, upon being asked by those two witnesses whether the Booth who killed the President was the one who had been there last fall, he answered that he did not know whether it was that man or one of his brothers, but he understood he had some brothers, and added, that if it was the Booth who was there last fall, *he knew that one*, but concealed the fact that this man had been at his house on that day and was then at his house, and had attempted in his presence to disguise his person? He was sorry, very sorry, that the thing had occurred, but not so sorry as to be willing to give any evidence to these two neighbors, who were manifestly honest and upright men, that the murderer had been harbored in his house all day, and was probably at that moment, as his own subsequent confession shows, lying concealed in his house or near by, subject to his call. This is the man who undertakes to show by his own declaration, offered in evidence against my protest, of what he said afterwards, on Sunday afternoon, the 16th, to his kinsman, Dr. George D. Mudd, to whom he then stated that the assassination of the President was a most damnable act — a conclusion in which most men will agree with him, and to establish which his testimony was not needed. But it is to be remarked that this accused did not intimate that the man whom he knew the evening before was the murderer had found refuge in his house, had disguised his person, and sought concealment in the swamp upon the crutches which he had provided for him. Why did he conceal this fact from his kinsman? After the church services were over, however, in another conversation on their way home, he did tell Dr. George Mudd that two suspicious persons had been at his house, who had come there a little before daybreak on Saturday morning; that one of them had a broken leg, which he bandaged; that they got something to eat at his house; that they seemed to be laboring under more excitement than probably would result from the injury; that they said they came from Bryantown, and inquired the way to Parson Wilmer's; that while at his house one of them called for a razor and shaved himself. The witness says, "I do not remember whether he said that this party shaved off his whiskers or his moustache, but he altered somewhat, or probably materially, his features." Finally, the prisoner, Dr. Mudd, told this witness that he, in company with the younger of the two men, went down the road towards Bryantown in search of a vehicle to take the wounded man away from his house. How comes it that he concealed in this conversation the fact proved, that he went with Herold towards Bryantown and left Herold outside of the town? How comes it that in this second conversation, on Sunday, insisted upon here with such pertinacity as evidence for the defense, but which had never been called for by the prosecution, he concealed from his kinsman the fact which he had disclosed the day before to Hardy and Farrell, that it was Booth who assassinated the President, and the fact which is now disclosed by his other confessions given in evidence for the prosecution, that it was Booth whom he had sheltered, concealed in his house, and aided to his hiding place in the swamp? He volunteers as evidence his further statement, however, to this witness, that on Sunday evening he requested the witness to state to the military authorities that two suspicious persons had been at his house, and see if anything could be made of it. He did not tell the witness what became of Herold, and where he parted with him on the way to Bryantown. How comes it that when he was in Bryantown on the Saturday evening before, when he knew that Booth was then at his house, and that Booth was the murderer of the President, he did not himself state it to the military authorities then in that village, as he well knew? It is difficult to see what kindled his suspicions on Sunday, if none were in his mind on Saturday, when he was in possession of the fact that Booth had murdered the President and was then secreting and disguising himself in the prisoner's own house.

His conversation with Gardner on the same Sunday at the church is also introduced here to relieve him from the overwhelming evidences of his guilt. He communicates nothing to Gardner of the fact that Booth had been in his house; nothing of the fact that he knew the day before that Booth had murdered the President; nothing of the fact that Booth had disguised or attempted to disguise himself; nothing of the fact that he had gone with Booth's associate, Herold, in search of a vehicle, the more speedily to expedite their flight; nothing of the fact that Booth had found concealment in the woods and swamp near his house upon the crutches which he had furnished him. He contents himself with merely stating "that we ought to raise immediately a home guard to hunt up all suspicious persons passing through our section of country and arrest them, for there were two suspicious persons at my house yesterday morning."

It would have looked more like aiding justice and arresting felons if he had put in execution his project of a home guard on Saturday, and made it effective by the arrest of the man then in his house who had lodged with him last fall, with whom he had gone to purchase one of the very horses employed in this flight after the assassination, whom he had visited last winter in Washington, and to whom he had pointed out the very *route* by which he had escaped by way of his house, whom he had again visited on the 3d of last March, preparatory to the commission of this great crime, and who he knew, when he sheltered and concealed him in the woods on Saturday, was not merely a suspicious person, but was, in fact, the murderer and assassin of Abraham Lincoln. While I deem it my duty to say here, as I said before, when these declarations uttered by the accused on Sunday, the 16th, to Gardner and George D. Mudd, were attempted to be offered on the part of the accused, that they are in no sense evidence, and by the law were wholly inadmissible, yet I state it as my conviction that, being upon the record upon motion of the accused himself, so far as these declarations to Gardner and George D. Mudd go, they are additional indications of the guilt of the accused in this, that they are manifestly suppressions of the truth and suggestions of falsehood and deception; they are but the utterances and confessions of guilt.

To Lieutenant Lovett, Joshua Lloyd, and Simon Gavican, who, in pursuit of the murderer, visited his house on the 18th of April, the Tuesday after the murder, he denied positively, upon inquiry, that two men had passed his house, or had come to his house on the morning after the assassination. Two of these witnesses swear positively to his having made the denial, and the other says he hesitated to answer the question he put to him; all of them agree that he afterwards admitted that two men had been there, one of whom had a broken limb, which he had set; and when asked by this witness who that man was, he said he did not know — that the man was a stranger to him, and that the two had been there but a short time. Lloyd asked him if he had ever seen any of the parties — Booth, Herold, and Surratt, — and he said he had never seen them; while it is positively proved that he was acquainted with John H. Surratt, who had been in his house; that he knew Booth, and had introduced Booth to Surratt last winter. Afterwards, on Friday, the 21st, he admitted to Lloyd that he had been introduced to Booth last fall, and that this man who came to his house on Saturday, the 15th, remained there from about four o'clock in the morning until about four in the afternoon; that one of them left his house on horseback, and the other walking. In the first conversation he denied ever having seen these men.

Colonel Wells also testifies that, in his conversation with Dr. Mudd on Friday the 21st, the prisoner said that he had gone to Bryantown, or near Bryantown, to see some friends on Saturday, and that as he came back to his own house he saw the person he afterwards supposed to be Herold passing to the left of his house toward the barn, but that he did not see the other person at all after he left him in his own house about one o'clock. If this statement be true, how did Dr. Mudd see the same person leave his house on crutches? He further stated to this witness that he returned to his own house about four o'clock in the afternoon; that he did not know this wounded man; said he could not recognize him from the photograph which is of record here, but admitted that he had met Booth some time in November, when he had some conversation with him *about lands* and horses; that Booth had remained with him that night in November, and on the next day had purchased a horse. He said he had not again seen Booth from the time of the introduction in November up to his arrival at his house on the Saturday morning after the assassination. Is not this a confession that he did see John Wilkes Booth on that morning at his house and knew it was Booth? If he did not know him, how came he to make this statement to the witness: that " he had not seen Booth *after* November *prior* to his arrival there on the Saturday morning "?

He had said before to the same witness he did not know the wounded man. He said further to Colonel Wells, that when he went upstairs after their arrival he noticed that the person he *supposed* to be Booth had shaved off his moustache. Is it not inferable from this declaration that he *then* supposed him to be Booth? Yet he declared the same afternoon, and while Booth was in his own house, that Booth was the murderer of the President. One of the most remarkable statements made to this witness by the prisoner was that he heard for the first time on Sunday morning, or late in the evening of Saturday, that the President had been murdered! From whom did he hear it? The witness (Colonel Wells) volunteers his "impression" that Dr. Mudd had said he had heard it after the persons had left his house. If the "impression" of the witness thus volunteered is to be taken as evidence — and the counsel for the accused, judging from their manner, seem to think it ought to be — let this question be answered: how could Dr. Mudd have made that impression upon anybody truthfully, when it is proved by Farrell and Hardy that on his return from Bryantown, on Saturday afternoon, he not only stated that the President, Mr. Seward, and his son had been assassinated, but that Boyle had assassinated Mr. Seward, and Booth had assassinated the President? Add to this the fact that he said to this witness that he left his own house at one o'clock and when he returned the men were gone, yet it is in evidence, by his own declarations, that Booth left his house at four o'clock on crutches, and he must have been there to have seen it or he could not have known the fact.

Mr. Williams testifies that he was at Mudd's house on Tuesday, the 18th of April, when he said that strangers had *not* been that way, and also declared that he heard, *for the first time*, of the assassination of the President on Sunday morning at church.

Afterwards, on Friday, the 21st, Mr. Williams asked him concerning the men who had been at his house, one of whom had a broken limb, and he confessed they had been there. Upon being asked if they were Booth and Herold, he said they were not — *that he knew Booth.* I think it is fair to conclude that he did know Booth when we consider the testimony of Wiechmann, of Norton, of Evans, and all the testimony just referred to, wherein he declares, himself, that he not only knew him, but that he had lodged with him, and that he had himself gone with him when he purchased his horse from Gardner last fall, for the very purpose of aiding the flight of himself or some of his confederates.

All these circumstances taken together, which, as we have seen upon high authority, are stronger as evidences of guilt than even direct testimony, leave no further room for argument and no rational doubt that Doctor Samuel A. Mudd was as certainly in this conspiracy as were Booth and Herold, whom he sheltered and entertained; receiving them under cover of darkness on the morning after the assassination, concealing them throughout that day from the hand of offended justice, and aiding them, by every endeavor, to pursue their way successfully to their co-conspirator, Arnold, at Fortress Monroe, and in which direction they fled until overtaken and Booth was slain.

We next find Herold and his confederate Booth, after their departure from the house of Mudd, across the Potomac in the neighborhood of Port Conway, on Monday, the 24th of of April, conveyed in a wagon. There Herold, in order to obtain the aid of Captain Jett, Ruggles, and Bainbridge, of the confederate army, said to Jett, "We are the assassinators of the President"; that this was his brother with him, who, with himself, belonged to A. P. Hill's corps; that his brother had been wounded at Petersburg; that their names were Boyd. He requested Jett and his rebel companions to take them out of the lines. After this Booth joined these parties, was placed on Ruggles's horse, and crossed the Rappahannock River. They then proceeded to the house of Garrett, in the neighborhood of Port Royal, and nearly midway between Washington City and Fortress Monroe, where they were to have joined Arnold. Before these rebel guides and guards parted with them, Herold confessed they were traveling under assumed names — that his own name was Herold, and that the name of the wounded man was John Wilkes Booth, "who had killed the President." The rebels left Booth at Garrett's, where Herold revisited him from time to time, until they were captured. At two o'clock on Wednesday morning, the 26th, a party of United States officers and soldiers surrounded Garrett's barn where Booth and Herold lay concealed, and demanded their surrender. Booth cursed Herold, calling him a coward, and bade him go, when Herold came out and surrendered himself, was taken into custody, and is now brought into court. The barn was then set on fire, when Booth sprang to his feet, amid the flames that were kindling about him, carbine in hand, and approached the door, seeking, by the flashing light of the fire, to find some new victim for his murderous hand, when he was shot, as he deserved to be, by Sergeant Corbett, in order to save his comrades from wounds or death by the hands of this desperate assassin. Upon his person was found the following bill of exchange: —

"No. 1492. The Ontario Bank, Montreal Branch. Exchange for £61 12s. 10d. Montreal, 27th October, 1864. Sixty days after sight of this first of exchange, second and third of the same tenor and date, pay to the order of J. Wilkes Booth £61 12s. 10d. sterling, value received, and charge to the account of this office. H. Stanus, manager. To Messrs. Glynn, Mills & Co., London.

Thus fell, by the hands of one of the defenders of the republic, this hired assassin, who, for a price, murdered Abraham Lincoln, bearing upon his person, as this bill of exchange testifies, additional evidence of the fact that he had undertaken, in aid of the rebellion, this work of assassination by the hands of himself and his confederates, for such sum as the accredited agents of Jefferson Davis might pay him or them, out of the funds of the Confederacy, which, as is in evidence, they had in "any amount" in Canada for the purpose of rewarding conspirators, spies, poisoners, and assassins, who might take service under their false commissions, and do the work of the incendiary and the murderer upon the lawful representatives of the American people, to whom had been entrusted the care of the republic, the maintenance of the Constitution, and the execution of the laws.

The court will remember that it is in the testimony of Merritt and Montgomery and Conover that Thompson and Sanders and Clay and Cleary made their boasts that they had money in Canada for this very purpose. Nor is it to be overlooked or forgotten that the officers of the Ontario Bank at Montreal testify that during the current year of this conspiracy and assassination Jacob Thompson had on deposit in that bank the sum of six hundred and forty-nine thousand dollars, and that these deposits to the credit of Jacob Thompson accrued from the negotiation of bills of exchange drawn by the Secretary of the Treasury of the so-called Confederate States on Frazier, Trenholm, & Co., of Liverpool, who were known to be the financial agents of the Confederate States. With an undrawn deposit in this bank of four hundred and fifty-five dollars, which has remained to his credit since October last, and with an unpaid bill of exchange drawn by the same bank upon London, in his possession and found upon his person, Booth ends his guilty career in this work of conspiracy and blood in April, 1865, as he began it in October, 1864, in combination with Jefferson Davis, Jacob Thompson, George N. Sanders, Clement C. Clay, William C. Cleary, Beverly Tucker, and other co-conspirators, making use of the money of the rebel confederation to aid in the execution and in the flight, bearing at the moment of his death upon his person their money, part of the price which they paid for his great crime, to aid him in its consummation and secure him afterwards from arrest and the just penalty which by the law of God and the law of man is denounced against treasonable conspiracy and murder.

By all the testimony in the case it is, in my judgment, made as clear as any transaction can be shown by human testimony, that John Wilkes Booth and John H. Surratt and the several accused, David E. Herold, George A. Atzerodt, Lewis Payne, Michael O'Laughlin, Edward Spangler, Samuel Arnold, Mary E. Surratt, and Samuel A. Mudd, did, with intent to aid the existing rebellion and to subvert the Constitution and laws of the United States, in the month of October last and thereafter, combine, confederate, and conspire with Jefferson Davis, George N. Sanders, Beverly Tucker, Jacob Thompson, William C. Cleary, Clement C. Clay, George Harper, George Young, and others unknown, to kill and murder, within the military department of Washington, and within the intrenched fortifications and military lines thereof, Abraham Lincoln, then President of the United States and Commander-in-Chief of the army and navy thereof; Andrew Johnson, Vice-President of the United States; William H. Seward, Secretary of State; and Ulysses S. Grant, lieutenant general in command of the armies of the United States; and that Jefferson Davis, the chief of this rebellion, was the instigator and procurer, through his accredited agents in Canada, of this treasonable conspiracy.

It is also submitted to the court, that it is clearly established by the testimony that John Wilkes Booth, in pursuance of this conspiracy, so entered into by him and the accused, did, on the night of the 14th of April, 1865, within the military department of Washington, and the intrenched fortifications and military lines thereof, and with the intent laid, inflict a mortal wound upon Abraham Lincoln, then President and Commander-in-Chief of the army and navy of the United States, whereof he died; that in pursuance of the same conspiracy and within the said department and intrenched lines, Lewis Payne assaulted, with intent to kill and murder, William H. Seward, then Secretary of State of the United States; that George A. Atzerodt, in pursuance of the same conspiracy, and within the said department, laid in wait, with intent to kill and murder Andrew Johnson, then Vice-President of the United States; that Michael O'Laughlin, within said department, and in pursuance of said conspiracy, laid in wait to kill and murder Ulysses S. Grant, then in command of the armies of the United States; and that Mary E. Surratt, David E. Herold, Samuel Arnold, Samuel A. Mudd, and Edward Spangler did encourage, aid, and abet the commission of said several acts in the prosecution of said conspiracy.

If this treasonable conspiracy has not been wholly executed; if the several executive officers of the United States and the commander of its armies, to kill and murder whom the said several accused thus confederated and conspired, have not each and all fallen by the hands of these conspirators, thereby leaving the people of the United States without a President or Vice-President; without a Secretary of State, who alone is clothed with authority by the law to call an election to fill the vacancy, should any arise, in the offices of President and Vice-President; and without a lawful commander of the armies of the republic, it is only because the conspirators were deterred by the vigilance and fidelity of the executive officers, whose lives were mercifully protected on that night of murder by the care of the Infinite Being who has thus far saved the republic and crowned its arms with victory.

If this conspiracy was thus entered into by the accused; if John Wilkes Booth did kill and murder Abraham Lincoln in pursuance thereof; if Lewis Payne did, in pursuance of said conspiracy, assault with intent to kill and murder William H. Seward, as stated, and if the several parties accused did commit the several acts alleged against them in the prosecution of said conspiracy, then it is the law that all the parties to that conspiracy, whether present at the time of its execution or not, whether on trial before this court or not, are alike guilty of the several acts done by each in the execution of the common design. What these conspirators did in the execution of this conspiracy by the hand of one of their co-conspirators they did themselves; his act, done in the prosecution of the common design, was the act of all the parties to the treasonable combination, because done in execution and furtherance of their guilty and treasonable agreement.

As we have seen, this is the rule, whether all the conspirators are indicted or not; whether they are all on trial or not. "It is not material what the nature of the indictment is, provided the offense involve a conspiracy. Upon indictment for murder, for instance, if it appear that others, together with the prisoner, conspired to perpetrate the crime, the act of one done in pursuance of that intention would be evidence against the rest." (1 Whar. 706.) To the same effect are the words of Chief Justice Marshall, before cited, that whoever leagued in a general conspiracy, performed any part, however MINUTE, or however REMOTE, from the scene of *action*, are guilty as principals. In this treasonable conspiracy to aid the existing armed rebellion by murdering the executive officers of the United States and the commander of its armies, all the parties to it must be held as principals, and the act of one in the prosecution of the common design the act of all.

I leave the decision of this dread issue with the court, to which alone it belongs. It is for you to say, upon your oaths, whether the accused are guilty.

I am not conscious that in this argument I have made any erroneous statement of the evidence, or drawn any erroneous conclusions; yet I pray the court, out of tender regard and jealous care for the rights of the accused, to see that no error of mine, if any there be, shall work them harm. The past services of the members of this honorable court give assurance that, without fear, favor, or affection, they will discharge with fidelity the duty enjoined upon them by their oaths. Whatever else may befall, I trust in God that in this, as in every other American court, the rights of the whole people will be respected, and that the republic in this, its supreme hour of trial, will be true to itself and just to all — ready to protect the rights of the humblest, to redress every wrong, to avenge every crime, to vindicate the majesty of law, and to maintain inviolate the Constitution, whether assailed secretly or openly, by hosts armed with gold, or armed with steel.

THE CONTROVERSY BETWEEN PRESIDENT JOHNSON AND JUDGE HOLT.

A Paper read by GEN. HENRY L. BURNETT, *late U. S. V., at a Meeting of the Commandery, State of New York, Military Order, Loyal Legion, April 3, 1889.*

PERHAPS no incident connected with the trial of the assassins of President Lincoln created more general interest — was so much discussed and commented upon by the public press, or aroused deeper feeling of antagonism and bitterness between two public men, than the charge by President Johnson that the Judge Advocate General, Judge Holt, had withheld or suppressed the recommendation to mercy of Mrs. Surratt, signed by five members of the commission, when he represented to him, the President, the record for his official action. While this charge had circulation and was asserted in the press during the time Mr. Johnson was occupying the presidential office, Mr. Johnson never openly made the charge until after his term had expired, some time in 1873.

No graver charge could be made against a public officer than this against Judge Holt, and, if true, no more cruel and treacherous betrayal of a public trust was ever committed by a man in high official position. It would be murderous in intent and effect. This charge rested, so far as human testimony went, upon the solemn assertion alone of President Johnson, and, if untrue, was one of the most cruel wrongs ever perpetrated by one man against another. I propose to give a brief abstract of the testimony produced by Judge Holt to disprove this charge, and also a statement of my connection with, and what little personal knowledge I had of the matter.

In a communication addressed to the Washington *Chronicle*, dated August 25, 1873, Judge Holt gives a copy of a letter addressed by him to the Secretary of War, on the 14th of that month, in which he sets forth evidence tending to disprove the charge originating with Andrew Johnson, of his suppression of the petition, signed by five of the nine members of the commission, recommending, in consideration of her age and sex, a commutation of the death sentence of Mary E. Surratt to imprisonment for life in the penitentiary. The petition read as follows: "To the President: The undersigned, members of the military commission appointed to try the persons charged with the murder of Abraham Lincoln, etc., respectfully represent that the commission have been constrained to find Mary E. Surratt guilty, upon the testimony, of the assassination of Abraham Lincoln, late President of the United States, and to pronounce upon her, as required by law, the sentence of death; but in consideration of her age and sex, the undersigned pray your Excellency, if it is consistent with your sense of duty, to commute her sentence to imprisonment for life in the penitentiary."

In a letter dated February 11, 1873, addressed to Hon. John A. Bingham, one of the special Judge Advocates during the trial, Judge Holt states: "In the discharge of my duty when presenting that record to President Johnson, I drew his attention to that recommendation, and he read it in my presence, and before approving the proceedings and sentence. He and I were together alone when this duty on his part and on mine was performed. . . . The President and myself having, as already stated, been alone at the time, I have not been able to obtain any positive proof on the point, although I have been able to collect circumstantial evidence enough to satisfy any unbiased mind that the recommendation was seen and considered by the President, when he examined and approved the proceeding and sentence of the court. Still, in a matter so deeply affecting my reputation and official honor, I am naturally desirous of having the testimony in my possession strengthened as far as practicable, and hence it is that I trouble you with this note. While I know that the question of extending to Mrs. Surratt the clemency sought by the petition was considered by the President at the time mentioned, I have, in view of its gravity, been always satisfied that it must have been considered by the Cabinet also; but from the confidential character of Cabinet deliberations I have thus far been denied access to this source of information." He then proceeds to inquire whether or not he (Judge Bingham) had any conversation with Secretary Seward or Mr. Stanton in reference to this petition, and if so to please give him as nearly as he (Judge Bingham) could, all that Secretary Seward or Mr. Stanton had said upon the subject.

Judge Bingham replied under date of February 17, 1873, and among other things said:—

"Before the President had acted upon the case, I deemed it my duty to call the attention of Secretary Stanton to the petition for the commutation of sentence upon Mrs. Surratt, and did call his attention to it, before the final decision of the President. After the execution, the statement which you refer to was made that President Johnson had not seen the petition for the commutation of the death sentence upon Mrs. Surratt. I afterwards called at your office, and, without notice to you of my purpose, asked for the record of the case of the assassins; it was opened and shown me, and there was then attached to it the petition, copied and signed as hereinbefore stated. Soon thereafter I called upon Secretaries Stanton and Seward and asked if this petition had been presented to the President before the death sentence was by him approved, and was answered by each of those gentlemen that the petition was presented to the President, and was duly considered by him and his advisers before the death sentence upon Mrs. Surratt was approved, and that the President and Cabinet, upon such consideration, were a unit in denying the prayer of the petition; Mr. Stanton and Mr. Seward stating that they were present.

"Having ascertained the fact as stated, I then desired to make the same public, and so expressed myself to Mr. Stanton, who advised me not to do so, but to rely upon the final judgement of the people."

In replying to this letter, Judge Holt very justly remarks: "It would have been very fortunate for me indeed could I have had this testimony in my possession years ago. Mr. Stanton's advice to you was, under all the circumstances of the case, most extraordinary.

"The asking you 'to rely upon the final judgment of the people,' and at the same time withholding from them the proof on which the judgment — to be just — must be formed, was a sad, sad mockery."

The next is a letter from ex-Attorney General Speed, dated March 30, 1873, in which he says: "After the finding of the military commission that tried the assassins of Mr. Lincoln and before their execution, I saw the record of the case in the President's office, and attached to it was a paper, signed by some of the members of the commission, recommending that the sentence against Mrs. Surratt be commuted to imprisonment for life; and according to my memory, the recommendation was made because of her sex.

"I do not feel at liberty to speak of what was said at Cabinet meetings. In this I know I differ from other gentlemen, but feel constrained to follow my own sense of propriety."

So that it is most clear from this statement of Attorney General Speed, unless he, without interest or motive, stated a most deliberate falsehood, that Judge Holt did *not* "withhold" or "suppress" the recommendation to mercy, but carried it with the record and "*attached to it,*" as Mr. Speed says, and delivered it in the President's office. Certainly every intelligent mind will concede that this testimony of Mr. Speed utterly disposes of the charge of Andrew Johnson that Judge Holt "suppressed" or "withheld" this recommendation to mercy. If Mr. Johnson did not see it or read it when in his office, that was his neglect, his failure to perform a solemn official duty. But on this question of his having *read* and *considered* it, how stands the evidence? Judge Holt states that he drew his attention to it, and that Mr. Johnson read it in his presence. Judge Bingham says both Mr. Stanton and Mr. Seward stated to him that this petition had been presented to the President and was duly considered by him and his advisers before the death sentence upon Mrs. Surratt was approved. Under date of May 27, 1873, James Harlan, a former member of Mr. Johnson's Cabinet, addressed a letter to Judge Holt, in which he said: "After the sentence and before the execution of Mrs. Surratt, I remember distinctly the discussion of the question of the commutation of the sentence of death pronounced on her by the Court to imprisonment for life had by members of the Cabinet in presence of President Johnson. I can not state positively whether this occurred at a regular or a called meeting, or whether it was at an accidental meeting of several members, each calling on the President in relation to the business of his own department. The impression on my mind is, that the only discussion of the subject by members of the Cabinet, which I ever heard, occurred in the last-named mode, there being not more than three or four members present — Mr. Seward, Mr. Stanton, and myself, and probably Attorney General Speed and others — but I distinctly remember only the first two. When I entered the room, one of these was addressing the President in an earnest conversation on the question whether the sentence ought to be modified on account of the sex of the condemned. I can recite the precise thought, if not the very words, used by this eminent statesman, as they were impressed on my mind with great force at the time, and I have often thought of them since, viz.: 'Surely not, Mr. President, for if the death penalty should be commuted in so grave a case as the assassination of the head of a great nation, on account of the sex of the criminal, it would amount to an invitation to assassins hereafter to employ women as their instruments, under the belief that if arrested and condemned, they would be punished less severely than men. An act of executive clemency on such a plea would be disapproved by the government of every civilized nation on earth.'"

Judge Harlan adds that he made inquiry at the time, and "was told that the whole case had been carefully examined by the Attorney General and the Secretary of War; and that the only question raised was whether the punishment shall be reduced on account of the sex of the party condemned. I do not remember that any differences of opinion were expressed on that point."

This is indirect but very conclusive evidence that the petition was attached to the record submitted to the President and examined by the Attorney General and Secretary of War; and that the subject of the mitigation of Mrs. Surratt's sentence was considered by the President and these members of his Cabinet, because in no part of the record was there the slightest allusion to the question of clemency to Mrs. Surratt, or to any of the other convicted persons, except in the petition signed by the five members of the Court.

The next is a letter from the Rev. J. George Butler, pastor of St. Paul's Church, Washington. Under date of December 5, 1868, in describing an interview he had with President Johnson, he says: "The interview occurred during a social call upon the family of the President in the evening, a few hours after the execution.

"I had been summoned by the Government, I then being a hospital chaplain, to attend upon Atzerodt, and was present at the execution.

"Concerning Mrs. Surratt, the remarks of the President, by reason of their point and force, impressed themselves upon my memory. He said, in substance, that very strong appeals had been made for the exercise of executive clemency; that he had been importuned; that telegrams and threats had been used; but he could not be moved, for, in his own significant language, Mrs. Surratt *'kept the nest that hatched the eggs.'*

"The President further stated that no plea had been urged in her behalf, save the fact that she was a *woman*, and his interposition upon that ground would license female crime."

This harmonizes entirely with the " thought " which Secretary Harlan heard uttered with so much force by a member of the Cabinet in Mr. Johnson's presence— either Mr. Stanton or Mr. Seward— and from his language, " this eminent statesman, " I take it to have been Mr. Seward.

The Rev. Mr. Butler adds: "I feel it due to a Christian soldier and personal friend (General Eakin) to make this statement, showing clearly that at the time of the execution the President's judgment wholly accorded with the judgment of the military commission; and that no appeals could then change his purpose to make ' treason odious.' "

General R. D. Mussey, under date of August 19, 1873, writes to Judge Holt:—

" In a few days after the assassination I was detailed for duty with Mr. Johnson and acted as one of his secretaries, and was an inmate of his household until some time in the fall of 1865.

" About the time the military court that tried Mrs. Surratt concluded its labors, I was, if I remember aright, for some days the only person acting as private secretary at the White House, my associate being absent on a visit.

" On the Wednesday previous to the execution (which was on Friday, July 7, 1865), as I was sitting at my desk in the morning, Mr. Johnson told me that he was going to look over the findings of the Court with Judge Holt, and should be busy and could see no one. I replied, ' Very well, sir, I will see that you not interrupted, ' or something to that effect, and continued my work. I think it was two or three hours after that that Mr. Johnson came out of the room where he had been with you, and said that the papers had been looked over and a decision reached. I asked what it was. He told me, approval of the findings and sentence of the Court; and he then gave me the sentences as near as he remembered them, and said that he had ordered the sentence where it was death to be carried into execution on the Friday following. I remember looking up from my desk with some surprise at the brevity of this interval, and asking him whether the time wasn't rather short. He admitted that it was, but said that they had had ever since the trial began for 'preparation'; and either then or later on in the day spoke of his design in making the time short, so that there might be less opportunity for criticism, remonstrance, etc. I do not pretend to use his precise language as to this, but the purport of it was that 'it was a disagreeable duty, and there would be endeavors to get him not to perform it, and he wished to avoid them as much as possible.' . . . I am very confident, though not absolutely assured, that it was at this interview Mr. Johnson told me that the Court had recommended Mrs. Surratt to mercy on the ground of her sex (and age, I believe). But I am certain he did so inform me about that time; and that he said he thought the grounds urged insufficient, and that he had refused to interfere; that if she was guilty at all, her sex did not make her any the less guilty; that he, about the time of her execution, justified it; that he told me there had not been women enough hanged in this war."

This evidence would seem to establish most conclusively that the " petition " was not only attached to the record, and delivered by Judge Holt at the President's office in the Executive Mansion, but that he read the same and afterward considered and discussed it with at least three members of his Cabinet; and intelligent charity can reach no further than to say that President Johnson, when he charged Judge Holt with having withheld this recommendation to mercy when he delivered the record of the trial at the President's Mansion, made a cruel and untruthful charge; and that when he asserted in 1873 that he had not seen, read, or heard of this recommendation to mercy, at the time he approved the sentences on the 5th day of July, 1865, had forgotten the facts — that his " forgettery " was much better than his memory.

One of the main points in President Johnson's response to this evidence was that in the published volume of the record of the trial of the assassins, prepared by Mr. Ben. Pittmann, of Cincinnati, under my official supervision, this recommendation to mercy does not appear. There is no force in this. The petition or recommendation to mercy constituted properly no part of the official record of the trial. Mr. Pittmann, who had his desk and place in my office at the War Department, was one of the official stenographers of the court, and had special charge and custody of the record from day to day. The other reporters sent in to him their portions of the testimony as they were written up, and thereafter he was responsible for them. My recollection is also that as the testimony was written up a press copy was made of it, which he (Mr. Pittmann) took with him to Cincinnati, and used, after he had received permission from the War Department to publish.

The commission met with closed doors at 10 A. M. on the 29th of June to consider its findings, and continued and concluded its labors with closed doors on the 30th. From these meetings all stenographic reporters were excluded. The findings and sentences, when finally made and recorded, were handed to me to be attached to the record, or to go with the record to the Judge Advocate General's office, as was then the course of procedure. By the oath administered, all the members of the commission, as well as the Judge Advocates, were bound not to reveal those findings and sentences. I therefore retained them in my possession, instead of passing them on to the stenographers. When the recommendation to mercy was drawn, and signed by five members of the commission, that was also handed to me to accompany the findings.

Mr. Pittmann never saw, I presume, either the original findings or the recommendation to mercy, and the first knowledge he had of the former doubtless was after they were promulgated by the Adjutant General on the 5th day of July. This is evidenced by the fact that the Adjutant General, in promulgating the proceedings, took Mrs. Surratt's name from the position it occupies in the records, and placed it next that of Payne, evidently for the purpose of grouping together the four persons condemned to death. Mr. Pittmann gives the findings and sentence in the order promulgated by the Adjutant General — that is to say, he places the findings and sentence in Mrs. Surratt's case next after that of Lewis Payne; while the Court, in making up its findings, followed the order named in the charge and specifications, where Mrs. Surratt's name follows that of Samuel Arnold.

When I reached my office at the War Department on the 30th — possibly on the morning of the 1st of July — I attached the petition or recommendation to mercy of Mrs. Surratt to the findings and sentence, and at the end of them, and then directed some one — probably Mr. Pittmann — to carry the record of the evidence to the Judge Advocate-General's office. I carried the findings and sentences and the petition or recommendation and delivered them to the Judge Advocate General in person or to the clerk in charge of court-martial records. Before leaving the War Department I may have attached these findings and sentences and petition to the last few days of testimony, and carried that to the Judge Advocate General's office. I never saw the record again until many years after — I think in 1873 or 1874.

I left Washington several days before, and was not there on the day of the execution. My recollection is, that I left there either on the evening of the 5th or on the morning of the 6th of July. On the 5th day of July, when Judge Holt had his conference with President Johnson over the record and proceedings of the military commission, when the President considered and passed upon the findings and sentences of the accused persons, after that interview Judge Holt came directly to Mr. Stanton's office in the War Department. I happened to be with Mr. Stanton as Judge Holt came in. After greetings, the latter remarked, "I have just come from a conference with the President over the proceedings of the military commission." "Well," said Mr. Stanton, "what has he done?" "He has approved the findings and sentence of the Court," replied Judge Holt. "What did he say about the recommendation to mercy of Mrs. Surratt?" next inquired Mr. Stanton. "He said," answered Judge Holt, "that she must be punished with the rest; that no reasons were given for his interposition by those asking for clemency, in her case, except age and sex. He said her sex furnished no good ground for his interfering; that women and men should learn that if women committed crimes they would be punished; that if they entered into conspiracies to assassinate, they must suffer the penalty; that were this not so, hereafter conspirators and assassins would use women as their instruments; it would be mercy to womankind to let Mrs. Surratt suffer the penalty of her crime." After some futher conversation, and after making known to Mr. Stanton that the President had fixed Friday, the 7th, as the day of execution, Judge Holt left. In giving the above conversation I cannot say that I have given the exact words; but the substance of what Judge Holt said I know I have given. It is indelibly impressed upon my memory. This conversation, while it does not constitute legal evidence of the fact of President Johnson's consideration of the recommendation to mercy, has always been a circumstance strong and convincing to my mind that President Johnson's charge was totally false. It showed that Mr. Stanton had knowledge of the recommendation — probably had examined the record in the four or five days which had intervened since the trial. As Secretary of War he was at that time daily — almost hourly — in consultation with the President over the disbandment of the military forces; the occupation by the army of the rebel States; the powers and duties of officers there, and the innumerable questions semi-military in character arising out of the chaotic political and social condition of the rebel States; and they could hardly have come together at that time without the question of the conviction and execution of the assassins coming up. The circumstances of the assassination, the plot or conspiracy to assassinate President Lincoln and his Cabinet, the Vice President himself, and General Grant; who were concerned in it; the evidence submitted to the Court, the weight given to it by the Court, and the conclusion reached by the Court, were matters in which the President and the Secretary of War could not fail to take, and, as is well known, did take the deepest possible interest. It is past human credulity to believe that they would thus come together during the time intervening between the conclusion of the trial on the 30th day of June and the execution of the sentences on the 7th of July, and the result of the trial, together with the recommendation to mercy, not be discussed between them. It is inconceivable to me that Judge Holt, even if he were so malicious and murderous in purpose, could be so reckless and foolish in execution of such purpose as to withhold from and try to conceal from President Johnson this recommendation to mercy, when the fact of its existence was known to Mr. Stanton, and was so certain to be made known to the President by him, and its contents discussed between them.

The historian in passing judgment upon this event, and in weighing evidence as to the truth or falsity of this charge made by President Johnson, will take into consideration the mental characteristics and moral fibre of the two men, and what adequate motive there was actuating one occupying the exalted position of President Johnson to make the charge, or of Judge Holt to commit so wicked and cruel a wrong.

Andrew Johnson's mental make-up is well known to the officers of the old Union army, and to the American people. His life, his acts, and his speeches are still remembered, and the public judgment formed and registered. I do not propose here to-night to take your time in going into a statement or discussion of this subject. It is sufficient to say that he was endowed by nature with more than ordinary intellectual abilities, and that he had risen from the lowest walks of life by the vigor of his own will, energy, and mental power, through many intermediate places of honor and trust, to the second place in the gift of the American people — the Vice-Presidency of the United States. He was a man of controlling prejudices and strong personality. He was ambitious, bold, hot-tempered, obstinate, and in the achievement of the ends and aims he sought — right ends and aims he may have thought them — he was unscrupulous in the means he used. This is well illustrated in the instance given by General Sheridan in his memoirs of President Johnson's treatment of him while he was in command of New Orleans in 1866.

You will recall the intense feeling aroused throughout the country by the wanton and bloody massacre of the convention assembled at New Orleans, on the 30th of July, that year, to remodel the constitution of that State. General Sheridan had been absent several days in Texas, and was returning, when the riot occurred. He reached New Orleans August 1st, made an investigation, and on the same day sent the following telegraphic report to General Grant: —

"You are doubtless aware of the serious riot which occurred in this city on the 30th. A political body styling themselves the 'Convention of 1864,' met on the 30th for, as it alleged, the purpose of remodeling the present constitution of the State. The leaders were political agitators and revolutionary men, and the action of the convention was liable to produce breaches of the public peace. I had made up my mind to arrest the head men if the proceedings of the convention were calculated to disturb the tranquility of the department, but I had no cause for action until they committed some overt act.

In the meantime official duty called me to Texas, and the mayor of the city, during my absence, suppressed the convention by the use of the police force, and in so doing attacked the members of the convention and a party of two hundred negroes with fire-arms, clubs, and knives, in a manner so unnecessary and atrocious as to compel me to say that it was murder. About forty whites and blacks were thus killed, and about one hundred and sixty wounded. Everything is now quiet, but I deem it best to maintain a military supremacy in the city for a few days, until the affair is fully investigated. I believe the sentiment of the general community is great regret at this unnecessary cruelty, and that the police could have made any arrest they saw fit without sacrificing lives. "P. H. SHERIDAN,
"*Major General commanding.*"

General Sheridan adds: "On receiving the telegram, General Grant immediately submitted it to the President. Much clamor being made at the North for the publication of the despatch, President Johnson pretended to give it to the newspapers. It appeared in the issues of August 4th, but with this paragraph omitted, viz.: —

"'I had made up my mind to arrest the head men, if the proceedings were calculated to disturb the tranquilty of the department, but I had no cause for action until they committed some overt act. In the meantime official duty called me to Texas, and the mayor of the city, during my absence, suppressed the convention by the use of the police force, and in so doing attacked the members of the convention and a party of two hundred negroes with fire-arms, clubs, and knives, in a manner so unnecessary and atrocious as to compel me to say it was murder.'"

General Sheridan adds: "Against this garbling of my report, done by the President's own order, I strongly demurred, and this emphatic protest marks the beginning of Mr. Johnson's well-known personal hostility toward me."

It will be observed that the omission of this portion of the despatch — this "garbling," done by President Johnson's own order — changes its whole tenor and meaning; made General Sheridan say exactly contrary to what he did in fact say. Omitting the part struck out, and connecting the two sentences that come together, the President made the despatch read: "The leaders were political agitators and revolutionary men, and the action of the convention was liable to produce breaches of the public peace. About forty whites and blacks were *thus* killed, and about one hundred and sixty wounded."

Observe — this makes General Sheridan say that the action of the convention was liable to produce breaches of the public peace, and thus, — in this wise, — about forty whites and blacks were killed and about one hundred and sixty wounded. General Sheridan said nothing of the kind — nothing in the whole despatch had any such implication or meaning. What he did say was that the mayor of the city "suppressed the convention by the use of the police force, and in so doing attacked the members of the convention and a party of two hundred negroes with fire-arms, clubs, and knives, in a manner so unnecessary and atrocious as to compel me to say that it was murder"; and "thus" by this means, by this mayor and his police, about forty whites and blacks were killed and about one hundred and sixty wounded.

Is it too much to say that a man who could do this wrong to General Sheridan, — could mutilate and corrupt a despatch so as to cause him to make a false report about a people over whom he was placed in government; to cause him to state falsely the facts and circumstances about an event in which forty persons had lost their lives, and one hundred and sixty had been grievously wounded, — would hesitate to state a falsehood about Judge Holt? Is it too much to say that a man who could do this, and then try to mislead and deceive the people of the United States as to this tragic event, about which they were clamoring to know the truth, perpetrating a lie upon them by mutilating and corrupting a despatch and promulgating it as the true one, would hesitate to deceive the people about the fact as to whether he did or did not see the recommendation to mercy of Mrs. Surratt? Is it not fair to say that he was of such mental structure and moral fibre as to do this wrong?

And now the motive: —

It is known of all men that Andrew Johnson had only fairly settled himself in the presidential chair of the great Lincoln, before he began to dream, to scheme, and to intrigue for an election by the people to that office.

The presidential bee was buzzing under the accidental presidential hat. The Southern leaders, clever diplomats and long-headed politicians as they are, soon took the measure of the man, and began to consider how best they could use him, and his ambition for their own purposes. It was noticed that Andrew Johnson had not been many months in the White House before there was a decided change in the style and type of visitors passing in and out under the great white portico. The men of the North, — the old "Union Republican group" of the House and Senate that were daily visitors there in the days of Lincoln, began to find the atmosphere of the White House less kind and congenial; there was a lack of warmth in the welcome, and a constraint in talk and exchange of ideas, progressing gradually to actual antagonism over the questions of amnesty, reconstruction, and constitutional guarantees to the freedmen. Then the Northern men dropped away; seemed not to go there any more. Men from the South who but lately had borne arms against the government, and who had not yet taken the oath of allegiance, were found plentiful about the White House, and apparently basking in the sunshine of presidential favor, as in the rays of a southern sun. It became the reign of the unreconstructed and unreconciled. Somebody had whispered loud enough for Mr. Johnson to hear, — perhaps the bee buzzed it, — that if the Southern States could be reconstructed previous to the presidential convention of 1868, and he (President Johnson) should be found friendly and faithful to the South in that work, there were fifteen Southern States whose electoral votes might be found solid for him as the Democratic nominee, and he would only need the votes of two or three Northern States in addition to carry off the nomination. You know how the poison took — how from the most radical of Union Republicans he became the most extreme — the leader — of the "strictest sect" of the Democrats; how the words "treason should be made odious," "traitors should take back seats," "a few traitors should be hung," with which his mouth was filled when elected, and were still sounding in the air when he sat down in Lincoln's vacant chair, had hardly died away before he had turned against and upon all those who had upheld the Union cause — all his old Union friends; how he fought the Congress with a bitterness and a boldness unparalleled in history. He took issue with it on every measure by which the Congress sought to fix in statute and in the fundamental law what the sword had achieved, what war had enacted. Thus he stood.

And now turning to Mrs. Surratt and her case. Over her execution a great clamor was raised throughout the country, not only by those who were lately in rebellion, and those in the North who were in sympathy with that rebellion, but almost universally by the Roman Catholics of the country, she being a member of that Church, they believing her innocent and a martyr. Mr. Johnson heard this clamor, and "his startled ambition grew sore afraid." He bethought him of some means to turn this wrath away from himself. The press kept referring to the fact that a recommendation to mercy had been signed by a majority of the Court; and his new friends and allies were calling upon him with a loud voice to know why he had not heeded the appeal for mercy, and saved this hapless woman. His fears whispered that the storm might grow so fierce and strong as to sweep away his carefully constructed political fabric. How could he turn away this wrath and clamor? How turn the fury of the storm? Were here not motive and interest enough? He doubtless remembered that, when he examined the record, he and Judge Holt had been alone. How easy to shift the blame, to turn the storm of wrath and execration upon another head by having it circulated that the recommendation had been suppressed by Judge Holt, and that he had never seen nor heard of it up to the time of the execution! Here was a sufficient motive — the motive of ambition — the motive which, as we have seen, changed the whole nature of the man, — changed his political thought and attitude — spoiled the purpose of his life.

Of Judge Holt's life little need be said. Born and reared in Kentucky, of the best blood of the State, he had achieved fame and stood in the front rank with the great lawyers and orators of that State before the rebellion began, and before he was called to the Cabinet of James Buchanan, first, as Postmaster-General, and afterward as Secretary of War, to fill the place made vacant by the retirement of the traitor John B. Floyd. Judge Holt was a man of collegiate education, a student and a scholar of wide and varied reading, and a rhetorician and logician second to few men in the country. Of the next generation after Henry Clay, he was of the time and type in intellectual grasp and power of the Marshalls, the Breckinridges, and the Crittendens of that State. He breathed in the spirit of loyalty, patriotism, and love of the Union of Clay, and never doubted, never swerved in giving all his powers — in dedicating his life to the work of saving the Union. It is related by the historian that at one of the Cabinet meetings of President Buchanan, when several of the Southern secretaries were still occupying their places and were boldly demanding that the forts at Charlestown should be evacuated, and Mr. Buchanan was too weak to take a position against them, Mr. Stanton, who had been called to fill the office of Attorney General, sprang to his feet and said, " Mr. President, it is my duty, as your legal adviser, to say that you have no right to give up the property of the government, or abandon the soldiers of the United States to its enemies, and the course proposed by the Secretary of the Interior, if followed, is treason, and will involve you and all concerned in treason!" For the first time in this Cabinet treason had been called by its true name. Floyd and Thompson, who had had everything their own way, sprang fiercely to their feet, while Mr.'Holt sprang to Mr. Stanton's side, indorsing his utterances, and ready to uphold him in any struggle. Mr. Buchanan begged that there would be no violence, and for the gentlemen to resume their seats. Thus bolstered by Mr. Stanton and Judge Holt, the President determined not to withdraw Major Anderson. Soon after this meeting, Floyd resigned, and Judge Holt was appointed Secretary of War in his place.

Save this charge of Andrew Johnson, no stain or blot, nor the least spot or soilure, has ever rested on the fair name and fame of Joseph Holt. For the last year or two of the war I was brought in close official and personal relations with him. I learned to know him well. He was most refined and sensitive in his nature, gentle and kindly in his intercourse, and in all his relations with those about him, pure in his private life, exalted in his ideas and ideals, dignified, and courtly in his bearing, yet always thoughtful, considerate, and courteous. He had traveled much, read much, and held as his friends, strongly attached to him, the best men of the land. I can now as little associate him in my mind with the commission of a dishonorable action as any man I have ever known.

One of the interesting episodes connected with this charge against Judge Holt is his appeal to Mr. Speed, Mr. Lincoln's Attorney General, to "speak out" and state the fact whether or not the recommendation to mercy was before President Johnson and his Cabinet, and considered by them. The correspondence between Judge Holt and Mr. Speed is published in the *North American Review* for July, 1888. It will be remembered that Mr. Speed, in his letter to Judge Holt of March 30, 1873, had said:—

"After the finding of the military commission that tried the assassins of Mr. Lincoln, and before their execution, I saw the record of the case in the President's office, and attached to it was a paper, signed by some of the members of the commission, recommending that the sentence against Mrs. Surratt be commuted to imprisonment for life; and according to my memory the recommendation was made because of her sex."

As I have heretofore said, this settled, so far as the testimony of James Speed could settle it, that the charge of Andrew Johnson that Judge Holt had withheld the recommendation to mercy was false. It settled the fact that previous to the execution the recommendation to mercy was in the President's office, and was attached to the record. But in this letter Mr. Speed added: "I do not feel at liberty to speak of what was said at Cabinet meetings. In this case I know I differ from other gentlemen, but feel constrained to follow my own sense of propriety."

Judge Holt had learned, through the statements of Mr. Seward and Mr. Stanton to Judge Bingham, that the recommendation to mercy had been presented to the President, and had been considered by him and members of the Cabinet before the execution. But when this information came to him, both Mr. Seward and Mr. Stanton were dead, and the statement of Judge Bingham of what they told him was secondary evidence; and Judge Holt was anxious, therefore, to get the direct evidence of Mr. Speed that his recommendation was, to his personal knowledge, before Mr. Johnson and his Cabinet, and considered by them. His appeals to Mr. Speed are pathetic in the earnestness and depth of feeling they reveal. What could be more profoundly sorrowful or touching than this, in his letter of April 18, 1883: "Allow me to add that we are now, each of us, far advanced in years, so that whatever is to be done for my relief should be done quickly. While, however, it is sadly apparent that I can remain here but a little while longer, I have not been able to bring myself to the belief that you will suffer the closing hours of my life to be darkened by a consciousness that this cloud, or even a shred of it, is still hanging over me — a cloud which can be dissipated at once and forever by a single word spoken by yourself in defense of the truth and in rebuke of a calumny, the merciless cruelty of which none can better understand than yourself. I make this final appeal to your honor as a man to do me the simple justice, which, under the same circumstances, I would render to you at once and joyfully."

But Mr. Speed would not speak — finally saying, in his letter of October 25, 1883, "After very mature and deliberate consideration, I have come to the conclusion that I cannot say more than I have." Neither would he enter into consideration or discussion of his determination not "to speak of what was said at Cabinet meetings." It seems to me that Judge Holt was right and Mr. Speed was wrong in their relative positions upon this question. In his letter of April 18, 1883, addressed to Mr. Speed, to which

I have referred, Judge Holt forcibly presents his view: "You were a member of his (President Johnson's) Cabinet, and I have the strongest reasons for believing that this atrocious accusation is known to you to have been false in its every intendment. It originated with President Johnson, and for years was industriously circulated by his unscrupulous abettors, though he did not dare make open proclamation of it until he felt assured, through your letter of the 30th of March, 1873, that no damaging disclosures were to be apprehended from yourself. . . . The question whether a President of the United States, as a craven refuge from accountability for official action, did seek to blacken the reputation of a subordinate officer holding a confidential interview with him, is in no just sense a private question; it is essentially a public one, which concerns the whole country, and one of which the country may well expect to speak, seeing that you were a member of that President's Cabinet, at the time of this disgraceful transaction. Your unwillingness thus to speak of it in 1873, seemed to have arisen from an exaggerated estimate of a rule which once prevailed with regard to the inviolability of Cabinet councils and secrets. But whatever may have been, in the remote past, the recognized force of this rule, the frequent and conspicuous disregard of it during the last two decades, by statesmen of the highest probity and rank, leaves the impression that the rule itself has lived its day and is now practically dead and inoperative. Waiving, however, this view, it is clear to me that, were the rule accepted as now binding in its utmost rigor, it could have no application to this case. I can not be misled in supposing that the relations between the President and the Cabinet are relations of honor, and that, therefore, they cannot be held to oblige any member of his Cabinet to protect, by his concealment, and thus become a moral accomplice in it — any criminal or wrongful act into which the President may be drawn by a guilty ambition, or by any other unworthy passion or purpose. In a word, the rule never has been and never should be so construed as to become a shelter for perjury or crime.

"Your associates in the Cabinet, — Messrs Seward and Stanton, — condemning the rule by which I have been so long victimized, declared the truth fully to Judge Bingham, as he has so forcibly set forth in his letter to which you are referred."

But, as I have said, Mr. Speed would not speak. I can only account for it by the life, circumstances, and education of the man. In the old slave States, in the *antebellum* days, there existed many of the ideas, traditions, and rules of personal conduct of the feudal times. Things touching personal honor, or trusted to it, or that partook of the knightly and chivalrous, were esteemed above common right, common honesty, or common sense. Restrained by these limitations of birth and tradition, and controlled by his chivalrous idea of not revealing what he regarded as Cabinet secrets, Mr. Speed would not speak, even to save a public officer from a great wrong, or his personal friend from a calumny which he knew would walk beside him, shadowing and embittering a life, noble and void of wrong, down to its close. In this I think the judgment of mankind will be that he erred. He knew that this charge of Andrew Johnson was a cruel falsehood. Not only what he said, but what he refused to say, proves this. His letter of March 30, 1873, states that he saw the record, with the recommendation attached to it, in the President's office before the execution. Judge Holt did not, therefore, "withhold," as the President alleged. But, stronger than this, and conclusive, I believe, in the mind of every honest and unprejudiced man, were Mr. Speed's utterances, less than two years ago, at a meeting of the Loyal Legion at Cincinnati. Mr. Speed read a paper at the meeting of this society, held there on the 4th of May, 1887, in which he said: —

"Only the group of fiends who stilled the pulsations of Lincoln's great heart, paid the penalty of the crime. A maudlin sentiment has sought to cast blame on the officials who dealt out justice to these. One in particular is my distinguished friend, the then Judge Advocate General of the army. Judge Holt performed his duty kindly and considerately. In every particular he was just and fair. This I know; but Judge Holt needs no vindication from me nor any one else. I only speak because I know reflections have been made, and because my position enabled me to know the facts, and because I know the perfect purity and uprightness of his conduct." Could any words say in stronger form, he knew that in this matter Judge Holt did his whole duty, and that President's Johnson's charges were false? Could he have said, "In every particular he was just and fair, this I know," if he did not *know* and intended to say that he knew Judge Holt did his whole duty and had presented this recommendation to mercy to President Johnson? But what he refused to say is as strongly convincing to my mind of the fact that the recommendation to mercy was, to his knowledge, duly brought to the President's attention, and was read and considered by him and members of his Cabinet, as anything he has affirmatively stated.

He was asked by Judge Holt to state whether this paper was or was not before President Johnson and his Cabinet. He refused to answer "because he did not feel at liberty to speak of what was said at Cabinet meetings." If nothing was said about the recommendation, if no such paper ever came before the Cabinet, might he not have so stated; might he not have said, "No such matter ever came before the Cabinet?" This would not reveal any Cabinet secret, would come nowhere near the limitations he had prescribed for himself "not to speak of what was said at Cabinet meetings."

Is it not the inevitable logical conclusion that it was because of this knowledge that this recommendation had been before, and had been discussed by, the President and his Cabinet, and his determination "not to speak of what was said at Cabinet meetings," that he would not speak?

But, finally, my friends, has not the faith of Judge Holt been realized? Has not time caused the truth to shine forth and his innocence to appear? In 1873, he said: "An abiding faith, however, remains with me that the public will do these witnesses justice, and myself, also; and that if truth has power to disarm the cloud of calumny of its lightnings, that then, standing in their presence and under their shelter, I may well feel that for the future this cloud can have no terrors for me."

Saith an old poet: —

" . . . I have ever thought
Nature doth nothing so great for great men
As when she's pleased to make them lords of truth.
Integrity of life is fame's best friend,
Which nobly beyond death shall crown the end.'

www.ingramcontent.com/pod-product-compliance
Lightning Source LLC
Chambersburg PA
CBHW050324230426
43663CB00010B/1737